Agriculture and conservation in the hills and uplands

ITE symposium no. 23

Edited by
M BELL and R G H BUNCE

ITE, Merlewood Research Station

INSTITUTE OF TERRESTRIAL ECOLOGY

Printed in Great Britain by Galliard (Printers) Ltd, Great Yarmouth, Norfolk

Published in 1987 by
Institute of Terrestrial Ecology
Merlewood Research Station
GRANGE-OVER-SANDS
Cumbria
LA11 6JU

BRITISH LIBRARY CATALOGUING-IN-PUBLICATION DATA
Agriculture and conservation in the hills and uplands
(ITE symposium, ISSN 0263-8614; no. 23)
1. Nature conservation - Great Britain
3. Landscape conservation - Great Britain
I. Bell, M II. Bunce, R G H
III. Institute of Terrestrial Ecology. V. Series
333. 76'16'0941 QH77. G7
ISBN 1 870393 03 1

COVER ILLUSTRATION
North Pennine Dales Environmentally Sensitive Area, a landscape created by farming, retaining semi-natural vegetation and hay meadows whereon traditional management practices are crucial to the maintenance of floral diversity. New national and European Commission grants can assist conservation and the small farm structure which underpins the area. It is no longer tenable to consider farm, conservation or rural social policies in isolation (Photograph R Scott)

The **Institute of Terrestrial Ecology** was established in 1973, from the former Nature Conservancy's research stations and staff, joined later by the Institute of the Tree Biology and Culture Centre of Algae and Protozoa. ITE contributes to, and draws upon, the collective knowledge of the 14 sister institutes which make up the **Natural Environment Research Council,** spanning all the environmental sciences.

The Institute studies the factors determining the structure, composition and processes of land and freshwater systems, and of individual plant and animal species. It is developing a sounder scientific basis for predicting and modelling environmental trends arising from natural or man-made change. The results of this research are available to those responsible for the protection, management and wise use of our natural resources.

One quarter of ITE's work is research commissioned by customers, such as the Department of Environment, the European Economic Community, the Nature Conservancy Council and the Overseas Development Administration. The remainder is fundamental research supported by NERC.

ITE's expertise is widely used by international organizations in overseas projects and programmes of research.

Drs M Bell & R G H Bunce
Institute of Terrestrial Ecology
Merlewood Research Station
GRANGE-OVER-SANDS
Cumbria
LA11 6JU

044 84 (Grange-over-Sands) 2264

CONTENTS

Preface

It has always seemed an axiom of environmental and ecological study that the scholar needs to consider links, overlaps and relationships with a wide range of influences. Thus, it was a welcome move when the Economic and Social Research Council, and their sister organization the Natural Environment Research Council came together to sponsor their first joint Fellowship. This volume is one output of that experiment.

There has been a number of roles and themes within the Fellowship. One has been the attempt to convey the knowledge and insights of different disciplines to those outside who could use them in their own work. Related to this attempt has been a broader aim of assisting different interests in the countryside to understand each other's viewpoint and concerns. As so often, Eric Carter of the Farming and Wildlife Advisory Group (FWAG) was the catalyst for ensuring that efforts in this area were directed to those at the 'sharp end'. In planning the conference, inviting speakers, but above all in attracting people to attend, one tried to look for a wide spread of individuals sharing a core interest in enhancing the countryside. The target audience was the planner, ranger, warden, FWAG advisor, agent or someone else with mud on their boots and the job of advising hard-nosed farmers and landowners. It was of great assistance when some of those with the muddiest wellies, the Association of Countryside Rangers, offered their guidance and help. It was perhaps of even greater assistance that a fair sprinkling of hard-nosed farmers were able to give up time to attend and to make clear that, whatever opportunities the present rethinking of the Common Agricultural Policy might raise, it felt like income pressure to them at the moment.

There is always a danger in acknowledging the contributions made by some bodies and peoples; an inadvertent omission could give great offence. It would be cowardice to permit that to deter, and the starting point must be to thank the speakers who made a conference organizer's job easy. Indeed, it is equally important to thank the odd speaker who did not, because recalcitrance was no more than a reflection of their commitments. The adage stood about asking a busy person if you want something doing. In no case was that more true than in regard to the Chairmen. To Messrs Bowers, Dunning, Harwood and Gordon Duff-Pennington go grateful thanks for their aplomb and efficiency.

On the evening of the conference, we were entertained, encouraged and occasionally admonished by Sir Derek Barber. This means that all concerned are doubly in the debt of the Countryside Commission: for its Chairman's excellent talk and for its financial support, which made the gathering viable and has underwritten this publication. It would be a tragedy if the wealth of information presented were not widely available. It is the editors' hope that this volume will fill a notable gap on the shelves: an accessible guide to research undertaken —or in train — regarding the hills and uplands.

A number of people worked tirelessly to assist with the conference and the publication. Margaret Whittaker was the lynchpin of the operation, Mrs P A Ward a painstaking proofreader and guide, whilst Chris Benefield handled graphics and illustrations. Thanks are due to all who assisted, and it is hoped their partial reward is this collection which we feel sure will be of assistance to farmers, landowners, advisors, students, and even to researchers — who are often a far more worldly bunch than popular myths would imply.

Malcolm Bell

Effects of man on upland vegetation

J MILES
Institute of Terrestrial Ecology, Banchory Research Station, Hill of Brathens, Banchory, Kincardineshire, Scotland

1 Introduction
This paper discusses the nature of vegetation in the British uplands, how it is influenced by man, and how it can be managed. It can only skim these subjects, and several later papers in this volume deal in more detail with specific management techniques.

Most available management techniques are, as actions, very simple, eg mowing, burning, fertilizing, draining, planting, applying herbicide. However, their consequences are exceedingly difficult to predict in detail, because vegetation is usually complex in structure and composition, and varies from place to place over even small distances. This variation, in turn, is a result of differences in the many factors that shape vegetation, in particular:

i. topography and location (aspect, altitude, etc);

ii. the chemical composition of bedrocks, and thus of soil parent materials (eg, the calcium content of a granite or gabbro can vary 8-fold, that of a sandstone 80-fold (Clarke 1924));

iii. drainage, structure and lithology of the soil (Beckett & Webster 1971; Lyford 1974), especially in transported materials such as glacial drifts (Robinson & Lloyd 1915; Kantey & Morse 1965);

iv. the chance nature of plant dispersal and the incidence of past catastrophes (eg extreme climatic events, outbreaks of disease or insect attack) (Miles 1979);

v. past management, land use and vegetation cover (Van Goor 1954; Armson 1959; Miles 1985a);

vi. clonal longevity and persistence (Miles 1979, 1981).

There are a number of basic points that every vegetation manager should know.

i. The composition of any patch of vegetation reflects its aggregate response to its past environment. Current environmental factors and events only control its future composition.

ii. No 2 patches of vegetation are ever exactly alike (ie in the combinations, proportions and spatial arrangement of the different species present).

iii. All vegetation is constantly changing in time, for various reasons (Miles 1985b), as individuals die and are replaced, though rates of change do vary greatly. Stability is thus only relative. Figure 1 shows the changes that occurred in the control plots of a grazing experiment, ie where there was no experimental treatment, over a 21-year period. These changes were so large that they would have been gratifying if they had been the results of the experimental treatment!

iv. Vegetation always responds to changes in its environment, whether the change is a single brief event (eg a fire), or of longer duration (eg the imposition or removal of grazing by sheep). Such changes, and the reaction of the vegetation, can vary from the gradual to the abrupt, and from the subtle to the obvious.

2 The nature of upland vegetation
The crucial point about upland vegetation is that, below the natural tree-line, it is almost all man-made, directly or indirectly. After the last Ice Age, man returned to Britain as game recolonized, and has been progressively changing the character of upland vegetation ever since. Burning, felling, and grazing by domestic livestock, and by wild herbivores such as red deer (*Cervus elaphus*) whose other predators had been exterminated, have destroyed all but fragments of the once predominant forest cover. In its place, the familiar moorland landscapes have developed, including the forest-zone

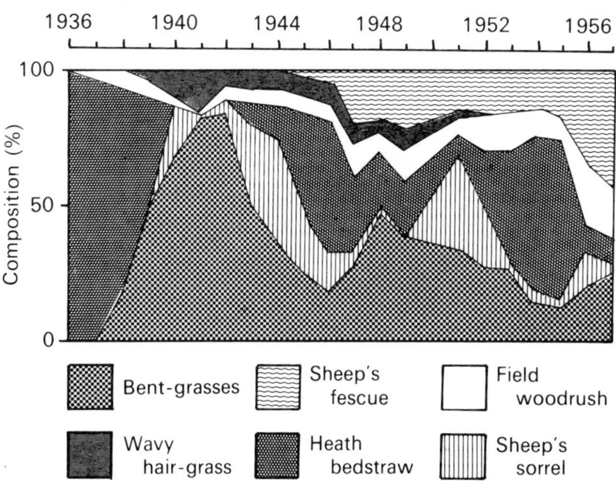

Figure 1. Changes in percentage composition (by cover) of species in a Breckland grass heath, 1936–57 (source: Watt 1960)

blanket bogs (Moore 1973; Merrifield & Moore 1974); even the great peatlands of Caithness may have been initiated by man tipping the ecological balance (Moore 1987). The extent of change to vegetation above the natural tree-line is problematic, but much has been subjected to burning, and all has been influenced by sheep grazing in particular (Thompson 1987). Thus, perhaps only a few cliff ledges, mountain peaks and islets today carry largely natural vegetation.

Man-made vegetation ('plagioclimax') within the potential natural forest zone will revert to forest if it can (a process termed secondary succession). In places with a heavy 'rain' of tree seeds, especially where soils are relatively fertile, this tendency is so strong that it creates severe problems for land managers who do not want the spread of trees (eg on many grouse moors, heathland nature reserves and limestone-dale sheepwalks). Often, however, the vegetation reverts very slowly to woodland, even when not heavily grazed and regularly burnt. This biological inertia results from 3 factors in particular: species poverty (especially light or negligible tree-seed rains), soil infertility (often exacerbated by the effects of the vegetation), and the effects of the vegetation. These points are discussed further because some knowledge of them is needed to understand why the response of upland vegetation to management is so variable.

2.1 Species poverty

As a result of deforestation, and because subsequent repeated burning eliminated fire-intolerant species, large expanses of relatively uniform vegetation in the uplands generally lack successional species, especially shrubs and trees, that can invade and thus change the vegetation, or that give diversity during succession or during regeneration cycles. Thus, heather (*Calluna vulgaris*)-dominant swards often redevelop directly after fire, a simplified course of events associated naturally only with very species-poor vegetation such as that in desert or arctic tundra.

The effects of species poverty were shown experimentally at 3 heather moor sites in north-east Scotland. When ground was bared, recolonization tended to regenerate the surrounding vegetation directly (Miles 1973a). However, when seeds of 107 species, most of which did not currently grow at these sites, were sown on the bared soil, from 28% to 67% of the species established, depending on the soil fertility (Miles 1974a). These new species included many that were probably present at the sites when they were wooded.

2.2 Soil infertility

Most non-calcareous upland soils are relatively infertile, partly intrinsically, because of the prevalence of base-poor rocks, but partly because of the loss of the natural woodland cover, and the subsequent acidifying effects of many moorland plant species, particularly heather (Miles 1985c). This secondary soil infertility now often controls species richness. For example, when soil was bared experimentally at 3 heather moor sites in north-east Scotland, only one species of flowering plant colonized that was not already growing in the surrounding vegetation. In contrast, when the soil was given a dressing of fertilizer, 10 new species colonized naturally (Miles 1973a). Also, in the experiments noted earlier in which seeds of 107 species were sown, 68-86% of the species established on fertilized soil, compared with only 28-67% on unfertilized ground (Miles 1974a).

2.3 Effects of vegetation

Three ways by which plants influence each other are discussed here: competition, the resistance of vegetation to new plants establishing, and the effects of plants on soil properties.

2.3.1 *Competition*

Competition between plants is the ubiquitous means by which they sort themselves into the assemblages we see. Many examples are of common experience; for example, mowing a lawn close to the ground in autumn tends to result in more moss than grass being present in spring. The main point for the upland manager is that many tall plants such as ox-eye daisy (*Chrysanthemum leucanthemum*) and red campion (*Silene dioica*) will only persist when grazing is light or absent for much of the summer, as in hay meadows. In contrast, intrinsically low-growing plants, such as white clover (*Trifolium repens*) and thyme (*Thymus drucei*), predominate in short swards. Management influences vegetation mainly by changing the competitive balance between species.

2.3.2 *Resistance of vegetation to immigration*

Many studies have shown that seedlings commonly establish very poorly in undisturbed grassland and dwarf shrub stands (Tamm 1956; Cavers & Harper 1967; Miles 1972, 1974b). Few moorland plant species can tolerate heavy shade; most can establish from seed only

Table 1. Mean percentage establishment after one growing season from seed sown experimentally in heather-dominant vegetation on a brown podzolic soil with different layers of the vegetation removed (source: Miles 1974a)

	Control	Canopy removed	Canopy and moss layer removed	Canopy, moss, & litter layers removed
Common bent-grass (*Agrostis tenuis*)	0	0.5	4	24
Wavy hair-grass (*Deschampsia flexuosa*)	0	0	2	5
Yorkshire fog (*Holcus lanatus*)	0	1	0.8	23
Cat's ear (*Hypochaeris radicata*)	0	2	4	22
Greater woodrush (*Luzula sylvatica*)	0	0.2	0.5	14
Sorrel (*Rumex acetosa*)	0	0	0.5	27
Broom (*Sarothamnus scoparius*)	0.5	4	6	10
Gorse (*Ulex europaeus*)	0	0	10	6

in gaps, though what constitutes a 'gap' varies from species to species. Table 1 shows how the physical structure of a heather stand influenced its receptivity to colonizers. There was negligible establishment when seeds were sown experimentally into the untouched sward, but, when different layers were successively removed, there was a progressive and substantial increase in establishment. This resistance of many vegetation types to colonization by seedlings can make them very stable. Good examples seen in the uplands are stands of rhododendron (*Rhododendron ponticum*) and bracken (*Pteridium aquilinum*), which by layering and rhizome growth respectively can maintain dense thickets that are highly resistant to tree invasion.

Small gaps tend to be filled by vegetative ingrowth rather than by seedlings.When different-sized patches of soil were bared experimentally in a species-rich heather-dominant sward, the cover after 3 years in patches of 25 cm^2 was mainly from plants that had vegetatively spread in from the edges (Figure 2). In contrast, most cover in patches of 2500 cm^2 was from plants regenerated from seed. Not all apparent gaps may be suitable niches. For example, a study of 20 fresh molehills in an alluvial bent/fescue (*Agrostis/Festuca*) grassland showed that, after 2 years, all had 100% cover derived entirely from vegetation regeneration (Miles, unpublished).

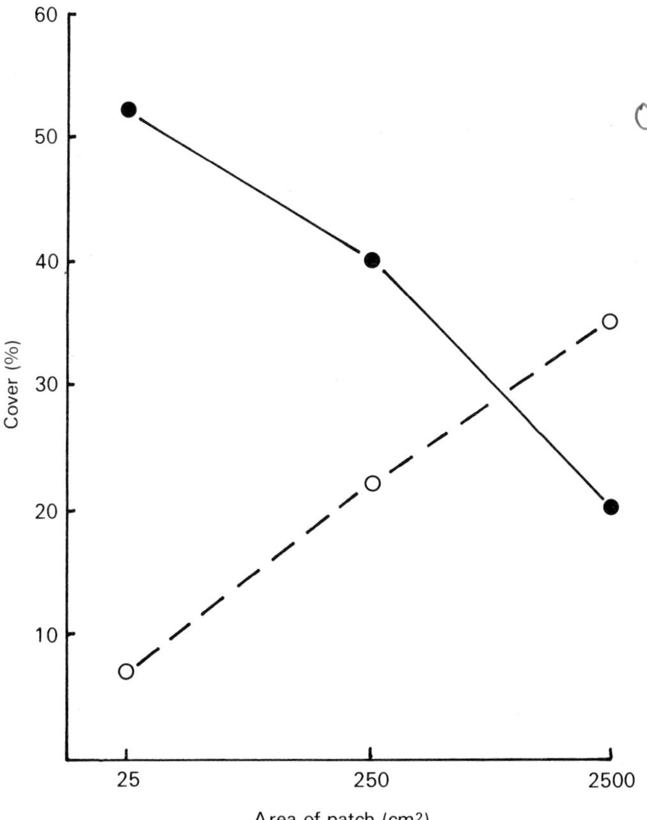

Figure 2. Mean percentage cover after 3 growing seasons of flowering plants regenerated from seed (o–––––o) and by vegetative means (●———●) in different-sized patches of experimentally bared ground (source: Miles 1974b)

2.3.3 Effects on the soil

Excluding peats, upland soils can conveniently be classed as having either mull or mor humus, or humus transitional between these 2 forms. This distinction is of fundamental importance. Mull soils have pH values 4.5–5 or greater, are biologically active, with rapid turnover of nutrients, and usually support species-rich vegetation. In contrast, mor soils are acid (pH<4.5), have lower rates of nutrient cycling, and are typically associated with species-poor vegetation. In the poorly buffered sandy soils prevalent in the uplands, mull and mor conditions are often interchangeable. Heather and other ericaceous species, pines (*Pinus* spp.) and spruces (*Picea* spp.) tend to produce acid mor soils, and can accelerate podzolization. In contrast, bracken, bent/fescue grassland, birch (*Betula pendula* and *B. pubescens*), aspen (*Populus tremula*), and juniper (*Juniperus communis*) typically produce mull or mull-like humus, and may in time bring about depodzolization through the greater biological activity in the soil (Miles 1985c). When one vegetation type gives way to another, the pH of the surface soil may increase or decrease by 0.5–1.5 units in 10–50 years from initial values between 4 and 6. Changes of this order can markedly influence the species composition and richness of vegetation (Miles 1985a, 1987). For example, when birch colonizes heather moorland, the number of flowering plant species growing under the canopy can more than double as a result of increased pH and associated changes in other soil properties (Miles & Young 1980).

3 *Effects of management*

Most upland vegetation has changed markedly in the past, much is changing now, and, for biological, political and socio-economic reasons, much will inevitably continue to change. Although there are many gaps in our knowledge, we do know a good deal about how to create and maintain the main vegetation types in the uplands. If land managers say what kind of vegetational landscapes they want, vegetation scientists at any point in time can, just like the agricultural advisory services, always advise how to create and maintain what is wanted, on the basis of the best available information. For most of the uplands within the forest zone, the range of potential vegetation types that can exist at any given place is very broad. Most upland soils, apart from areas of limestone and blanket peat, have pH values within the range 3.8–5.5, which accommodates most of the common vegetation types (Figure 3). There is thus considerable scope for creating vegetational diversity.

The most important management practices influencing plagioclimax vegetation in the uplands are grazing and burning. The former is ubiquitous, the latter confined to combustible material (dwarf shrub and shrub stands, bracken and grasslands with an accumulation of dead material), but both have had major and widespread effects. Other practices have been used only locally, though their effects can be equally or more profound. The sections that follow discuss the effects of different management techniques that influence vegetation.

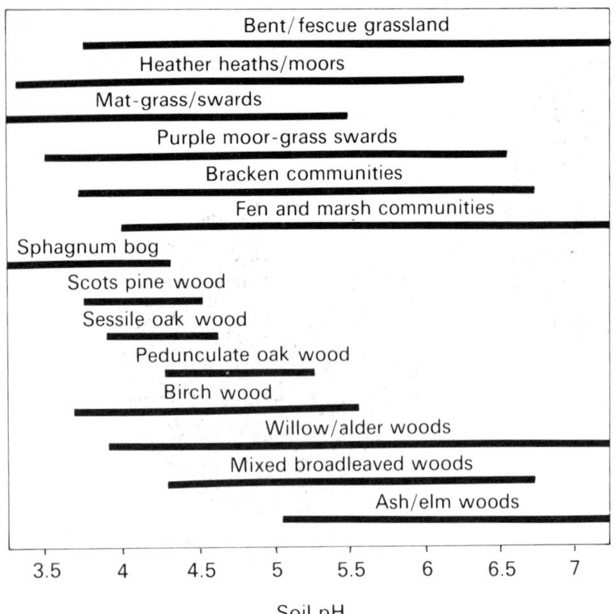

Figure 3. Distribution of vegetation types in relation to pH (source: Miles *et al.* 1978)

3.1 Grazing

Grazing by domestic livestock in the uplands, mainly sheep and cattle, is superimposed on a varying background level of grazing by wild herbivores. Under free-range conditions, the effective grazing intensity on any patch of vegetation depends on the general stock density and the attractiveness of that vegetation, and thus varies widely. One study in the north Pennines showed that the effective density of sheep varied from 5 ha^{-1} on bent/fescue grassland to 3 on mat-grass (*Nardus stricta*)-dominant grassland, one on heath rush (*Juncus squarrosus*)-dominant swards, 0.3 on cotton-grass (*Eriophorum* spp.) bog and 0.1 on heather-dominated bog (Rawes & Welch 1969).

Grazing has a critical effect on the composition of plagioclimax vegetation. All grasslands within the forest zone in Britain are maintained by grazing (or by artificial defoliation, eg mowing). Sheep, in particular, and also red deer in the Highlands, prevent tree regeneration over much of the uplands. Away from moorland, rabbits (*Oryctolagus cuniculus*) and roe deer (*Capreolus capreolus*) also often prevent woodland regeneration. Small rodents eat seeds and seedlings, and sometimes debark and kill saplings, while molluscs also kill seedlings, including those of trees (Howells 1966; Scarratt 1966; Miles & Kinnaird 1979b). Stands of mature trees can be killed by caterpillars, eg birch by those of the moth *Operinia autumnata* (Kallio & Lehtonen 1975), and lodgepole pine (*Pinus contorta*) by those of the pine beauty moth (*Panolis flammea*) (Stoakley 1977). Grazing by heather beetle (*Lochmaea suturalis*) can kill heather plants. On lowland Dutch heaths, death of heather stands from this cause rather than old age seems the rule, and has led to replacement of heather by wavy hair-grass (*Deschampsia flexuosa*) and purple moor-grass (*Molinia caerulea*) (de Smidt 1977; Diemont & Heil 1984). Extensive dieback of heather certainly occurs in the south of England, but further north in Britain only small patches ever seem to be killed.

Controlling grazing by wild herbivores is at best difficult, and often impossible. However, grazing by domestic livestock can, in contrast, be carefully controlled. Figure 4 shows some results from a classic experiment on a north Cardiganshire hill. Two swards evolved under free-range grazing by sheep were studied: one with dominant sheep's fescue (*Festuca ovina*) overlying a well-drained brown podzolic soil, the other with dominant purple moor-grass overlying peat. When sheep were excluded for 2 years, the cover of heather and bilberry (*Vaccinium myrtillus*) in the fescue sward had increased from 1% to 30%, while the more desirable bent-grasses decreased from 9% to 2%. In the other sward, purple moor-grass increased from 55% to 85%, while the bents neared extinction. In contrast, after 2 years of summer grazing at an annual rate of 2 sheep ha^{-1}, the proportion of bent more than doubled in both swards, and less desirable species declined in abundance. Identical grazing pressures probably have different effects in different parts of Britain. For example, in north-east Scotland, heather-dominant stands begin to change to bent/fescue grasslands when grazing levels exceed 2.5 sheep ha^{-1} (Welch 1984).

Patterns of change between upland vegetation types are complex and multidirectional (Miles *et al.* 1978). Figure 5 shows the known successional transitions between 8 common upland vegetation types, divided according to the 3 broad levels of grazing pressure under which they occur. The available information about rates of change between types is summarized by Miles *et al.* (1978). These sequences are poorly understood, and little is known about regional variations in the frequency or occurrence of particular transitions. The main reason for particular transitions occurring at particular sites at particular grazing levels may be simple proximity. Thus, at low grazing pressures, dying birch woods with grassy field layers seem initially to give way to heather unless bracken is present, in which case dense bracken stands quickly develop and prevent heather colonization.

Grazing animals influence vegetation in many ways other than by defoliation. For example, vertebrate herbivores influence soil nutrient status by their dunging and urination (Wolton 1955; Peterson *et al.* 1956), and thus increase herbage production and change the floristic composition (Wheeler 1958; Weeda 1967), while their saliva stimulates plant growth (Reardon *et al.* 1972, 1974). Trampling creates niches for seedling establishment (Miles 1973b); excluding livestock from grassland leads to loss of species diversity (Watt 1960), and from deciduous woodland can lead to a lack of tree regeneration (Shaw 1974; Miles & Kinnaird 1979a). Equally, soil bared by trampling exposes previously buried seeds. Gorse (*Ulex europaeus*) and broom

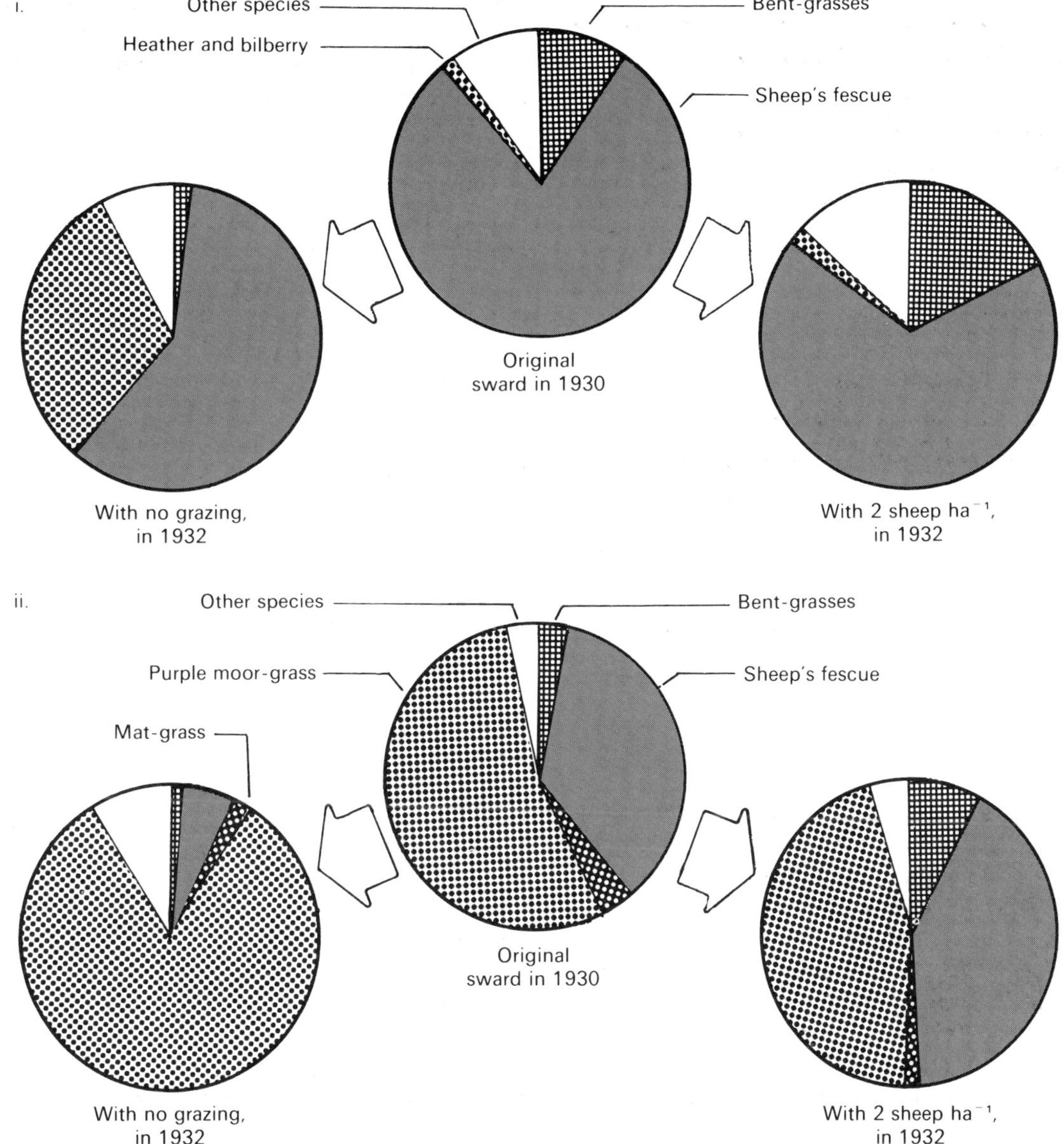

Figure 4. Changes in percentage composition (by weight) of (i) a bent/fescue grassland, and (ii) a purple moor-grass-dominated grassland, at 290 m in north Cardiganshire, after 2 years with protection from sheep grazing and with grazing at 2 sheep ha^{-1} yr^{-1} (source: Jones 1967)

(*Sarothamnus scoparius*) stands, rush infestations and, in woodlands, showy displays of foxgloves (*Digitalis purpurea*) can all originate in this way. Animals also carry fruits and seeds of many plants, internally as well as externally (eg goosegrass (*Galium aparine*) (Ridley 1930)). They are significant agents of plant dispersal in the uplands, depositing many agronomically important species in their dung, eg white clover, bent-grasses, sweet vernal-grass (*Anthoxanthum odoratum*), smooth-stalked meadow-grass (*Poa pratensis*) and rye-grass (*Lolium perenne*) (Welch 1985).

3.2 Fire

Fires are frequent in the uplands. Some are caused by accident or by lightening (Anon 1970), but most are deliberate acts of management to prevent:

i. the accumulation of old woody stems and litter in heather-dominated dwarf shrub heath, and thus to encourage the growth of new sprouts near the ground for consumption by sheep and red grouse (*Lagopus l. scoticus*) in particular;

ii. the accumulation of dead leaves and surface litter in grasslands, especially where purple moor-grass predominates;

iii. the establishment of trees and shrubs on grazings and grouse moors, and to kill existing scrub.

After a fire, heather and other dwarf shrub stands show a fairly regular pattern of early predominance and changing abundance of many of the associated species. Figure 6 gives an example from north-east Scotland, with a sequence of predominance by grasses, mainly wavy hair-grass, bell-heather (*Erica cinerea*), bearberry (*Arctostaphylos uva-ursi*) with heather, and finally heather with an underlayer of feather mosses. On peatier

i.

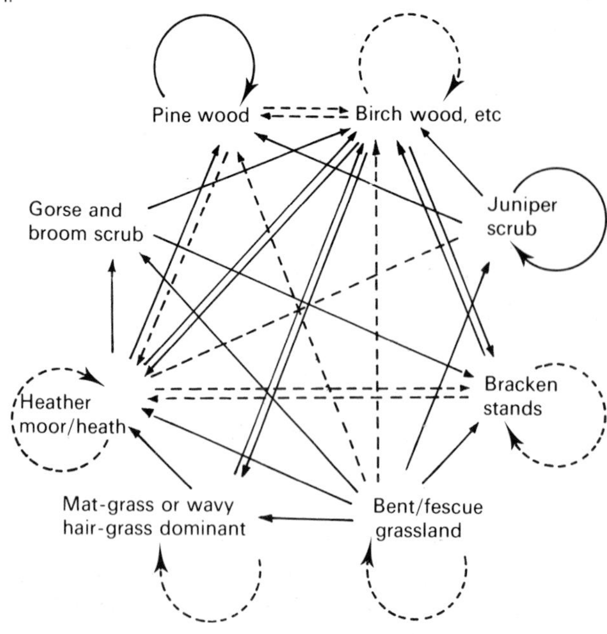

ii.

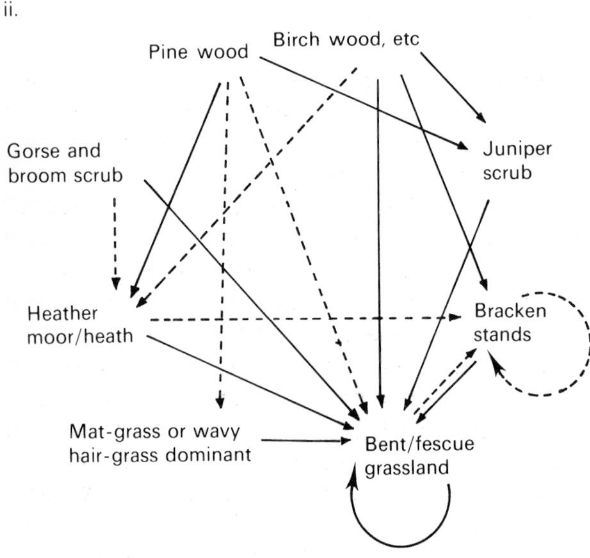

iii.

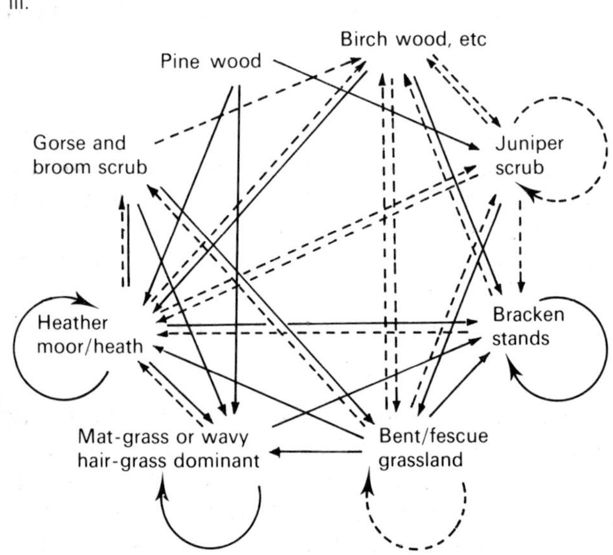

soils, bilberry and cowberry (*Vaccinium vitis-idaea*) tend to predominate early on, while on wetter soils cross-leaved heath (*Erica tetralix*) is the more usual early dominant. These sequences occur because many moorland species grow and spread faster than heather after a fire, but are eventually overtopped by the heather and become only minor components of the stand.

Heather regenerates best if it is burnt when about 25–35 cm tall, a height usually reached 8–15 years after the last fire. A well-managed heather moor has a mosaic of small patches (Watson & Miller 1976; Muirburn Working Party 1977). For grouse, a moor should be burnt as small strips about 0.5–1 ha in size, but for sheep or red deer grazings the patches can be bigger. For nature conservation purposes, there should be greater variation in the time to burning, with some patches burnt more frequently than every 8–15 years. This timing increases the abundance of species such as bell-heather that grow rapidly after fire. Equally, some patches should be burnt less frequently than every 15 years to allow fuller development of moss- and lichen-rich layers, but this is not practicable when there is a substantial rain of tree seeds because infrequent burning allows trees to establish.

Lightly grazed areas of hill grassland are also often burnt to remove dead material which would otherwise mask, perhaps for weeks, the spring flush of growth of critical value to livestock. Such grasslands are customarily burnt either annually, as on the purple moor-grass and bent/fescue grasslands of the Exmoor Forest, or every few years, as in the southern uplands and north-west Highlands of Scotland. On mineral soils, repeated burning of grassland can help to maintain species diversity (Lloyd 1968). However, frequent burning favours purple moor-grass when it is present in the sward, and can cause it to become dominant (Grant *et al.* 1963). The difficulty is that purple moor-grass is deciduous, and produces substantial amounts of litter, so that burning it merely further increases the need to burn.

Scrub, particularly gorse stands, is frequently burnt as an attempted control measure. However, burning gorse is usually quite ineffective. Like most broadleaved woody species, gorse bushes, unless very old, sprout vigorously from the base after burning or cutting, thus regenerating the plants. Many other woody species are also burnt,

Figure 5. Successional transitions between common types of semi-natural vegetation on well-drained, acid mineral soils that occur with (i) low grazing pressures ($<$1 sheep equivalents ha^{-1} yr^{-1}) and without burning, (ii) high grazing pressures ($>$2–3 sheep equivalents ha^{-1} yr^{-1}) and frequent burning, and (iii) intermediate levels of grazing (1–2 sheep equivalents ha^{-1} yr^{-1}) and burning. Solid lines represent the most frequent transitions, dashed lines less common transitions (source: Miles 1985c, courtesy of the British Society of Soil Science)

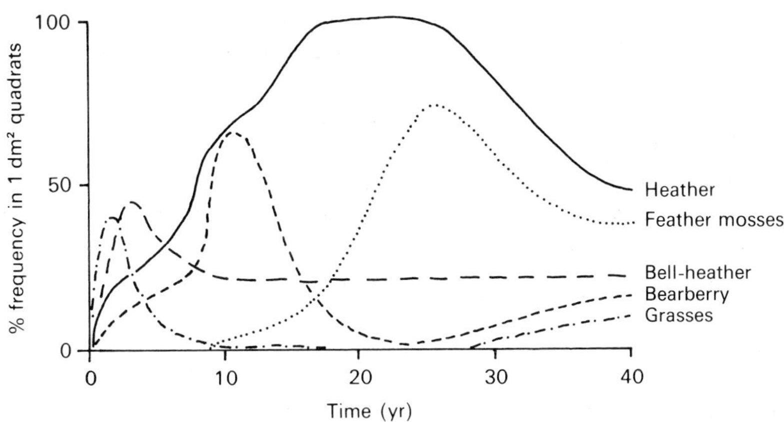

Figure 6. Generalized sequence of vegetation change with time after fire in Dinnet Moor, Aberdeenshire (source: Hobbs *et al.* 1984)

usually during heather, bracken or grass fires. In the uplands, bushes of broom, and saplings and young trees of birch, rowan (*Sorbus aucuparia*), willow (*Salix* spp.), hawthorn (*Crataegus monogyna*), and oak (*Quercus robur* and *Q. petraea*) are often cut back in this way, but generally resprout. Bushes of juniper and saplings and young trees of Scots pine (*Pinus sylvestris*) and other conifers naturalized in Britain are fire-sensitive, however, and are almost always killed by fire.

Carefully planned and executed fires are a useful and positive management tool. Although there was probably a general loss of soil fertility as Britain's moors developed from fires, and when burning began, these losses may now have reached an asymptote, so that careful burning now causes little if any net loss of nutrients from the system. In contrast, inappropriate burning can have serious negative effects on both vegetation and soil (McVean 1959; Gimingham 1985). Burning dwarf shrub heath, too, frequently reduces, and can eliminate, heather and *Erica* spp., and instead causes increases in:

i. wavy hair-grass, fescues, bent-grasses and bracken on well-drained mineral soils;

ii. purple moor-grass and deer-grass (*Trichophorum cespitosum*) on wetter and peatier soils;

iii. cotton-grasses (*Eriophorum vaginatum* and *E. angustifolium*) and, where present, cloudberry (*Rubus chamaemorus*) on blanket peat (Taylor & Marks 1971; Miles *et al.* 1978; Currall 1981; Hobbs 1984).

For example, too frequent burning over much of north-west Scotland has greatly reduced the cover of heather, and thus the amount of green forage available in winter.

Burning heather produces a good seed bed for a few years until a heather canopy redevelops. A heather fire close to trees capable of colonizing moorland is inviting tree invasion, especially by birch. Seedlings of birch are never found in abundance more than 50–100 m from seed-bearing trees (Sarvas 1948; Brown 1984) because most seeds are not dispersed far. The problem for managers, though, is that even an unburnt cordon of heather beside woodland will be invaded eventually by trees, unless the heather is maintained as a vigorous stand by, for example, periodic mowing. This is because gaps otherwise appear in the heather canopy with old age which allow colonization.

Burning on very steep slopes is inadvisable, as even temporary removal of the stabilizing cover of vegetation can allow the onset of gulley erosion, a phenomenon which can happen anyway during periods of prolonged heavy rainfall (eg the summer of 1985) even on wooded slopes. However, perhaps the most important, though commonly overlooked, result has been when burning too frequently or during drought conditions has either destroyed the surface covering of humus or peat, or allowed its loss by erosion, on infertile soils where this layer comprised a high proportion of the readily available nutrient capital. Such devastated areas are particularly common in the north-west Highlands of Scotland, the result of traditionally uncontrolled burning over poor soils in a high rainfall region. They also occur too frequently elsewhere, at least in the Highlands, especially on higher and steeper ground. Peat erosion in the Pennines and on the North York Moors has also been attributed to injudicious burning (Imeson 1971; Tallis 1973).

3.3 Fertilizing

The addition of nutrients to vegetation acts to swing the balance of composition towards dominance by species with high relative growth rates. While the nature of any change depends on the nutrient status of the soil in question, addition of either nitrogen or phosphorus to upland soils with plagioclimax vegetation invariably causes considerable floristic change, while liming causes lesser changes.

Light dressings of nitrogen fertilizer can increase heather growth and flowering (Miller 1968; Miller *et al.* 1970; Helsper *et al.* 1983), but heavier or repeated dressings result in its gradual replacement by other species. Which species replace heather depends on the soil type, and on what species are present and thus able to take advantage of the changed nutrient availability. The sparse available information suggests that additions of nitrogen and/or phosphate in the absence of imposed grazing tend to cause increases at the expense of heather in:

i. mosses and lichens respectively on the poorest podzols, where graminoid species are sparse or absent, while lime also favours mosses (Helsper *et al.* 1983; Miles 1968);

ii. fescues and bent-grasses on more fertile soils (eg brown podzolic soils), which usually support relatively species-rich stands (Jones 1967; Heil & Diemont 1983);

iii. purple moor-grass on soils that are poorly drained or have high water tables (Jones 1967; Vermeer 1986; Miles, unpublished).

In one experiment, addition of nitrogen, phosphorus and potassium at agricultural rates increased the percentage of purple moor-grass in 2 grassy mires from 44 and 62 to 97 and 95 respectively (Miles, unpublished).

The effects of fertilizer interact strongly with grazing, and can be speeded up. Figure 7 shows the dramatic changes that occurred in 5 years, with rotational grazing to maintain short swards, from a single addition of 800 kg ha^{-1} of ground limestone, and from annual additions of nitrogen, phosphorus and potassium at 80, 67 and 27 kg ha^{-1} respectively, with bents and sheep's fescue becoming dominant in place of purple moor-grass.

Patches of hillside in northern England and the southern uplands of Scotland were in the past irrigated with lime-rich water to improve soil fertility, a practice begun by Cistercian monks and continued into the 19th century. The effects on vegetation composition were similar to those from liming (Heddle & Ogg 1936).

3.4 Draining

It has never been economic to install tile or other buried drains on unimproved ground, but there was an earlier vogue for making open drains on moorland (moor gripping) to try to improve grazing values, including improving heather growth on grouse moors. However, draining any but the wettest ground has little effect on vegetation, except immediately beside open drains (Stewart & Lance 1983). Of the common and abundant upland species, *Sphagnum* mosses and cotton-grasses are the most drought-sensitive. Open drains do increase sediment runoff, a phenomenon particularly associated with modern afforestation. Thus, deep ploughing of land for drainage in part of Galloway prior to tree planting was shown to cause a 20-fold increase in sediment runoff (Battarbee *et al.* 1985). Such pulses of soil erosion last for about 10 years, and can damage the stream spawning beds of salmon and trout and interfere with the water industry.

Over much of the uplands, buried drains are an essential part of creating improved pastures. In recent decades, the increasing availability of mechanical diggers, coupled with Government subsidies, has markedly increased the areas of reclaimed moorland, and thus changed landscapes. One consequence has been the spread of tall rushes. These rushes naturally occur on marshy and boggy ground, especially on acid soils, but stands are never extensive on unreclaimed moorland. Several species occur, with similar ecology, though soft rush (*Juncus effusus*) is generally the commonest. However, rush infestations are common in grasslands on intrinsically poorly drained soils, especially in the high-rainfall areas in the west of Britain. These sites commonly give the 2 factors needed for rush germination and

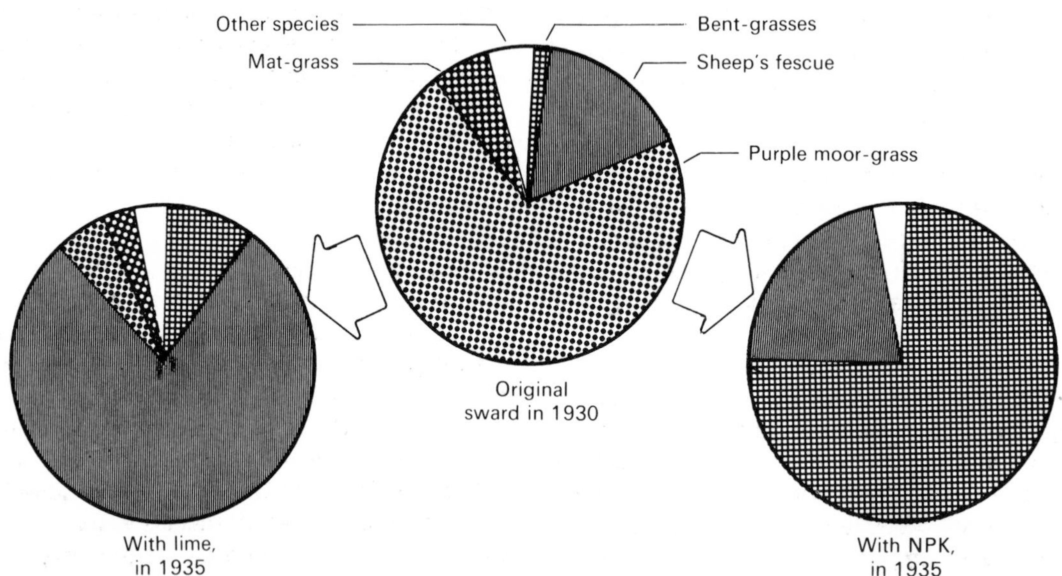

Figure 7. Changes in percentage composition (by weight) of a purple moor-grass-dominated grassland after 5 years, following a single application of ground limestone and annual additions of NPK (source: Jones 1967)

establishment: wet surface soil (Lazenby 1955) and, because of poaching by livestock, small patches of bare soil (Agnew 1961). On many soils it is likely that no drainage system will ever reduce surface moisture enough to prevent rushes establishing from seed. Seed production is prolific, and seeds are dispersed by wind when dry, and by various animals when wet because their seed coats become sticky (Richards & Clapham 1941). Further, seeds can stay dormant in soil for decades; over 15 000 seeds per square metre of ground may be present (Milton 1948). Thus, on unsuitable soils, prevention of rush infestations means either not reclaiming the ground in the first place, or else mowing the grass crop. When livestock grazes reseeds on such ground, it is usually only a matter of time before some poaching occurs and the first rushes colonize.

3.5 Weedkiller use

Selective chemical weedkillers (herbicides) have been developed and used since the 1940s. With the range of selective and total weedkillers and ways of application now available (Fryer & Makepeace 1978; Marrs 1981; Johansson 1985), there is no upland weed that cannot be controlled in principle.

All trees and shrubs (including gorse, birch and rhododendron) can be killed by either foliar spraying or stump treatment. The most commonly used effective chemicals are 2,4,5-T, glyphosate ('Roundup'), ammonium sulphamate ('Amcide') and fosamine ammonium ('Krenite'); all except the last are recommended for stump application as well as foliar sprays.

Bracken control was revolutionized by the discovery in 1967 that asulam ('Asulox'), a non-persistent weedkiller of low toxicity marketed 2 years earlier to control docks (*Rumex* spp.), was very effective at killing bracken (McKelvie & Scragg 1972). Spraying following the manufacturer's recommendations will give a 95–96% kill in the first year, and respraying in the second year can give 99+% control (Miller *et al.* 1984). Follow-up spraying or cutting is essential; otherwise the 4–5% of fronds that reappear after a single treatment will regenerate a dense stand in a few years.

Purple moor-grass and deer-grass can be controlled by the selective weedkiller dalapon. Using it, heather dominance has been recreated experimentally in part of Wester Ross where too frequent burning had resulted in these species becoming codominant (Miller *et al.* 1984).

3.6 Mowing and cutting

In the absence of grazing, grasslands can be maintained by mowing, which need not be more often than once a year. Indeed, this is how species-rich hay meadows have traditionally been maintained, sometimes for centuries. Road and railway verges and river banks are also commonly managed by periodic mowing or cutting.

Cutting woody vegetation rejuvenates the stand, which is the basis of woodland management by coppicing. Heather stands can also be maintained by cutting, though if the brash is left where it falls regeneration is impeded. Roadside gorse stands are often cut by local authorities, apparently as a control measure, but unless the plants are very old the stands are merely rejuvenated. To eliminate broadleaved scrub after cutting, stump treatment with an appropriate weedkiller is needed.

3.7 Soil disturbance

Ploughing and/or harrowing or discing are routinely done during agricultural reseeding. Ploughing kills many grassland species. Usually these species will quite readily recolonize small ploughed patches that are still surrounded by intact grassland. However, the larger the disturbed patch, the slower this process is.

When large areas are ploughed, there can to all intents and purposes be an absolute loss of species diversity, especially if adjacent seed sources are minimal. Soil disturbance can nevertheless be used to positive effect for nature conservation purposes, because it allows short-lived, ruderal species to establish from buried seed, which, if not controlled, increase the species diversity of the swards for 2-3 years. Soil disturbance has been used by nature reserve managers to maintain early successional species in chalk grassland (Duffey *et al.* 1974). Crofters in South Uist still practise shifting cultivation of small plots of machair grassland to grow potatoes and forage crops. This practice results in scattered patches of successional grassland of different ages and species composition, which enhance the floristic diversity of the machair.

Historically, heather-dominated heathlands in Flanders, the Netherlands and north-west Germany were maintained largely as a result of periodic sod removal (deturfing), with the heather regenerating from buried seeds. Sods were used as bedding and litter for inwintered livestock, and the resulting muck was used to fertilize arable fields (Gimingham & de Smidt 1983). Today, sod removal is a practical way of regenerating heather or *Erica*-dominant stands in heathland that has changed to grassland, eg as a result of grazing (Bakker 1978). Heather seed populations persist for decades in acid soils, so that, provided seeds remain in reasonable numbers, sod removal is a useful tool for nature reserve managers.

3.8 Planting and sowing

The advantage of transplants is that they generally establish under conditions in which seedlings would fail. Tree planting is done routinely throughout Britain, for production, amenity and nature conservation purposes. Shrubs and herbs can also be successfully planted in the wild, as was shown even in the last century (Bonnier 1890, 1920; MacDougal 1921). It is quite feasible to establish a wide variety of species in upland areas where the species in question grew, or probably grew, in the past (Park *et al.* 1962), or even where they may never have grown, at least not for centuries (Miles 1974a, 1975). However, introducing uncommon species to sites outside their putative natural range is a debatable activity, and may cause ill-feeling among nature conservationists and students of plant geography!

Planting can use individual plants or turves (Park *et al.* 1962; Humphries 1979; Gilbert & Wathern 1980); Miles (unpublished) has successfully established heather-dominant stands in patches of felled birch wood in a long-term experiment on the effects of heather on soil fertility. Eighteen-month-old heather plants were spaced at 25 cm intervals after the field layer had been killed with 2,4-D and dalapon, and the stand achieved >95% cover in 4 years.

Species diversification can also be achieved by direct seeding, both of trees and shrubs (McVean 1966) and of herbs (Wathern & Gilbert 1978; Wells 1979, 1980, 1983). Slot-seeding can be used to give a linear seed bed, and thus minimize the damage to the vegetation (Haggar 1980).

3.9 Fences, walls and hedges

The chief use of fences, etc, is to control livestock movements, and thus only indirectly to influence vegetation. However, boundary barriers, especially fences and hedges, are used as perches by fruit-eating birds, and seeds are voided. Woody species that are commonly dispersed and established in this way are rowan, rose (*Rosa* spp.), juniper, hawthorn, brambles (*Rubus fruticosus* agg.), holly (*Ilex aquifolium*), raspberry (*Rubus idaeus*), gean (*Prunus avium)* and bird-cherry (*P. padus*).

4 Conclusions

Vegetation management has a strong claim to being the oldest profession (Egler 1977)! All of the ways of managing vegetation discussed earlier, with the exception of the use of mineral fertilizers and chemical weedkillers, were known to our Bronze Age, and perhaps even our Stone Age, ancestors. Our advantage is that from systematic study of the ecology of our flora and vegetation, and of the processes of vegetation change, we know more about how the techniques operate, and are thus better able to predict and direct the course of change. Despite the paucity of original management tools, there is great scope for positive management in the uplands. Although precise prediction of the course of change is, from the nature of vegetation, usually impossible, more general prediction, using known principles, is increasingly feasible.

5 References

Agnew, A. D. Q. 1961. The ecology of *Juncus effusus* L. in north Wales. *J. Ecol.*, **49,** 83-102.

Anon. 1970. Forest fires in Scotland for the year ending 31st July 1970. *Scott. For.*, **24,** 292-293.

Armson, K.A. 1959. An example of the effects of past land use on fertility levels and growth of Norway spruce (*Picea abies* (L.) Karst). *Univ. Toronto For. Tech. Rep.*, **1.**

Bakker, J. P. 1978. Some experiments on heathland conservation and regeneration. *Phytocoenosis*, **7,** 351-370.

Battarbee, R.W., Appleby, P.G., Odell, K. & Flower, R.J. 1985. ^{210}Pb dating of Scottish lake sediments, afforestation and accelerated soil erosion. *Earth Surf. Process. Landf.*, **10,** 137-142.

Beckett, P.H.T. & Webster, R. 1971. Soil variability: a review. *Soils Fertil., Harpenden*, **34,** 1-15.

Bonnier, G. 1890. Cultures experimentales dans les Alpes et les Pyrenees. *Revue gen. Bot.*, **2,** 513-546.

Bonnier, G.1920. Nouvelles observations sur les cultures experimentales a diverses altitudes. *Revue gen. Bot.*, **32,** 305-326.

Brown, I.R. 1984. *Management of birch woodland in Scotland.* Perth: Countryside Commission for Scotland.

Cavers, P.B., & Harper, J.L., 1967. Studies in the dynamics of plant populations. I. The fate of seed and transplants introduced into various habitats. *J. Ecol.*, **55,** 59-71.

Clarke, F.W. 1924. The data of geochemistry. *U.S. Geol. Surv. Bull.*, no. 770.

Currall, J.E.P. 1981. *Some effects of management by fire on wet vegetation in western Scotland.* PhD thesis, University of Aberdeen.

Diemont, W.H. & Heil, G.W. 1984. Some long-term observations on cyclical and seral processes in Dutch heathlands. *Biol. Conserv.*, **30,** 283-290.

Duffey, E., Morris, M.G., Sheail, J., Ward, L.K., Wells, D.A. & Wells T.C.E. 1974. *Grassland ecology and wildlife management.* London: Chapman & Hall.

Egler, F.E. 1977. *The nature of vegetation: Its management and mismanagement.* Aton Forest: F.E. Egler.

Fryer, J.D. & Makepeace, R.J. 1978. *Weed control handbook. Vol. II. Recommendations including plant growth regulators.* 8th ed. Oxford: Blackwell Scientific.

Gilbert, O.L., & Wathern, P. 1980. The creation of flower-rich swards on mineral workings. *Reclam. Rev.*, **3,** 217-221.

Gimingham, C.H. 1985. Muirburn. In: *Vegetation management in northern Britain*, edited by R.B. Murray, 71-71. (British Crop Protection Council monograph no. 30.) Croydon: British Crop Protection Council.

Gimingham, C.H. & Smidt, J.T. de. 1983. Heaths as natural and semi-natural vegetation. In: *Man's impact on vegetation*, edited by W. Holzner, M.J.A. Werger & I. Ikusima, 185-199. The Hague: Junk.

Grant, S.A., Hunter, R.F. & Cross, C. 1963. The effects of muirburning *Molinia*-dominant communities. *J. Br. Grassld Soc.*, **18,** 249-257.

Haggar, R.J. 1980. Weed control and vegetation management by herbicides. In: *Amenity grassland: an ecological perspective*, edited by I.H. Rorison & R. Hunt, 163-173. Chichester: Wiley.

Heddle, R.G. & Ogg, W.G. 1936. Irrigation experiments on a Scottish hill pasture. *J. Ecol.*, **24,** 220-231.

Heil, G.W. & Diemont, W.H. 1983. Raised nutrient levels change heathland into grassland. *Vegetatio*, **53,** 113-120.

Helsper, H.P.G., Glenn-Lewin, D. & Weger, M.J.A. 1983. Early regeneration of *Calluna* heathland under various fertilization treatments. *Oecologia*, **58,** 208-214.

Hobbs, R.J. 1984. Length of burning rotation and community composition in high-level *Calluna-Eriophorum* bog in N England. *Vegetatio*, **57,** 129-136.

Hobbs, R.J., Mallik, A.V. & Gimingham, C.H. 1984. Studies on fire in Scottish heathland communities. III. Vital attributes of the species. *J. Ecol.*, **72,** 963-976.

Howells, G. 1966. *Some factors affecting development of natural regeneration of Sitka spruce.* PhD thesis, University of Wales.

Humphries, R.W. 1979. Some alternative approaches to the establishment of vegetation on mined land and on chemical waste materials. In: *Ecology and coal resource development*, edited by M.K. Wali, 461-475. New York: Pergamon.

Imeson, A.C. 1971. Heather burning and soil erosion on the north Yorkshire moors. *J. appl. Ecol.*, **8,** 537-542.

Johansson, T. 1985. Herbicide injections into stumps of aspen and birch to prevent regrowth. *Weed Res.*, **25,** 39-45.

Jones, L.I. 1967. Studies on hill land in Wales. *Welsh Pl. Breed. Sta. Tech. Bull.*, no. 4.

Kallio, P. & Lehtonen, J. 1975. On the ecocatastrophe of birch forests caused by *Operinia autumnata* (Bkh.) and the problem of reforestation. In: *Fennoscandian tundra ecosystems. Part 2. Animals and system analysis*, edited by F.E. Wielgolaski, 174-180. Berlin: Springer.

Kantey, B.A. & Morse, R.K. 1965. A modern approach to highway materials sampling. *Proc. 5th int. Conf. Soil Mech. Fdn Eng.*, **1,** 55-58.

Lazenby, A. 1955. Germination and establishment of *Juncus effusus* L. II. The interaction effects of moisture and competition. *J. Ecol.*, **43,** 595-605.

Lloyd, P.S. 1968. The ecological significance of fire in limestone grassland communities of the Derbyshire dales. *J. Ecol.*, **56,** 811-826.

Lyford, W.H. 1974. Narrow soils and intricate soil patterns in southern New England. *Geoderma*, **11,** 195-208.

MacDougal, D.T. 1921. The reactions of plants to new habitats. *Ecology*, **2,** 1-20.

McKelvie, A.D. & Scragg, E.B. 1972.The control of bracken by asulam. *Scott. Agric.*, **51,** 474-480.

McVean, D.N. 1959. Muir burning and conservation. *Scott. Agric.*, **39,** 79-82.

McVean, D.N. 1966. Establishment of native trees and shrubs on Scottish nature reserves by direct seed sowing. *Scott. For.*, **20,** 26-36.

Marrs, R. 1981. Scrub control on lowland heaths. In: *Heathland management*, edited by L. Faarrell, 59-67. Hutingdon: Nature Conservancy Council.

Merrifield, D.L. & Moore, P.D. 1974. Prehistoric human activity and blanket peat initiation on Exmoor. *Nature, Lond.*, **250,** 439-441.

Miles, J. 1968. Invasion by *Bryum bornholmense* Winkelm & Ruthe of heathland treated with calcium carbonate. *Trans. Br. Bryol. Soc.*, **5,** 287.

Miles, J. 1972. Experimental establishment of seedlings on a southern English heath. *J. Ecol.*, **60,** 225-234.

Miles, J. 1973a. Natural recolonization of experimentally bared soil in Callunetum in north-east Scotland. *J. Ecol.*, **61,** 399-412.

Miles, J. 1973b. Early mortality and survival of self-sown seedlings in Glenfeshie, Inverness-shire. *J. Ecol.*, **61,** 93-98.

Miles, J. 1974a. Experimental establishment of new species from seed in Callunetum in north-east Scotland. *J. Ecol.*, **62,** 527-551.

Miles, J. 1974b. Effects of experimental interference with stand structure on establishment of seedlings in Callunetum. *J. Ecol.*, **62,** 527-551.

Miles, J. 1974c. Effects of experimental interference with stand structure on establishment of seedlings in Callunetum. *J. Ecol.*, **62,** 675-687.

Miles, J. 1975. Performance after six growing seasons of new species established from seed in Callunetum in north-east Scotland. *J. Ecol.*, **63,** 891-902.

Miles, J. 1979. *Vegetation dynamics.* London: Chapman & Hall.

Miles, J. 1981. Problems in heathland and grassland dynamics. *Vegetatio*, **46,** 61-74.

Miles, J. 1985a. Soil in the ecosystem. In: *Ecological interactions in soil*, edited by A.H. Fitter, D. Atkinson, D.J. Read & M.B. Usher, 407-427. (British Ecological Society special publication no. 4.) Oxford: Blackwell Scientific.

Miles, J. 1985b. The ecological background to vegetation management. In: *Vegetation management in northern Britain*, edited by R.B. Murray, 3-20. (British Crop Protection Council monograph no. 30.) Croydon: British Crop Protection Council.

Miles, J. 1985c. The pedogenic effects of different species and vegetation types and the implications of succession. *J. Soil Sci.*, **36,** 571-584.

Miles, J. 1987. Soil variation caused by plants – a mechanism of floristic change in grassland? In: *Disturbance in grasslands: species and population responses*, edited by J. van Andel, R.W. Snaydon & J.P. Bakker. The Hague: Junk. In press.

Miles, J. & Kinnaird, J.W. 1979a.The establishment and regeneration of birch, juniper and Scots pine in the Scottish Highlands. *Scott. For.*, **33,** 102-119.

Miles, J. & Kinnaird, J.W. 1979b. Grazing with particular reference to birch, juniper and Scots pine in the Scottish Highlands. *Scott. For.*, **33,** 280-289.

Miles, J. & Young, W.F. 1980. The effects on heathland and moorland soils in Scotland and northern England following colonization by birch (*Betula* spp.). *Bull. Ecol.*, **11,** 233-242.

Miles, J., Welch, D. & Chapman, S.B. 1978. Vegetation and management in the uplands. In: *Upland land use in England and Wales*, edited by O.W. Heal, 77-95. (CCP111.) Cheltenham: Countryside Commission.

Miller, G.R. 1968. Evidence for selective feeding on fertilized plots by red grouse, hares and rabbits. *J. Wildl. Mgmt*, **32,** 849-853.

Miller, G.R., Miles, J. & Heal, O.W. 1984. *Moorland management: a study of Exmoor.* Cambridge: Institute of Terrestrial Ecology.

Miller, G.R., Watson, A. & Jenkins, D. 1970. Response of red grouse populations to experimental improvement of their food. In: *Animal populations in relation to their food resources*, edited by A. Watson, 323-335. Oxford: Blackwell Scientific.

Milton, W.E.J. 1948. The buried viable seed content of upland soils in Montgomeryshire. *Emp. J. exp. Agric.*, **16,** 163-177.

Moore, P.D. 1973. The influence of prehistoric cultures upon the initiation and spread of blanket bog in upland Wales. *Nature, Lond.*, **241,** 350-353.

Moore, P.D. 1987. A thousand years of death. *New Scient.*, **113,** 46-48.

Muirburn Working Party. 1977. *A guide to good muirburn practice.* Edinburgh: HMSO.

Park, K.J.F., Rawes, M. & Allen, S.E. 1962. Grassland studies on the Moor House National Nature Reserve. *J. Ecol.*, **50,** 53-62.

Peterson, R.G., Woodhouse, W.W. & Lucas, H.L. 1956. The distribution of excreta by freely grazing cattle and its effect on pasture fertility. II. Effect of returned excreta on the residual concentrations of some fertility elements. *Agron. J.*, **48,** 444-449.

Rawes, M. & Welch, D. 1969. Upland productivity of vegetation and sheep at Moor House National Nature Reserve, Westmorland, England. *Oikos (suppl.)*, **11,** 1-72.

Reardon, P.Q., Leinweber, C.L. & Merrill, L.B. 1972. The effect of bovine saliva on grasses. *J. Anim. Sci.*, **34,** 897-898.

Reardon, P.Q., Leinweber, C.L. & Merrill, L.B. 1974. Response of sideoats grama to animal saliva and thiamine. *J. Range Mgmt*, **27,** 400-401.

Richards, P.W. & Clapham, A.R. 1941. Biological flora of the British Isles: *Juncus effusus. J. Ecol.*, **29,** 375-380.

Ridley, H.N. 1930. *The dispersal of plants throughout the world.* Ashford: Reeve.

Robinson, G.W. & Lloyd, W.E. 1915. On the probable error of sampling in soil surveys. *J. agric. Sci., Camb.*, **7,** 144-153.

Sarvas, R. 1948. A research on the regeneration of birch in south Finland. *Comm. inst. for. fenn.*, **35**(4), 1-91.

Scarratt, J.B. 1966. *Investigations into the germination, early growth and survival of Sitka spruce seedlings under natural and artificial conditions.* PhD thesis, University of Wales.

Shaw, M.W. 1974. The reproductive characteristics of oak. In: *The British oak. Its history and natural history*, edited by M. G. Morris & F. H. Perring, 162-181. Farringdon: E. W. Classey.

Smidt, J.T. de. 1977. Interactions of *Calluna vulgaris* and the heather beetle (*Lochmaea suturalis*). In: *Vegetation and fauna*, edited by R. Tuxen, 179-186. Vaduz: Cramer.

Stewart, A. J. A. & Lance, A. N. 1983. Moor-draining: a review of impacts on land use. *J. environ. Manage.*, **17,** 81-89.

Stoakley, J. T. 1977. A severe outbreak of the pine beauty moth on lodgepole pine in Sutherland. *Scott. For.*, **31,** 113-125.

Tallis, J.H. 1973. Studies on southern Pennine peats. V. Direct observations on peat erosion and peat hydrology at Featherbed Moss, Derbyshire. *J. Ecol.*, **61,** 1-22.

Tamm, C. O. 1956. Further observations on the survival and flowering of some perennial herbs. I. *Oikos*, **7,** 273-292.

Taylor, K. & Marks, T.C. 1971. The influence of burning and grazing on the growth and development of *Rubus chamaemorus* L. in *Calluna-Eriophorum* bog. In: *The scientific management of animal and plant communities for conservation*, edited by E. Duffey & A.S. Watt, 153-166. Oxford: Blackwell Scientific.

Thompson, D.B.A., Galbraith, H. & Horsfield, D. 1987. Ecology and resources of Britain's mountain plateaux: land use conflicts and impacts. In: *Agriculture and conservation in the hills and uplands*, edited by M. Bell & R.G.H. Bunce, 22-31. (ITE symposium no. 23.) Grange-over-Sands: Institute of Terrestrial Ecology.

Van Goor, C.P. 1954. The influence of tillage on some properties of dry sandy soils in the Netherlands. *Landbouwk. Tijdschr., 's-Grav.*, **66,** 175-181.

Vermeer, J.G. 1986. The effect of nutrients on shoot biomass and species composition of wetland and hayfield communities. *Acta Oecol., Oecol. Plant.*, **7,** 31-41.

Wathern, P. & Gilbert, O.L. 1978. Artificial diversification of grassland with native herbs. *J. environ. Manage.*, **7,** 29-42.

Watson, A. & Miller, G.R. 1976. *Grouse management.* 2nd ed. Fordingbridge: Game Conservancy.

Watt, A.S. 1960. Population changes in acidophilous grass-heath in Breckland, 1936-1957. *J. Ecol.*, **48,** 605-629.

Weeda, W.C. 1967. The effect of cattle dung patches on pasture growth, botanical composition, and pasture utilization. *N.Z. J. agric. Res.*, **10,** 150-159.

Welch, D. 1984. Studies on the grazing of heather moorland in north-east Scotland. III. Floristics. *J. appl. Ecol.*, **21,** 209-225.

Welch, D. 1985. Studies on the grazing of heather moorland in north-east Scotland. IV. Seed dispersal and plant establishment in dung. *J. appl. Ecol.*, **22,** 461-472.

Wells, T.C.E. 1979. Habitat creation with reference to grassland. In: *Ecology and design in amenity land management,* edited by S.E. Wright & G.P. Buckley, 128-145. Wye: Wye College and Recreation Ecology Research Group.

Wells, T.C.E. 1980. Management options for lowland grassland. In: *Amenity grassland: an ecological perspective,* edited by I.H. Rorison & R. Hunt, 175-195. Chichester: Wiley.

Wells, T.C.E. 1983. The creation of species-rich grasslands. In: *Conservation in perspective,* edited by A. Warren & F.B. Goldsmith, 215-232. Chichester: Wiley.

Wheeler, J.L. 1958. The effect of sheep excreta and nitrogenous fertilizer on the botanical composition and production of a ley. *J. Br. Grassld Soc.*, **13,** 196-202.

Wolton, K.M. 1955. The effect of sheep excreta and fertilizer treatments on nutrient status of a pasture. *J. Br. Grassld Soc.*, **10,** 240-253.

The extent and composition of upland areas in Great Britain

R G H BUNCE
Institute of Terrestrial Ecology, Merlewood Research Station, Grange-over-Sands, Cumbria, England

1 Introduction

Despite the many conferences on the uplands, the difficulties inherent in producing an adequate definition have led to no generally accepted figure being available for the area involved. This deficiency is due to (i) the difficulty of defining the upland characteristics, and (ii) the problem of obtaining national coverage.

The main purpose of the present paper is, therefore, to define the area concerned, and then to use the Institute of Terrestrial Ecology's Merlewood land classification system data base to estimate the upland area of Britain and its vegetation composition.

Bunce and Heal (1984) summarized the current situation regarding information on the rural environment, and concluded that the disparate nature of much of the information available on vegetation and land use meant that there was no adequate, co-ordinated data base for defining the composition of the countryside. A comparable situation exists in the uplands, although a relatively restricted area is involved.

The first problem is recognized in many publications, with particularly useful summaries being given by MacEwen and Sinclair (1983) and Sinclair (1983). The problem is caused by the range of latitude in Britain, with sea level in Cornwall supporting vegetation generally considered as lowland in character, whilst in Shetland, at the same altitude, vegetation of upland character would be present. A further confusing factor is that, in general, it is easier to identify the affinities of species as upland in character, rather than to analyse the complex of controlling environmental factors. There is, therefore, an element of circularity in the discussion, in that upland character (an environmental definition) is frequently inferred indirectly from the species composition.

Altitude is the most widely used parameter (eg Ball *et al.* 1983) and gives a useful general overall estimate, but underestimates the area in the north. Birse (1970) provides more sophisticated integrated classes, but the information is given as maps, and only covers Scotland. The agricultural land classification does not provide adequate figures because valley-bottom grade 3 land in the uplands cannot be separated from the general occurrence of that category elsewhere. The soils pose comparable problems, although, as Ball (1978) has shown, estimates can be obtained from appropriate soil types. The soil maps of Avery *et al.* (1975) and Bibby (1980) could, therefore, be used to obtain useful estimates, although the problem remains of the better soil types in upland areas. Concerning vegetation, the classification of Robertson (1984) defines upland types in Scotland but gives no figures for their relative coverage. Likewise, the classification of Ward (1971) defines the major upland types, as does the national vegetation classification currently being produced at the University of Lancaster, but gives no consistent areal estimates.

Turning now to the consistency of coverage, the various publications by the Countryside Commission contain a range of figures for England and Wales, but do not cover Scotland. The disparate nature of such information is well summarized by the Centre for Agricultural Strategy (1978). Published figures by the Hill Farming Research Organisation are related to the agricultural land classification, and other general statements available do not provide adequate definition of the way they were derived.

In conclusion, the best available figures seem to be those derived from the designation of Less Favoured Areas (LFAs) under European Community Directive 75/268. These figures are useful because of the indirect correlation between part of the definition used, that of declining population, with upland characteristics. A separate 'mountain area' definition is not applied in Britain. The map of LFAs corresponds closely to the generally considered area of uplands as shown by Ball *et al.* (1982), and the figure for this category is used for comparison with those derived independently below. It should be noted that the area of LFA was extended in 1983 to include marginal areas of hill land.

2 Upland definition

The figures presented in Table 1 are derived from a dual system of definition reflecting the difficulties mentioned above.

i. The land classes (defined by the Merlewood land classification system (Bunce *et al.* 1983), which have a combination of high rainfall, low evapotranspiration, low insolation and generally poor soils, provide the basic upland area.

ii. Within that area, vegetation which is of upland character, ie comprises species such as deer-grass (*Trichophorum cespitosum*), mat-grass (*Nardus stricta*) and purple moor-grass (*Molinia caerulea*), is separated from the mainly agricultural grasslands of predominantly lowland species, such as rye-grass (*Lolium perenne*), which can still exist in the uplands following improvement.

Table 1. A comparison of 2 methods of estimating the major components of upland vegetation in Britain

i. derived from areal measurements of land cover types in 256 sample squares (8 from 32 classes);

ii. derived from the proportion of 1280 200 m² quadrats placed at random within the 32 classes, classified according to TWINSPAN and summarized at a similar level (proportion only — areal measurements not applicable)

Total area of Britain (excluding water and urban) = 19.8 Mha

Total area of uplands (including forest and agricultural grass) = 7.7 Mha (39%)

Area of upland vegetation (bog, moorland and grassland) = 4.6 Mha (23%)

	Bog	Moorland	Grassland
i.	Bog	Moorland	Grassland
	1.5 Mha	1.7 Mha	1.4 Mha
	(32%)	(37%)	(31%)
ii.	Bog	Moorland	Grassland
	Sundew *(Drosera rotundifolia)*, cotton-grass *(Eriophorum angustifolium)*	Heather *(Calluna vulgaris)*, tormentil *(Potentilla erecta)*	Bent-grass *(Agrostis tenuis)*, heath bedstraw *(Galium saxatile)*
	34%	37%	28%

Table 2. Major upland species covering land in the uplands, determined from cover in 1280 200 m² quadrats (40 in each of 32 classes)

	Mha	GB %	% upland
Heather *(Calluna vulgaris)*	1.4	6	25
Bent-grass *(Agrostis tenuis)*	0.8	3	14
Purple moor-grass *(Molinia caerulea)*	0.6	3	10
Mat-grass *(Nardus stricta)*	0.3	1	6
Bracken *(Pteridium aquilinum)*	0.3	1	6
Deer-grass *(Trichophorum cespitosum)*	0.2	1	3
Sheep's fescue *(Festuca ovina)*	0.2	1	3
Wavy hair-grass *(Deschampsia flexuosa)*	0.2	1	3
Sweet vernal-grass *(Anthoxanthum odoratum)*	0.2	1	3
Bilberry *(Vaccinium myrtillus)*	0.1	1	1

Taking the upland land class definition, the uplands cover 7.7 Mha (39%) of GB as compared with the figure of 8.7 Mha for LFAs, redefined and extended in 1983. On the other hand, only 4.6 Mha (23% of GB) is upland vegetation. This reduction is due, in part, to inherently better soils in otherwise upland situations, but also to agricultural improvement converting upland soils and vegetation to more productive species of predominantly lowland character. Further details of the breakdown of the individual categories are given by Bunce *et al.* (1984) but, for present purposes, the types were grouped into 3 broad categories, bog, moorland and grassland. Two methods were then used to compare their relative cover within the upland land class:

i. by areal measurements of land cover types in 256 sample squares (Bunce *et al.* 1983), which can then be converted to national estimates from their occurrence within land classes;

ii. by classifying sample quadrats, within which all species are recorded into classes for the comparable groupings described under (i).

Although the sampling system was identical, the results from the contrasting methods of survey show a high degree of consistency, which would suggest that the figures are reasonable estimates of the major breakdown of upland vegetation in Britain. This suggestion is supported further by the comparison of 7.4 Mha from LFA measurements. Further details of the areal coverage of more detailed categories are given by Bunce *et al.* (1984).

A further important aspect of upland vegetation is the coverage by individual species. Within 1280 200 m² quadrats, the percentage cover of individual species was also recorded, and was used to obtain the national estimates of cover in Table 2. This Table shows that surprisingly few species, with heather (*Calluna vulgaris*) being outstanding, are involved in the vegetation cover of the uplands, and that the residual cover is provided by a limited range of other species.

A further example of the use of the sampling framework to estimate the extent of upland areas is given in Table 3. In this case, the land classes containing the upland plateaux referred to by Thompson (1987) were extracted. Whilst the plateaux themselves will form a relatively small proportion of the uplands, the Table shows how the relative proportions change when different categories are considered. In particular, the example of the extent of bare rock shows how an individual component of a resource can be estimated and shown to have a restricted distribution — an essential activity when making recommendations about the conservation of an individual ecosystem.

Table 3. Contribution of land classes 23 and 24 to the uplands of Great Britain

Britain 19.8 Mha

Mountain core 1.35 Mha Uplands 7.7 Mha	= 6.8% of Britain
Mountain core 1.35 Mha Upland vegetation 4.6 Mha	= 17.5% of uplands
Mountain core 1.35 Mha	=29.3% of upland vegetation

Bog	Moorland	Grassland	Rock
1.5 Mha	1.7 Mha	1.4 Mha	0.14 Mha
MC = 0.4 Mha	0.44 Mha	0.6 Mha	0.05 Mha
26.3%	25.9%	4.3%	39.0%

MC, mountain core

3 Discussion

The above results show how the land classification system has been used to produce the first co-ordinated estimates of the extent and composition of the uplands. In the present case, only general categories are used, but further details on vegetation or habitats could be added, if required. Such basic statistics concerning the resource are essential for strategic planning purposes, as they provide the baseline against which changes can be assessed. Other studies are currently in progress to examine various impacts, eg afforestation (Bunce 1987), on the uplands so that the extent of the impact can be determined. In this particular case, the very wet deer-grass/cotton-grass (*Trichophorum/Eriophorum*) bog was affected to a much lesser degree than other semi-natural vegetation types. The impact also differs according to the extent of the category — a loss of 70% of 10 000 ha is more significant than 70% of 100 000 ha. A monitoring programme is, therefore, required to follow the changes that are taking place, together with the consequences, so that pressure can be brought to bear for the necessary policy changes to be made.

4 References

Avery, B.W., Finlay, D.C. & Mackney, D. 1975. *Soil map of England and Wales 1:1,000,000.* Southampton: Ordnance Survey.

Ball, C.F. 1978. The soils of upland Britain. In: *The future of upland Britain*, 397-417. (CAS Report no. 2.) Reading: Centre for Agricultural Strategy, University of Reading.

Ball, D.F., Dale, J., Sheail, J. & Heal, O.W. 1982. *Vegetation change in upland landscapes.* Cambridge: Institute of Terrestrial Ecology.

Ball, D.F., Radford, G.L. & Williams, W.M. 1983. *A land characteristic data bank for Great Britain.* (Bangor occasional paper no. 13.) Bangor: Institute of Terrestrial Ecology.

Bibby, J.S. 1980. Soil research and land use capability interpretative maps. In: *Land assessment in Scotland*, edited by M.F. Thomas & J.T. Coppock, 25-36. Aberdeen: University Press.

Birse, E.L. 1970. *Assessment of climatic conditions in Scotland.* Aberdeen: Macaulay Institute for Soil Research.

Bunce, R.G.H. 1987. The potential impact of afforestation on semi-natural vegetation in Britain. In: *Proceedings of Annual Conference of Institute of Chartered Foresters.* In press.

Bunce, R.G.H. & Heal, O.W. 1984. Landscape evaluation and the impact of changing land-use on the rural environment: the problem and an approach. In: *Planning and ecology*, edited by R.D. Roberts & T.M. Roberts, 164-188. London: Chapman & Hall.

Bunce, R.G.H., Barr, C.J. & Whittaker, H.A. 1983. A stratification system for ecological sampling. In: *Ecological mapping from ground, air and space*, edited by R.M. Fuller, 39-46. (ITE symposium no. 10.) Cambridge: Institute of Terrestrial Ecology.

Bunce, R.G.H., Tranter, R.B., Thompson, A.M.M., Mitchell, C.P. & Barr, C.J. 1984. Models for predicting changes in rural land use in Great Britain. In: *Agriculture and the environment*, edited by D. Jenkins, 37-44. (ITE symposium no. 13.) Abbots Ripton: Institute of Terrestrial Ecology.

Centre for Agricultural Strategy. 1978. *The future of upland Britain.* (CAS Report no. 2.) Reading: Centre for Agricultural Strategy, University of Reading.

MacEwen, M. & Sinclair, G. 1983. *New life for the hills.* London: Council for the National Parks.

Robertson, J.G.. 1984. *A key to the common plant communities of Scotland.* Aberdeen: Macaulay Institute for Soil Research.

Sinclair, G. 1983. *The upland landscape study.* Environment Information Services, Dyfed.

Thompson, D.B.A., Galbraith, D. & Harsfield, D. 1987. Ecology and resources of Britain's mountain plateaux: land use conflicts and impacts. In: *Agriculture and conservation in the hills and uplands*, edited by M. Bell & R.G.H. Bunce, 22-31. (ITE symposium no. 23.) Grange-over-Sands: Institute of Terrestrial Ecology.

Ward, S.D. 1971. *A dichotomous key to upland acidic plant communities.* Bangor: Institute of Terrestrial Ecology.

Ecology and resources of Britain's mountain plateaux: land use conflicts and impacts

D B A THOMPSON, H GALBRAITH and D HORSFIELD
Chief Scientist Directorate, Nature Conservancy Council, 12 Hope Terrace, Edinburgh, Scotland

1 *Introduction*

Many people find mountain scenery inspiring. The dissected plateaux of Cairn Gorm and Lochnagar in the central Scottish Highlands are excellent examples. Deep, steep-sided valleys gouged out by glacial activity and erosion, together with variations in geology, aspect and flora, promote the stark features and contrasts which look so dramatic. The plateaux are attracting increasing numbers of people, and concern is mounting over vegetation damage, soil erosion and potential disturbance to birds. Grazing impacts are mentioned frequently, yet data are rarely produced.

This paper outlines the land use issues as they affect the biotic resource of the plateaux. Ski development and recreation-related intrusions are fairly localized, whereas grazing impacts are widespread, particularly south of the Scottish Highlands. Grazing pressures far exceed the others in terms of area affected. Nevertheless, we discuss recreational impacts first, because these are traditionally viewed as the main conflict with conservation. This is a misconception: the broader, but more gradual, changes inflicted by grazing sheep and deer are responsible for the main transformation of the natural montane landscape. Relevant material has been drawn from UK and abroad in this first attempt to produce a general overview.

2 *The dimensions of the resource*

Hills, moorland and mountains cover at least 25% of Britain's land surface (Ratcliffe & Thompson 1988). Above 611 m (2000 ft), there are 396 km^2, 5039 km^2 and 226 km^2 in England, Scotland and Wales, respectively (Ball *et al.* 1983). The total comprises some 2.5% of Britain's surface, with only 0.2% lying above 914 m (3000 ft). Towards the north and west, there is a gradual descent in altitudinal life zones; the natural tree-line lies at about 650 m in the Cairngorms, but at no more than 300 m in north-west Sutherland, and virtually down to sea level on exposed northern coasts (Ratcliffe 1987). We are interested in the higher zones, and take as the lowermost threshold the level above which heather (*Calluna vulgaris*) becomes prostrate (at around 700 m in the Cairngorms and central Grampians, dropping to 550 m in Sutherland, 350 m in farthest north-west Sutherland, and only 300 m in Orkney and Shetland). Here, heather gives way to moss, lichen, small-shrub or sedge heaths, or to ablation surfaces. Most high-level plateaux are located in the north and west (Figure 1), and cover some 0.6–0.8% of Britain's land surface. These are among the largest most natural habitats, and comprise a resource nearest to that found in unspoilt arctic/alpine areas. The high altitude, shallow infertile soils and severe climate, however, render the plateaux vulnerable to both natural and human-induced damage.

3 *Land use issues*

High, flat-topped mountains are important to hill-walkers, climbers and mountain skiers. Many are attracted to them by the remoteness and dramatic beauty which afford a physical and psychological detachment from more commonplace areas. This impression of wilderness may be reinforced in winter when the high plateaux are at their most hostile. For most people, this experience probably depends more on the general ambience than on any aspect of the biota. Wildlife nevertheless certainly enhances the aesthetic quality (Thompson 1986).

We see 5 main threats to Britain's montane ecological resource: (i) downhill ski developments in Scotland; (ii) hill-walking disturbance; (iii) overgrazing by sheep and deer, mainly in Wales and England, and on a smaller scale in Scotland; (iv) acid deposition which has affected much of the English Pennines and parts of Wales; and (v) mineral extraction and quarrying. The first 2 effects can be closely intertwined (see Watson 1985; Bayfield *et al* 1988; and reviews in Bayfield & Barrow 1985); the others are quite different, though more difficult to evaluate. We do not deal with (iv) because relevant information is unavailable for the plateaux (for studies at lower altitudes, see, for example, Lee *et al.* 1986, 1988); (v) is left aside because traditional activities fluctuate with the world mineral markets. Depletion of stocks of certain metals, however, might result in renewed working of low-grade cores (see Ratcliffe 1974, 1987).

3.1 Ski developments

Compared with countries such as France, Switzerland, Austria, USA and Canada, the British skiing industry is tiny. It is growing, however, being comparable in rate of increase, but certainly not scale, with the USA (Dearden & Sewell 1985). Organized skiing began in Scotland around 1949, when some hoteliers in Speyside offered special rates and additional attractions. The uptake was slow until the late 1950s, but by 1962 there were commercial ski developments at Cairnwell and Cairn Gorm, both near mountain plateaux. During the 3 winters post-1962–63, there was a 10-fold increase in numbers of people using the lifts or tows at Cairn Gorm (Watson 1967). There are now 4 main ski developments, and another 6 are proposed; numbers of skiers appear to be rising annually (Bayfield *et al.* 1988).

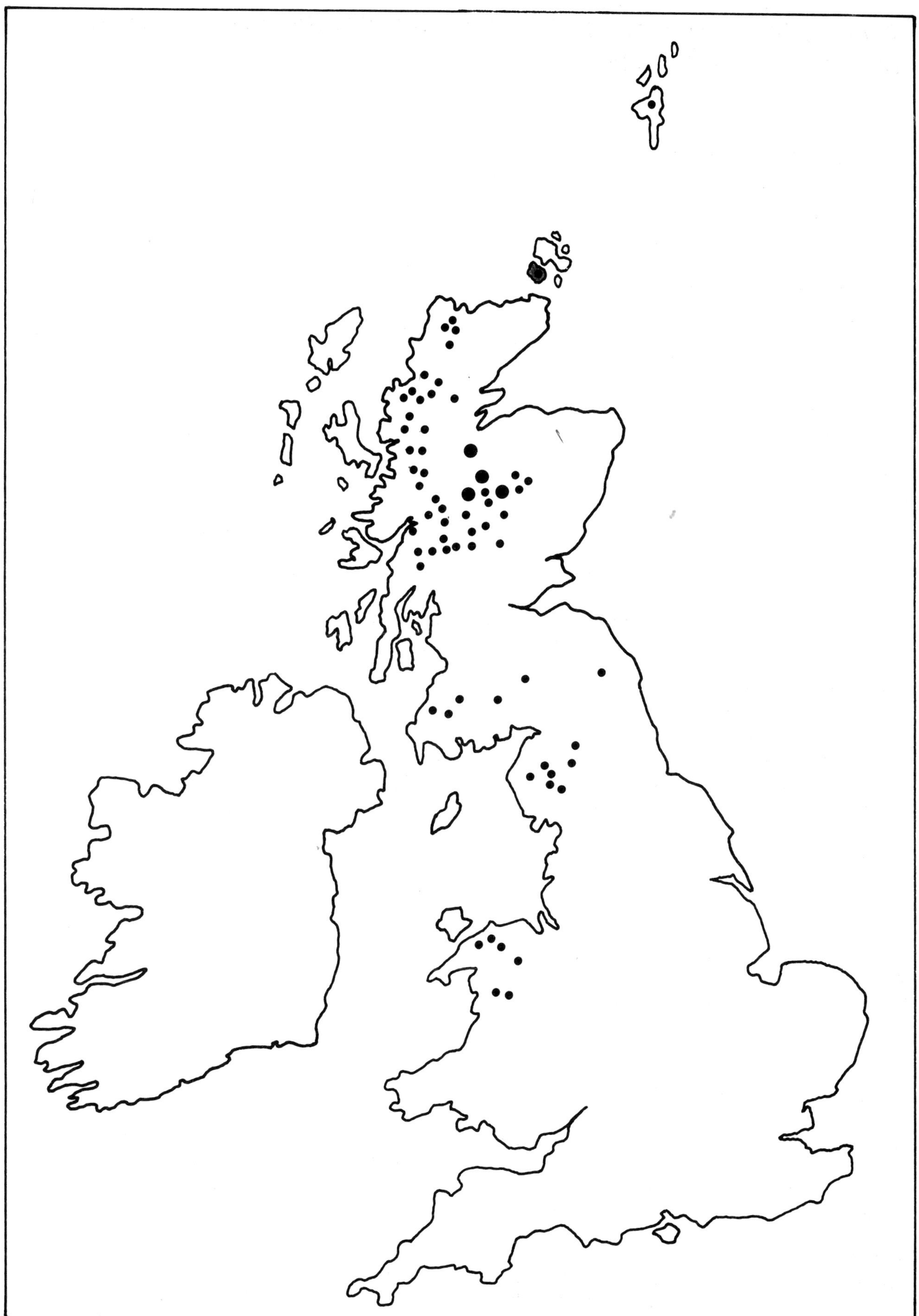

Figure 1. The occurrence of Britain's mountain plateaux. Most small closed circles indicate flat areas above 760 m (2500 ft) larger than approximately one km^2, though in Orkney and Shetland 2 sites above only 456 m (1500 ft) have been included on botanical grounds. Large symbols denote massifs (eg Cairngorms)

Downhill skiing and conservation clash for 3 main reasons. First, the highest, broad summit ridges, containing the most outstanding and extensive natural montane plant and animal communities, adjoin corries and slopes coveted by skiers. Second, the severe climate and fragile soils combine to render the plateaux extremely vulnerable to damage. At resorts abroad, such as in Switzerland, France, Germany and Austria, most skiing pistes occur on the ecologically more resilient zones below the timber-line, or within the timber or the agricultural zones; recovery from damage is better there (eg Grabherr 1985; Price 1985). Third, ski developments can facilitate the year-round use of mountains, with the paraphernalia of new roads, car parks, chairlifts and cafés open in summer to supplement winter incomes. As Watson (1967, 1984a), Bayfield (1985) and Bayfield *et al.* (1988) point out for the Cairngorms, the rapid increase in footpaths is mainly attributable to the development of uplift facilities in the past 25 years. Many of the more recreational impacts related to downhill skiing are considered in the next Section. However, some of the damage is restricted to skiing, and can be considered under 2 headings.

3.1.1 Construction damage

Heavy-tracked vehicles used for transporting materials, creating pistes and clearing snow have caused extensive damage. The most insidious effects have occurred on slopes with sparse snow cover, where vegetation has been bruised, ripped out or buried under debris (Miller 1986). Both gully erosion and slumping occur, especially where drainage ditches are inadequate (as on Cairn Gorm and Glenshee). A combination of heavy rain, considerable snowmelt, shallow frosts and rapid thawing of barer ground speeds up erosion and alluvial movement. The water catchment is sometimes very large, and water may be shed quickly. Tracks and paths often conduct the runoff, altering the natural pattern of streamflow, taking water into less stable areas, and depositing grit and stones on to previously damage-free ground. Contractors now use helicopters or people to transport materials, and fences to retain snow on the major runs, and sow plant-damaged areas with mixtures of fast-growing agronomic grasses. This practice has reduced the damage considerably. Features such as pylons and overhead wires, however, remain eyesores. They are also a problem for red grouse (*Lagopus l. scoticus*) and ptarmigan (*Lagopus mutus*), especially males, which often die from flying into them (Watson 1979, 1982). Nevertheless, they do not deter some breeding birds: ptarmigan, meadow pipits (*Anthus pratensis*) and wheatears (*Oenanthe oenanthe*) have nested within a few metres of pylons.

3.1.2 Ski damage

Skiing cuts up vegetation where snow cover is shallow or incomplete, and bruises or kills plants, inducing soil erosion where snow becomes compacted. On undulating ground, where the snow cover is shallow, hummocks may be bared and will recover only if skiing ceases. Hamilton (cited in Price 1985) looked at ski damage at Marmot Basin, North America, and found that 48% of convex slopes were damaged, with regrowth on only 4%; few concave or flat areas were damaged.

Around tows and at each end of chairlifts, erosion is frequent and widens as people seek to avoid wetter, churned patches. The artificial redistribution and prolongation of snow cover affect the natural spatial pattern of plants. Heather can be killed by snow mould (*Fusarium* spp.) when under snow for long periods. Snow-tolerant species (eg mat-grass (*Nardus stricta*), bilberry (*Vaccinium myrtillus*)) may move in to colonize the ground freed by heather dieback (Miller 1986). Graminoids tend to be more successful colonizers than dwarf shrubs and mosses, leading to local changes in cover. Mat-grass produces large numbers of tillers in late summer/autumn which overwinter to emerge early in spring, facilitating rapid colonization of bare, damaged ground (eg Pryor 1985). Whether or not colonized ground was unnaturally damaged is often not clear.

3.2 Recreational damage and disturbance

3.2.1 An international perspective

Since the later 1940s, the growth in recreational use of the high mountains has been immense. The rate of increase in Scotland has been steep since the early 1970s (Aitken 1983), while in the Lake District there was probably a 4-fold increase between 1939 and 1975 (Fishwick 1985). Abroad, the story is much the same; harmful impacts have been described in Sweden (Emanuelsson 1985), North America (Price 1985; Dearden & Sewell 1985), Austria, Germany (Grabherr 1985) and in parts of the USA (Willard & Marr 1971; Cole 1985; Studlar 1985). Most of the damage has been due to trampling and tends to be located around paths and traditionally popular destinations. Hence, figures quoted for overall damage to mountain areas tend to be small, eg <2% in Eagle Cap Wilderness, Oregon (Cole 1981). Such figures are rarely comparable anyway, because of methodological differences: some workers measure only bare soil extent, others contrast damaged and undamaged vegetation, and few quantify natural damage. Reliable counts of people are few. Exceptionally, over 200 walkers have been counted on the Cairn Gorm–Ben Macdui plateau on a fine summer day. In winter, sometimes over 7000 use the Cairn Gorm and Glenshee ski grounds (Nethersole-Thompson & Watson 1981). A daily average of 440 (maximum 900) people have been counted on Helvellyn summit (Fishwick 1985), and overall about 500 people per day visit Snowdon summit (Archer 1985).

The loss or modification of natural montane plant communities (Figure 2) from recreation (as well as grazing and acidification) on British plateaux is now being estimated by us and colleagues. Three vegetation types appear to be particularly vulnerable: closed moss (*Racomitrium*) heath, lichen-rich heath, and high-altitude springs and flushes. To date, the best data on change with time are

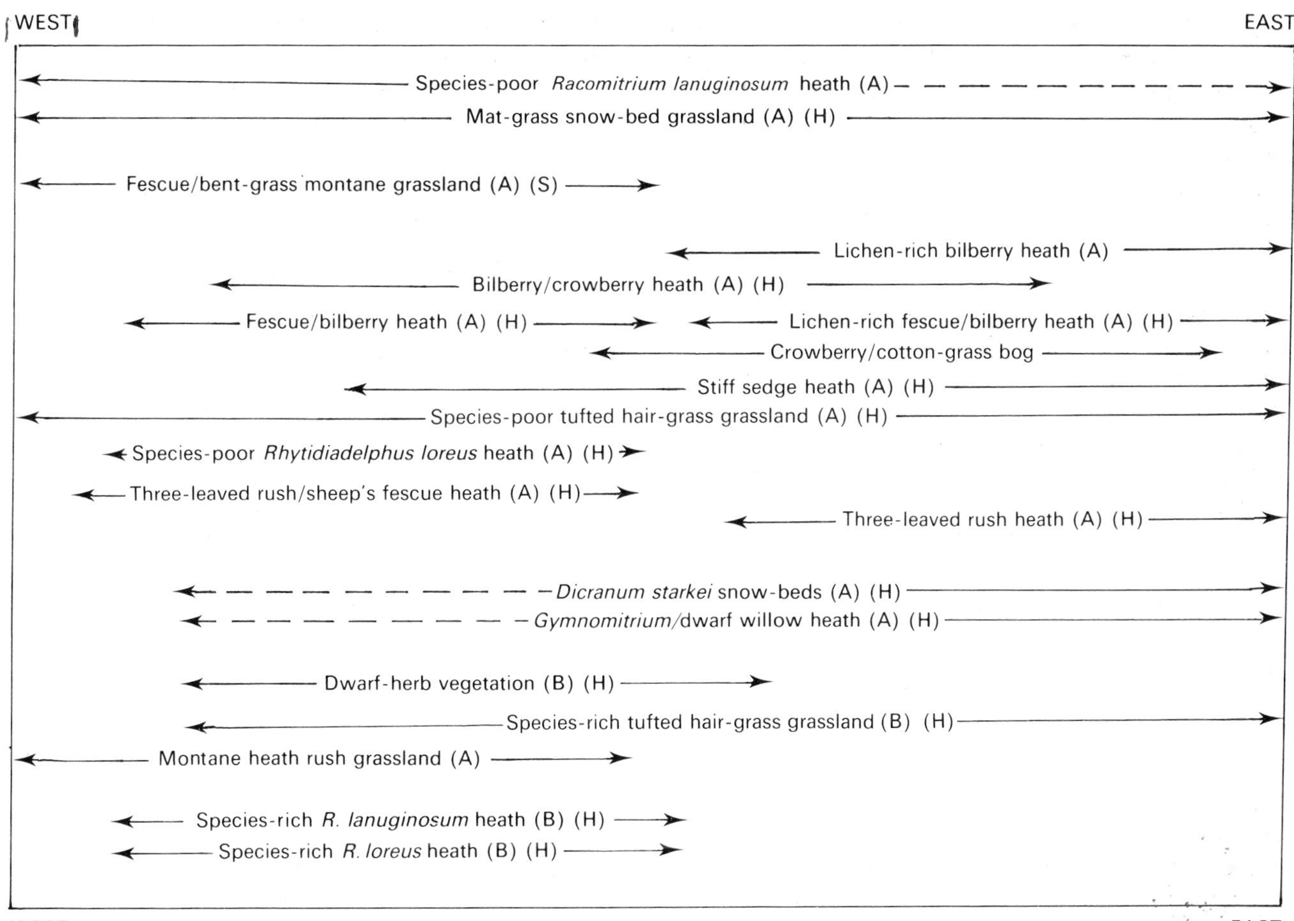

Figure 2. Plant communities of Britain's mountain plateaux. Distribution across upland Britain and approximate descending order of prevalence are indicated A, acidic soils; B, basic soils, H, found mainly in Scottish Highlands; S, found mainly south of the Scottish Highlands

mainly for footpaths and some well-researched areas on or close to ski slopes. Baugh (1979), Bayfield (1985), Watson (1984a) and Aitken (1983) summarize much of the work on mountain footpaths; Bayfield quotes data collected since 1969 for path numbers, changes in width, and compaction of bare ground. Path widths were broadly related to levels of use, but were wider on peatier than mineral soils.The paths monitored on the Cairn Gorm plateau (mineral soil) increased in width by 0.1–0.2 m per year, with 2 supporting up to 200 and 60 people daily. Total footpath length on the same plateau increased from 1.3 km to 7.2 km to 17.1 km in 1961, 1968 and 1980, respectively (Watson 1984a).

3.2.2 Specific impacts and recovery

Some of the best examples are recorded outside Britain. Grabherr (1985) working in the Austrian Tyrol studied alpine lichens and grasslands, and quantified inverse curvilinear relationships between plant biomass and trampling intensity for (in descending order of damage) lichens, then grasses and forbs, and finally a species of sedge (*Carex curvula*). On the Salt Pond mountain plateau in Virginia, USA, Studlar (1985) looked at 7 mosses fragmented by trampling: *Sphagnum recurvum* recovered badly from 1600 walks but well from only 300; *Ditrichum pallidium* and *Hypnum imponens* showed good recovery after one year from 4200 walks, but were later displaced by vascular plants; *Polytrichum commune, Thuidium delicatulum, Sphagnum palustre* and *S. hemynse* recovered well and expanded. Other good examples from outside Britain are reviewed by Willard and Marr (1971), Price (1985) and Cole (1985). Once the topsoil has vanished, decades, or even centuries, may pass before natural vegetation is restored (eg Willard & Marr 1971).

In Britain, relevant research on the plateaux has been undertaken only in the Cairngorms. Salient results of research by Bayfield (1979, 1985) and Bayfield *et al.* (1981) are summarized in Table 1. Following experimental trampling, wet heather/deer-grass (*Trichophorum*) heath tended to be most resilient and heather/bearberry (*Arctostaphylos uva-ursi*) most susceptible, with a slow recovery after mineral soils were exposed (Bayfield 1979). Moss heath was less fragile than anticipated, with the carpet appearing to cushion the impact of feet and provide a suitable substrate for replacement growth (taking 8 years, but 70–80% complete after only 2 years when previously subjected to 240 tramples). Emanuelsson's (1985) findings from experimentally trampled alpine and sub-alpine vegetation in Lapland are very similar.

Table 1. Response and recovery (after 3 months–8 years) of 4 montane heath communities on Cairn Gorm in relation to variation in intensity of trampling (0–240 tramples) (source: Bayfield 1979, 1985; Bayfield *et al.* 1981)

Heath community	Damage increased with trampling intensity	Bare ground or peat remained	Recovery Rate	Recovery Completion
1. Lichen-rich heather/deer-grass	Yes**	Some	Moderate	Complete
2. Heather/deer-grass	Yes**	Yes*	Fast	Complete
3. Heather/bearberry	Yes*	Yes*	Slow	Incomplete
4. Moss heath	Yes**	No	Gradual	Complete

* P<0.05, ** P<0.01; F-ratio for ANOVA indicating significant increase with trampling intensity

Altitude of plots: 620 m (1), 640 m (2), 750 m (3) and 1050 m (4). Soil types: blanket peat (1 & 2), mountain podzol (3 & 4). Bayfield (1974) controlled for temporal and spatial dynamic change in plant cover by estimating 'relative cover', involving initial and final measurements on control and experimental plots

In 1, 2 and 3, damage was crushing of deer-grass, with a significant amount of broken heather only occurring in 1. In 4, the heath consisted of significantly crushed crowberry and bog bilberry (*Vaccinium uliginosum*) (P<0.01) and dead *Racomitrium* (P<0.05)

Of other species studied, bilberry recovered slowly but completely after 8 years, stiff sedge (*Carex bigelowii*) recovered extremely quickly, crowberry, lichens and cotton-grass (*Eriophorum* spp.) recovered slowly and incompletely, and *Sphagnum rubellum* damage increased with trampling intensity (P<0.05) and showed barely any recovery over the years

Interestingly, weather appears to interact with moss heath resilience, for in drier weather, when more people are on the tops (Morris *et al.* 1974; Anderson Semens Houston 1981; Watson unpubl.), smaller fragments break off making recovery harder. Lichens (*Cladonia* spp.) are also more susceptible during dry weather (Bayfield *et al.* 1981). Only small differences were found between summer and winter responses to trampling. Vulnerability should be greatest from late summer through to early spring when the vegetation is dormant or slow-growing. Seasonal changes in relative cover of 6 vegetation types exposed to summer trampling (300 walks) in the northern Cairngorms were recorded by Pryor (1985). He found recovery to be most complete in mat-grass (75%), 3-leaved rush (*Juncus trifidus*) (50%), moss heath (45%), crowberry (*Empetrum*)/bilberry (35%) and heather/deer-grass (30%). Recovery was poorest in lichen-rich dwarf heather heath (15%). There were significant improvements in recovery between spring and summer in total plant cover, mainly accounted for by an expansion of 3-leaved rush. Looking more closely at the population dynamics of this species, Pryor found that moderate, but not high, disturbance was associated with the presence of relatively more smaller, younger individual plants. Three-leaved rush seed stores average 900 seeds m^{-2}, with perhaps only 12% of seedlings at high altitudes dying in their first winter, compared with 56% mortality for sedges, and 99–100% for dwarf shrubs and dicotyledonous herbs (Miller 1986). Other studies of how disturbance affects montane plant demography are published by Marchand and Roach (1980), Gartner *et al.* (1983), and Fletcher and Shaver (1983). Miller (1986, pp13-18) gives a good summary of the reproductive capabilities of Scottish montane plants: many large patches of mat-grass above 1000 m are sterile; 3-leaved rush frequently fails to set good seeds in cold, wet summers; and the viable buried seed pool is virtually restricted to organic rather than mineral soils.

3.2.3 Broader impacts

Most of this work has been concerned with obvious intrusions, such as ski developments, paths or trampled areas. To what extent has the wider plateau been degraded by recreation? Watson (1985) provides the best answers for the Cairn Gorm plateau and corries. He devoted considerable effort to distinguishing between man-induced and widespread natural damage, the latter being due to the severe climate in open, exposed ground. Features of natural disturbance included tiny rills, partially torn clumps of vegetation facing the prevailing winds, and grit lying 5 m to the leeside of big patches of grit along a one metre band on the clump's windward side. Grit was blown easily over icy snow for distances of up to 100 m, and after thaws it occurred over about 2% of undisturbed areas. Human-disturbed areas had paths, torn plants with crushing or poaching beside footprints, bare soils with vegetation present only on the underside of boulders, much more grit on vegetation, and lateral or linear erosion. Foot slippage increased on steep slopes in disturbed areas. Human-disturbed areas covered 403 ha, 17% being in the Cairngorms National Nature Reserve. Watson (1985) also found that disturbed soil had a lower content of organic material and fewer fine particles (<0.5 mm). Table 2 summarizes paired comparisons of vegetation cover in disturbed and undisturbed areas, and reveals that disturbance was associated with reduced cover and occurrence of plants.The differences were significant, being highest for the shrubs, mosses and lichens.

3.2.4 Effects on animal communities

Any adverse effects on invertebrate populations are almost unknown (despite many being rare or relict, and

Table 2. The average percentage cover of plants in pairs of human-disturbed and undisturbed (though 'naturally' disturbed) transects on Cairn Gorm (data collated from 3 transects) (source: Watson 1985)

Species	% cover in areas Disturbed	Undisturbed
Dwarf willow (*Salix herbacea*)	0.67	8.77***++
Bilberry	0.00	2.40***+++
Cladonia spp. and *Cetraria* spp. lichens on ground vegetation	0.10	3.90***++
Mosses (Musci) on ground vegetation	4.87	28.6***++
Others[1]	0.2	2.0***

*** P<0.001; Mann-Whitney U test for % cover comparisons

Data for 20 pairs per transect (200 m long; 0.25 m^2 quadrats)

++ P<0.01, +++ P<0.001; Fisher exact probability test for frequency of occurrence comparisons

[1] Other species: alpine lady's-mantle (*Alchemilla alpina*), crowberry (*Empetrum hermaphroditum*), moss campion (*Silene acaulis*), grasses, sedges and rushes

forming the food resource of scarce dotterel (*Charadrius morinellus*), snow buntings (*Plectrophenax nivalis*) and other birds). Welch (in Watson 1976) found disturbed soils held fewer mountain top beetles (*Liogluta nitidiuscula*). On sub-montane grasslands, invertebrates responded to levels of human trampling that had little effect on plant communities (Duffey 1975).

The effects on birds and mammals have been quantified in Britain only in the Cairngorms and at Cairnwell (Watson 1979, 1988, unpubl.; Nethersole-Thompson & Watson 1981). Breeding densities of ptarmigan and red grouse, meadow pipit and wheatear were no lower on disturbed ground, though the breeding success of ptarmigan and grouse was very low on the heavily disturbed Cairn Gorm. The main cause of poor breeding was heavy predation by crows (*Corvus* spp.) attracted by food scraps left by tourists (Watson 1982). Watson (unpubl.) found no differences between spring numbers or breeding success of dotterel before and after ski developments. On the more base-rich hills of the Moinian and Dalradian schists, breeding densities and productivity of ptarmigan and dotterel appear to be highest (Nethersole-Thompson 1973; Watson *et al.* 1970; Watson & Rae 1987. Breeding surpluses on these sites may continually restock the poorer acidic hills. Any egg or chick losses due to predation or egg collecting may, therefore, reduce numbers of birds exported elsewhere, and yet be insufficient to influence population size on disturbed areas; but we have no evidence. On some blanket bog areas in the Peak District, northern England, Yalden (1986) has suggested that golden plover (*Pluvialis apricaria*) numbers have declined because of considerable human disturbance. Yalden and Yalden's (unpubl.) observations of people and dogs indicate that over 30% of walkers may leave paths, and that 60% of dogs are not on a lead (with 8% running wild).

On Cairn Gorm, more sheep, reindeer (*Rangifer tarandus*) and mountain hares (*Lepus timidus*) concentrate on the reseeded areas, where they graze the lusher, fertilized grasses (Watson 1979).

3.3 Impacts of grazing animals

The large extent of grazer-determined sub-montane and montane plant communities in Britain has no other European counterpart (Ratcliffe 1987; Ratcliffe & Thompson 1988). In the USA packstock (horses and mules) affect alpine vegetation by trampling, preferentially grazing, and introducing 'alien' species. They exert a pressure per m^2 3–4 times greater than that of humans, causing trampling to be the most serious problem (Price 1985). Cole (1985) mentions serious packstock damage in almost half of the USA wilderness areas, with animals causing much damage to meadows. In the Sierra Nevada, packstock impacts are superimposed on the 'even more drastic effects of past grazing by sheep and cattle' (Cole 1985, p150): during the past 20 years, restrictions placed on stock density and movements have led to much improvement.

Whereas recreational impacts tend to be highly concentrated, those of sheep and deer are widespread, although sheep can be selective in their choice of food patches (eg Grant *et al.* 1978, and see reviews by Grant & Maxwell 1988; Hobbs & Gimingham 1987; Mowforth & Sydes 1988). Deer are more abundant than ever before (Albon & Clutton-Brock 1988) and sheep numbers have doubled since 1947 (Anderson & Yalden 1981; Hudson 1985; Hobbs & Gimingham 1987; Sydes & Miller 1988). Many sheep, however, are now supported by supplementary feeding on inbye land to enhance ewe productivity. Comparisons between the impacts of grazing and people are usually hampered by the lack of hard facts. The good data collected by Lamb and Watson (1986) and Watson (unpubl.) are needed for many other mountains. Lamb and Watson's (1986) distribution maps indicate maximum densities on the Wyvis plateau (Ross, Scotland) in summer of almost 15 people km^{-2}, 15–16 sheep km^{-2} and 3–4 red deer (*Cervus elaphus*) km^{-2}. There was a significant inverse relationship between densities of sheep and deer, with sheep tending to favour the main grasslands.

3.3.1 Indications of overgrazing

There is much confusion about the term 'overgrazing' for it means different things to ecologists and agriculturalists. It is used here in reference to situations where particularly high numbers of sheep or deer have caused a shift in the vegetation cover from natural to semi-natural, or from semi-natural to artificial (see Sydes & Miller 1988; Ratcliffe & Thompson 1988). Our own research indicates at least 5 signs of overgrazing on the plateaux. Some of these are still speculative and merit experimental validation.

i. Obvious trampling, eg on paths, ruts and gullies; moss heath and bilberry show this damage clearly.

ii. Torn vegetation, such as detached mosses or small amounts of mat-grass ripped by deer and sheep.

iii. Moss heath with co-dominant sheep's fescue (*Festuca ovina*) or wavy hair-grass (*Deschampsia flexuosa*) (see Table 3; Birks & Ratcliffe 1980). This modification is probably due to trampling and ripping of mosses favouring rapid colonization by graminoids (eg Pryor 1985), and sheep or deer urine and faeces killing the mosses but enhancing growth conditions for grasses. There are photographs of this conversion in parts of north-west England (D A Ratcliffe, pers. comm.); on Helvellyn, only the grazing-free ledges contain semi-extensive moss heath. In the Cairngorms, 3-leaved rush may supplant damaged moss heath (A Brown, pers. comm.).

iv. Bent/fescue (*Agrostis/Festuca*) grasslands, with sheep's fescue or viviparous fescue (*F. vivipara*) and wavy hair-grass covering much ground, are widespread on sheep-grazed montane summits and plateaux above 760 m south of the Highlands.

Table 3. Percentage cover of natural and modified moss heath on mountain summit plateaux in Britain. The degree of grazing modification increases towards the right of the Table (we thank Anne Burn of the Welsh Field Unit for supplying data from Wales)

Plateaux	E1a	E1c	C1b	% modified to C1b
	Percentage cover[1]			
Wales				
Snowdon	—	11	25	69
Carneddau	—	8	30	79
Glyders	—	35	7	17
Northern England				
Buttermere	+	2	97	97
Helvellyn	—	+	94	99
Cross Fell	—	100	+	<1
South Scotland				
Rinns of Kells	—	33	67	67
Cairnsmore of Carsphairn	—	20	80	80
North Scotland				
Greag Meagaidh	100	—	—	0
Ben Wyvis	100	—	—	0
Ben Armine	100	—	—	0

Altitude ranges from 630–643 m (Ben Armine) to 850–1110 m (Creag Meagaidh), and surface area from 1 km² (Cross Fell) to 8 km² (Creag Meagaidh)

[1] Codes according to Birks and Ratcliffe (1980):

E1a: *Racomitrium lanuginosum*/stiff sedge heath dominated by an almost continuous carpet of *R. lanuginosum;*

E1c: sheep's fescue/wavy hair-grass/*Racomitrium* heath with an abundance of grasses (including sheep's fescue, viviparous fescue, wavy hair-grass and brown bent-grass), among the *R. lanuginosum;*

C1b: sheep's fescue/wavy hair-grass/brown bent-grass grassland, with little or no *R. lanuginosum.*

The remaining ground is covered by mat-grass and heath/rush grassland, dwarf-shrub heaths, or bare soil and rock

They are probably derived from the plant community in (iii) above as a continuation of the succession.

v. Tufted hair-grass (*Deschampsia cespitosa*) confined to corries and steep slopes in the Scottish Highlands can be associated with fairly prolonged snow cover, and may be derived from overgrazed tall-herb or fern-dominated communities (see also Ratcliffe 1977).

Whilst studying food selection in west Greenland caribou (*Rangifer tarandus groenlandicus*), Thing (1984) quantified comparable herbivore-induced plant succession. Under heavy grazing pressure (>25 animals km^{-2}), a species of willow (*Salix glauca*) and dwarf birch (*Betula nana*) disappeared over several years; several grass species, including nitrophilic smooth-stalked meadow-grass (*Poa pratensis*), overwhelmed them and grew rapidly. Caribou preferred meadow-grass, and, as they accumulated and spent longer on the grass, there was further fertilization, enhancing the growth and spread of grassland.

3.3.2 *Where has the vegetation been modified?*

During 1979–86, the Nature Conservancy Council's Upland Survey Team surveyed and mapped the vegetation of all upland Sites of Special Scientific Interest (SSSIs) throughout Britain (almost 0.5 Mha). These sites tend to be more semi-natural or natural, particularly in the Scottish Highlands. Table 3 shows the percentage cover of natural and modified moss heath communities (as defined above) for a selection of plateaux (17 have been measured to date; the 11 shown make up a nationally representative sample). In England and Wales, fragmented moss heath (E1a) was located only in small areas of Buttermere. Moss heath with co-dominant fescue and wavy hair-grass was found fairly extensively on Cross Fell only, and in small patches in Wales. Most of the southern tops have become grassy. In south Scotland, the moss heath was apparently modified, whereas further north it was not. South of the Highlands, the best moss heath is on Corserine and Carlin's Cairn in Galloway. There are no sheep grazing there now, and the heath appears to be improving (D A Ratcliffe, pers. comm.). Considerable amounts of bare rock now exist in the Welsh mountains (10–55% cover in the 3 sample sites), of which some is due to sheep- and human-induced erosion. We conclude that grazing effects on the montane plateaux are most marked in Wales and northern England, then central Scotland, and only locally in the Scottish Highlands.

The vegetation will not revert, unless sheep or deer numbers are reduced. No data are yet available to indicate the stocking rate at which moss heath or even shrubs such as crowberry have diminished. On areas such as Helvellyn, where people and dogs cause serious harassment of sheep (pers. obs.), the energy requirements of sheep may be higher than normal, which might contribute to a more rapid modification of natural vegetation. In bighorn sheep (*Ovis canadensis*), there is a significant decrease in heart rate (and presumably energy demands) further away from the roads, and significantly higher rates in sheep exposed to people appearing over ridges with dogs (Geist *et al.* 1985).

3.3.3 *Consequences for wild fauna*

There is little reliable information. In the highest north Wales mountains, the change in vegetation is likely to be most serious for food plant-dependent invertebrates because some of their communities must be the most south-westerly relicts of arctic/alpine habitat.

The disappearance of ptarmigan from south-west Scotland was possibly due to heavy sheep grazing of dwarf shrubs in the early 19th century (Thom 1986; Galbraith *et al.* 1988). Dotterel are scarce in north-west England (Nethersole-Thompson 1973) and in places this scarcity may be related to overgrazing. Only about 5 pairs per year have been found in northern England (cf 'guesstimated' 50–75 pairs prior to 1860, Nethersole-Thompson 1973, pers. comm.). Ratcliffe (1973) considered persecution, human disturbance, climatic change and increased predation in northern England, but found all but the last explanation wanting. Crows, gulls (*Larus* spp.) and foxes (*Vulpes vulpes*) may have increased because of greater recreational use of the hills, and might be implicated. Perhaps the increase in sheep numbers has caused trampling of some nests and the loss of moss heath. Combined with disturbance, it would probably render this very marginal habitat less attractive for breeding. Farther north, where there is a stronghold, similar amounts of disturbance but less grazing activity and a more intact vegetation presumably act as less of a deterrent. In parts of Scotland, moss heath is important for feeding, provides nest camouflage and may buffer eggs, incubating adults and chicks against chilling (see Kålås & Lofaldhi 1987).

4 *Conclusions*

4.1 The problems

We have described the 3 major land use impingements on the mountain plateaux. The resource is outstanding in nature conservation value, fascinating to ecologists and geomorphologists with an academic interest in natural formations and change, and important to farmers, hill-walkers, mountaineers and skiers.

The land use conflicts occur at 2 levels. First, there are the changes arising from widespread grazing pressures (and acid deposition). These changes occur gradually and seem acceptable to many farming or recreating in the uplands. We have indicated how and where several natural plant communities have been lost or modified. Except where unnatural erosion has been the end point, the main impact has been on the range and complement of natural communities. At the second level, the more concentrated damage due to downhill ski development and excessive recreational use (as well as mineral extraction and mining) covers the range of Britain's mountains, but is local in occurrence. However, damage is most severe at the higher altitudes on some of the least common and most fragile soils or plant communities. Recovery rates of shrub, moss or lichen-rich heaths are very slow, but restitution is possible if the disturbance ceases. Although ski-related problems occur mainly in the Scottish Highlands (Dun Fell on Moor House NNR has some skiing), they should not be dismissed as parochial. The impacts affect a disproportionately large number of internationally important or distinctive sites.

4.2 What should be done?

In England, Wales and southern Scotland, a reduction in stocking densities of sheep should bring back the more natural montane plant communities. We wish to see rural, hill-farming communities remain viable, so obviously accept the need for subsidies. The independent adverse effects of tourists and hill-walkers are virtually impossible to control. In Scotland, however, restricting the use of all chairlifts to the skiing season should help reduce localized damage.

When considering ski developments, we ought to use quantitative criteria for measuring site potential. Davison (1981) attempted this;he did not weight any factors, and concluded that Glenshee and Newtonmore were best and Beinn a' Bhuird and Creag Meagaidh poorest for development. Development should be geared to preserving the local rural community, and not just supporting marginal enterprises relying on labour drawn from elsewhere. Abroad, the skiing industry faces problems, with 35% of the 115 ski centres in Switzerland and 26–42% of the 131 centres in North America in financial difficulties (Davison 1985).

Long-term scenic value, water catchment and flood damage may be incalculable. The importance of the plateaux for containing northern and alpine European outliers of vegetation types and animal communities has yet to be assessed. It certainly cannot be calculated in strict monetary terms, and wider heritage values would be more apposite. The penetration of the high tops by access tracks for stalking and grouse shooting has wrought much damage. In the north-east Scottish hills, over 1000 km of new tracks have been bulldozed during the last decade, including 49% along new lines and 9% on former footpaths (Watson 1984b). Apart from marring the scenery, these tracks provide motor cyclists and tourists with easier access (in 1982, motor cyclists were seen on at least 5 Scottish summit plateaux (Watson 1984b)), causing erosion, disturbance to wildlife and sheep, and encouraging the spread of litter. Although district councils officially control the construction of tracks in National Scenic Areas, they are not always consulted beforehand. In 3 cases where tracks were bulldozed, the council gave retrospective planning permission to 2, and the Secretary of State over-ruled the Countryside Commission for Scotland on the third. We believe that there should be a firmer adherence to council controls, and that retrospective concessions should not be made.

Much more attention should be given to rehabilitating damaged ground (eg Bayfield 1980, 1985). Laying strong aggregates on some heavily used footpaths (such as those on Cairn Gorm summit) would probably reduce damage away from the path. Miller (1986) proposes measures such as the use of mulches and soil stabilizers, repeated applications of nitrogenous fertilizer, sowing with macerated moss fragments, and establishment with native species, as well as the exclusion of deer and sheep from badly damaged areas.

We have far to go before catching up with countries such as the USA. There, in 1964, the Wilderness Act led to the establishment of National Wilderness Parks covering some 3200 km (just over 1% of the land surface). High mountain landscapes and arctic tundra account for most of these Parks; some are closed to all recreational use and mechanized recreation is widely banned (Lucas 1985). Management of visitors tends to be active, with party size limited in 50% of all areas! Lucas argues convincingly that associations between visitors' experiences, ecological and scenic impacts, and restrictions need to be quantified to discover what conditions human behaviour and perceptions. The same might be said for Britain.

4.3 Research priorities

Outside the Cairngorms area, the significance of human-induced compared with natural damage remains to be investigated. Galbraith, Thompson and Watson are currently refining the definition and delineation of the plateaux, and will try to clarify international and national ecological contexts. The threats posed to these areas are to be quantified in 2 ways. First, on a range of sites throughout Britain, they will monitor changes in plant cover due to natural processes, livestock and anthropogenic factors. A small number of exclosures will enable them to quantify recovery rates and to compare recreation with grazing. Second, on 3 geologically distinct study areas in the Scottish Highlands, Galbraith *et al.* will examine the effects of topography, geology, soil type and aspect on erosion and damage to plant and animal communities. Feeding and nesting associations between birds and important environmental variables will be examined to understand factors underpinning distribution and breeding success, and birds will be marked to determine whether or not local populations depend on more than one massif. Time/energy budgets of birds will be recorded in relation to the activities of livestock and people, and the presence and effects of predators and scavengers will be recorded.

More specialized studies are required to quantify the importance of invertebrates as a food source; to compare severe climate, recreation and grazing impacts on soil erosion and flood damage; to examine the feasibility of rehabilitating damaged areas with indigenous species; to determine the effects of acid deposition on the ombrotrophic high-level blanket bogs and large moss heaths; and to quantify the notions of site integrity and wilderness, and how these are perceived by people living in or simply enjoying the uplands.

5 Acknowledgements

We are immensely grateful to Adam Watson, Derek Ratcliffe, Desmond Nethersole-Thompson, Neil Bayfield and Gordon Miller for their obvious contributions to this review; Chris Sydes, Anne Burn, Alan Brown, Robin Payne, Lindsey Kinnes, Steven Ridgill and Alison Hobbs for collecting most of the data in Table 3 and for many discussions; David Stroud and Mike Pienkowski for detailed comments; Malcolm Bell for soliciting the manuscript; Derek Langslow for support; and the NCC for funding.

6 References

Aitken, R. 1983. *Scottish mountain footpaths.* Perth: Countryside Commission for Scotland.

Albon, S.D. & Clutton-Brock, T.H. 1988. Population dynamics of red deer in the Highlands. In: *Ecological change in the uplands,* edited by D.B.A. Thompson & M.B. Usher. Oxford: Blackwell Scientific. In press.

Anderson, P. & Yalden, D.W. 1981. Increased sheep numbers and the loss of heather moorland in the Peak District, England. *Biol. Conserv.,* **20,** 195-213.

Anderson Semens Houston. 1981. *Environmental impact analysis. Proposed extension of downhill skiing facilities, Coire an t-Sneachda, Coire an Lochain and Lurchers Gully, Cairngorm.* Glasgow: ASH.

Archer, D. 1985. Managing public pressures in Snowdon. In: *The ecological impacts of outdoor recreation in mountain areas in Europe and North America,* edited by N.G. Bayfield & G.C. Barrow, 155-161. Ashford: Recreation Ecology Research Group.

Ball, D.F., Radford, G.L. & Williams, W.M. 1983. *A land characteristic data bank for Great Britain.* (Bangor occasional paper no. 13.) Bangor: Institute of Terrestrial Ecology.

Baugh, I. 1979. *The condition of some footpaths in the northern Cairngorms.* Edinburgh: Nature Conservancy Council.

Bayfield, N.G. 1979. Recovery of four montane heath communities on Cairngorm, Scotland, from disturbance by trampling. *Biol. Conserv.,* **15,** 165-179.

Bayfield, N.G. 1980. Replacement of vegetation in disturbed ground near ski lifts in the Cairngorm Mountains, Scotland. *J. Biogeogr.,* **7,** 249-260.

Bayfield, N.G. 1985. Effects of extended use of footpaths in mountain areas in Britain. In: *The ecological impacts of outdoor recreation in mountain areas in Europe and North America,* edited by N.G. Bayfield & G.C. Barrow, 100-111. Ashford: Recreation Ecology Research Group.

Bayfield, N.G. & Barrow, G.C., eds. 1985. *The ecological impacts of outdoor recreation in mountain areas in Europe and North America.* Ashford: Recreation Ecology Research Group.

Bayfield, N.G., Urquhart, U.H. & Cooper, S.M. 1981. Susceptibility of four species of *Cladonia* to disturbance by trampling in the Cairngorm Mountains, Scotland. *J. appl. Ecol.,* **18,** 303-310.

Bayfield, N.G., Watson, A. & Miller, G.R. 1988. Assessing and managing the effects of recreational use on British hills. In: *Ecological change in the uplands,* edited by D.B.A. Thompson & M.B. Usher. Oxford: Blackwell Scientific. In press.

Birks, H.J.B. & Ratcliffe, D.A. 1980. *Classification of upland vegetation types.* Edinburgh: Nature Conservancy Council. (Unpublished.)

Cole, D.N. 1981. Vegetation changes associated with recreational use and fire suppression in the Eagle Cap Wilderness: some management implications. *Biol. Conserv.,* **20,** 247-270.

Cole, D.N. 1985. Management of ecological impacts in wilderness areas in the United States. In: *The ecological impacts of outdoor recreation in mountain areas in Europe and North America,* edited by N.G. Bayfield & G.C. Barrow, 138-154. Ashford: Recreation Ecology Research Group.

Davison, R. 1981. Ski developments in Scotland - what lies ahead? *Scott. Geogr. Mag.,* **97,** 110-123.

Davison, R. 1985. The measurement of site potential for downhill skiing. In: *The ecological impacts of outdoor recreation in mountain areas in Europe and North America,* edited by N.G. Bayfield & G.C. Barrow, 188-197. Ashford: Recreation Ecology Research Group.

Dearden, P. & Sewell, W.R.D. 1985. From gloom to glory and beyond: the North American mountain experience. In: *The ecological impacts of outdoor recreation in mountain areas in Europe and North America,* edited by N.G. Bayfield & G.C. Barrow, 1-17. Ashford: Recreation Ecology Research Group.

Duffey, E. 1975. The effects of human trampling on the fauna of grassland litter. *Biol. Conserv.,* **7,** 255-274.

Emanuelsson, U. 1985. Recreation impact on mountainous areas in Northern Sweden. In: *The ecological impacts of outdoor recreation in mountain areas in Europe and North America,* edited by N.G. Bayfield & G.C. Barrow, 63-73. Ashford: Recreation Ecology Research Group.

Fishwick, A. 1985. Planning and management responses to recreational pressures in the Lake District National Park. In: *The ecological impacts of outdoor recreation in mountain areas in Europe and North America,* edited by N.G. Bayfield & G.C. Barrow, 18-33. Ashford: Recreation Ecology Research Group.

Fletcher, N. & Shaver, G.R. 1983. Life histories of tillers of *Eriophorum vaginatum* in relation to tundra disturbance. *J. Ecol.,* **71,** 131-147.

Galbraith, H., Kinnes, L., Watson, A. & Thompson, D.B.A. 1988. Pressures on ptarmigan populations. *Annu. Rev. Game Conservancy.* In press.

Gartner, B.L., Chapin, F.S. & Shaver, G.R. 1983. Demographic patterns of seedling establishment and growth of native graminoids in the Alaskan tundra disturbance. *J. appl. Ecol.,* **20,** 965-980.

Geist, V., Stemp, R.E. & Johnston, R.H. 1985. Heart-telemetry of bighorn sheep as a means to investigate disturbances. In: *The ecological impacts of outdoor recreation in mountain areas in Europe and North America,* edited by N.G. Bayfield & G.C. Barrow, 92-99. Ashford: Recreation Ecology Research Group.

Grabherr, G. 1985. Damage to vegetation by recreation in the Austrian and German Alps. In: *The ecological impacts of outdoor recreation in mountain areas in Europe and North America,* edited by N.G. Bayfield & G.C. Barrow, 74-91. Ashford: Recreation Ecology Research Group.

Grant, S.A. & Maxwell, T. 1988. Hill vegetation and grazing animals: the biology and definition of management options. In: *Ecological change in the uplands,* edited by D.B.A. Thompson & M.B. Usher. Oxford: Blackwell Scientific. In press.

Grant, S.A., Barthram, G.T., Lamb, W.I.C. & Milne, J.A. 1978. Effects of season and level of grazing on the utilization of heather by sheep. 1. Responses of the sward. *J. Br. Grassld Soc.,* **33,** 289-300.

Hobbs, R.J. & Gimingham, C.H. 1987. Vegetation, fire and herbivore interactions in heathland. *Adv. ecol. Res.,* **16,** 87-173.

Hudson, P.J. 1985. Some effects of sheep management on heather moorlands in northern England. In: *Agriculture and the environment,* edited by D. Jenkins, 143-149. (ITE symposium no. 13.) Abbots Ripton: Institute of Terrestrial Ecology.

Kålås, J.A. & Lofaldhi, L. 1987. Costs of incubation in the dotterel. *Ornis scand.* In press.

Lamb, L. & Watson, A.J. 1986. *The vegetation and land-use of Ben Wyvis, Ross-shire.* Nature Conservancy Council. (Unpublished.)

Lee, J.A., Press, M.C., Woodin, S.J. & Fergusson, P. 1986. Responses to acidic deposition in ombrotrophic mires. In: *Effects of acidic deposition and air pollutants on forests, wetlands and agricultural ecosystems,* edited by T.C. Hutchinson & K.M. Meema. Berlin: Springer.

Lee, J.A., Tallis, J.H. & Woodin, S.J. 1988. Acidification and the British uplands. In: *Ecological change in the uplands,* edited by D.B.A. Thompson & M.B. Usher. Oxford: Blackwell Scientific. In press.

Lucas, R.C. 1985. The management of recreational visitors in wilderness areas in the United States. In: *The ecological impacts of outdoor recreation in mountain areas in Europe and North America,* edited by N.G. Bayfield & G.C. Barrow, 122-138. Ashford: Recreation Ecology Research Group.

Marchand, P.J. & Roach, D.A. 1980. Reproductive strategies of pioneering alpine species: seed production, dispersal and germination. *Arct. Alp. Res.,* **12,** 137-146.

Miller, G.R. 1986. *Ecological impact of downhill skiing developments in north-east Scotland.* Natural Environment Research Council contract report to the Nature Conservancy Council. Banchory: Institute of Terrestrial Ecology. (Unpublished.)

Morris, D., Hammond, E.C. & Kessler, C.D.J. 1974. *Cairngorms National Nature Reserve. A report on the characteristics of visitor use.* Nature Conservancy Council. (Unpublished.)

Mowforth, M. & Sydes, C. 1988. *Moorland management: a literature review.* Peterborough: Nature Conservancy Council.

Nethersole-Thompson, D. & Watson, A. 1981. *The Cairngorms.* Perth: Melven.

Price, M. 1985. A review of research into the impacts of recreation on alpine vegetation in western North American. In: *The ecological impacts of outdoor recreation in mountain areas in Europe and North America,* edited by N.G. Bayfield & G.C. Barrow, 34-52. Ashford: Recreation Ecology Research Group.

Pryor, P. 1985. The effect of disturbance on open *Juncus trifidus* heath in the Cairngorm mountains, Scotland. In: *The ecological impacts of outdoor recreation in mountain areas in Europe and North America,* edited by N.G. Bayfield & G.C. Barrow, 53-62. Ashford: Recreation Ecology Research Group.

Ratcliffe, D.A. 1974. Ecological effects of mineral extraction in the United Kingdom and their significance to nature conservation. *Proc. R. Soc.,* **339,** 355-372.

Ratcliffe, D.S. 1977. *A nature conservation review.* Vol. 1. Cambridge: Cambridge University Press.

Ratcliffe, D.A. 1987. The British upland scene. In: *The upland seminar,* edited by D.B.A. Thompson & S. Whyte. (Research and Survey Series.) Peterborough: Nature Conservancy Council. In press.

Ratcliffe, D.A. & Thompson, D.B.A. 1988. An introduction to the British uplands and their international significance. In: *Ecological change in the uplands,* edited by D.B.A. Thompson & M.B. Usher. Oxford: Blackwell Scientific. In press.

Studlar, S.M. 1985. Trampling effects on mosses near Mountain Lake, Virginia: damage and recover. In: *The ecological impacts of outdoor recreation in mountain areas in Europe and North America,* edited by N.G. Bayfield & G.C. Barrow, 182-187. Ashford: Recreation Ecology Research Group.

Sydes, C. & Miller, G.R. 1988. Range management for nature conservation in Britain. In: *Ecological change in the uplands.* edited by D.B.A. Thompson & M.B. Usher. Oxford: Blackwell Scientific. In press.

Thing, H. 1984. Feeding ecology of the west Greenland caribou *(Rangifer tarandus groenlandicus)* in the Sisimiut-Kangerlussuaq Region. *Dan. Rev. Game Biol.,* **12,** 1-53.

Thom, V. 1986. *Birds of Scotland.* Calton: Poyser.

Thompson, D. 1986. Conflict on the high tops. *Scott. Birds News,* **4,** 6-7.

Watson, A. 1967. Public pressures on soils, plants and animals near ski lifts in the Cairngorms. In: *The biotic effects of public pressures on the environment,* edited by E. Duffey, 38-45. London: Nature Conservancy.

Watson, A. 1979. Bird and mammal numbers in relation to human impacts at ski lifts on Scottish hills. *J. appl. Ecol.,* **16,**753-764.

Watson, A. 1982. Effects of human impact on ptarmigan and red grouse near ski lifts in Scotland. *Annu. Rep. Inst. terr. Ecol. 1981,* 48-50.

Watson, A. 1984a. Paths and people in the Cairngorms. *Scott. Geogr. Mag.,* **100,**151-160.

Watson, A. 1984b. A survey of vehicular hill tracks in north-east Scotland for land use planning. *J. environ. Manage.,* **18,**345-353.

Watson, A. 1985. Soil erosion and vegetation damage near ski lifts at Cairn Gorm, Scotland. *Biol. Conserv.,* **33,** 363-381.

Watson, A. 1988. Dotterel, *Charadrius morinellus,* numbers in relation to human impact in Scotland. *Biol. Conserv.* In press.

Watson, A. Unpublished. Increases of people and their impact on the Cairn Gorm plateau following ski developments. Submitted.

Watson, A. & Rae, R. 1987. Dotterel numbers, habitat and breeding success in Scotland. *Scott. Birds.* In press.

Watson, A., Bayfield, N.G. & Moyes, S.M. 1970. Research on human pressures on Scottish mountain tundra, soils and animals. In: *Productivity and conservation in the northern circumpolar lands,* edited by W.A. Fuller & P.G. Kevan, 256-266. (New Series 16.) Morges: IUCN.

Willard, B.E. & Marr, J.W. 1971. Recovery of alpine tundra under protection after damage by human activities in the Rocky Mountains of Colorado. *Biol. Conserv.,* **3,**181-190.

Yalden, D.W. 1986. The status of golden plovers in the Peak Park England in relation to access and recreational disturbance. *Wader Study Group Bull.,* **46,** 34-35.

Yalden, P.E. & Yalden, D.W. Unpublished. *The level of recreation pressure on blanket bog in the Peak District National Park, England.* (Report to Chief Scientist Directorate.) Peterborough: Nature Conservancy Council.

Ecology and management of improved, unimproved and reverted hill grasslands in mid-Wales

J B DIXON
Department of Applied Biology Field Centre, University of Wales Institute of Science and Technology (Cardiff), Newbridge-on-Wye, Powys, Wales

1 Introduction

The Cambrian Mountains massif of mid-Wales are typically rounded, steep-sided hills rarely exceeding 600 m. The slopes, the 'ffriddlands', with which this paper is concerned, on the edge of the block and of the valleys, are covered by thin layers of moderately acidic, mineral-rich brown earth or brown podzolic soils, of the Manod Association (Rudeforth *et al.* 1984).

Reclamation in upland Wales began with the forest clearance of the first farmers of the early Neolithic period (6000-5000 BP), and this influence is well documented for mid-Wales (Moore 1968). There is also evidence of further moorland enclosures dating from that period until modern times. Despite the exhortations of pioneer land improvers between the wars (Stapledon 1935), the greatest period of land improvement did not begin until the recent post-war period. Parry and Sinclair (1985) have documented this and other land uses for the Cambrian Mountains, recording an increase in forestry plantations as the most significant change. However, in the latter years of their study (1978–83), they consider agricultural reclamation to have occurred more rapidly than new forestry plantations and at a rate in mid-Wales higher than in other upland areas in the UK. This reclamation reached a peak rate of 1120 hectares per year, 73% accountable to agricultural reclamation during the period 1978–83.

Parry and Sinclair recorded a high degree of reversion, from improved grassland to rough grassland, especially on the small, old fields on valley-sides. In my experience, many of the larger, more recently reseeded ffriddlands have also reverted. They also recorded that 30% of the land reclaimed between 1978 and 1980 had reverted to rough pasture within 3–5 years, and that there was an increased likelihood of further reclamation of these reverted pastures.

2 Loss of moorland vegetation types to reclamation

Figure 1 indicates that, over an 11-year period (Dixon 1984), heather (*Calluna vulgaris*) moor and other blanket peat communities and vegetation communities characteristic of valley-side brown earth soils, gorse (*Ulex europaeus*) scrub and fescue (*Festuca*) grassland, have been preferentially chosen for land improvement in the Cambrian Mountains. This finding concurs with Parry and Sinclair (1985). These vegetation types are chosen for forestry (blanket bog and ffriddland), surface treatment of moorland (blanket bog) and standard agricultural reclamation (ffriddland). Stagnopodzol soils, often mat-grass (*Nardus*)-dominated, are not chosen so readily. Similar results have recently been obtained by Davies *et al.* (1985) in the uplands east of the Cambrian Mountains where, according to a Welsh Office survey of reclaimed land for the period 1948–64 (Welsh Office 1971), land improvement has occurred more rapidly than in the central Cambrian Mountains massif.

3 Ecology of ffriddlands

Brown earth and brown podzolic soils of the Manod Association occupy 3744 km^2 or 18% of Wales (Rudeforth *et al.* 1984), and are thus significant in land use terms. These soils are generally free-draining, fine loamy soils, on steep-sided valleys, the steepness of which often limits their agricultural value. Plate 1 illustrates the typical vegetation found. It is the most productive vegetation community of hill rough grazing, or sheepwalk, dominated by sheep's fescue (*Festuca ovina*), bent-grasses (*Agrostis* spp.) and often encroaching bracken (*Pteridium aquilinum*). Annual production is between 2000 and 4000 kg dry matter ha^{-1} (Newbould 1985), supporting grazing densities of up to 6 ewes ha^{-1}. In comparison with other hill grasslands, these areas have a high palatability to stock (Newbould 1985) and a longer growing season of up to 7 months, the attribute considered by Stapledon (1935) of most value. They also respond well to applications of lime and fertilizer (Iorweth-Jones 1967). The exact botanical composition and productivity of these pastures are dependent on soil base status, soil moisture, grazing pressure and selective grazing, and these factors together influence the range of variation in a floristic continuum (King 1961), although, in practice, these areas appear relatively uniform. Semi-natural bent/fescue grasslands are clearly one of the most significant resources of extensive pastoral farming in mid-Wales.

The bent/fescue grasslands represent part of the mosaic of semi-natural sub-montane habitats for which the north and west of Britain are of repute (Ratcliffe 1977). Although species-poor, the ffriddlands of Wales support a characteristic invertebrate and bird fauna and are of especial importance to carrion-feeding birds (Royal Society for the Protection of Birds, unpublished). Where soils are sufficiently deep and often adjacent to reseeded pastures or woodland, and where earthworm (Lumbricidae) populations are high (Neal 1977), badger (*Meles meles*) setts of great antiquity may be found, giving rise to a local mid-Wales name for these soils as 'badger

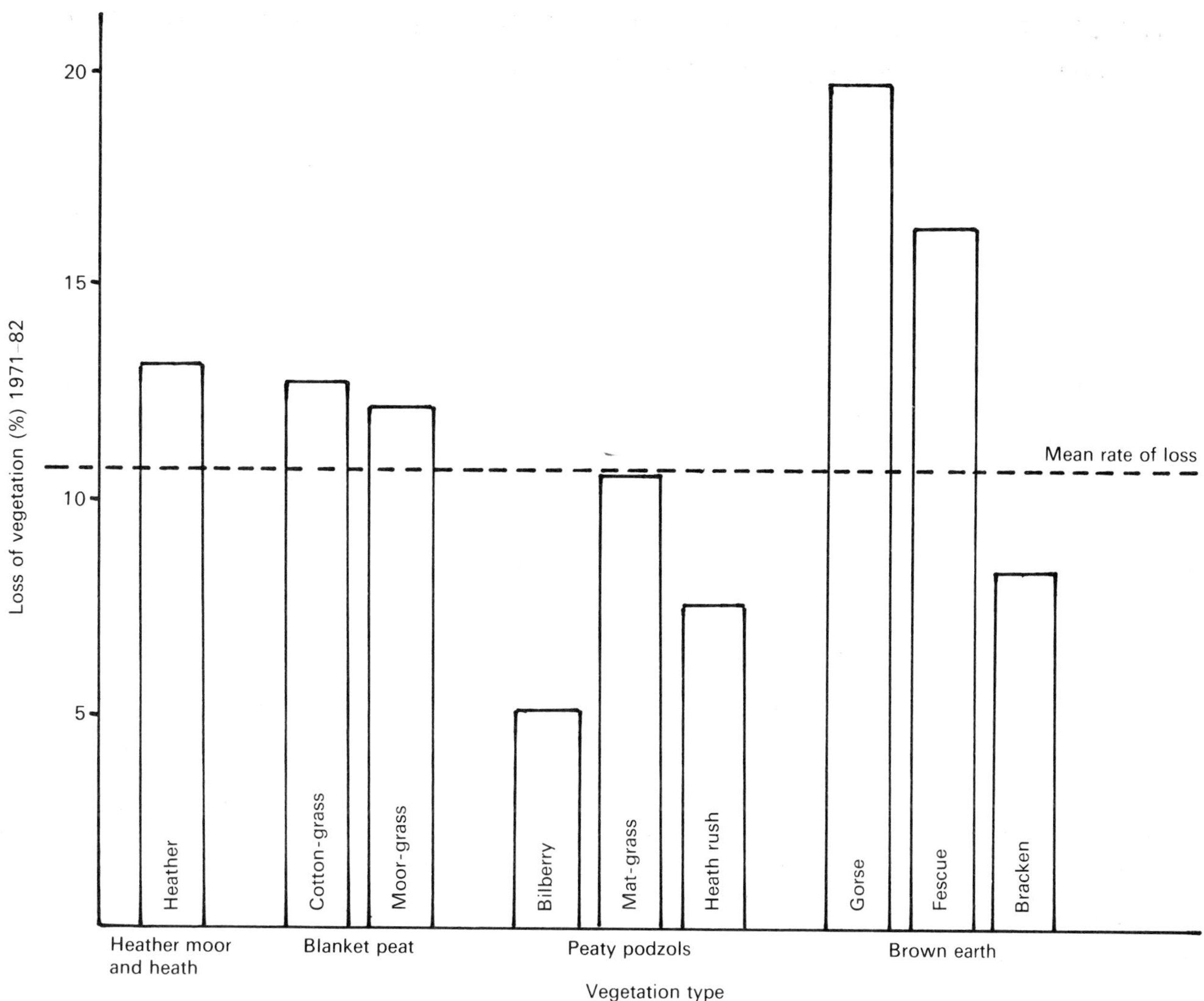

Figure 1. Loss of moorland vegetation types to afforestation and agricultural reclamation in Montgomery study area, 1971–82

sands'. Hydrologically, these freely drained mineral-rich soils form substantial parts of the catchments of economically and ecologically valuable rivers such as the Wye. Twenty per cent of the soils of this type support plantation woodland or native broadleaved woodland.

In the future development of marginal farming, environmental and other land uses will increase in prominence; the proposed Cambrian Mountains Environmentally Sensitive Area is perhaps the forerunner of support for multiple-objective upland land use.

4 *Successional change on ffriddland*

In the management of change, information on directional change in vegetation and related ecology, ie ecological succession, is of prime importance. The wide range of recently reseeded and reverting fields in mid-Wales, perhaps unique in Wales, has afforded an opportunity to examine the ecology of succession. This phenomenon is analogous to the widespread and intensively documented old-field succession of the USA. Methods used by North American ecologists often involve comparing a chronosequence of fields of known history, of similar geology, aspect, soil type and climate, where fields of varying successional age substitute for successional time (Booth 1941). Ball *et al.* (1981) proposed a rough pathway for the truncated succession (limited by continuous grazing) from reseeded to rough pasture in upland areas, but commented that the exact nature of this succession was unclear and probably dependent on environmental influences. It would vary for different soil type and management.

5 *Botanical and soil succession*

Thirty sites representing vegetational succession were examined and, from soil and vegetation data to be published elsewhere, groups of indicator species have been determined representing this succession (Table 1).

Succession is a continuum, as illustrated by Figure 2, probably controlled by soil factors such as soil acidity and consequent reduced nutrient turnover, and not all phases may be represented in this series. In the intermediate phases of succession, common bent-grass (*Agrostis capillaris*) does not replace rye-grass (*Lolium perenne*) in direct proportion (dotted line of Figure 2). In

Plate 1. Fence-line between cattle (lower diagonal) and sheep (upper diagonal) plots grazed with animal numbers of both species adjusted twice weekly as necessary to maintain the sward surface height of the between-tussock grasses at 4.5 cm (Photograph Hill Farming Research Organisation)

the later phases of succession as diversity increases, other indigenous grasses, herbs and lower plants contribute to the sward and so depress the relative importance of common bent-grass.

There is evidence for the mechanisms of vegetative ingress of weed grass species into reseeded swards from lowland grass leys and, in general, root competition between species is implicated (Snaydon & Howe 1986). Soil status is clearly important and, indeed, Kirkwood (1959) concluded that poor nutrient status, phosphate and lime, in particular, in reseeded pastures inhibited organic matter cycling, contributing a competitive advantage to indigenous species and hence generating reversion. Davies (1967) also implicated these and other management inadequacies, particularly poor drainage, in reversion, although he did not record serious reversion in mineral soils.

This vegetational successional sequence suggests that soil conditions are important in the general trend, but that interactions between species and external environmental influences, such as drought, frost or grazing management, can accelerate vegetation succession in advance of soil succession. The converse would not be true and, for the maintenance of productive permanent pasture, it has long been known that soil fertility must be maintained (Crompton 1953; Davies 1967).

The rapid decline of fertility here must be of concern in agricultural terms but may, if considered desirable, be harnessed to the reinstatement of semi-natural grassland. In the later stages of succession under grazing, 2 end points are recognizable. On the lower slopes, old fields have developed as relatively species-rich (50–60 species) and on the thinner soils higher up the slopes, vegetation more typical of the open ffriddland has developed.

6 *Past and future vegetation: buried seeds in succession*

Although seed banks rarely show close correlation with the surface vegetation, they represent a vital element in plant population dynamics (Fenner 1985). The presence of persistent seed banks may indicate the nature of historical surface vegetation (eg Milton 1948), and they may also have a role in its future development. As

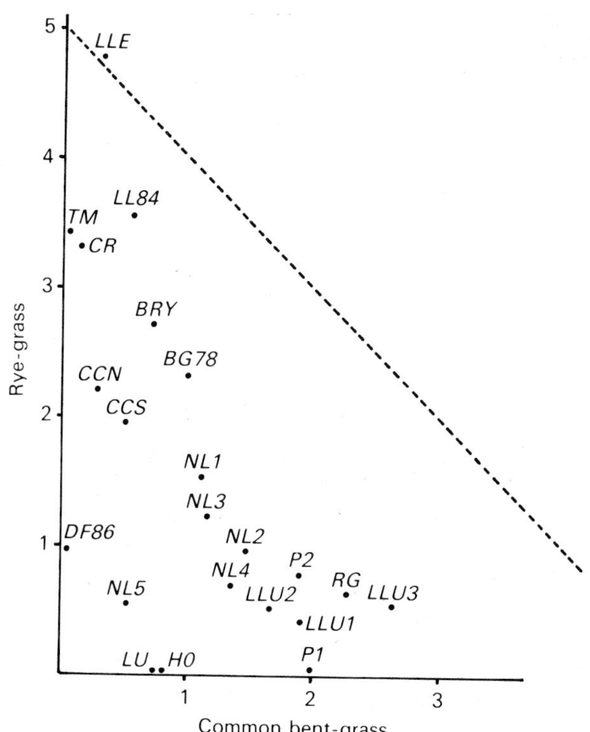

Figure 2. Replacement of rye-grass by common bent-grass on a series of reseeded brown earth soils (5=100%)

Thompson (1978) points out, succession often begins with a high degree of disturbance and then tends towards stability, with a corresponding decline in nutrient availability.

Species found in the early stage of succession are highly dependent on complex seed dispersal, dormancy, germination patterns and the accumulation of persistent seed banks. Species of later stages will produce fewer propagules, grow more slowly, depend more on vegetative growth, and hence accumulate smaller seed banks. It follows that, as succession progresses, seed banks will tend to decline in size, and much of the seed present may originate from the early stages of succession (Oosting & Humphrey 1940; Livingstone & Allessio 1968; Thompson 1978).

The buried viable seed population of 10 representative sites is shown in Figure 3, indicating an initial development of a large seed bank with a subsequent decline. The proportion of seeds of species prominent in vegetation succession, eg common bent-grass, is apparently low in the early stages, with seeds of improved phases predominating (mainly fat hen (*Chenopodium album*), procumbent pearlwort (*Sagina procumbens*), dove's-foot cranesbill (*Geranium molle*) and annual meadow-grass (*Poa annua*)), with densities comparable with arable situations (Harper 1977). Common bent-grass only appears to develop a significant seed bank in the later successional phases, with the apparent exception of one site where vegetation succession is advanced.

Table 1. Summary of vegetation succession from improved to reverted hill grasslands on south-facing brown earth soils

Successional stage	Characteristic species	Soil condition
Improved I	Sown species of little persistence, eg timothy (*Phleum pratense*) Associated 'arable' weeds, eg fat hen (*Chenopodium album*) and chickweed (*Stellaria media*)	pH 6–6.5 Nutrient-rich
Improved II	More persistent sown grasses, eg rye-grass (*Lolium perenne*) and associated grassweeds, eg annual meadow-grass (*Poa annua*), and dicotyledonous weeds, eg procumbent pearlwort (*Sagina procumbens*)	pH 6–6.5 Nutrient-rich
Improved III	Weed species of open grass swards, eg field madder (*Sherardia arvensis*) and dove's-foot cranesbill (*Geranium molle*)	pH 6–6.5 Nutrient-rich/ moderate
Improved/ Reverted I	Species characteristic of the period of replacement of sown species, especially common bent-grass (*Agrostis capillaris*), also thistles (*Cirsium* spp.) and self heal (*Prunella vulgaris*)	pH 5–6 Nutrient-moderate/ poor
Reverted II	Species of thinner soils where vegetation succession advanced through sward damage, eg bracken (*Pteridium aquilinum*), lop-grass (*Bromus hordaceus*) and common bent-grass	pH 5.5–6 Nutrient-moderate
Reverted III	Species found on lower slopes, older fields tolerant of acidity and organic matter accumulation, eg sweet vernal grass (*Anthoxanthum odoratum*), Yorkshire fog (*Holcus lanatus*), red fescue (*Festuca rubra*) sheep sorrel (*Rumex acetosella*)	pH 5–5.5 Nutrient-poor
Reverted IV	Species mix similar to reverted III but more diverse (50–60 spp ha^{-1}), including eyebright (*Euphrasia officinalis*) and meadow buttercup (*Ranunculus acris*)	pH 4.5–5 Nutrient-poor
Reverted V	Species of old reverted and unimproved sites, eg wavy hair-grass (*Deschampsia flexuosa*) and heath bedstraw (*Galium saxatile*)	pH 4.5–5 Nutrient-moderate/ poor

The densities found in the later phases of succession are comparable with estimates for permanent grasslands elsewhere (Williams 1984, 1985), and the diversity increases as the diversity of the surface vegetation increases and as species of each successional phase contribute seed.

The absence of tree seeds (with the exception of small numbers of birch (*Betula pendula*) at one site) belies their significance in succession, in keeping with other studies (Thompson 1978), as they were widespread as seedlings in many sites in the series. Densities of birch and hawthorn (*Crataegus monogyna*) of up to one m^{-2} were found in the vegetation assessments of the sites, and oak (*Quercus* spp.) and alder (*Alnus glutinosa*) were also recorded. Although grazing pressure is high and few, if any, of these species survive as seedlings, in the older reverted fields scattered hawthorn trees and bushes were found, presumably originating from periods of lower grazing intensity. The apparent absence or scarcity of tree seeds from the seed bank has a good ecological explanation: trees are the last stage of succession and therefore tend not to accumulate seed banks. It would

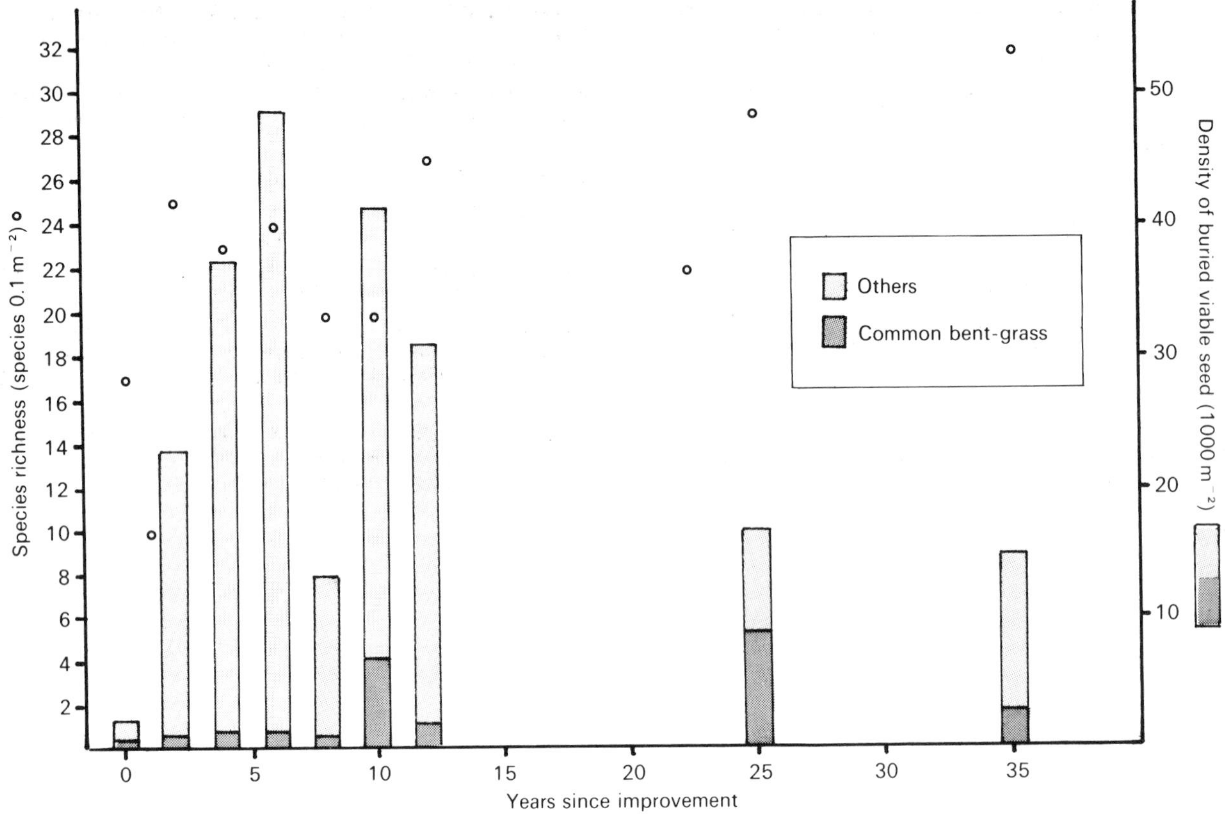

Figure 3. Species richness and density of buried viable seed population of a series of hill grasslands

clearly be no impediment to the continued succession towards scrub communities and thence to mature woodland, if grazing pressure were reduced on these fields.

7 Management options

7.1 The *status quo* could be maintained, which would see further reversion of recently reseeded fields tending to relatively species-rich swards on the lower hills and bent/fescue grassland on the higher hills. Periodic reseeding would be expensive and, in the current climate, unlikely.

7.2 Increased agricultural value could be achieved by the correct application of fertilizers (particularly lime and phosphate) and grazing practice.

7.3 Forestry, where water catchment, nature conservation and amenity interests allow, at the farm scale could well be accommodated on these soils.

7.4 The nature conservation interest could best be achieved by a mosaic of the most species-rich lower hill pastures, regenerating and retained woodland and open, grazed, higher hill grassland.

7.5 Wood pasture would, perhaps, achieve many of these objectives.

8 Acknowledgements

The help and advice of the staff and students of Llysdinam Field Centre and the Department of Applied Biology, particularly Drs F M Slater and P F Randerson, are gratefully acknowledged. The Llysdinam Charitable Trust and the University of Wales are acknowledged for facilities provided. My thanks are also due to the many landowners and farmers who so freely allowed access to their farms.

9 References

Ball, D. F., Dale, J., Sheail, J., Dickson, K. E. & Williams, W. M. 1981. *Ecology of vegetation change in upland landscapes. Part 1, general synthesis.* Bangor: Institute of Terrestrial Ecology.

Booth, W. E. 1941. Revegetation of abandoned fields in Kansas and Oklahoma. *Am. J. Bot.*, **28**, 415-422.

Crompton, E. 1953. Grow the soil to grow the grass. *Agriculture, Lond.*, **60**, 301-308.

Davies, H. 1967. The influence of soil and management on the botanical composition of 20 years old reclaimed hill-pasture in mid Wales. *J. Br. Grassld Soc.*, **22**, 141-147.

Davies, M., Green, M. & Knight, A. 1985. *Upland land use study 1985.* Newtown: Royal Society for the Protection of Birds. (Unpublished.)

Dixon, J. B. 1984. *The impact of agricultural change on the ecology of the Welsh uplands.* BSc dissertation, University of Wales Institute of Science and Technology, Cardiff.

Fenner, M. 1985. *Seed ecology.* London: Chapman & Hall.

Harper, J. 1977. *Population biology of plants.* London: Academic Press.

Iorweth-Jones, Ll. 1967. *Studies on hill land in Wales.* (Technical bulletin no. 2.) Aberystwyth: Welsh Plant Breeding Station.

King, J. 1961. The *Festuca-Agrostis* grassland complex in south-east Scotland. *J. Ecol.*, **49**, 321-355.

Kirkwood, R. C. 1959. *Factors affecting mat formation and decomposition in reseeded hill pastures.* PhD thesis, University College of Wales, Aberystwyth.

Livingstone, R.B. & Allessio, M. L. 1968. Buried viable seed in successional field and forest stands. Harvard Forest, Massachusetts. *Bull. Torrey bot. Club,* **95,** 58-69.

Milton, W.E.J. 1948. The buried viable seed content of upland soils in Montgomeryshire. *Emp. J. exp. Agric.,* **16,** 163-177.

Moore, P.D. 1968. Human influence upon vegetational history in north Cardiganshire. *Nature, Lond.,* **217,** 1006-1009.

Neal, E.G. 1977. *Badgers.* Poole: Blandford.

Newbould, P. 1985. Improvement of native grassland in the uplands. *Soil Use Manage.,* **1** (2), 43-50.

Oosting, H.J. & Humphrey, M.E. 1940. Buried viable seeds in a series of old field and forest soils. *Bull. Torrey bot. Club,* **67,** 253-273.

Parry, M.L. & Sinclair, G. 1985. *Mid Wales uplands study.* Cheltenham: Countryside Commission.

Ratcliffe, D.A. 1977. *A nature conservation review.* Cambridge: Cambridge University Press.

Royal Society for the Protection of Birds. Unpublished. *The ffriddland report.* Newtown: RSPB.

Rudeforth, C.C., Hartnup, R., Lea, J.W., Thompson, T.R.E. & Wright, P.S. 1984. *Soils and their use in Wales.* (Bulletin no. 11.) Harpenden: Soil Survey of England & Wales.

Snaydon, R.W. & Howe, C.D. 1986. Root and shoot competition between established ryegrass and invading grass seedlings. *J. appl. Ecol.,* **23,** 667-674.

Stapledon, R.G. 1935. *The land.* London: Faber & Faber.

Thompson, K. 1978. The occurrence of buried viable seeds in relation to environmental gradients. *J. Biogeogr.,* **5,** 425-430.

Welsh Office. 1971. *Distribution of reclaimed land in the Welsh uplands, January 1965.* Cardiff: Welsh Office. (Unpublished.)

Williams, E.D. 1984. Changes during 3 years in the size and composition of the seed bank beneath a long-term pasture as influenced by defoliation and fertilizer regime. *J. appl. Ecol.,* **21,** 603-615.

Williams, E.D. 1985. Long-term effects of fertilizer on the botanical composition and soil seed population of a permanent grass sward. *Grass Forage Sci.,* **40,** 479-483.

The effect of fertilizers on the conservation interest of traditionally managed upland meadows

R S SMITH
Department of Agricultural & Environmental Science, University of Newcastle, Newcastle-upon-Tyne, England

1 Summary
The effects on plant species composition and diversity of different, relatively low, amounts of fertilizer are described from a short-term trial on turves from a traditionally managed meadow in the Yorkshire Dales. There was a reduction in the diversity of vascular plants over time at all the levels of nitrogen and phosphorus used, as well as with increased amounts of nitrogen fertilizer. Comparisons are made with long-term trials at Rothamsted Experimental Station (the Park Grass Experiment) and at Cockle Park, Northumberland (the Palace Leas Meadow Trial). It is suggested that loss of diversity is a consequence of the use of nitrogen fertilizer, and the removal of winter grazing by sheep and cattle.

2 Introduction
Of the many grassland types used for grazing and fodder conservation in the hills and uplands of England and Wales, those within meadows are the most productive and most important to farmers. The number of livestock that can be overwintered on an upland farm is dependent upon the amount of conserved forage that can be made. This amount depends upon the area of meadow land and its yield of hay or silage. The former is usually fixed by physical constraints and land ownership, but the latter can be increased by the use of herbicides and fertilizers, and by reseeding with productive grasses such as rye-grass (*Lolium perenne*) and Timothy (*Phleum pratense*). Large increases in yield are possible, and there are very few meadows in the north Pennine Dales that have not been treated to some extent, even if only with a small amount of mineral fertilizer. Large amounts of nutrients are removed in the hay crop. Under traditional management, their return is achieved by the recycling of farmyard manure (FYM). There are consequential changes in the plant species composition of the swards associated with increased production, often involving an increase in the yield of the more competitive grasses and a decrease in the herbs. This change is only one of many that accompany the move from low input/low output traditional farming to modern farming methods that aim to increase the carrying capacity of upland farms through appropriate changes in management (Allaby 1983; Sinclair 1983).

The extent to which this change has occurred has resulted in the designation of Environmentally Sensitive Areas in some 13 000 ha in the north Pennines. These sites are distributed in 8 separate blocks in Weardale, Teesdale, Arkengarthdale and Swaledale, Waldendale, Wharfedale and Langstrothdale, Dentdale and Deepdale. Their boundaries follow the upper limits of the inbye land. One of the management objectives of this designation is to encourage farmers to improve the plant diversity of their hay meadows. The overall aim is to retain traditional grassland management in order to preserve the traditional appearance of the landscape in these upland areas. The following are included in the general prescription first proposed for meadow management.

i. Their use for grazing and hay-making should be with no applications of artificial or chemical fertilizers, maintained, pesticides or herbicides and no ploughing or artificial reseeding.

ii. Applications of farmyard manure to any one field should be restricted to a maximum of one year in 3.

iii. Stock should be excluded at least 7 weeks before the first hay cut, which should be made no earlier than mid-July, and no silage should be cut.

The traditional meadow types in the north Pennines vary in species composition according to soil conditions and management. Those that have been cut for hay have been divided into 6 types, ranging from relatively unproductive swards on thin limestone soils, and swards on acid boulder clay and peat soils, through moderately productive swards including the typical Dales buttercup (*Ranunculus* spp.) meadow, to traditional productive swards on alluvial soils characterized by the presence of wood cranesbill (*Geranium sylvaticum*) (Smith 1985). This latter type is particularly distinctive and is restricted to the upper reaches of the Dales. It is the same as the sweet vernal-grass (*Anthoxanthum odoratum*)/wood cranesbill neutral grassland identified by the national vegetation classification (Rodwell, in preparation). Its occurrence on relatively flat fertile sites suggests that the few examples that remain are likely to be agriculturally improved, unless active steps are taken to conserve them. They often persist only because they are owned by elderly farmers who do not wish to change their management. Otherwise, they may be isolated fields away from the main farmstead or they are under some form of conservation management, eg the Yorkshire Wildlife Trust's nature reserve of Yellands Meadow in upper Swaledale. This area is managed under licence by a local farmer.

3 *A fertilizer trial with old meadow turves*

The effect of fertilizers has been investigated by means of a small-scale turf experiment using 36 turves taken at random from a wood cranesbill/cock's-foot (*Dactylis glomerata*) meadow near Sedbergh, in the Yorkshire Dales. Four levels of nitrogen were used, equivalent to 0, 25, 50 and 75 kg ha^{-1}, with 3 levels of phosphorus, equivalent to 0, 17 and 34 kg ha^{-1}. There were 3 replicates of each of the 12 treatments. A base dressing of potassium, equivalent to 37 kg ha^{-1}, was applied to all the turves. Nitrogen was applied as ammonium nitrate, phosphorus as calcium hydrogen orthophosphate and potassium as potassium chloride. Turves were 25 cm deep and 25 cm square, and were laid out in boxes in a randomized split-plot design on a layer of sand separated from the underlying soil by a sheet of polythene. The hay crop was cut with shears in mid-July of each year and hand-sorted into its constituent species, which were dried and weighed.

The data were subjected to analysis of variance and detrended correspondence analysis (Hill 1979). Changes in the yield of hay and its species composition, the vascular plant species diversity and the presence of competitive species were assessed.

A total of 42 species were found, with a maximum of 23 species in a turf in the first year. The mean number of species per square metre of this vegetation type was 22.2 (Smith 1985). The high number of species in the turves suggests that the variation between turves is likely to be high.

Yields differed considerably from year to year, with overall means of 615 g m^{-2}, 1670 g m^{-2} and 939 g m^{-2} in 1984, 1985 and 1986. These differences probably reflect climatic differences, with 1984 having a very dry summer, as well as being the first year and 'settling down period' for the experiment; 1985 had a very wet summer. There were no significant differences in yield as a result of the fertilizer treatment in any year. Compared with published data for hay yields in other fertilizer trials, these yields are high, almost twice to 4 times the expected level. This increased yield may be due to the use of turves transported from the field. Under this experimental regime, there may be changes in the amount of nutrients released in the decomposition of soil organic matter. Larger amounts may be released through increased soil aeration in the turves. Alternatively, increased yield may be a consequence of the cessation of early spring grazing, growth normally grazed off by sheep being harvested later with the summer hay cut. This harvesting of the turves is also likely to be much more efficient than normal hay-timing, possibly leading to a greater hay yield.

The overall species composition of the turves changed during the course of the experiment. Separate ordinations of each year's data showed that the main trends were significantly related to applied nitrogen rather than phosphorus (Table 1). These trends reinforced one another in succeeding years, so that there is a temporal as well as a nitrogen trend. Species characteristic of the first year are self-heal (*Prunella vulgaris*), eyebright (*Euphrasia officinalis*), yellow-rattle (*Rhinanthus minor*), common mouse-ear chickweed (*Cerastium fontanum*), cuckoo flower (*Cardamine pratensis*), daisy (*Bellis perennis*), hairy oat (*Avenula pubescens*) and lop-grass (*Bromus hordeaceus*). These species have been lost from the turves, and there has been a rise in the relative abundance of Yorkshire fog (*Holcus lanatus*) and cock's-foot. Even the unfertilized controls have changed over time with an increase in these latter species.

Table 1. Analysis of variance of the fertilizer trial on the wood cranesbill/cock's-food sward

Date	Yield 84,85,86	Species composition Axis 1 84,85,86	Species composition Axis 2 84,85,86	Competitiveness 84,85,86	Number of species 84,85,86	Shannon-Weiner diversity index 84,85,86
Nitrogen	NS NS NS	* ** NS	NS NS **	* * *	NS * NS	NS NS NS
Phosphorus	NS NS NS	NS NS NS	NS NS NS	NS NS NS	NS NS NS	NS NS NS
Nitrogen x phosphorus interaction	NS NS NS	NS NS NS	NS NS NS	NS NS NS	NS NS NS	NS NS *

NS = not significant; *P<0.05; **P<0.01

The extent of the changes in diversity can be seen in Figure 1. In the first year, there was no difference

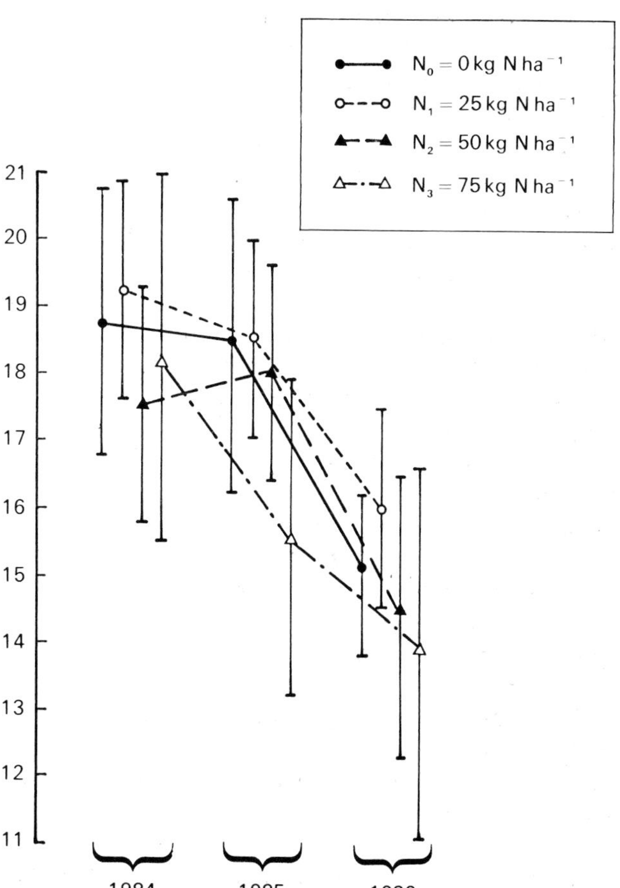

Figure 1. Wood cranesbill/cock's-foot meadow turves: change in the number of species with time, at different levels of fertilizer nitrogen

between treatments, but by the end of the second year all treatments had shown a drop of about 30%. When the relative amounts of each species are taken into account, it can be seen that there has been a loss of diversity at all nitrogen levels in the second year (Figure 2). This loss continues for the highest nitrogen treatment but levels off for the lower ones.

Grime (1979) classifies species according to their reaction to stress and disturbance. Competitive species are found in situations of low stress and no disturbance. Ruderals are found in low stress but disturbed situations, and stress tolerators are found where stress is high but disturbance is low. These 3 primary strategies are complemented by intermediate secondary strategies. Of the 42 species found in the turves, only cock's-foot is a competitor in the strict sense. Common mouse-ear chickweed and lop-grass are ruderals and there are 5 competitive ruderals, ie Yorkshire fog, white clover (*Trifolium repens*), rough-stalked meadow-grass (*Poa trivialis*), cow parsnip (*Heracleum sphondylium*) and creeping buttercup (*Ranunculus repens*). The majority of the species are C-S-R strategists typical of old meadow land. The increase in cock's-foot, both with time and with the amount of applied nitrogen, is typical of such species when freed from stress (Figure 3). Its increase in time without any applied nitrogen suggests that some other factor has also been holding it back.

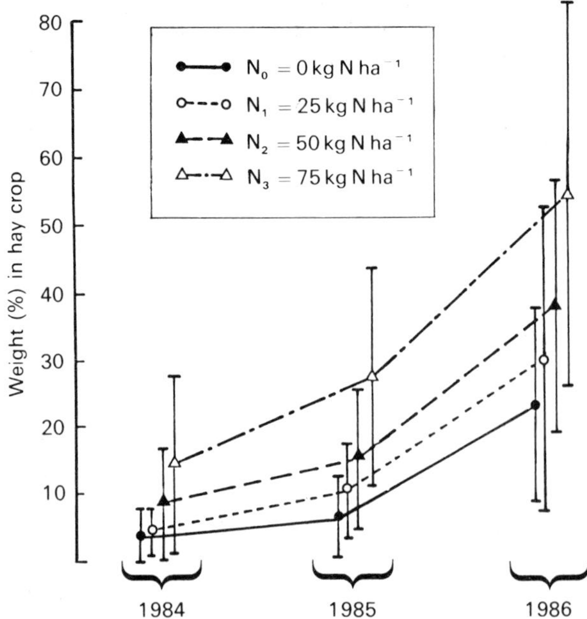

Figure 3. Wood cranesbill/cock's-foot meadow turves: change in yield of cock's-foot with time, at different levels of fertilizer nitrogen

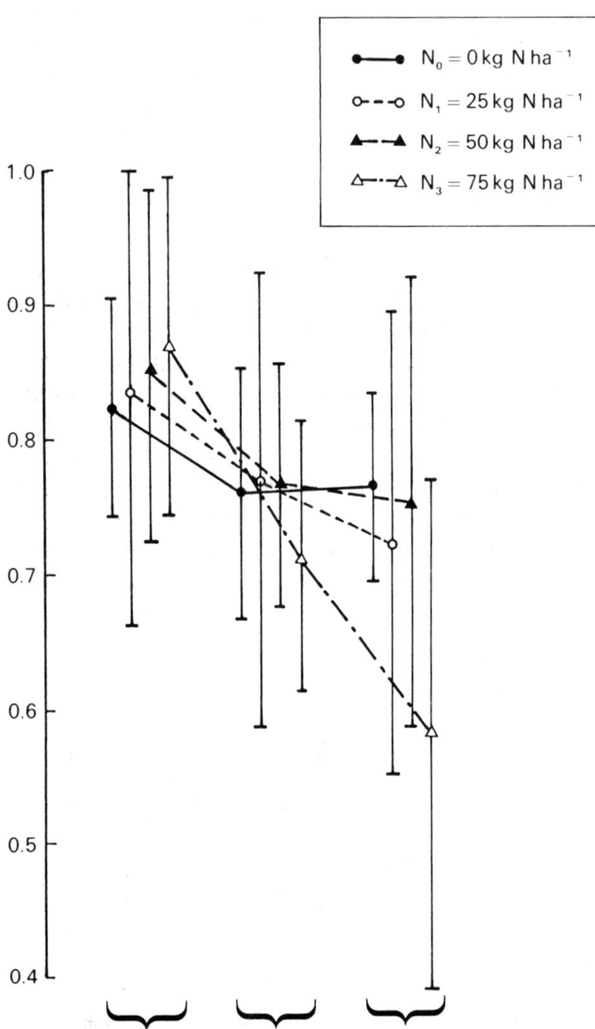

Figure 2. Wood cranesbill/cock's-foot meadow turves: change in diversity (Shannon-Weiner index) with time, at different levels of fertilizer nitrogen

It seemed likely that the ability of a turf to respond to applied fertilizer would depend upon whether or not it contained competitive species capable of reacting to the changed conditions. Each turf was, therefore, allocated a competitiveness index (CI), based on the proportion of the competitive, the ruderal and the competitive-ruderal species and the proportion of the hay yield attributed to them.

$$CI = \Sigma(\%\text{ competitive species } i \times \%\text{ yield from competitive species } i)$$

The competitive index of each turf in each year is significantly related to the amount of applied nitrogen (Table 1) and increases in subsequent years, although not linearly (Figure 4).

4 *Some long-term agricultural trials*

The Park Grass Experiment is a well-known classic meadow experiment described in detail by Lawes *et al.* (1882) and by Brenchley and Warrington (1958). It has been summarized by Thurston (1969), and used by Harper (1971) and Rorison (1971) to illustrate the fact that the fertilizer regime applied to grassland has a major influence on the botanical composition of meadow swards. The experiment is laid out as a series of plots of various sizes, and the fertilizer treatments suffer from a lack of replication and randomization. This shortcoming is characteristic of its time (1856) and is also a problem with the Palace Leas Meadow Trial established in 1896

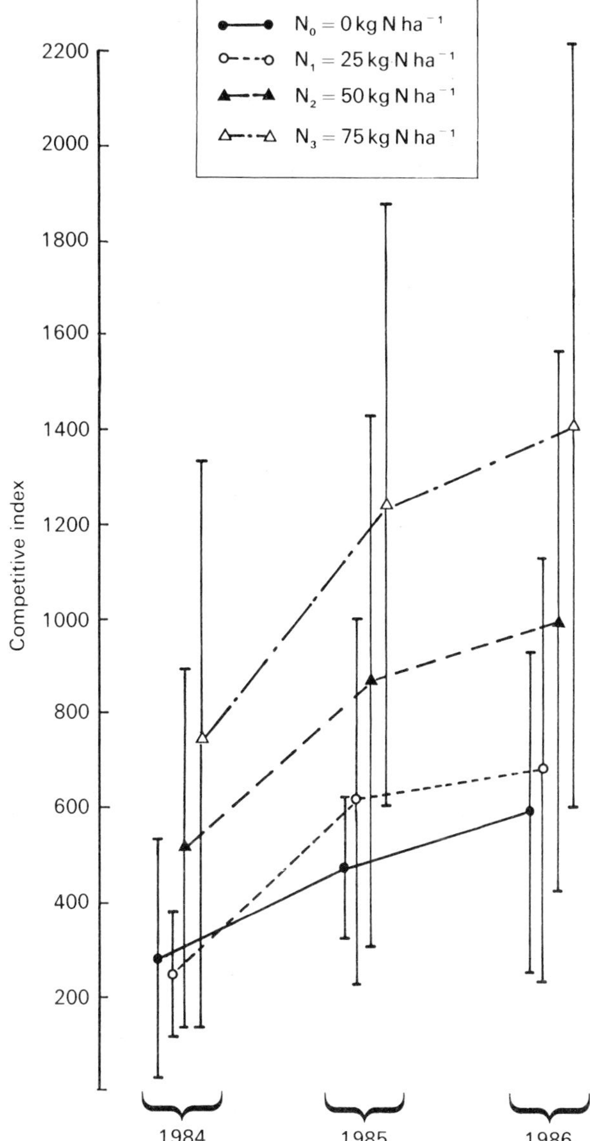

Figure 4. Wood cranesbill/cock's-foot meadow turves: change in the competitiveness index with time, at different levels of fertilizer nitrogen

at Cockle Park, the University of Newcastle-upon-Tyne's experimental farm near Morpeth, Northumberland.

The fertilizer treatments at the Park Grass Experiment fall into 3 main groups: no nitrogen, nitrogen applied as ammonium sulphate, and nitrogen applied as sodium nitrate. Within each group, plots are present with or without phosphorus and potassium, sodium and magnesium sulphates. Various farmyard manure treatments are applied. The plots were originally cut for hay in June, this being made on the plot, and subsequently grazed. From 1873, the grazing stopped and a second hay cut was made in the autumn. The experiment has been complicated by changes in the fertilizer and lime regimes over its life-time.

The Palace Leas Meadow Trial differs from the Park Grass Experiment in that there has been no alteration in the amounts of fertilizer applied since 1897 when the trial

Table 2. The Palace Leas Meadow Trial: fertilizer regimes (kg ha^{-1})

Plot	FYM[1]	Sulphate of ammonia	Nitrate of soda	Muriate of potash	Basic slag
2	20 000				
1	20 000	42.2	56.3	56.3	168.8
3	20 000	42.2	56.3	56.3	168.8
	FYM and artificial fertilizers are alternated annually				
5	50 000	42.2	56.3	56.3	168.8
	FYM every fourth year, artificial fertilizers in other years				
4	20 000				
	FYM applied in alternate years				
12				112.5	337.5
8					337.5
13		168.8		112.5	337.5
6	Control				
10		168.8			337.5
7		168.8			
9				112.5	
11		168.8		112.5	

[1] Plots are ordered according to the main trend in species composition from fertile to infertile plots; FYM = farmyard manure

began (Table 2). Only one hay cut is taken; the aftermath growth is grazed by cattle and sheep and has been since the trial was started (Pawson 1960).However, detailed botanical data are only available irregularly throughout its life. In fact, the only reasonably comparable data are for the species composition immediately after the start of the trial and for 1984 (Walker 1985).

One important trend in the Park Grass plots is their loss of species between 1862 and 1949 (Figure 5). Even the unmanured and FYM plots lose species, although this loss is less than in the other plots. On diversity grounds, the best fertilizer treatments are those which do not use mineral nitrogen, eg plots 3, 7 and 19, where the overall loss of species is smaller than on the mineral nitrogen plots. There are also more equitable amounts of each species, as indicated by the relatively constant values of the Shannon-Weiner diversity index (Figure 6).

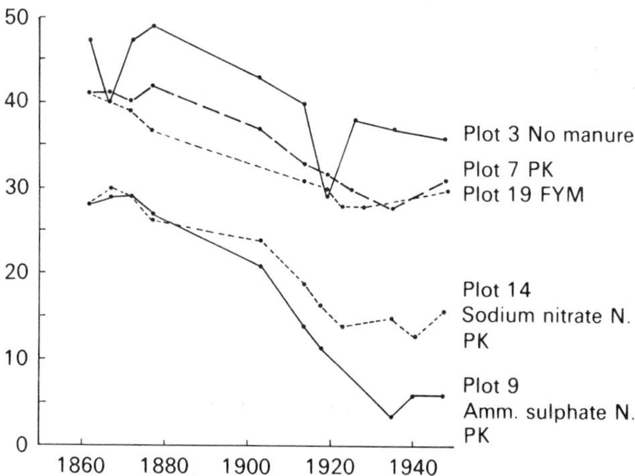

Figure 5. The Park Grass Experiment: change in the number of species in selected plots from 1862 to 1949

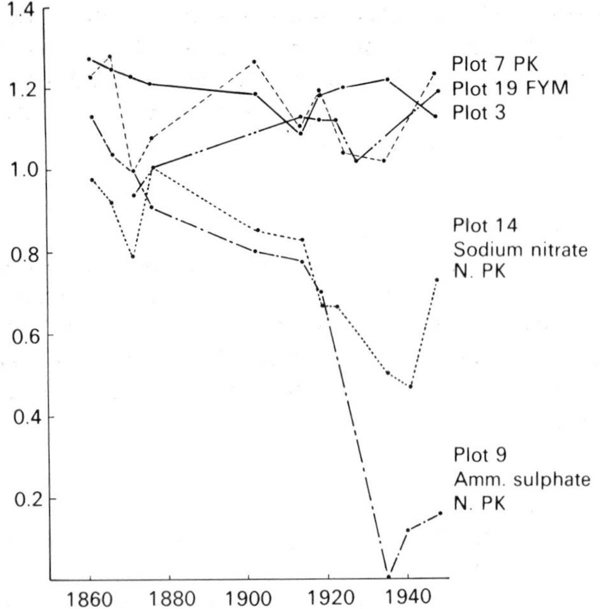

Figure 6. The Park Grass Experiment: change in plant species diversity (Shannon-Weiner index) in selected plots from 1862 to 1949

In 1897, the Palace Leas Meadow Trial was dominated by bent-grasses (*Agrostis* spp.) (86% of the hay from the unmanured plot in that year). All other species made less than a 2% contribution to the hay and included sweet vernal-grass, yellow oat (*Trisetum flavescens*), crested dog's-tail (*Cynosurus cristatus*), cock's-foot, red fescue (*Festuca rubra*), Yorkshire fog, rye-grass, rough-stalked meadow-grass, white clover, birdsfoot-trefoil (*Lotus corniculatus*), vetch (*Lathyrus* spp.), field woodrush (*Luzula campestris*) and ribwort (*Plantago lanceolata*). Timothy and red clover (*Trifolium pratense*) were also noted from the field in the first year. Other species generally noted as weeds in 1899 were purging flax (*Linum catharticum*), dock (*Rumex* spp.), common mouse-ear chickweed, ox-eye daisy (*Leucanthemum vulgare*), creeping buttercup, rush (*Juncus* spp.), horsetail (*Equisetum* spp.), yellow-rattle and cat's ear (*Hypochaeris radicata*). There were at least 15 species in the unmanured plot 6 in 1897. By 1985, this plot had at least 20 species, with 13.3 species m^{-2}, and seems to

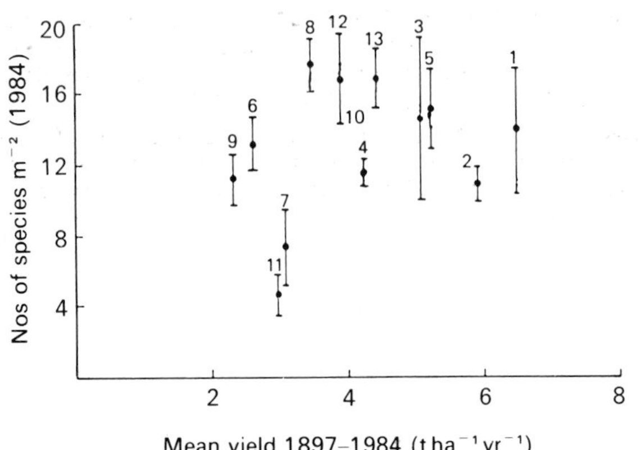

Figure 7. The Palace Leas Meadow Trial: the yield and species richness of plots 1–13

have increased its species richness over the 88-year period.

In terms of its wildlife interest, the Palace Leas Trial tells the same story as the Park Grass Experiment. High plant species diversity is associated with moderate fertility, particularly phosphatic fertilizer and moderate pH (Figure 7; Table 3) (Thurston *et al.* 1976). The maintenance of its overall species richness throughout its life and the predominance in some plots of species that regenerate by seed in vegetation gaps suggest that grazing in winter is an important feature for the conservation management of species-rich meadow land.

Table 3. Soil pH and diversity of the Palace Leas Meadow Trial (source: Walker 1985)

Plot[1]	Soil pH	Number of species m^{-2}	Total number of species $plot^{-1}$
2	5.8	11	18
1	5.9	14	25
3	5.8	15	25
5	5.9	15	25
4	5.8	11	18
12	5.4	17	25
8	5.7	18	26
13	4.8	17	25
6	4.6	13	20
10	5.1	15	22
7	3.8	7	12
9	4.8	11	18
11	3.8	5	7

[1] Plots are arranged according to the main trend in species composition from fertile to infertile plots

5 *Conclusions*

In the ungrazed situation at the long-term Park Grass Experiment and the short-term experiment on the Dales meadow turves, there has been a loss of species at all fertilizer levels. In the Park Grass Experiment, this loss seems to have stabilized after about 60–80 years and at a higher number in those treatments that did not involve mineral nitrogen fertilizer. The balance between species has stabilized more quickly, with the Shannon-Weiner index remaining comparatively high, when mineral nitrogen was not applied. The most extreme results are obtained when high levels of ammonium sulphate are used. This fertilizer acidifies the soil and results in grass-dominated, low-diversity swards.

Whilst there are no continuous data for changes in the species composition of the Palace Leas Trial, the available data at the start of the experiment suggest that the loss of species shown by the other 2 experiments has not occurred, perhaps because of the different management outside the period when the hay is grown. The Park Grass Experiment is cut for hay twice a year. It has not been grazed outside the period of hay growth since the year 1873, and the loss of species from most of the plots used here has occurred after this change in management.

The turves cut from the wood cranesbill/cock's-foot sward were originally grazed in the winter and spring, and this grazing would have been particularly heavy when the ewes were in the field for tupping and lambing, but ceased when the turves were moved to the experimental site. There will have been no trampling, dung or urine effects and no selective grazing. The heavy winter grazing is likely to have resulted in the grasses being particularly heavily grazed when the herbs were generally dormant. Apart from this effect, there is likely to be a reduced seed supply through isolation of the turves from a surrounding meadow, and the fact that hay was not allowed to lie, dry and lose its seed as in traditional management. The sampling method may, in fact, be analogous to silage-making in this respect. The lack of grazing may well be the factor underlying the change in species composition and diversity of the unfertilized controls. Alternatively, it may be an effect of the base dressing of potassium chloride or a result of soil changes consequent upon turf cutting. The most likely explanation from the long-term trials is that the diverse swards are the result of the maintenance of conditions unfavourable for the vigorous growth of competitive grasses, and this maintenance is achieved by keeping the soil nutrient status at relatively modest levels and by the use of grazing livestock outside the period when the hay is grown.

If grazing is the other factor at work here, then it suggests that the species composition of meadows can be carefully manipulated by controlling the grazing, soil pH and fertilizer applications. The exact balance between these factors has yet to be defined by experiment, but this points the way to defining management prescriptions for the maintenance of diverse meadow swards in the uplands. The blanket refusal to accept any fertilizers on important Sites of Special Scientific Interest is justified in terms of the effect of even low levels of fertilizer on some species, eg adder's tongue (*Ophioglossum vulgatum*). However, it is likely that an appropriate compromise management regime can be devised for those meadows that are not quite so significant to wildlife conservation but which are still an important amenity. Whilst grazing regimes cannot yet be defined, the principles underlying the fertilizer regimes can be suggested. Organic manures and mineral fertilizers that do not contain any nitrogen are preferable to nitrogenous mineral fertilizer, the manure being applied at a rate of less than 20 tonnes ha^{-1}. Nitrogen fertilizer may be applied to increase hay yields but should not be used at rates greater than 25 kg ha^{-1}. This rate represents about one cwt $acre^{-1}$ of a proprietary 20:10:10 fertilizer. The soil pH should not be allowed to fall below 5, and the soil should be limed when this is likely to occur.

6 *Acknowledgements*

E Smith typed the manuscript and assisted in some of the data collection. Vegetation data from the Palace Leas Meadow Trial were collected by S Walker; R S Shiel and W Stelling helped to set up the turf trial. The work was funded by a small grant from the Northumberland National Park.

7 *References*

Allaby, M. 1983. *The changing uplands.* (CCP 153.) Cheltenham: Countryside Commission.

Brenchley, W.E. & Warrington, K. 1958. *The Park Grass plots at Rothamsted 1856-1949.* Harpenden: Rothamsted Experimental Station.

Grime, J.P. 1979. *Plant strategies and vegetation processes.* London: Wiley.

Harper, J.L. 1971. Grazing, fertilisers and pesticides in the management of grassland. In: *The scientific management of animal and plant communites for conservation,* edited by E. Duffey & A. S. Watt, 15-32. (Symp. British Ecological Society no. 11.) Oxford: Blackwell Scientific.

Hill, M.O. 1979. *DECORANA: a FORTRAN program for detrended correspondence analysis and reciprocal averaging.* Ithaca, N.Y.: Section of Ecology and Systematics, Cornell University.

Lawes, J.B., Gilbert, J.H. & Masters, M.T. 1882. Agricultural, botanical and chemical results of experiments on the mixed herbage of permanent grassland, conducted for many years in succession on the same land. Part II. The botanical results. *Phil. Trans. R. Soc.,* **173,** 1181-1413.

Pawson, H.C. 1960. *Cockle Park Farm.* Oxford: Oxford University Press.

Rorison, I.H. 1971. The use of nutrients in the control of the floristic composition of grassland. In: *The scientific management of animal and plant communities for conservation,* edited by E. Duffey & A. S. Watt, 65-77. (Symp. British Ecological Society no. 11.) Oxford: Blackwell Scientific.

Sinclair, G. 1983. *The upland landscapes study.* Narberth: Environment Information Services.

Smith, R.S. 1985. *Conservation of northern upland meadows.* Bainbridge: Yorkshire Dales National Park.

Thurston, J.M. 1969. The effect of liming and fertilisers on the botanical composition of permanent grassland, and on the yield of hay. In: *Ecological aspects of the mineral nutrition of plants,* edited by I.H. Rorison, 1-10. (Symp. British Ecological Society no. 9.) Oxford: Blackwell Scientific.

Thurston, J.M., Williams, E.D. & Johnston, A.E. 1976. Modern developments in an experiment on permanent grassland started in 1856: effects of fertilisers and lime on botanical composition and crop and soil analyses. *Annls agron.,* **27,** 1043-1082.

Walker, S. 1985. *A study of the effects of long term fertiliser applications on the diversity of species and the botanical composition at Palace Leas meadow, Northumberland.* BSc thesis, University of Newcastle-upon-Tyne.

The nitrogen cycle in upland agriculture: its understanding, control and use

P INESON
Institute of Terrestrial Ecology, Merlewood Research Station, Grange-over-Sands, Cumbria, England

1 *Introduction*

Paradoxically, the air around us is composed mainly of nitrogen (N), yet it is this element which is the greatest limiting nutrient to agricultural productivity throughout the world. Although molecular N constitutes about 80% of the earth's atmosphere, it is chemically inert and therefore cannot be used directly by most living organisms. The conversion of N from the gaseous form into compounds suitable for uptake by living organisms is called N fixation and this is principally achieved by the chemical industry and by N-fixing bacteria. It is man's efforts to overcome this limiting factor to productivity which have led to the annual expenditure of vast quantities of energy, and to major problems in the pollution of the environment.

The production of one kg of fertilizer by the chemical industry currently requires an energy input equivalent to that provided by burning 2 kg of oil. The UK demand for nitrogenous fertilizers is on the increase, and Figure 1 clearly shows the consistent and upward trend in the use of N fertilizers, contrasting it with the trends shown for the 2 other principal nutrients used in agriculture. Unfortunately, large quantities of the nitrogen currently applied to agricultural land often miss the target crop, finding their way into aquatic systems and back into the atmosphere. It is estimated that farmers in the UK spend 400 million on N fertilizers each year and, because of this enormous financial commitment, together with the importance of N in polluting natural ecosystems, we need to be aware of the fate, efficiency, and environmental consequences of these compounds.

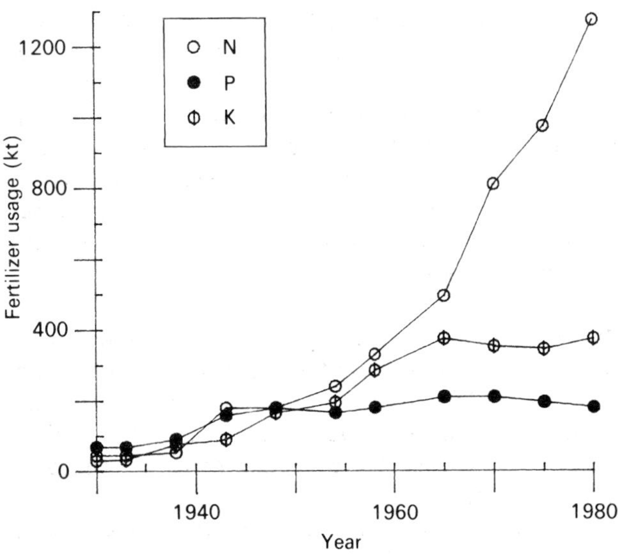

Figure 1. Trends in UK fertilizer usage

2 *Understanding nitrogen*

The movement of N through the environment is cyclic and any atom of N can move between gaseous, liquid or solid phase. The main components of the N cycle can be seen in Figure 2, which shows the principal forms of N and the pathways between them.

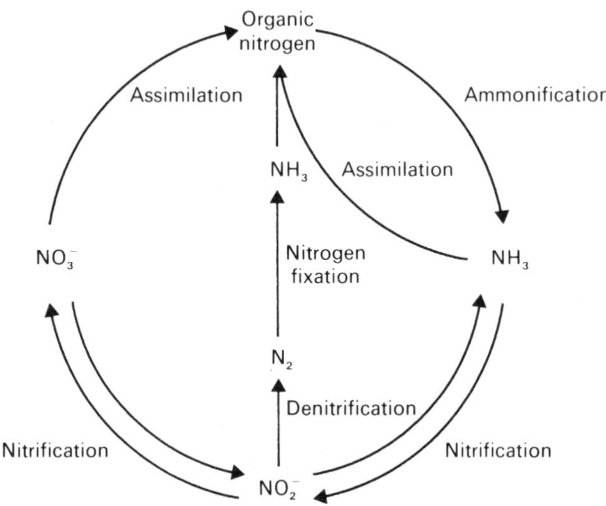

Figure 2. The nitrogen cycle

2.1 N fixation

It has been emphasized above that one major feature of the N cycle is the fact that the largest pool of N is in the atmosphere, in the form of dinitrogen gas (N_2). N can move from this pool into organisms *via* the route of N fixation. The vast supply of N gas in the atmosphere, coupled with the relative scarcity of combined N on the earth's surface, suggests that the process of N fixation is the major rate-limiting step in the N cycle. N fixation is the conversion of dinitrogen from the air to ammonium, a process which can be achieved biologically at normal ambient temperatures and air pressures, or artificially by chemical processes requiring high temperatures and pressures. Additionally, N can be converted from gaseous to liquid forms as a consequence of lightening, and by dry deposition of oxides of N to surfaces.

Only a small number of bacteria are capable of fixing N biologically, and the organisms involved can be divided into 2 groups: free-living bacteria which carry out non-symbiotic N fixation and symbiotic bacteria which exist in a mutualistic partnership with plants. Quantitatively, the most important N fixers belong to the genus *Rhizobium*, and members of this genus live symbiotically in the roots of leguminous plants, where they form characteristic nodules. The fixation of N is accomplished by enzymes produced by the bacterium, and the host plant provides carbohydrates and an environment suitable for the bacterium to carry out this fixation.

The most important agents of non-symbiotic N fixation are certain members of the blue-green bacteria, which are capable of fixing both carbon and N from the atmosphere. Although their role in N fixation in temperate agriculture is often assumed to be negligible, there is still some evidence that they may make a significant contribution to the N economy of certain arable lands (Powlson & Jenkinson 1988). Evidence is also accumulating that free-living N-fixing bacteria may exist in close association with plant roots, and fix significant quantities of N in the rhizosphere.

2.2 Assimilation

Nitrogen is essential for life, being a necessary component of amino acids, which are the fundamental building blocks of structural and enzymatic proteins. Plants are able to assimilate N in inorganic forms, mainly from the soil, and incorporate them into organic N compounds, with the principal nitrogenous compounds taken up by plants being ammonium and nitrate.

In turn, animals, including man, obtain N by consuming plants and other animals. During incorporation into animal tissue, the complex nitrogenous compounds of plants are hydrolyzed by varying degrees, with the N remaining largely in reduced organic form. Animals, unlike plants, excrete a significant quantity of metabolically produced nitrogenous compounds, and the form of excretory N differs markedly between animal species. Principal excretory products include ammonia, urea, uric acid and some organic nitrogenous compounds.

2.3 Ammonification

Much of the N assimilated by plants and animals remains in plant and animal tissues until the death of the organism, at which stage decomposition occurs and N is released. The process of decomposition is carried out mainly by micro-organisms, which attack proteins and nucleic acids liberating ammonium (ammonification). Part of the N is assimilated by the micro-organisms themselves (immobilization) and converted into microbial constituents, which will in due course be released when the microbe dies. The process results in a net release of N and is referred to as N mineralization, so called because organic N is converted to mineral, inorganic, form. Under anaerobic conditions, some of the amino acids are converted to amines (with their characteristic odour) and this process is referred to as putrefaction.

2.4 Nitrification

Although very small amounts of nitrate may be liberated on decomposition of organic matter, the principal inorganic N form released during decomposition is ammonium, as outlined above. However, there are groups of bacteria in the soil, collectively known as nitrifiers, which are able to convert ammonium to nitrate. These organisms are unusual in that they use the process of nitrification to provide energy for growth and reproduction, instead of the oxidation of organic matter. Their activity is very important, because certain plants preferentially assimilate nitrate, and nitrate is far more readily leached from soils than ammonium.

2.5 Denitrification

Denitrification is the biological conversion of nitrate to gaseous N products, such as dinitrogen and nitrous oxide. It is the major route by which fixed N is returned to the atmosphere. Again, it is a microbiological process achieved by a wide variety of organisms, but only occurs under certain environmental conditions. The process uses nitrate as a substrate, and requires anaerobic conditions and a source of energy for the organisms.

Although recent research has demonstrated that denitrification may be a major route for fertilizer losses in agricultural systems, it must be remembered that this process is also responsible for helping to shed excess nitrate from waters, and has an important function in preventing nitrate accumulation in aquatic systems.

3 *The nitrogen cycle in the uplands*

Figure 3 shows the overall inputs and outputs of N to agricultural land in the UK, with estimated total inputs and outputs being balanced at around 3 M t N yr^{-1}. This figure represents the overall situation for agricultural land in the UK, and the relative amounts have to be modified when considering upland areas alone. The specific use made of a particular area in the uplands also modifies this picture.

Unfortunately, the information we have about the N cycle in upland soils is limited to a few studies, yet we do know that there are certain important differences between these sites. The overall picture is presented in Figure 3 (Batey 1982). The unfavourable climate in the upland areas has important consequences for N cycling. Because of high rainfall rates and low temperatures, the soils are heavily leached, and organic matter accumulates, which leads to acid soils with low levels of available nutrients. The low levels of productivity also preclude expensive management options.

The results of one intensive study performed on a montane grassland ecosystem dominated by common bent-grass (*Agrostis capillaris*) and sheep's fescue (*Festuca ovina*) are considered here as an example of an upland N cycle. The study was performed at Llyn Llydaw and is described in detail by Perkins (1978). A summary diagram of the N cycle for this sheep-grazed grassland is illustrated in Figure 4, which shows the various pools and the fluxes between them.

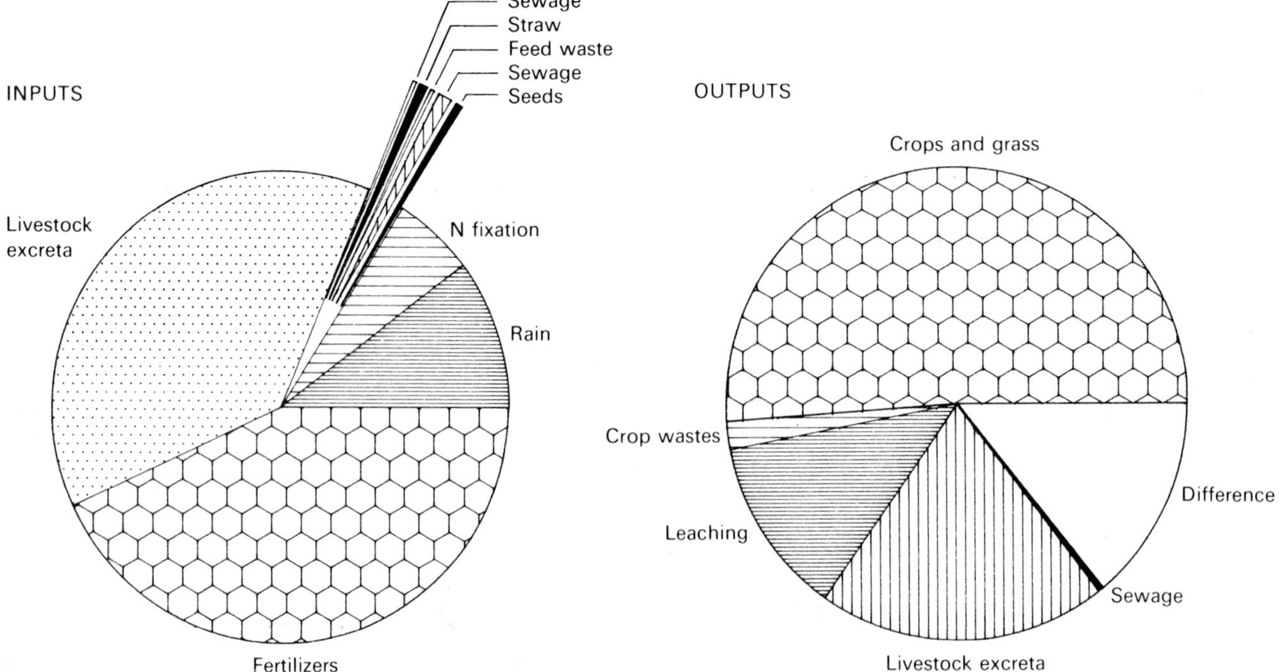

Figure 3. Overall nitrogen inputs and outputs for UK agriculture

3.1 Inputs

The relative overall inputs of N to agriculture in the UK are presented in Figure 3, with an estimated total input of around 3 M t N yr^{-1}. The major inputs are from fertilizers and animal excreta, which far exceed those from rainfall, N fixation and other sources.

The situation in the upland grassland ecosystem is very different, with no inputs from fertilizer or external sources other than rain, which contributed an estimated 18.4 kg ha^{-1} in the Llyn Llydaw study. The low occurrence of N-fixing plants in the sward gave rise to a negligible input from this source. Thus, this upland system represents one which is dependent on rainfall N, and which could be changed by different deposition rates. The suggestion that the concentration of nitrate in rainfall is increasing as a consequence of anthropogenic sources could have important effects in an area such as this, and it has indeed been seen as an important factor in affecting the floral composition of upland areas (Woodin & Lee 1987).

It has been estimated that a clover (*Trifolium* spp.) sward without added fertilizer can fix nearly 200 kg N ha yr^{-1} (Cowling 1982), which compares with an average fertilizer input to UK agricultural crops and grasslands of around 130 kg N per hectare and year (Church 1982). A review of N fixation in upland and marginal areas of the UK by Newbould (1982) emphasized the commercial advantages of adding to the nitrogen income by the use of clovers, especially white clover (*Trifolium repens*).

The contribution of wild white clovers and other N fixers to rough grazings is low because of their low density on acid soils. However, by the addition of lime, phosphorus (P) and potassium (K), it is possible to improve the percentage of white clover in upland soils, and the N they contribute. The pH of the soil must be increased above 5.2 before the wild clover will grow well, and a correct balance of added nutrients is necessary to achieve the establishment of a significant clover component (Floate *et al.* 1981). These workers demonstrated a large increase in rye-grass (*Lolium perenne*) herbage production on deep peat in response to a combined application of lime, P and K, which was mainly due to extra N transferred from the clover to the grass by urine from grazing animals. Figure 4 shows the importance of the excretory route in cycling N at Llyn Llydaw.

Using the above improvement techniques, clovers may become established on soils which either lack or have inefficient strains of *Rhizobia*, and experiments have shown that inoculation with effective strains can increase fixation levels. However, these experiments show a strong interaction with soil type, deep peats showing a positive response to inoculation and mineral soils showing a lack of response (Newbould 1982). The reason for these interactions is not clearly understood, but may be due to the interaction between lime and N mineralization. Addition of lime to acid, organic soils often results in increased mineralization of nitrogen, and it is known that increasing the inorganic N concentration in soils frequently results in an inhibition of nodule formation in leguminous plants. Also, for this reason, it is difficult to determine the extent to which improvements in the fixation of nitrogen by clover lead to increased nitrogen availability to swards, or the extent to which this increase is due to improved N mineralization caused by the addition of lime. However, despite these uncertainties, it has been suggested that fixation in the order of 125 kg N ha^{-1} yr^{-1} can be achieved through the establishment of white clover in upland systems (Newbould 1982).

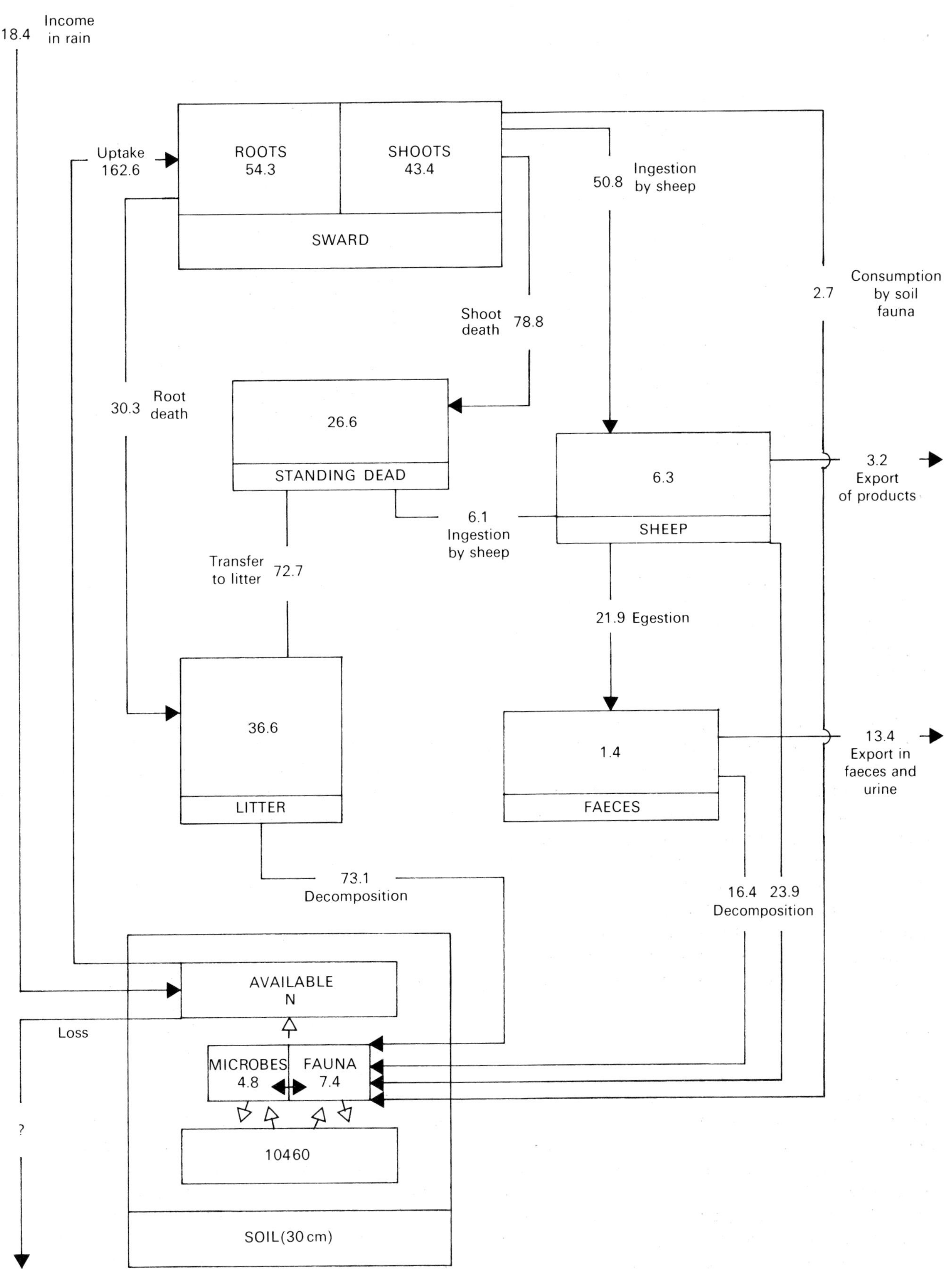

Figure 4. The nitrogen cycle at Llyn Llydaw. Pools are represented by boxes, and are given in kg ha^{-1}. Fluxes are shown as lines, with the quantities in kg ha^{-1}

3.2 N turnover

Perhaps the most surprising feature in Figure 4 is the discrepancy between the size of the pool of organic nitrogen in the soil and the relatively small quantities of nitrogen in circulation. The rate of ammonification of the organic matter in these soils is very low, dictated by the low temperatures and soil acidity at upland sites. Thus, despite the high nitrogen capital held in the soil (to 30 cm), less than 2% is mineralized per annum.

In upland regions, the nitrogen assimilated by the sward is mainly obtained as ammonium, derived from the decomposition of soil organic matter. Low soil temperature is probably the main factor controlling mineralization of N (Floate *et al.* 1981), but soil acidity will inhibit both decomposition and nitrification. Nitrification in acid soils such as these is usually negligible, unless the soil is limed, fertilized or disturbed by ploughing.

The majority of N taken up by the sward enters the detrital pathway *via* root and shoot death, with only a small fraction being ingested by the sheep. As mentioned above, the return of N to the soil as urine and faeces is an important source of available N for the sward, but there is often a transfer of N to the dry or sheltered areas used as resting places by the sheep, resulting in patches of higher fertility (O'Connor 1981).

Surprisingly, more N is contained in the soil fauna than in the sheep, and the amount of N held in microbial tissues also approaches this level.

3.3 Outputs

The N-deficient nature of upland pastures causes the cycling of nitrogen to be very tight, in that little nitrogen leaves the site. One of the principal reasons is the low concentration of nitrate in soil solution, the inorganic soil N pool being dominated by ammonium. Ammonium is less readily leached than nitrate, being retained on soil cationic exchange sites. Because the concentrations of ammonium in the soil will also remain relatively low, due to poor mineralization rates and uptake by the vegetation, the opportunity for nitrification is limited.

Few estimates of nitrogen leaching from upland areas have been made, yet catchment studies suggest losses in the order of 3–6 kg ha^{-1} yr^{-1} (Batey 1982). This aspect of the N cycle was not studied at Llyn Llydaw, and estimates are difficult to make. The main known source of N loss in this study was its export in faeces, which is largely the result of high transference to night camping sites, by the sheep. Strictly speaking, this does not represent a loss to the grassland site as a whole, but simply emphasizes the heterogeneous nature of the study site.

Livestock and wool represent the most obvious export route for N from upland pastures, but at Llyn Llydaw the total N loss was only 17% of the income in rain. This export represents less than 5% of the N ingested, the remainder being recycled in faeces and urine. Other livestock losses include grouse and deer removal, which may be important for certain specific areas, yet generally represent insignificant components of the cycle.

Losses of N from upland sites to the atmosphere are very difficult to quantify. The process of denitrification, recently identified to be a major N route in fertilized lowland systems, probably has little significance in the uplands. Upland soils do not receive fertilizer N inputs and, consequently, soil concentrations of nitrate will never be sufficiently high to support denitrification. However, this situation may not apply at points where faeces are deposited and where anaerobic conditions and nitrification may provide conditions for denitrification to occur. Again, this export is likely to be small, due to the limited occurrence of suitable microsites.

The other principal route by which N may be released to the atmosphere is through burning, which may represent a considerable loss, according to the frequency of burning, vegetation and soil type, and severity of burn. In very severe fires, not only is the standing vegetation combusted, but also large quantities of organic matter in the upper soil horizons.

Allen (1964) showed that losses of N in a single burn could amount to 45 kg ha^{-1}, yet he suggested that the stimulation of mineralization of organic soil N as a consequence of the burn could compensate for these losses. Comparable field measurements of N losses through straw-burning suggest that a single burn may release around 10 kg ha^{-1} (Fowler *et al.* 1985). Batey (1982) gives a range of 4–6 kg ha^{-1} yr^{-1} for burning losses on upland pastures, but emphasizes that, for any particular site, losses may be substantially greater or less. In the Llyn Llydaw situation, for example, the level of sheep grazing is so great that burning is not practised.

4 *Conclusions*

Upland soils are strongly influenced by climate, with high leaching and weathering leading to losses of bases and increasing acidity. Together with low temperatures, this situation leads to low rates of nutrient return through decomposition, and an accumulation of organic nitrogen in unavailable forms in the soil. Typically, only a few per cent of the total soil pool N is mineralized every year and, of this amount, only a fraction ends up in the grazers. The vegetation on these soils is usually strongly N limited.

Herbage production of upland rough grazings can be markedly improved by liming and fertilization, and there is substantial scope for increasing the use of legumes as sources of fixed N. Usually, the only other inputs of N in these areas are from rainfall, yet losses tend to be small. Leaching losses and losses through denitrification are reduced because of the absence of nitrate in the soils. However, losses of N through burning may be substantial.

5 References

Allen, S.E. 1964. Chemical aspects of heather burning. *J. appl. Ecol.*, **1,** 347-367.

Batey, T. 1982. Nitrogen cycling in upland pastures of the U.K. *Proc. R. Soc. B,* **296,** 551-556.

Church, B.M. 1982. Use of fertilisers in England and Wales, 1981. *Rep. Rothamsted exp. Stn, 1981,* Part 2, 123-128.

Cowling, D.W. 1982. Biological nitrogen fixation and grassland production in the United Kingdom. *Proc. R. Soc. B,* **296,** 405-417.

Floate, M.J.S., Rangeley, A. & Bolton, G.R. 1981. An investigation of problems of sward improvement on deep peat with special reference to potassium responses and interactions with lime and phosphorus. *Grass Forage Sci.,* **36,** 81-90.

Fowler, D.N., Mullock, S., Leith, I.D., Cape, J.N. & Unsworth, M.H. 1985. Production of oxides of nitrogen during strawburning. *Annu. Rep. Inst. terr. Ecol. 1984,* 61-62.

Newbould, P. 1982. Biological nitrogen fixation in upland and marginal areas of the U.K. *Proc. R. Soc. B,* **296,** 405-417.

O'Connor, K.F. 1981. Comments on Dr. Floate's paper on grazing effect by large herbivores. *Ecol. Bull. Stockh.,* **33,** 707-714.

Perkins, D.F. 1978. The distribution and transfer of energy and nutrients in the *Agrostis-Festuca* grassland ecosystem. In: *Production ecology of British moors and montane grasslands,* edited by O.W. Heal & D.F. Perkins, 375-395. Berlin: Springer.

Powlson, D.S. & Jenkinson, D.S. 1988. Quantifying inputs of non-fertilizer nitrogen into agro-ecosystems. In: *Field methods in terrestrial ecosystem nutrient cycling,* edited by A.F. Harrison, P. Ineson & O.W. Heal. London: Elsevier Applied Science. In press.

Woodin, S.J. & Lee, J.A. 1987. The fate of some components of acidic deposition in ombrotrophic mires. *Environ. Pollut.,* **45,** 61-72.

Phosphorus in grasslands: its understanding, control and use

A F HARRISON[1] and K TAYLOR[2]
[1]Institute of Terrestrial Ecology, Merlewood Research Station, Grange-over-Sands, Cumbria, England
[2]Department of Biology, University College London, Gower Street, London

1 Introduction

Hill and upland sheep-grazed grasslands are frequently deficient in phosphorus (P) and to a variable extent, and this deficiency, together with the effects of poor climate, restricts sward productivity (Reith 1973; Newbould 1974; Newbould & Floate 1979). The maintenance or improvement of the productivity of grasslands depends on sustained or improved soil fertility, whilst the conservation of the varied and often special floristic composition of grasslands may depend on a relatively low or delicately balanced level of fertility. Clearly, therefore, if we are to manage hill and upland grasslands to maximize farm outputs and financial returns, yet also conserve their wildlife value, we need to understand the processes involved in the phosphorus cycle of these ecosystems and how to manipulate them to our advantage.

2 Soil phosphorus

The first question which needs answering is 'Why are hill and upland grassland soils P deficient, when they contain 500–3000 kg P ha^{-1} in the top 0.5 m of the soil profile?' (Floate 1962; Newbould & Floate 1979; Perkins 1978). The basic reason is that the vast majority of the phosphorus in the acid hill soils is 'unavailable' to plants, being bound in relatively stable organic matter or complexed in insoluble compounds with iron and aluminium. The organic form of phosphorus is often 65–80% of the total amount in the top 0.5 m of soil, and may approach 95% of that in the surface soil layers. Generally, the amount and proportion of phosphorus in the organic form increase with the altitude and rainfall of the site, the organic matter content of the soil and the thickness of the mat layer on the soil surface (Floate 1962; Harrison 1985, 1987). However, the plant production potential, shown using the common bent-grass (*Agrostis capillaris*) and white clover (*Trifolium repens*) as test plants (Harrison & Hornung 1983), is highly significantly negatively related to the proportion of the soil phosphorus in the organic form (Harrison 1985). There is a tendency for hill soils to accumulate organic matter because of its slow decomposition, both in the mineral (Clement & Williams 1964) and surface mat layers (Floate 1970a; Shiel & Rimmer 1984), particularly in areas with low grazing pressure (Gillingham 1980). Acidification of the soil through leaching of soil bases (Newbould & Floate 1979) and the addition of nitrogenous fertilizer (Shiel & Rimmer 1984) promotes the accumulation of organic phosphorus in the soil (Floate 1962, 1973; Walker 1962). Fertilizer phosphorus may end up in either or both of the surface mat and soil humus (Blair *et al.* 1976; Parfitt 1980). Accumulation of phosphorus in the organic form exacerbates the problems of P deficiency, by reducing the amount of phosphorus available in the soil (Jackman 1964a, b; White *et al.* 1976).

3 Phosphorus cycling

The phosphorus available to plants (2–10 kg P ha^{-1} Newbould & Floate 1979) is usually a very small proportion of the total present in the soil. Generally, as the available phosphorus is taken up from the soil by the roots of the grass sward, it is replenished through the processes of organic matter decomposition and organic phosphorus mineralization by the soil micro-organisms and fauna, and by leaching of the surface mat by rain. The availability of phosphorus is, indeed, largely controlled by the mineralization processes. These are dynamic processes changing in rates with the seasonal, climatic and soil conditions, and play a vital role in the maintenance of the phosphorus cycle, and hence the fertility of the soil.

A typical phosphorus cycle of an upland grassland is presented in Figure 1, which is that for a phosphorus-deficient bent-grass/fescue (*Agrostis/ Festuca*) sward at Llyn Llydaw, Snowdonia, north Wales (Perkins 1978). The site is at 500 m elevation, has an annual rainfall of 380 cm, a mean annual temperature of 7.2°C and is grazed by sheep (12.5 animals ha^{-1}) from April to October.

In this grassland ecosystem, only a small proportion (0.5%) of the total phosphorus capital is in the living biomass and about half is below ground. The living vegetation contains about 7.7 kg P ha^{-1} and an estimated 4 kg P ha^{-1} is in soil fauna and micro-organisms, the latter being more than in the sheep. A further 5.7 kg P ha^{-1} occurs in standing dead grass and litter mat on the soil surface. The annual plant uptake of phosphorus (16 kg P ha^{-1} yr^{-1}) is higher than the total amount returned to the soil in plant litter, by root death and in sheep faeces (14 kg P ha^{-1} yr^{-1}), because an estimated 1.2 kg P ha^{-1} yr^{-1} is lost from the site in faeces excreted by sheep on to lower ground when they camp at night. Transfer of phosphorus by sheep from one area to another has been recorded elsewhere (Gillingham & During 1973), and 0.8 kg P ha^{-1} yr^{-1} is removed in sheep products. Cycling phosphorus may also be reduced through some accumulation of soil organic matter, but the loss has not been estimated for this site. The available phosphorus in the soil is, however, largely replenished by decomposition

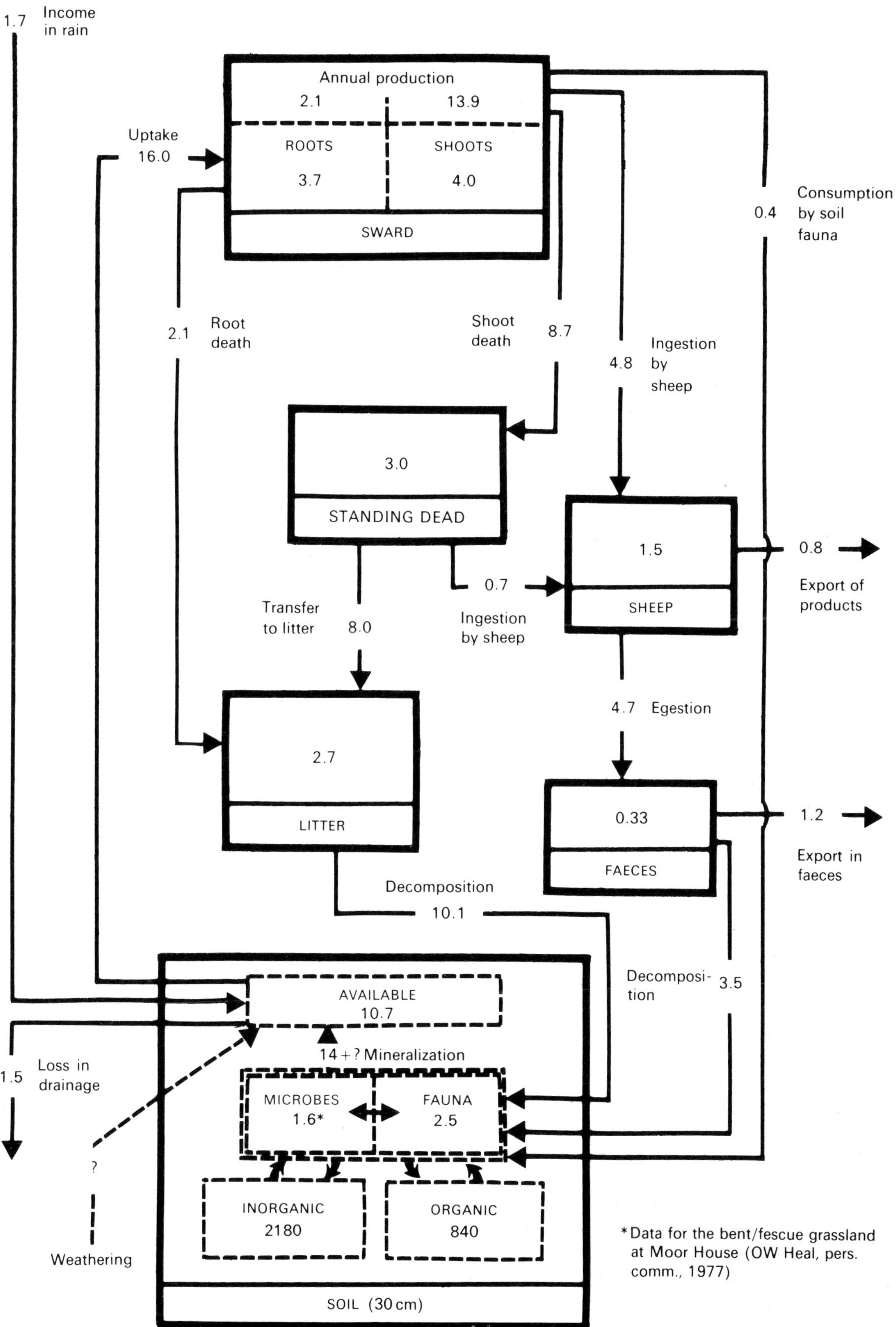

Figure 1. Phosphorus cycle of a bent/fescue grassland (Llyn Llydaw, Snowdonia, north Wales), based on Perkins (1978): contents in kg P ha^{-1} and transfers in kg P ha^{-1} yr^{-1} (source: Harrison 1985)

of the organic matter returned to the soil and the consequent release of the phosphorus contained to the available supply.

The processes of organic matter decomposition and release of the phosphorus for recycling are dynamic, and the rates are constantly changing. Temperature and moisture conditions in the soil are important factors governing the release of phosphorus from organic matter in hill grasslands (Floate 1970b, c, d), so there is a marked seasonal variation in the availability of phosphorus in the soil (Gupta & Rorison 1975). Changes in grazing pressure by seasonal grazing management may alter the amounts of phosphorus returned in urine and faeces, and hence amplify the natural seasonal pattern of available phosphorus. Phosphorus availability also varies in different layers of the soil, probably being greatest at the soil surface (Gupta & Rorison 1975).

The uptake of phosphorus by the grass sward varies with its seasonal growth pattern and is also affected by temperature and moisture conditions. In low-phosphorus soils, P taken up by some plants in one period of the year may be temporarily stored to support growth in other periods when conditions are unfavourable for uptake or when the soil is depleted (Grime 1979). In addition, the patterns of phosphorus uptake by the sward may be influenced by rooting depths of the different plant species present (Goodman & Collison 1982). The vesicular/arbuscular mycorrhizal development on the root systems of the sward species stimulates phosphorus uptake by plants by increasing the effective root system surface area and soil volume for phosphorus absorption (Sanders & Tinker 1971; Sparling & Tinker 1978; Fitter 1986). Whilst mycorrhizal infection may improve total sward production, selective mycorrhizal development may be an important competitive factor in the survival of particular plant species in a complex P-deficient sward (Read *et al.* 1976).

4 *Grassland improvement*

Several management practices can be employed to improve the rate of phosphorus cycling and thus the productivity of hill grasslands: (i) fertilizing; (ii) liming; (iii) increasing stocking rate; (iv) ploughing and reseeding; (v) introduction of earthworms; and (vi) inoculation with mycorrhizas.

The main way to improve the phosphorus status of hill and upland grassland soils, particularly when there is a net outflow of the element (see Figure 1), is to apply phosphorus either as slurry or as fertilizer. Slurry applications may not be as effective as fertilizer per unit phosphorus applied, as much of the phosphorus contained is in slowly mineralizing organic forms, but it has a cost advantage where its application is practical. There may be some disadvantages, however, as it may induce unfavourable soil conditions for micro-organisms and fauna (McAllister 1977). Fertilizer applications of 25–75 kg P ha^{-1} are often recommended (Newbould 1974; Newbould & Floate 1979) at various intervals of 2–8 years, depending on soil and pasture conditions.

Liming soils to increase soil pH (Pearson & Hoveland 1974) brings about an increase in microbiological activity (Jackman 1960; Macdonald 1979) which, in turn, stimulates the decomposition of soil organic matter (Jackman 1960; Broadbent 1962). Increasing soil pH through liming also increases the solubility of iron and aluminium complexes with organic and inorganic phosphorus (Jackman & Black 1951; Hsu & Jackson 1960) and increases the rate of mineralization of organic phosphorus in soils (Thompson *et al.* 1954). Together, these increases improve the rate of cycling of phosphorus and increase grassland productivity (Floate 1962; Floate *et al.* 1973).

Under increased grazing pressure generated by raising the stocking rate, there is an increase in the degree of pasture utilization. This results in a lowering of the rate of return of dead plant material to the soil, and thus a reduction in the thickness of the surface mat of organic matter and a decrease in the carbon/organic phosphorus of the soil profile (Floate 1970a, b). In addition, there are the increased returns of phosphorus to the soil in urine and faeces, the phosphorus in the latter being potentially more available than that in decaying plant material (Floate 1970a). Both processes improve phosphorus cycling, enhance sward productivity (Rawes & Welch 1969; Floate 1970a, 1973) and improve properties of these hill soils (Floate 1962, 1970a; Walker 1962). However, increased grazing pressure may result in an accumulation of organic phosphorus in the soil, possibly through increased faecal returns (McLachlan 1968; Floate 1973), so, in the longer term, fertilizer phosphorus applications are also necessary.

Ploughing of upland grassland soils often results in an increase in the rate of decomposition of accumulated organic matter, as soil disturbance improves aeration, stimulates microbial activity and makes the organic matter more accessible for decomposition (Rovira & Greacen 1957; Maltby 1979, 1984). Phosphorus locked up in the organic matter may, therefore, be mobilized for potential plant uptake (Thompson *et al.* 1954; Jackman 1964b). However, the mobilized phosphorus may be directly fixed by iron and aluminium to become unavailable to plants, particularly if the ploughing should expose iron-rich layers – many hill grassland soils have a high capacity to fix phosphate and render it unavailable to plants. Thus, ploughing may not have the desired effect on all soils, of actually increasing the amount of phosphorus cycling. For reseeding with an improved grass species and clover, it may be necessary therefore to apply lime and fertilizer (Munro *et al.* 1979; Newbould & Floate 1979).

The introduction of earthworms into grasslands has been shown to enhance the grassland productivity (Stockdill 1966, 1982; Hoogerkamp *et al.* 1983). In acid upland grasslands, it may be necessary to apply some lime to adjust soil pH, before attempting to introduce earthworms of the right species (Syers & Springett 1984). Earthworms improve soil aeration, microbial activity and soil organic matter decomposition, and hence should stimulate phosphorus cycling. It is not known, however, if there have been any experimental attempts to introduce earthworms and assess their effects on grassland production in upland Britain.

As there are proven benefits of mycorrhizal infection of root systems on the phosphorus uptake by plants, attempts could be made to enhance the degree of plant infection by artificial inoculation. Attempts to inoculate plants in acidic hill soils with mycorrhizas may also necessitate prior liming to modify soil pH, as mycorrhizas most successfully develop at about pH 6.0 (Graw 1979; Newbould & Rangeley 1984). Some trials in mid-Wales have shown that grass plants may benefit from inoculation with appropriate mycorrhizal fungi (Hayman 1977). Though liming may increase the degree of mycorrhizal infection in plants, the productivity of the plants may not be improved (Newbould & Rangeley 1984).

5 *Floristic composition*

An inevitable problem with the above soil/site management practices is that the floristic composition of the swards will be changed. These changes frequently reduce, sometimes markedly, the conservation value of the upland grasslands. Some of the floristic changes may be directly attributable to the altered levels of phosphorus availability. Many of the species present in upland grasslands survive when the availability of phosphorus in the soil is low, and some species can react vigorously to increases in phosphorus supply (Bradshaw *et al.* 1960; Clarkson 1967; Rorison 1968; Jeffrey & Pigott 1973; Atkinson 1983). So, fertilizing grassland swards with phosphate causes major changes in the species composition (Milton 1940; Sears 1953; Jeffrey & Pigott 1973; Pigott 1982), and may result in a considerable reduction in the number present (Jeffrey & Pigott 1973).

Many changes in species composition of grasslands are also caused by liming (Milton 1940; Sears 1953; Pigott 1982), some of which may be indirectly induced by changes in phosphate availability. However, changes in calcium availability resulting from liming can have direct and marked influences on the growth and survival of many acidophilous plants. Varying the grazing pressure by changing the stocking rate can also result in changes in the floristic composition of swards. Some species, perhaps relatively rare ones, may flourish under heavy grazing pressure, whilst others become more abundant when sheep grazing is removed (Welch & Rawes 1964; Rawes 1981). In some sites, removal of sheep grazing causes a reduction in the number of plant species in the sward (Watt 1957; Welch & Rawes 1964), and some changes in the flora may still be occurring 24 years after grazing removal (Rawes 1981). Though some of the changes in species might be brought about by changes in availability of soil phosphate through recycling in urine and faeces, induced by grazing pressures, major direct effects result from the grazing itself and trampling by the sheep and, after grazing is removed, from competition for light as the sward grows denser.

From the available data, it is clear that altering the phosphate status of upland grasslands, by whatever management practice, will induce many changes in the species of plants present in a sward. It is important to realize, however, that the effects of the management procedures designed to 'improve grasslands' are only of a temporary nature. Without renewal of fertilizer applications or continuity of management, the grasslands are prone to revert to the previous acidifying, low microbial activity, organic matter-accumulating state of lower fertility (Jackman 1964a, b; Floate 1977; Maltby 1979). The timescale for the natural reconstitution of the poorer nutrient status, acid soil conditions which favour many of the plant species of conservation interest, from limed, highly fertilized and perhaps reseeded pasture, is as yet unknown.

6 *Management of soil phosphorus status*

Clearly, as indicated in the introduction to this paper, we need to understand the patterns and processes of phosphorus cycling in upland grasslands, if we are to manage efficiently the productivity and the floristic composition of grassland swards.

One of the very basic necessities for efficient management of upland and hill grasslands for optimum productivity and floristic composition is to determine the soil phosphorus status by sensitive, reliable and practical methods. However, assessment of phosphorus 'availability' in hill and upland soils by current routine soil analysis is in most cases unsatisfactory (Floate & Pimplaskar 1976; Pimplaskar et al. 1982), due largely to the complex nature of the soil phosphorus chemistry and the dynamics of the phosphorus cycle influenced by the grazing sheep, as discussed earlier.

A new approach (Harrison & Helliwell 1979) for assessing the phosphorus status of soils has recently been applied to grasslands and is showing considerable promise. The bioassay is based on the physiological responses of plant root systems rather than soil analysis. The root response is determined as the rate at which ^{32}P-labelled phosphorus is metabolically absorbed from a standardized solution in the laboratory. The uptake rate by roots is related negatively and exponentially to the supply of phosphorus in the rooting medium (Harrison *et al.* 1985, 1986). Preliminary studies, relying on the responses of sheep's fescue (*Festuca ovina*), a most common species in upland and hill swards, have shown that the bioassay can be used to predict fertilizer responses and total sward productivity in upland grasslands (Harrison *et al.* 1986). As this method is particularly sensitive, and its sensitivity increases with decreasing soil fertility (Harrison & Helliwell 1979), it could provide a useful means of determining the phosphorus status of hill and upland grasslands, particularly if there are specific conservation aspects of floristic composition which have to be taken into account. The bioassay has the potential to be used both as a research tool in complex biological studies and in the practical routine manner for assessing fertilizer requirements.

7 References

Atkinson, C.J. 1983. Phosphorus acquisition in four co-existing species from montane grassland. *New Phytol.*, **95**, 427-437.

Blair, G.J., Till, A.R. & Smith, R.C.G. 1976. The phosphorus cycle - what are the sensitive areas? *Rev. Rural Sci.*, **3**, 9-19.

Bradshaw, A.D., Chadwick, M.J., Jowett, D., Lodge, R.W. & Snaydon, R.W. 1960. Experimental investigations into the mineral nutrition of several grass species. III. Phosphate level. *J. Ecol.*, **48**, 631-637.

Broadbent, F.E. 1962. Biological and chemical aspects of mineralisation. *Trans. Comm. IV and V, Int. Soil Sci. Soc. New Zealand*, 220-229.

Clarkson, D.T. 1967. Phosphorus supply and growth rate in species of *Agrostis* L. *J. Ecol.*, **55**, 111-118.

Clement, C.R. & Williams, T.E. 1964. Leys and soil organic matter. I. The accumulationm of organic carbon in soils under different leys. *J. agric. Sci. Camb.*, **63**, 377-383.

Fitter, A.H. 1986. Effect of benomyl on leaf phosphorus concentration in alpine grasslands: a test of mycorrhizal benefit. *New Phytol.*, **103**, 767-776.

Floate, M.J.S. 1962. *Pedogenetic relationships concerning forms of soil phosphorus and soil organic matter.* PhD thesis, University of Durham.

Floate, M.J.S. 1970a. Plant nutrient cycling in hill land. *Rep. Hill Fmg Res. Org., 5th*, 15-34.

Floate, M.J.S. 1970b. Mineralisation of nitrogen and phosphorus from organic materials of plant and animal origin and its significance in the nutrient cycle in grazed upland and hill soils. *J. Br. Grassld Soc.*, **25**, 295-302.

Floate, M.J.S. 1970c. Decomposition of organic materials from hill soils and pastures. III. Effects of temperature on the mineralisation of carbon, nitrogen and phosphorus from plant materials and sheep faeces. *Soil Biol. Biochem.*, **2**, 187-196.

Floate, M.J.S. 1970d. Decomposition of organic materials from hill soils and pastures. IV. Effects of moisture content on the mineralisation of carbon, nitrogen and phosphorus from plant materials and sheep faeces. *Soil Biol. Biochem.*, **2**, 275-283.

Floate, M.J.S. 1973. Soils associated with grass and heather moorland and some long-term changes related to grazing influences. *J. Sci. fd Agric.*, **24**, 1149.

Floate, M.J.S. 1977. British hill soil problems. *Soil Sci.*, **123**, 325-331.

Floate, M.J.S. & Pimplaskar, M.S. 1976. Some anomalous results for 'available P' in hill soils and experimental attempts towards their resolution. *J. Sci. fd Agric.*, **27**, 591.

Floate, M.J.S., Eadie, J., Black, J.S. & Nicholson, I.A. 1973. The improvement of *Nardus* dominant hill pasture by grazing control and fertilizer treatment and its economic assessment. In: *Hill pasture improvement and its economic utilisation. Colloq. Proc.*, no.3, 33-46. Potassium Institute Ltd.

Gillingham, A.G. 1980. Phosphorus uptake and return in grazed steep hill pastures. I. Pasture production and dung and litter accumulation. *N.Z. J. agric. Res.*, **23**, 313-321.

Gillingham, A.G. & During, C. 1973. Pasture production and transfer of fertility within a long-established hill pasture. *N.Z. J. exp. Agric.*, **1**, 227-232.

Goodman, P.J. & Collison, M. 1982. Varietal differences in uptake of ^{32}P-labelled phosphate in clover plus ryegrass swards and monocultures. *Ann. appl. Biol.*, **100**, 559-565.

Graw, D. 1979. The influence of soil pH on the efficiency of vesicular arbuscular mycorrhiza. *New Phytol.*, **82**, 687-695.

Grime, J.P. 1979. *Plant strategies and vegetation processes.* Chichester: Wiley.

Gupta, P.L. & Rorison, I.H. 1975. Seasonal differences in the availability of nutrients down a podzolic profile. *J. Ecol.*, **75**, 521-534.

Harrison, A.F. 1985. Effects of environment and management on phosphorus cycling in terrestrial ecosystems. *J. environ. Manage.*, **20**, 163-179.

Harrison, A.F. 1987. *Soil organic phosphorus: a world literature review.* Wallingford: Commonwealth Agricultural Bureaux International.

Harrison, A.F. & Helliwell, D.R. 1979. A bioassay for comparing phosphorus availability in soils. *J. Ecol.*, **16**, 497-505.

Harrison, A.F. & Hornung, M. 1983. Variation in fertility of UK soils. *Annu. Rep. Inst. terr. Ecol. 1982*, 98-99.

Harrison, A.F., Dighton, J., Hatton, J.C. & Smith, M.R. 1985. A phosphorus-deficiency bioassay for trees and grasses growing in low nutrient status soils. In: *Proc. int. Colloq. for the Optimization of Plant Nutrition, Montpellier, September 1984*, edited by P. Martin-Prevel, 957-963. Montpellier: AIONP/GERDAT.

Harrison, A.F., Hatton, J.C. & Taylor, K. 1986. Application of a root bioassay for determination of P-deficiency in high-altitude grasslands. *J. Sci. fd Agric.*, **37**, 10-11.

Hayman, D.S. 1977. Mycorrhizal effects on white clover in relation to hill land improvement. *ARC Res. Rev.*, **3**, 82-85.

Hoogerkamp, M., Rogaar, H. & Eijsackers, H.J.P. 1983. Effect of earthworms on grassland on recently reclaimed polder soils in the Netherlands. In: *Earthworm ecology: from Darwin to vermiculture*, edited by J.E. Satchell, 85-105. London: Chapman & Hall.

Hsu, P.H. & Jackson, M.L. 1960. Inorganic phosphate transformations by chemical weathering in soils as influenced by pH. *Soil Sci.*, **90**, 16-24.

Jackman, R.H. 1960. Organic matter stability and nutrient availability in Taupo pumice. *N.Z. J. agric. Res.*, **3**, 6-23.

Jackman, R.H. 1964a. Accumulation of organic matter in some New Zealand soils under permanent pasture. I. Patterns of change of organic carbon, nitrogen, sulphur and phosphorus. *N.Z. J. agric. Res.*, **7**, 445-471.

Jackman, R.H. 1964b. Accumulation of organic matter in some New Zealand soils under permanent pasture. II. Rates of mineralisation of organic matter and the supply of available nutrients. *N.Z. J. agric. Res.*, **7**, 472-479.

Jackman, R.H. & Black, C.A. 1951. Solubility of iron, aluminium, calcium, and magnesium inositol phosphates at different pH values. *Soil Sci.*, **72**, 179-186.

Jeffrey, D.W. & Pigott, C.D. 1973. The response of grasslands on sugar-limestone in Teesdale to application of phosphorus and nitrogen. *J. Ecol.*, **61**, 85-92.

Macdonald, R.M. 1979. Liming and the growth of a mixed population of soil bacteria. *Soil Biol. Biochem.*, **11**, 633-636.

Maltby, E. 1979. Changes in soil properties and vegetation resulting from reclamation on Exmoor. *Rep. Welsh Soils Discuss. Grp*, no. 20, 83-118.

Maltby, E. 1984. Response of soil microflora to moorland reclamation for improved agriculture. *Pl. Soil*, **76**, 183-193.

McAllister, J.S.V. 1977. Spreading slurry on land. *Soil Sci.*, **123**, 338-343.

McLachlan, K.D. 1968. Stocking rate and the super phosphate requirements of sown pasture on an acid soil. *Aust. J. exp. Agric. Anim. Husb.*, **8**, 33-39.

Milton, W.E.J. 1940. The effect of manuring, grazing and cutting on the yield, botanical and chemical composition of natural hill pastures. *J. Ecol.*, **28**, 326-356.

Munro, J.M.M., Davies, D.A., Morgan, T.E.H. & Young, N.R. 1979. Pasture plant breeding and hill land improvement. *Rep. Welsh Soils Discuss. Grp*, no. 20, 49-79

Newbould, P. 1974. The improvement of hill pastures for agriculture. *J. Br. Grassld Soc.*, **29**, 241-247.

Newbould, P. & Floate, M.J.S. 1979. Problems of hill and upland soils. *Rep. Welsh Soils Discuss. Grp*, no. 20, 1-31.

Newbould, P. & Rangeley, A. 1984. Effect of lime, phosphorus and mycorrhizal fungi on growth, nodulation and nitrogen fixation by white clover (*Trifolium repens*) grown in UK hill soils. *Pl. Soil*, **76**, 105-114.

Parfitt, R.L. 1980. A note on the losses from a phosphate cycle under grazed pasture. *N.Z. J. exp. Agric.*, **8**, 215-217.

Pearson, R.W. & Hoveland, C.S. 1974. Lime needs of forage crops. In: *Forage fertilisation*, edited by D.A. Mays, 301-322. Madison, Wi: American Society of Agronomists, Crop Science Society of America and Soil Science Society of America.

Perkins, D.F. 1978. The distribution and transfer of energy and nutrients in the *Agrostis-Festuca* grassland ecosystem. In: *Production ecology of British moors and montane grasslands*, edited by O.W. Heal & D.F. Perkins, 375-395. Berlin: Springer.

Pigott, C.D. 1982. The experimental study of vegetation. *New Phytol.*, **90**, 389-404.

Pimplaskar, M.S., Floate, M.J.S. & Newbould, P. 1982. The suitability of different methods for assessing phosphorus status of hill soils. *J. Sci. fd Agric.*, **33**, 957-963.

Rawes, M. 1981. Further results of excluding sheep from high-level grasslands in the north Pennines. *J. Ecol.*, **69**, 651-669.

Rawes, M. & Welch, D. 1969. Upland productivity of vegetation and sheep at Moor House National Nature Reserve, Westmorland, England. *Oikos (suppl.)*, **11**, 7-72.

Read, D.J., Koucheki, H.K. & Hodgson, J. 1976. Vesicular arbuscular mycorrhiza in natural vegetation systems. 1. The occurrence of infection. *New Phytol.*, **77**, 641-653.

Reith, J.W.S. 1973. Soil conditions and nutrient supplies in hill land. In: *Hill pasture improvement and its economic utilisation. Colloq.Proc.*, no. 3, 5-17. Potassium Institute Ltd.

Rorison, I.H. 1968. The response to phosphorus of some ecologically distinct plant species. 1. Growth rates and phosphorus absorption. *New Phytol.*, **67**, 913-923.

Rovira, A.D. & Greacen, E.L. 1957. The effect of aggregate disruption on the activity of micro organisms in the soil. *Aust. J. agric. Sci.*, **8**, 659-673.

Sanders, F.E. & Tinker, P.B. 1971. Mechanism of absorption of phosphate from soil by *Endogone* mycorrhizas. *Nature, Lond.*, **233**, 278-279.

Sears, P.D. 1953. Pasture growth and soil fertility. 1. The influence of red and white clovers, superphosphate, lime, and sheep grazing, on pasture yields and botanical composition. *N.Z. J. Sci. Technol.*, **35**, (Suppl. 1), 1-29.

Shiel, R.S. & Rimmer, D.L. 1984. Changes in soil structure and biological activity on some meadow hay plots at Cockle Park, Northumberland. *Pl. Soil*, **76**, 349-356.

Sparling, G.P. & Tinker, P.B. 1978. Mycorrhizal infection in Pennine grassland. II. Effects of mycorrhizal infection on the growth of some upland grasses on γ-irradiated soils. *J. appl. Ecol.*, **15**, 951-958.

Stockdill, S.M.J. 1966. The effect of earthworms on pastures. *Proc. N.Z. ecol. Soc.*, no. 13, 68-75.

Stockdill, S.M.J. 1982. Effects of introduced earthworms on the productivity of New Zealand pastures. *Pedobiologia*, **24**, 29-35.

Syers, J.K. & Springett, J.A. 1984. Earthworms and soil fertility. *Pl. Soil*, **76**, 93-104.

Thompson, L.M., Black, C.A.& Zoellner, J.A. 1954. Occurrence and mineralisation of organic phosphorus in soils, with particular reference to associations with nitrogen, carbon and pH. *Soil Sci.*, **77**, 185-196.

Walker, T.W. 1962. Problems of soil fertility in a grass-animal regime. *Int. Soil Conf. N.Z., 1962*, 704-714.

Watt, A.S. 1957. The effect of excluding rabbits from grassland B (Mesobrometum) in Breckland. *J. Ecol.*, **45**, 861-878.

Welch, D. & Rawes, M. 1964. The early effects of excluding sheep from high-level grasslands in the north Pennines. *J. Ecol.*, **1**, 281-300.

White, E.M., Krueger, C.R. & Moore, R.A. 1976. Changes in total N, organic matter, available P and bulk densities of a cultivated soil 8 years after tame pastures were established. *Agronomy*, **68**, 581-583.

Land use in the hills and uplands: the work of the Hill Farming Research Organisation

T J MAXWELL, J EADIE and J HODGSON[1]
Hill Farming Research Organisation[2], Bush Estate, Penicuik, Midlothian, Scotland

1 Introduction

During the last decade, agriculture in the hills and uplands has come under close scrutiny. It remains, nevertheless, the primary economic activity and the principal sustainer of the population in these rural areas. As it depends heavily on national, and European, financial support, there has been a continuing debate about the relevance of such support in the context of agricultural surpluses. This debate has taken place despite the fact that, as yet, few of these surpluses can be attributed to hill and upland areas. In relation to cereal and dairy product surpluses, however, it has been pointed out that there may be opportunities for improving the efficiency of sheep meat production, in particular, by transferring that activity from the hills and uplands to the better-quality land resources of the lowlands. At the same time, there has been a continuing call to improve the net incomes of farms in the hill and upland sector. In response, this has led to the investigation and application of technologies which aim to improve the efficiency of use of resources on these farms and thereby improve their productivity.

There has been much suspicion, and indeed fear, of these production-oriented agricultural technologies, about their impact on the character of the hill and upland countryside. In response to this suspicion, and because of a general concern for the environment, public policy now requires that landowners and farmers weigh landscape and amenity values and good conservation practices more heavily in their decision-making. This policy is reflected in the Wildlife & Countryside Act and in the conditions which now apply to grants, as well as the levels of capital grants given for agricultural improvement and development in the hills and uplands.

It is recognized also that, as low-ground producers continue to move from cereal and dairy production into sheep, self-sufficiency in sheep meat within the European Community may be progressively inevitable. Out of this recognition has come a desire to seek alternative systems of production. For example, there is an increasing interest in finding ways of making farm/forestry integration both technically and financially possible, and environmentally attractive. Systems of deer production have become a small, but important and developing, part of commercial agricultural production. Agroforestry and the production of high-quality timber and of other non-food products, such as cashmere from goats, are seen as promising alternatives to sheep and beef.

A major interest competing for land is forestry, and much of the land in the hill farming sector qualifies for forestry authority grant aid. The bulk of timber used in this country is imported at considerable cost, and at a disadvantage to the balance of payments. Consequently, it can be reasonably assumed that the transfer of land out of hill agriculture is likely to continue to be encouraged by Government. The rate of transfer will continue to depend, in part, on the balance between the relative profitability of livestock farming and the fiscal incentives offered to forestry.

This brief summary of the changes taking place in the objectives for land use suggests that it is hardly surprising that there is so much uncertainty about the way in which the various pressures for change in the hills and uplands will be resolved. Indeed, prediction is made even more precarious by the difficult-to-define and unquantitative nature of some of the perceived non-market benefits and objectives which depend on aesthetics and other subjective human responses expressed as value judgements.

It is as well to recognize, however, that the emphasis given to, and the balance between, competing objectives will undoubtedly change. The status of the national economy will be one determining factor. If the resources can be provided, it will then depend on the extent to which there is the political will to sustain a reasonably populated countryside, especially in its remoter parts. There is unlikely to be disagreement about the general need to satisfy land use objectives in a cost-effective way. This does not imply that change will not take place, but that the rate of change may well be slower than those engaged in the arguments on either side may hope or fear. It seems reasonable to assume that there will be a continuing economic dependence on the production of sheep meat, wool, beef, and deer for some time.

Potentially achievable production, economic and social objectives will depend upon the nature of the land resources under consideration (Eadie 1984). In the uplands which include predominantly enclosed sown permanent grasslands, there seems to be a good possibility of obtaining worthwhile agricultural production

[1] now at Massey University, Department of Agronomy, Palmerston North, New Zealand

[2] now the Macaulay Land Use Research Institute

at reasonable levels of cost relative to animal production in the lowlands, and, at the same time, of achieving worthwhile social objectives. In the poorer, higher and more remote hills, agriculture may simply become a means of sustaining the best possible populations of resource managers, their main objective being the maintenance of grazed open hill landscapes. The role of the better hills in sustaining populations is important, given that much of the forestry is likely to come from this sector. It is at least arguable that the integration of agriculture in a framework which includes an element of agricultural development may well be the only way of harmonizing production possibilities, economic and social objectives and sensitive environmental planning.

Against this background and the title of the Conference, *The management of change*, it is not difficult to appreciate the need for research. Where, and if, change is needed, it is reasonable to hope that it be brought about with reasonable precision and predictability: to do so requires above all else a quantitative knowledge of the relevant biological mechanisms and processes, and an understanding of how to manipulate them.

2 *Upland agriculture, conservation and research*

Upland farms and their associated servicing industries contribute significantly to the economy and population of rural areas. Many of the farms are small businesses but are good subjects for the developing technologies in pasture production and utilization, and sheep and beef production. Farm amalgamation will most likely continue, but upland farms are also capable of a significant degree of intensification. Intensification is inevitable if net farm incomes are to be maintained at levels which provide individuals with an acceptable standard of living. A failure to sustain these farms as economic units would lead to a very rapid and obvious dereliction, which most people would regard as being unacceptable in terms of landscape and amenity value.

A significant part of the Organisation's research therefore, is devoted to developing a precise and quantitative biological understanding of systems of sheep, cattle and deer production. The aim is to provide information which allows the effective control of the operational management of such systems and their levels of output across a range of inputs.

One of the inputs which plays a crucial role in determining output and which increasingly causes concern in relation to the environment is nitrogen. Though the level of fertilizer use in the uplands is relatively much lower than that in the lowlands, nitrogen fertilizer can potentially provide the means whereby the small upland farm can overcome the problem of low output, and a low and inadequate net farm income, by substantially increasing herbage production and stock carrying capacity. It is important to find ways by which this improvement can be done efficiently.

At present, it is simply not possible to describe a site in terms which will allow a precise prediction of the environmental consequences or the herbage production that could be expected from an application of nitrogen fertilizer at a particular time of the year. This inability seriously limits the precise control of nitrogen inputs and the manipulation of herbage production from pastures. The identification and description of soil/pasture parameters which would provide a basis for determining the use of applied nitrogen in a predictable way are of great importance to the progressive improvement of grass production, utilization and the efficient use of nitrogen. In HFRO, considerable attention is being given to improving the understanding of processes of nitrogen cycling in soil/plant/animal systems and the factors which influence them. The quantitative significance of clover (*Trifolium* spp.) is also being examined within this context.

Work to establish the role of organic nitrogen for grass growth has begun, and includes measurements of the effects of excretal returns by grazing animals. The transfer of nitrogen via the grazing animal from ingested herbage to the available soil nitrogen pool is also being quantified. The effects of temperature, excretal return, level and type of nitrogen fertilizer on the fixation of nitrogen by clover are being investigated, and the rates and factors which affect the transfer of fixed nitrogen from clover to grass determined. Thus, a systematic approach to quantify the major pathways of nitrogen mineralization, fixation, transfer and uptake is being made. From such information, it will hopefully be possible to describe nitrogen response relationships more precisely, make more effective use of clover, and design more effective fertilizer strategies which are also environmentally acceptable (Hill Farming Research Organisation 1986).

The importance of this work cannot be overemphasized. The information obtained will have relevance for a range of systems, extending from those which may be wholly dependent on clover nitrogen, to those which use large amounts of inorganic nitrogen applied regularly throughout the grazing season.

Only by vigorously pursuing a research programme of the kind described will it be possible to develop an understanding of how to operate these systems in ways which satisfy both agricultural and environmental objectives.

As a means of diversifying production on upland farms, alternative production systems have been investigated. Venison production has already been mentioned and work on upland deer continues. More recently, agroforestry systems have been considered and appraised: they have been successfully tested with sheep and conifers in Australia and New Zealand, and there is a paper elsewhere in this volume describing some of the work carried out by HFRO in collaboration with the Forestry Commission, which indicates that the system could have relevance to the UK conditions (Sibbald *et al.* 1987a). The important economic implication for farmers is that agroforestry could provide a potential means of shifting the balance of their productive output away from food products, without seriously affecting their net farm income in the short term. The impact of agroforestry on the environment has so far received little attention, but in establishing agroforestry sites the impact of such change in land use on the wildlife, visual and amenity aspects of the environment, and the change in water balance and nutrient outflows from such areas will require to be investigated.

3 Hill farming, conservation and research

It is on the land on which the better hill farms exist that there is likely to be the greatest conflict between competing interests. Yet, if significant numbers of farms and people are to remain in these areas, without further substantial increases in Government financial support, in whatever form this may come, some land improvement will need to be carried out, despite existing conditions of grant. If this development is not acceptable, then the widespread sale of land for afforestation or a progressive decline towards dereliction is inevitable. A detailed account of the management practices required to integrate improved land successfully with open hill vegetation has been reported elsewhere (Armstrong *et al.* 1986), but, as Eadie (1985) has stated, 'there is neither any need for, nor any useful purpose to be served by, managing open hill semi-natural vegetation in other than an ecologically sound fashion, within such a management approach'. What is important, of course, is to establish an objective means of ecologically sound management.

The development of hill farming in this way also makes it possible to consider farm/forestry realistically on a sufficient scale to make it both visually and economically attractive. Some of our research in HFRO has been devoted to an examination of the potential for farm/forestry integration. Computer-based models suggest that considerable progress could be made by objectively examining the optimization of the allocation of land between farming and forestry enterprises (Maxwell *et al.* 1979; Sibbald & Eadie 1987). More appropriate solutions might be achieved if existing fiscal and/or business structural arrangements were changed. The alternatives suggested by Fothergill (1986), Denne *et al.* (1986) and by the Ministry of Agriculture, Fisheries and Food (unpublished) require further consideration and explanation.

An initial examination of the use of goats to maintain weed-free improved pastures, particularly the heath rush (*Juncus squarrosus*) (Russel *et al.* 1983), led to further studies of their grazing impact on indigenous and clover-based pastures. It is clear that goats may have a useful complementary role to play in the utilization of hill grazings. Some of this work is reported by way of a poster at this Conference (Lippert *et al.* 1987). As has been pointed out previously, goats also produce highly valued cashmere fibre, which again provides the means of shifting production away from products in potential surplus. Feral goats (*Capra hircus*) have been a part of the total ecology of some of our remoter hill areas for many years; their role and their impact within managed systems have yet to be fully determined.

The conflict of interests on hill land, however, is unlikely to be concerned, at least for some time, about the introduction of small populations of goats under controlled management. It will have much more to do with the conservation of the large expanses of indigenous vegetation. Such conservation will be an issue, not only on the better-quality hill land but also on poorer land where agriculture becomes a means of maintaining these usually remoter areas in their present state. It is clear that central to a resolution of the conflict between conservation and farming is the development of an understanding of the impact of the grazing animal on the indigenous vegetation and woodlands of hill and upland areas.

4 Objective moorland management

The basic assumption underpinning the Organisation's research in relation to this proposition is that control of vegetation in terms of community distribution and continued productivity is a desirable management objective and can be achieved most effectively by grazing animals (Hodgson 1985). Vegetation control is desirable from both a conservation and an agricultural point of view. In terms of conservation, there is a strong desire to protect the visual amenity inherent in the vistas and mosaics presented by expanses of indigenous vegetation maintained in their current state of low fertility. Open hill landscapes of the kind which have evolved through time as a consequence of varying degrees of agricultural activity are highly valued. For agriculture, it is important to understand the impact of grazing on the morphological and physiological characteristics of plants. It is important to understand the management regimes which secure their continued presence, productivity, and contribution to the nutrition of the animal populations utilizing them. The levels of nutrition provided by these communities have also to be characterized so that the potential for manipulating animal performance by grazing control or other inputs can be determined. Thus, though different emphasis may be placed on management strategies for conservation and productive agriculture, ultimately the objective in both cases must be the definition and attainment of sustainable balances between the plant species in particular communities, and between the plant and animal populations in a particular locality (Hodgson 1985).

There has been a number of studies which have clearly established the potential impact of grazing animals upon plant succession and vegetation characteristics (eg Burnett 1964); from such studies, it has been possible to produce a generalized hypothesis of the impact of grazing intensity on vegetation change. However, as

Hodgson (1985) has pointed out, while 'a framework of this kind provides a useful basis for planning strategies of vegetation management, it is unlikely to be adequate for decision-making in particular cases. This is especially so where circumstances require that vegetation change be controlled within fine limits. This is partly because of the limitations of existing evidence, which is concerned more with association rather than with causation. It is also because the stocking rate of grazing animals is at best an agent of change rather than its determinant. As such it is but one of a complex of variables influencing the balance between rates and patterns of herbage production and consumption'. Consequently, there is a need for a more objective definition of management strategies in terms of vegetation characteristics. A number of studies within the Organisation's programme of research can be used to illustrate the potential benefit of defining management strategies in this way.

Bent/fescue (*Agrostis/Festuca*) grassland which dominates much of the brown earth soils of the hill and upland areas is a vitally important component of the vegetation resources used on many of the more productive hill farms. There has long been recognition of the fact that it is used intensively by sheep for much of the year (Hunter 1962), and understandable concern has been expressed from time to time for its long-term productivity. Brasher and Perkins (1978) have shown that, as a community, levels of utilization of at least 40–50% of the herbage produced had no effect on its stability. The results of long-term studies from our own Organisation's research programme (Eadie *et al.* 1981) show that regular grazing to a residual herbage mass of only 500 kg dry matter ha^{-1} (about 2 cm sward surface height) had little impact on its botanical composition and resulted in a progressive increase in herbage production. Such quantitative information, linked to the nutritional consequences of grazing bent-grass/fescue communities to these levels, provides the basis of operating controlled grazing systems, and leads to an understanding of the consequences for vegetation stability and animal performance where controlled grazing is not practised.

However, bent-grass/fescue is frequently found in combination with mat-grass (*Nardus*)- and moor-grass (*Molinia*)-dominant communities, and provides the visual variety which is found to be attractive in many hill areas. Mat-grass is of very limited nutritional value for sheep and they tend to avoid grazing it; for this reason, it has been postulated that the species can spread rapidly in hill grassland communities. Work to investigate the impact of grazing by sheep and also by cattle (Grant *et al.* 1985) indicates that cattle may be more effective in controlling mat-grass where grazing management regimes are determined by controlling inter-tussock sward surface height. This degree and precision of management control is important because it sets the results in a quantifiable basis and allows the definition of management strategies to be objectively developed for other circumstances.This work is reported more fully in the poster presentations (Grant *et al.* 1987). It will be developed and extended to investigate long-term cumulative effects, mixed grazing strategies and the consequent production effects on breeding cows and ewes. Work on moor-grass has begun but, as yet, it remains to be seen whether appropriate management strategies can be described in the same objective terms as for mat-grass control.

Attempts to use similar criteria, however, are being investigated in a project, also presented as a poster at this conference (Mitchell 1987), to investigate and assess the impact of controlled variation in intensity and seasonality of grazing on tree regeneration and on ground flora in upland broadleaved woodland. The shelter and grazing provided by upland broadleaved woods can play an important role in upland agriculture, but these are also prime sites for nature conservation. The present study aims to find out whether it is possible to develop objective grazing strategies whereby both an agricultural use and a conservation interest can be satisfied.

Heather (*Calluna vulgaris*) vegetation is an important and extensive component of hill land resources in Scotland, northern England and parts of Wales. The morphology of the heather plant makes it tolerant of moderate defoliation. The regular removal of shoots helps to maintain the plant in a juvenile state in which growth is active and the development of potential competitors is suppressed (Gimingham 1972). Grant *et al.* (1982), however, have shown that the management strategies for heather stands can be defined effectively in terms of the level of utilization of the current season's shoots. Removal of 40% of the current season's shoots under grazing conditions can be tolerated, but 80% removal cannot. Low levels of defoliation allow the plant to mature, which encourages degenerative changes and gives rise to greater stand heterogeneity (Gimingham 1972). While this development may be desirable as an objective of conservation in most cases, it will lead to scrub regeneration unless checked by grazing or fire.

As a source of nutrients for sheep, heather is poor (Milne *et al.* 1979). It cannot support adequate levels of production from breeding ewes, unless they have access to grass communities. Though non-producing sheep may be sustained on a largely heather diet, the implications are that, where a heather stand is to be maintained in a juvenile state, it will be necessary to augment grazing regularly with fire (Gimingham 1972), or to provide areas of grassland which can be grazed in association with heather (Maxwell *et al.* 1986). Neither of these proposals will necessarily be without environmental repercussions.

However, objective control of heather communities as a result of these studies in relation to both agricultural and conservation objectives does seem possible. Sibbald *et al.* (1987b) have designed a computer-based model which has the potential for use as a guide to the management of heather moorland. Although the output is seen in terms of sheep numbers and frequency of burning, with assumptions about sheep performance and winter feeding, the management decisions are based on a quantitative understanding of the biological processes involved.

Such a management tool as that made possible by the computer-based model and the knowledge and understanding which it represents provides the means whereby existing balances between heather heterogeneity and animal population can be maintained. It can also be used to calculate the number of sheep which will prevent overgrazing and remove the risk of heather replacement by native grass species. It can be used to avoid underutilization and to prevent a degenerative change towards scrub regeneration and loss of the resource for agricultural purposes. Management plans in terms of sheep numbers, frequency of burning, and land improvement possibilities can be drawn up to achieve any one of a range of objectives.

The above examples illustrate how a series of well-chosen parameters can be used to control the management of a single plant community. It is clearly much more difficult to find a simple approach to the management of areas where animals have access to several plant communities simultaneously. The relevant questions in these circumstances have to do primarily with the factors determining choice between communities. So far, the only 2 communities which have received detailed study recently at HFRO are combinations of heather and sown rye-grass (*Lolium perenne*) swards (HFRO 1979). Animal responses to the experimental manipulation of vegetation characteristics of both components have been examined. The relationships derived from these studies were crucial to an understanding of how to integrate rye-grass reseeds dispersed throughout a dominant heather community, to control the morphology and productivity of that community and, at the same time, to achieve acceptable levels of nutrition for the breeding ewe.

The achievement of an understanding of those factors which influence the choice of a grazing site by an animal is a difficult research area. As far as indigenous communities are concerned, little real progress has been made since the classical studies of Hunter (1962). However, if there is to be any hope of controlling the management of mixed communities with some objectivity, it will need to be a research area which receives much more attention. The research problem is to design experiments which can be used to provide an adequate framework within which management decisions can be made. This framework requires the definition of management in terms which allow vegetation characteristics and distribution to be changed or maintained with reasonable predictability to achieve desired objectives. Some progress has been made, but more needs to be done.

Controlled experimentation in the hill environment is always difficult and, given the long-term nature of many of the studies, it is essential to make the most effective use of limited experimental resources. There is a strong case to be made for a determined effort to establish collaborative research on vegetation management in the widest possible context.

5 *Conclusion*

In discussing the future contribution of hill and upland areas to agricultural output, Eadie (1985) reminds us that research and development will have to take a broader view of hill land use than hitherto. Progress will continue to depend on detailed studies of quite specific aspects of the biology of component processes and of plant/animal function. The need for high-quality work of this kind to resolve problems and explore opportunities will not diminish. Increasingly, science will be called upon to illuminate interaction among land uses. Trade-offs and interactions of a kind which, to date, have been handled by instinct and 'feel' will have to be quantified more effectively. Novel interactions will require to be explored. Better bridges will have to be built between biologists whose interests lie in the various land uses, as well as between biologists and economists.

6 *References*

Armstrong, R.H., Eadie, J. & Maxwell, T.J. 1986. Hill sheep production a modified management system in practice. In: *Hill Land Symposium, Galway, 1984,* edited by M. O'Toole, 230-247. Dublin: An Foras Taluntais.

Brasher, S. & Perkins, D.F. 1978. The grazing intensity and productivity of sheep in the grassland ecosystem. In: *Production ecology of British moors and mountain grasslands,* edited by O.W. Heal & D.F. Perkins, 354-374. Berlin: Springer.

Burnett, J.H. 1964. *The vegetation of Scotland.* Edinburgh: Oliver & Boyd.

Denne, T., Bown, M.J.D. & Abel, J.A. 1986. *Forestry: Britain's growing resource.* London: UK Centre for Economic and Environmental Development.

Eadie, J. 1984. Trends in agricultural land use: the hills and uplands. In: *Agriculture and the environment,* edited by D. Jenkins, 13-20. (ITE symposium no. 13.) Cambridge: Institute of Terrestrial Ecology.

Eadie, J. 1985. The future contribution of the hills and uplands to agricultural output. In: *Hill and upland livestock production,* edited by T.J. Maxwell & R.G. Gunn, 123-130. (Occasional publication no. 10.) British Society of Animal Production.

Eadie, J., Hetherington, R.A., Common, T.G. & Floate, M.J.S. 1981. Long-term responses of grazed hill pasture types to improvement procedures. 1. Pasture production and nutritive value. In: *The effective use of forage and animal resources in the hills and uplands,* edited by J. Frame, 167-168. (British Grassland Society occasional symposium no. 12.) Penicuik: Hill Farming Research Organisation.

Fothergill, P. 1986. The potential for forestry. In: *The future of agriculture in the hills and uplands. Proc. Conf., Perth, 1986.* Edinburgh: Scottish Agricultural Colleges.

Gimingham, C.H. 1972. *Ecology of heathlands.* London: Chapman & Hall.

Grant, S.A., Milne, J.A., Barthram, G.T. & Souter, W.G. 1982. Effects of seasons and level of grazing on the utilisation of heather by sheep. 3. Longer term responses and sward recovery. *Grass Forage Sci.,* **37,** 311-320.

Grant, S.A., Suckling, D.E., Smith, H.K., Torvell, L., Forbes, T.D.A. & Hodgson, J. 1985. Comparative studies of diet selection by sheep and cattle; hill grasslands. *J. Ecol.,* **73,**1987-1004.

Grant, S.A., Torvell, L., Armstrong, R.G. & Beattie, M.M. 1987. The manipulation of mat-grass pasture by grazing management. In: *Agriculture and conservation in the hills and uplands,* edited by M. Bell & R.G.H. Bunce, 62-64. (ITE symposium no. 23.) Grange-over-Sands: Institute of Terrestrial Ecology.

Hill Farming Research Organisation. 1979. *Science and hill farming - twenty-five years of work at the Hill Farming Research Organisation*, 92-93. Penicuik: HFRO.

Hill Farming Research Organisation. 1986. *Biennial report 1984-85*, 1-14. Penicuik: HFRO.

Hodgson, J. 1985. Grazing and its influence on hill vegetation. *BCPC Monogr.*, no. 30, 21-31.

Hunter, R.F. 1962. Hill sheep and their pasture: a study of sheep grazing in south-east Scotland. *J. Ecol.*, **50,**651-680.

Lippert, M., Russel, A.J.F. & Grant, S.A. 1987. The use of goats in hill pasture management. In: *Agriculture and conservation in the hills and uplands*, edited by M. Bell & R.G.H. Bunce, 116-119. (ITE symposium no. 23.) Grange-over-Sands: Institute of Terrestrial Ecology.

Maxwell, T.J., Sibbald, A.R. & Eadie, J. 1979. The integration of forestry and agriculture - a model. *Agric. Syst.*, **4,**161-188.

Maxwell, T.J., Grant, S.A., Milne, J.A. & Sibbald, A.R. 1986. Systems of sheep production on heather moorland. In: *Hill Land Symposium, Galway, 1984*, edited by M. O'Toole, 188-211. Dublin: An Foras Taluntais.

Milne, J.A., Bagley, L. & Grant, S.A. 1979. Effect of season and level of grazing on the utilisation of heather by sheep. 2. Diet selection and intake. *Grass Forage Sci.*, **34,** 45-53.

Mitchell, F.J.G. 1987. Grazing in broadleaved upland woods. In: *Agriculture and conservation in the hills and uplands*, edited by M. Bell & R.G.H. Bunce, 125-126. (ITE symposium no. 23.) Grange-over-Sands: Institute of Terrestrial Ecology.

Russel, A.J.F., Maxwell, T.J., Bolton, G.R., Currie, D.C. & White, I.R. 1983. A note on the possible use of goats in hill sheep grazing systems. *Anim. Prod.*, **36,**313-316.

Sibbald, A.R. & Eadie, J. 1987. Optimum allocation of land between the farming and forestry enterprises. *Farming and Forestry*. In press.

Sibbald, A.R., Grant, S.A., Milne, J.A. & Maxwell, T.J. 1987a. Heather moorland management - a model. In: *Agriculture and conservation in the hills and uplands*, edited by M. Bell & R.G.H. Bunce, 107-108. (ITE symposium no. 23.) Grange-over-Sands: Institute of Terrestrial Ecology.

Sibbald, A.R., Maxwell, T.J., Griffiths, J.H., Hutchings, N.J., Taylor, C.M.A., Tabbush, P.M. & White, I.M.S. 1987b. Agroforestry research in the hills and uplands. In: *Agriculture and conservation in the hills and uplands*, edited by M. Bell & R.G.H. Bunce, 74-77. (ITE symposium no. 23.) Grange-over-Sands: Institute of Terrestrial Ecology.

The manipulation of mat-grass pasture by grazing management

S A GRANT, L TORVELL, R H ARMSTRONG and M M BEATTIE
Hill Farming Research Organisation, Bush Estate, Penicuik, Midlothian, Scotland

1 *Introduction*

A recent comparative study of diet selection by sheep and cattle grazing a mat-grass (*Nardus*)-dominated sward has indicated that cattle consistently ingest more mat-grass than do sheep, and also that the proportion of mat-grass in the diet is inversely related to the height or the biomass of the preferred between-tussock vegetation (Figure 1, after Grant *et al.* 1985). This information was used in the design of the currently reported study, the objective of which is to investigate the scope for manipulation of the floristic composition and nutritive value of mat-grass pasture by controlled grazing.

2 *The grazing experiments*

There are 2 trials, both situated in Fife; in one trial, the plots are grazed by cattle or by sheep only, and in the other by sheep or by goats. In both trials, the management aim is to maintain the preferred between-tussock grasses at one or other of a range of pre-determined mean sward surface heights. This objective is achieved by making twice-weekly measurements of sward height and by adjusting animal numbers as necessary. The trials were begun in 1984. Early results from the cattle and sheep site are reported here.

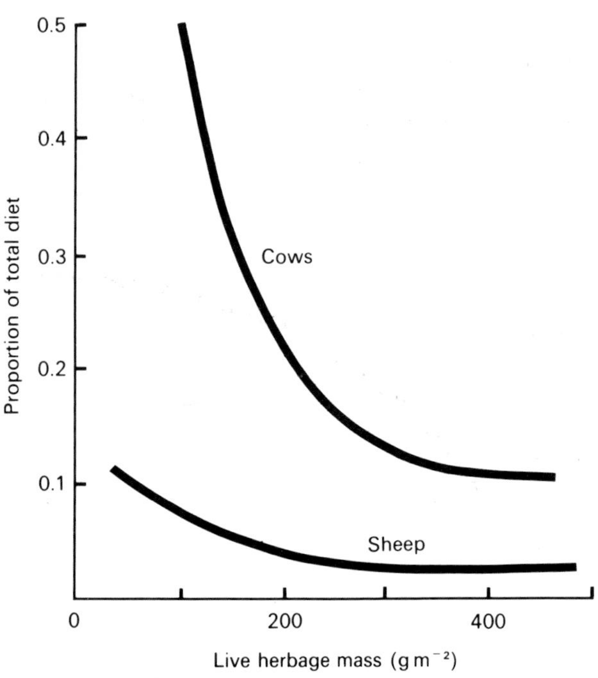

Figure 1. Relationship between the live aerial biomass of herbage between the mat-grass tussocks and the proportion of mat-grass in the diets of grazing cattle and sheep

3 *Results*

3.1 Utilization of mat-grass

The frequency and severity of grazing of mat-grass by cattle and sheep are compared in Figure 2. In swards in which the between-tussock vegetation was maintained at 4–5 cm surface height, cattle rapidly reduced the size of mat-grass tussocks, grazing both a higher proportion of leaves and also grazing the leaves more closely than did sheep.

These differences are illustrated in Plate 1 which compares the fence-line effect between the cattle-grazed sward (lower diagonal) and sheep-grazed sward (upper diagonal) at the same between-tussock grass height of 4–5 cm after 3 grazing seasons. Sheep failed to achieve the same control as cattle, even when pressure was increased by reducing the between-tussock height to 3–4 cm.

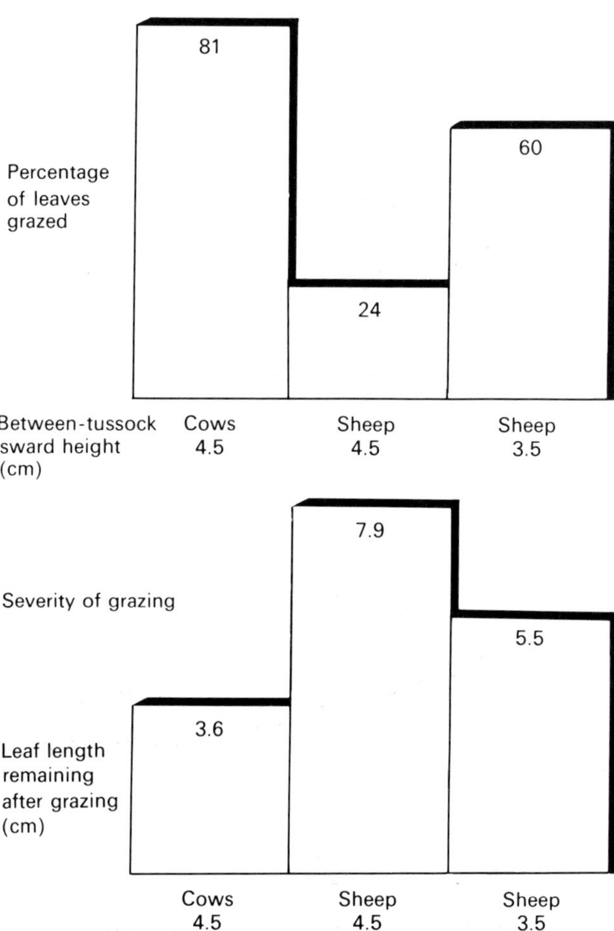

Figure 2. Frequency and severity of grazing of mat-grass in plots with sward height between the mat-grass tussocks maintained as stated by cattle or by sheep

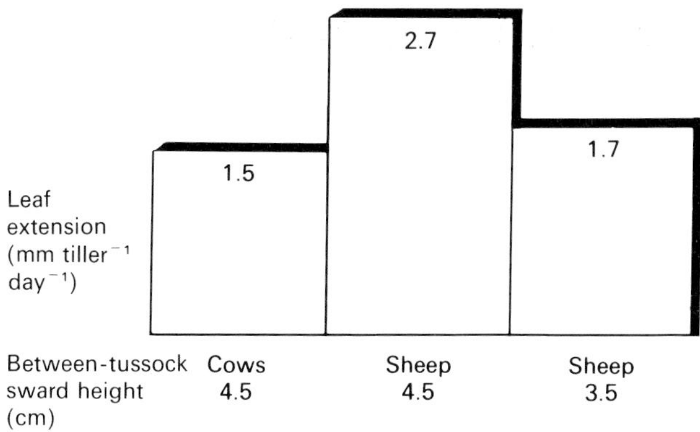

Figure 3. Rates of leaf exension of mat-grass tillers in grazed plots with sward height between the mat-grass tussocks maintained as stated by cattle or by sheep

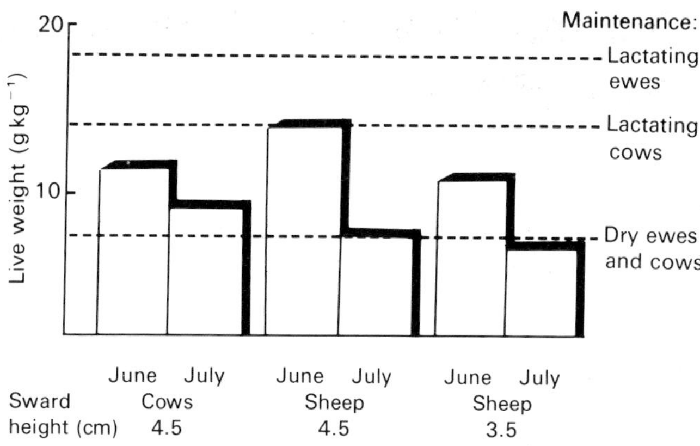

Figure 5. Digestible organic matter intake of cattle and sheep on plots with sward height between the mat-grass tussocks maintained as stated by cattle or by sheep

3.2 Sward responses

Observations were made on the rates of leaf extension of mat-grass tillers on the grazed plots (Figure 3) and on trends in the percentage of specific frequency and cover (Figure 4). The results suggest that the intensity of defoliation achieved by the cattle was adequate to control, and over time to reduce, mat-grass content in a pasture.

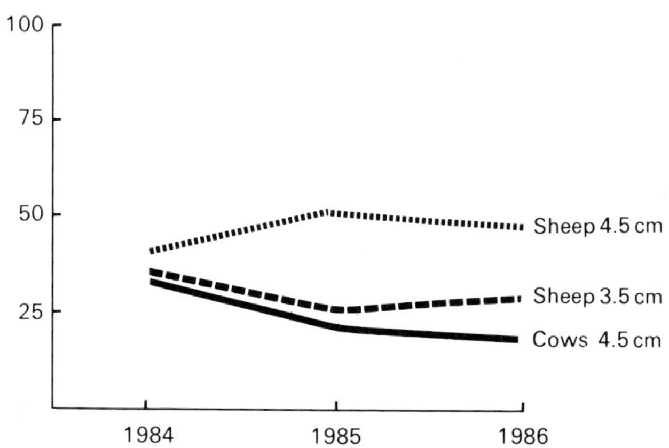

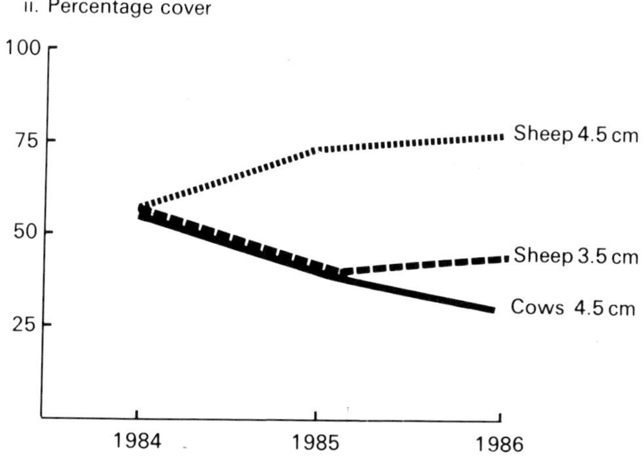

Figure 4. Trends in (i) percentage specific frequency, and (ii) percentage cover of mat-grass in grazed plots with sward height between the mat-grass tussocks maintained as stated by cattle or by sheep

3.3 Animal performance

In farming practice, it is important to consider the nutritional consequences of particular management regimes for the grazing stock. In these trials, adult dry cows and sheep, ie non-productive stock, were used. Data on digestible organic matter intake are still being assessed. Early results (Figure 5) have indicated that intake levels were adequate to meet the maintenance requirements of both cattle and sheep early in the season. Intake limitations were apparent later in the season, however, and were greater for sheep than for cattle. Changes in cattle live weights over the grazing season (Figure 6) showed that dry cows were able to gain weight in early summer within a grazing regime which controlled mat-grass.

4 *Further work*

Before recommendations for farm practice can be made, more information is required on (i) the performance of

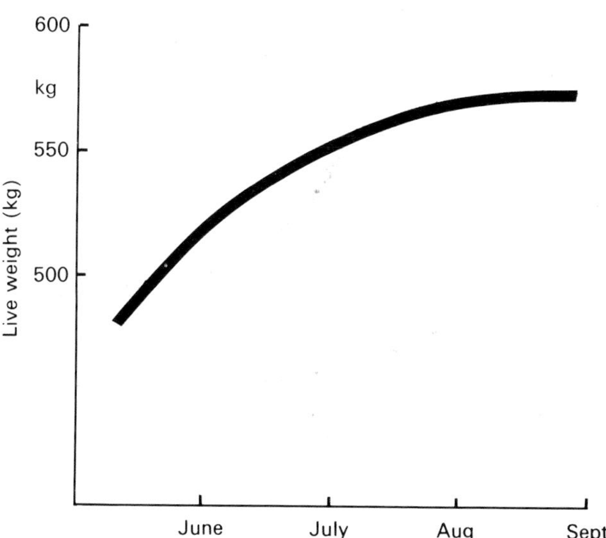

Figure 6. Changes in cattle live weights over the grazing season

productive animals (which have higher nutrient demands than dry stock), (ii) animal performance and mat-grass control in mixed grazing systems, eg using different ratios of cattle and sheep, and (iii) the timing and length of grazing period needed to control mat-grass. The early results are encouraging, however, and illustrate the use of objective sward criteria to define management strategies for vegetation control. Such an approach both advances understanding and has relevance for conservation, as well as for agricultural objectives.

5 Reference

Grant, S.A., Suckling, D.E., Smith, H.K. Torvell, L. Forbes, T.D.A. & Hodgson, J. 1985. Comparative studies of diet selection by sheep and cattle: the hill grasslands. *J. Ecol.,* **73,** 987-1004.

Vegetation surveys of upland sites in Wales: research note

Nature Conservancy Council (Wales Field Unit), Plas Penrhos, Bangor, Gwynedd, north Wales

A survey of the semi-natural vegetation of all the major blocks of upland in Wales is being carried out by the Nature Conservancy Council's Wales Field Unit. The survey was begun in 1979 and is programmed to finish in 1987. The aim of the survey is to map and describe the vegetation of all the upland blocks in Wales for the purpose of comparison and evaluation of their botanical interest, using a standard vegetation classification (Ratcliffe & Birks 1980). The survey will also give an overall picture of the present extent of each of the major upland plant communities in Wales and will provide a base-line for monitoring changes on particular sites, both in terms of habitat loss and of detrimental changes such as the spread of bracken (*Pteridium aquilinum*) or loss of heather (*Calluna vulgaris*).

1 *Survey method*

The survey uses aerial photographs, preferred scale 1:10 000, as a basis for mapping. The air photographs are encased in weather-proof transparent plastic envelopes and used for recording information in the field. Information on the vegetation types and boundaries is recorded in the field using fine waterproof felt-tip pens. This information is later used to produce a vegetation map of the site (1:25 000 or 1:10 000). The survey is primarily a mapping exercise, but the information recorded on the air photographs is supplemented by recording details of notable plants encountered during the survey, and by recording species lists from localities of interest, such as base-rich rock outcrops or species-rich flushes. Each site map is accompanied by a short report on the site describing the vegetation and drawing attention to features of interest.

Similar surveys are being carried out by NCC in the uplands of Scotland and northern England.

The vegetation classification used will be compatible with the upland types in the national vegetation classification.

2 *Reference*

Ratcliffe, D.A. & Birks, H.J.B. 1980. *Classification of upland vegetation types in Britain.* Peterborough: Nature Conservancy Council. (Unpublished.)

Hill livestock compensatory allowances and upland management

S EVANS and M FELTON
Economics Advisory Unit, Nature Conservancy Council, Northminster House, Peterborough, England

1 *Introduction*

Heather moorland is being lost through afforestation, agricultural intensification and inappropriate management, and the nature conservation interest of the remaining moorland is threatened by changes in management and grazing pressure. Moorland management involves shepherding, burning and the use of appropriate stocking levels, and, where economic or other factors change management input, ecological changes take place which are generally detrimental to the nature conservation interest. The wildlife typically associated with heather moorland is more abundant and more highly prized than that associated with the grass or bracken (*Pteridium aquilinum*) which replaces it.

Many organizations and individuals have suggested that a reduction in grazing pressure could be achieved by altering the current system of hill livestock compensatory allowances (HLCAs). We submit that, while the HLCA system has undoubtedly been one of the factors that has encouraged an overall increase in the number of hill and upland sheep, changes in the HLCA system alone **cannot** be used to control stocking rates. The HLCA system is only part of the total livestock subsidy available to the hill farmer. The main instruments of the European Community (EC) sheepmeat regime as implemented in the UK are the annual ewe premium and the variable premium on finished lambs. These premiums make up roughly two-thirds of the total livestock subsidy, the remainder being HLCA payments. The UK is the only Member State to opt for variable premiums; France uses ewe premiums alone. Unlike HLCAs, the annual ewe premium and the variable premium have never been subject to a stocking rate limit, so revenue from the sheepmeat regime continues to increase with the number of ewes, and this increase over-rides the effect of any limit to the number of ewes per hectare that can qualify for HLCA payments. Recent increases in overall grazing pressure are more likely to have been caused by these sheepmeat regime payments than by the long-established HLCA system. An increase in the area of improved hill land, encouraged by a previously generous system of capital grants, has allowed stocking rates to increase to take advantage of the support available through this sheepmeat regime.

On the type of semi-natural vegetation that the Nature Conservancy Council (NCC) is particularly concerned about, overall stocking rates are well within the current HLCA limit of 6 ewes ha^{-1}. Even if this limit were to be sharply reduced, the payment of the annual ewe premium, combined with returns from the resulting lambs, makes it worthwhile for the farmer to have as many sheep as is feasible, given the technical and financial limitations imposed by the individual business. Reducing total HLCA payments would reduce farm incomes severely, but there is no guarantee that it would reduce the number of sheep.

Farm incomes in the Less Favoured Areas are totally underpinned by livestock subsidies, and any proposal to alter the system of HLCA payments would cause considerable concern and uncertainty among the farming community, at a time when hill land prices are already weak. Such uncertainty could precipitate a further fall in land values and increase the risk of coniferous afforestation in the uplands, particularly in Scotland.

Until surplus problems precipitate a change in the sheepmeat regime, there is a need to encourage better management of moorland for multiple use. Consideration should be given to an alternative method of income support in designated moorland areas, with the intention that it would over-ride the sheepmeat regime and the HLCA payments. An Environmentally Sensitive Areas (ESA)-type approach could be considered, but it will take time to assess the effectiveness of existing ESAs.

We need to adopt a multidisciplinary approach to the problem of moorland management, bringing together ecological, agricultural and economic expertise. We accept that multiple-use systems may not be feasible in some areas, and realize that there are considerable problems regarding tenancies and common land. We also accept that future control of stocking rates with a revamped sheepmeat regime will not automatically solve problems caused more by inappropriate management than by sheep numbers.

2 *Background*

2.1 Loss of moorland habitat

A survey based on Government statistics (Royal Society for the Protection of Birds (RSPB) 1984) shows that, since 1946, 22% (122000 ha) of freehold rough grazing has been lost in England, 41% (197 000 ha) in Wales, and 11% (500 000 ha) in Scotland. The rate of loss appears to have slowed down in England, but has accelerated in Scotland and Wales. The evidence suggests that the loss of moorland in Scotland is primarily due to afforestation, whereas in England and Wales higher grazing pressures may be more of a contributing factor. NCC's own National Country Monitoring Scheme data for Cumbria show a 70% (approximately) loss of moorland between the mid-1940s and the mid-1970s, of which approximately 50% was due to conversion to grass through higher grazing pressures. Other studies confirm this general trend of loss of moorland habitat. Parry *et al.* (1982) found an overall 16% loss of rough land across upland areas, but did not determine what percentage of this loss was due to forestry. The NCC reported (1984) a 30% loss or significant damage to upland grasslands, heaths and blanket bogs through coniferous afforestation, hill land improvement and reclamation, burning and overgrazing. Livestock numbers have increased while the area available for rough grazing has decreased, and, although the level of data collected in the June agricultural returns does not allow the calculation of stocking on moorland, individual cases suggest that overgrazing contributes to moorland loss, particularly in England and Wales.

2.2 Loss of associated species

According to the Royal Society for the Protection of Birds (1984), there are 10 species of bird in the UK whose breeding populations are dependent on moorland habitats, and whose numbers are in danger of being significantly reduced. Other species are partially dependent on these habitats. Modification to the moorland habitat (as opposed to total loss) also causes detrimental change to the vegetation and fauna of the area.

2.3 Agricultural versus *ecological overgrazing*

Ecologists describe an area as 'overgrazed' where natural succession has been arrested, with tree and shrub seedlings being destroyed by wild or domestic animals. Agricultural overgrazing is the loss of palatable species by selective grazing. Where an area of hill is used for sheep but not grouse, localized 'ecological' overgrazing may not be considered an agricultural problem.

Where shooting is involved, the picture differs. The traditional moorland habitat was set by a use system that developed in Scotland and northern England, but not to such a great extent in Wales. Grazing management was adjusted to provide the particular mosaic of habitats that allowed the co-existence of a profitable sheep industry and a shooting sector. Modern technology has moved this balance further in the favour of grassland by:

- increasing the area and productivity of inbye land;

- reducing the importance of the contribution that heather (*Calluna vulgaris*) makes to survival by increasing the ease of supplementary feeding.

There is now a conflict between management by sheep farmers and the owners of sporting rights to the land, with the latter correctly convinced that overgrazing is contributing to a reduction in grouse numbers through loss of heather. Overgrazing also contributes to accelerating erosion, threatening future agricultural productivity. However, technology continues to reduce the contribution of the open hills to sheep nutrition and allows compensating investments to counteract the declining nutritional status of the hill. In some areas, particularly in Scotland, badly managed moor burning is thought to contribute more to the loss of heather moorland than does overgrazing.

2.4 Problems of defining stocking rate

The only currently collected national statistics from which any estimate of stocking rate can be made are the January livestock returns and the June agricultural census. These data are available on an individual farm basis to the Ministry of Agriculture, Fisheries and Food (MAFF) and the Department of Agriculture and Fisheries for Scotland (DAFS), and on a parish basis to everyone else. For the purpose of administering agricultural policies, MAFF and DAFS could calculate the average annual stocking rate on individual farms, and other researchers can calculate this rate on a parish basis. Neither of these measures gives any meaningful indication of grazing pressure, which is the result of year-long management practices and cannot be defined by a snapshot stocking rate. Parish level data suffer from the same problem, with the added one that sheep do not recognize parish boundaries. Neither measure can cope with common grazings, or with the different grazing pressures exerted by different breeds of sheep. Literature relating to sheep densities is confused by the measurement of stocking rates in terms of sheep per hectare or ewes per hectare, and by the problems of comparing year-round grazing densities with what may be a totally different short-term density arrived at during a critical period for vegetation damage (Yalden 1981). General year-round stocking rates in 1981 (RSPB 1984) ranged from 3.62 ewes ha^{-1} (Welsh Borders south) to 0.44 ewes ha^{-1} (north-west Scotland). While this range is wide in terms of differing effects on vegetation, it is a fairly narrow range to influence using the blunt instrument of blanket policy measures.

The maximum stocking rates recommended (Mowforth 1986) as being compatible with the nature conservation interest (2.0 sheep ha^{-1} on heather moor and 0.37 sheep ha^{-1} on blanket bog) are certainly exceeded in Wales, but not in all other areas. However, to allow the regeneration of heather, stocking rates need to be considerably below these levels. A maximum average of around 0.5 sheep ha^{-1} on heather moor and 0.1 sheep ha^{-1} on blanket bog has been suggested in this case.

3 *Factors affecting farm stocking rate decisions*

3.1 Market prices and level of subsidies

The main grazing enterprises in upland areas (equivalent to the Less Favoured Areas for broad policy considerations) are hill and upland sheep and suckler cows. Under present agricultural policies, there is a mixture of price (market) subsidy and structural support for these enterprises, as follows.

3.1.1 Hill livestock compensatory allowances (HLCAs)
Set up under the EC Less Favoured Areas Directive (75/268)
Under this scheme, a farmer with not less than 3 ha of land within a Less Favoured Area (LFA) may claim a per head allowance for the breeding ewes and cows (not dairy cows) present on the farm on the 1st January in each year. This headage payment varies as follows (1986):

SEVERELY DISADVANTAGED LAND

Highlands & Islands Development Board	Gradation A	B	C
Cows	£57.55	£62.48	£62.48
Hill flocks	£7.33	£7.33	£7.33
Upland flocks	£4.50	£4.50	£4.50

Elsewhere	
Cows	£54.50
Hill flocks	£6.75
Upland flocks	£4.50

DISADVANTAGED LAND

Cows	£27.25
Sheep	£2.25

HLCA payments are confined to not more than 6 ewes ha^{-1} on severely disadvantaged land, but this figure is way over the agricultural stocking capacity of unimproved moorland and does not limit stocking rates on this type of land. A farmer can claim for any number of stock, providing that this per hectare limit is not exceeded.

3.1.2 Sheep variable premium (VP)
Part of the EC sheepmeat regime - a market support mechanism
This premium is paid on all finished lambs and clean sheep after slaughter, providing that they meet certain standards. Many farmers in the LFAs will not receive much in the way of VP payment as they do not fatten many, if any, lambs, but all benefit from the improvement in the store lamb market as a result of the VP on finished lambs. (A beef variable premium system operates in a similar manner.)

3.1.3 Annual ewe premium (AEP)
Part of the EC sheepmeat regime - a market support mechanism
This scheme makes up the difference between the target revenue for sheep farmers (as determined by the EC reference price) and the actual revenue received (the market price plus VP). It is paid on a per head basis for all ewes, plus all gimmers and ewe hoggs tupped the preceding year. Cull ewes and flocks of fewer than 10 sheep are excluded from the premium. The AEP is totally EC-financed, makes up about half of the sheep support in the LFAs, and was about £6.75 per ewe in 1985.

(A suckler cow premium operates in a similar manner.)

In Scotland last year (1985), the breakdown of total sheep support was as follows:

HLCA	29%	
VP	34%	
EP	38%	(Leat 1986)

Net farm incomes in the LFAs are totally underpinned by livestock subsidies (livestock subsidy receipts have recently exceeded net farm income on Scottish LFA sheep and sheep/cattle farms (Crabtree *et al.* 1986). However, HLCAs are the only part of the livestock subsidy that is subject to a stocking rate limit, and the only part that varies to some extent with the type of land. This is the reason why HLCAs have been singled out as a potential vehicle through which stocking rates could be controlled. The EC legislation which enables Member States to set these values and limits is currently under review (ECC 1986).

3.1.4 Modifying the HLCA structure - the likely influence on stocking rate
By studying the cost and revenue structure of a 'typical' hill sheep farm under various levels and limits of HLCAs, it is possible to predict the effect of various policy options on stocking rates.

We explored 5 different policy options:

i. the *status quo*;
ii. reducing the limit on HLCA payment unchanged;
iii. increasing the HLCA payment to £24 per ewe and limiting the payment to one ewe ha^{-1};
iv. as for (iii), but with a 'fine' of £12 per ewe in excess of the one per hectare allowed;
v. removing all HLCA payments.

We have concentrated on the sheep enterprise as this has increased in importance relative to cattle. We have also based our analysis on the current UK support system.

We looked at economically optimum stocking rates, using a model based on a farmer selling store lambs only and with a fixed percentage of improved pasture.

We made various assumptions as follows.

TECHNICAL FACTORS

As stocking rate increases:
- Replacement rate increases due to higher mortality: from 20% at 1 ewe ha^{-1} to 23% at 3 and 26% at 6 ewes ha^{-1}.
- Lambing percentage falls over the same range from 95% to 82% to 59%.
- Lambs sold = ewes ha^{-1} x lambing % x (1-replacement %).

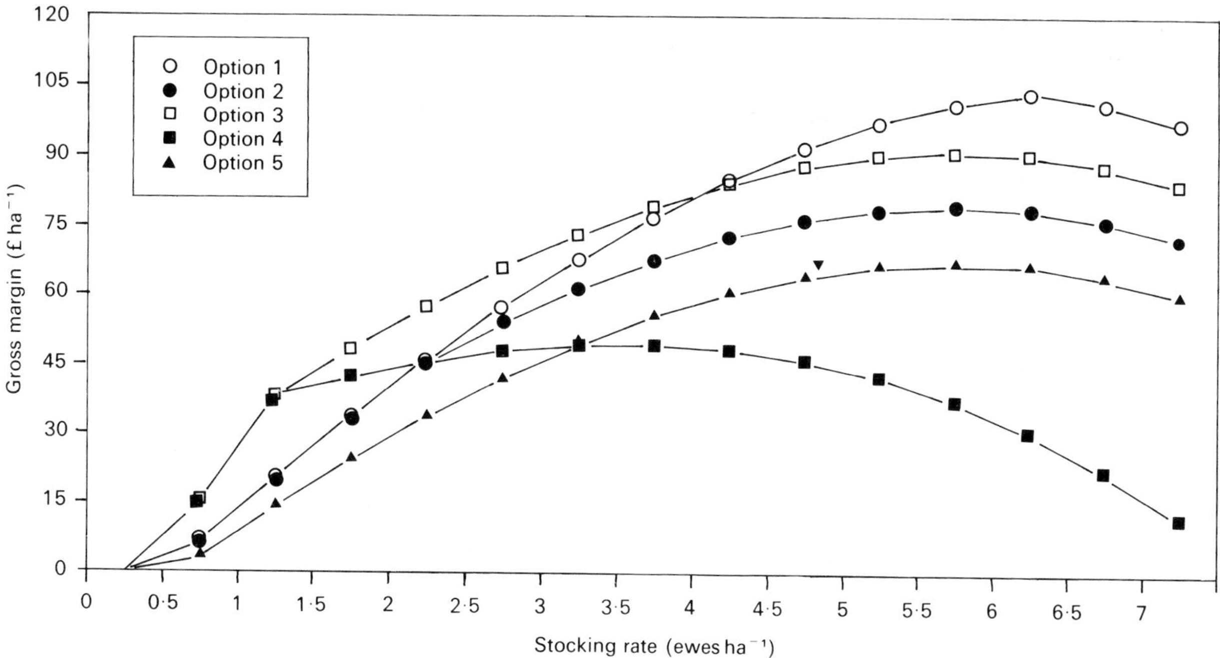

Figure 1. The effect of changes in hill livestock compensatory allowances on returns from store lamb production at varying stocking rates

FINANCIAL FACTORS

The analysis is based on a gross margin, which is:

INCOME (HLCAs, ewe premium, lamb sales, wool sales) minus
VARIABLE COSTS (grazing, shearing, feed, veterinary and medical)

We have assumed that, within constraints of technical stocking capacity and labour/capital availability, the chosen stocking rate will maximize gross margin per hectare. We have ignored cull sales, which would increase with stocking rate, and changes in capital stocks as represented by ewes and replacements.

We used the 1985–86 levels of the annual ewe premium throughout the analysis. Our analysis, the results of which are summarized in Figure 1, shows that, even if the maximum stocking rate allowed for the purposes of HLCA arrangements were to be reduced to one ewe ha^{-1}, and the headage payment for this one ewe substantially increased, this would still not remove the incentive to improve income by increasing the number of stock.

Removing the HLCA system completely merely reduces income, as does reducing the stocking limit from 6 to 2 ewes ha^{-1}. The only way to reduce current stocking rates using the HCLA system would be to fine farmers who exceeded a given rate, which is obviously an unacceptable option. Our analysis made various assumptions about changes in the performance of a sheep flock at differing stocking densities. These assumptions err on the side of caution; it is likely that we have underestimated rather than overestimated the resulting gross margin figures, and therefore the stocking rate is likely to be even less sensitive to changes in the HLCA system than our figures suggest.

In summary, revenue from non-HLCA sources continues to increase with the number of ewes (up to the technical stocking capacity of the land, see Section 3.2). This increase over-rides the effect of any changes that could feasibly be made to the HLCA system.

3.2 Technical and managerial factors

3.2.1 Sheep management

Sheep cannot live by heather alone, partly because it is deficient in certain essential minerals. The chief use of the heather moorland is to provide winter grazing at a maintenance-only level, thereby giving the 'improved' areas time to recover. Heather, unlike other grazable vegetation, remains palatable over the winter months and is also accessible through snow cover.

Sheep must have access to a better nutrient source in the autumn (before tupping) and in the spring (immediately before lambing and during lactation). This source is normally provided by grazing the ewes on inbye land and/or on 'improved' hill pasture at these times, and by providing supplementary feeding which is crucial to the profitability of hill sheep, and relevant to the nature conservation issue, as overgrazing and physical damage to the heather plant is a recognized problem around feeding areas.

Good grazing management for a hill sheep flock involves 'raking' the sheep so that they graze the lower ground during the day and move to higher ground in late afternoon and evening. This practice spreads grazing pressure over the hill and therefore reduces the risk of localized overgrazing. Raking is partly instinctive but is encouraged by good shepherding (Mowforth 1986).

A patchwork of muirburn is also part of good grazing management. This system increases the grazing capacity of the heather by keeping it edible. The danger of overgrazing the young plants is reduced by burning a patchwork of small areas, a practice which also gives patches of older heather for shelter.

Essentially, this type of upland management needs more labour than can presently be employed.

3.2.2 *Improvement of hill land*

A larger area of improved pasture on a hill farm, if well managed, can allow for an increase in overall stocking rate and a higher lambing percentage.

There are 4 basic methods of 'improving' hill ground, all of which are designed to cause a sustainable modification to the existing semi-natural vegetation:

i. fencing with controlled grazing;

ii. fencing, controlled grazing, lime and fertilizer;

iii. fencing, controlled grazing, lime and fertilizer and oversowing with clover (*Trifolium* spp.) or grass/clover mixtures;

iv. fencing with full reseed, with or without drainage.

Prospects for a further general increase in stocking rate due to hill land improvement may have been altered by a change in the capital grants available for this purpose. Until recently, capital grants of up to 50% (LFAs) were available for the drainage, fencing, reseeding and regeneration of existing grassland or moorland, so that many hill farmers were financially able to increase their acreage of improved pasture. Under the new agricultural improvement scheme (ECC 1986), these grants are down to 30%, but are available only for farmers participating in a development scheme and not for converting from moor to grassland. The previous grant scheme allowed farmers to claim a grant for hill land improvement on a one-off basis, without having to engage in a total farm development plan.

The impact of reducing grants on the profitability of hill land improvements has been considered (Carroll 1983). At a 30% grant rate, the investment was considered worthwhile, but a negative rate of return on the investment resulted from a total removal of the grant (as would now be the case if the farmer did not submit an improvement plan). Lack of grant for moorland conversion will reduce the number of situations in which such a measure becomes a viable proposition. Ploughing up of moorland may not stop altogether, because there are situations where such improvement will allow for an increase in stocking rate, which will turn the farm into a viable unit and hence increase its capital value. Moorland reclamation costs can be claimed as normal business expense under Schedule D taxation, and there is also evidence (Farmers Weekly 1986) that drainage contractors are lowering charges now that grants have been cut.

The maintenance of existing reseeds is essential to the continuation of the current farming system in hill areas, and to the maintenance of the capital value of the farm. It may also be a condition of tenancy. To this extent, the reseeding grants are a straight income supplement as the work would be carried out anyway.

The recent change in the capital grants structure is, therefore, unlikely to affect the maintenance of already reseeded areas, and so is unlikely to lead to a decline in the overall stocking rate. The extent to which technical improvements have increased the grazing pressure on heather moorland is almost impossible to determine. A higher overall stocking rate on a farm may not increase grazing pressure on the moor if the improved pasture can be used to reduce this grazing pressure at critical times. However, if sheep management is less than ideal, a higher stocking rate offers greater scope for an irreversible ecological change in the heather moorland.

Thus, our summary of the effect of technical and managerial factors on stocking rates is that the ratio of improved and/or inbye land to heather moorland, and the nutritional status of both, determines the technical limit to stocking rates.

It is possible for grazing management to change this technical limit by controlling grazing pressure, burning and supplementary feeding, and by the 'improvement' of grazing.

3.3 Labour and capital availability

Labour and capital availability affects stocking rate to the extent that physically similar farms may be managed in dissimilar ways; in the case of an elderly farmer, the physical work involved in looking after a large flock may be too taxing and employing help not financially justifiable, with the result that the stocking rate is well below the technical optimum and/or grazing management is poor. If the farm is owner-occupied and without serious debt, the farmer has a greater range of options than would be the case on a tenanted farm. The need to pay rent will force a tenant farmer to stock near to the economic optimum. An owner-occupier without debt can let grazing or exist with a lower stocking rate, although the return on capital will be poor.

Constraints on capital availability are also likely to lead to stocking rates below the technical optimum.

Thus, lack of labour and capital may cause concern from a nature conservation viewpoint, if the resulting low stocking rates decrease farm income to the extent that the farm is no longer viable. If the farmer has no alternative source of income, there is a possibility of all or part of the farm being sold for afforestation.

4 Policy considerations

4.1 A critique of proposals to date

HLCAs and ecological change are just one facet of the debate about the future of the uplands. Many organizations and individuals have proposed policy changes relating to the entire upland economy, including tourism, recreation and local services, as well as agriculture and conservation. Among authors who have contributed constructively to the uplands debate, and produced policy proposals, are the RSPB (1984), the Countryside Commission (1984), MacEwen and Sinclair (1983) and Smith (1985). It is not within the scope of this paper to comment on the broader socio-economic proposals made by some of these authors, but it is relevant to consider briefly the specific proposals they make for reform of the HLCA system.

The Countryside Commission recommended that MAFF and the Welsh Office Agriculture Department reassess stocking levels in LFAs, in consultation with the National Park authorities and local authorities, to achieve agricultural and environmental objectives. Additionally, they recommended that, where stocking levels are set to meet conservation interest, HLCA payments be raised to the EC maxima. This recommendation does not address the problem of grazing management. It would be ineffective at controlling localized overgrazing, as it could control stocking only on a farm basis, particularly on large upland areas grazed by farmers with hefted flocks (Smith 1985). Neither does it get round the problem that the level of returns available from the sheepmeat regime may make it worthwhile for the farmer to exceed the recommended stocking rate and forego the enhanced HLCAs available.

The RSPB recommend paying the maximum EC rates of HLCA to the areas of greatest handicap, lowering the per hectare stocking rate limit, and calculating the limit based on adjusted forage hectares. They also suggest an alternative, and administratively more feasible, scheme linking the HLCA payment to the area of rough grazing on the farm, so that the farms with the most rough grazing have the potential to receive higher payments. Lowering the per hectare stocking rate limit would be ineffective in reducing localized overgrazing, would not act as an incentive to reduce stocking rates and would lower the income-earning capacity of the farm. It would increase the risk of the coniferous afforestation which the RSPB are so rightfully keen to prevent. The use of rough grazing areas alone to determine HLCA payment would make no different to farms with a high percentage of rough grazing and would serve only to decrease the income of those with a greater proportion of better land. This measure, again, would increase the risk of afforestation.

McEwen and Sinclair proposed a system based on 4 handicap classes, each qualifying for a different percentage of a base rate of HLCA and subject to an upper limit of 250 livestock units per farm (approximately 1666 sheep). About 6% of farms in England and Wales have more livestock than this figure, and would experience a fall in farm income and a corresponding drop in land values. Smaller and more handicapped farms might, indeed, benefit but stocking rate would not be affected.

Smith (1985) proposes a zoning system similar to the one suggested by McEwen and Sinclair and to which the same comments apply. He also proposes that HLCAs should be paid on not more than 50 livestock units per farm (approximately 333 sheep). This proposal would affect all but 53.7% of the LFA farms in England and Wales (McEwen & Sinclair 1983) and would cause a severe drop in hill land values, and consequently an increased risk of afforestation.

Our critique of past policy proposals is, therefore, that all the proposals examined miss one critical factor, which is that the sheepmeat regime recognizes no stocking limits and constitutes roughly two-thirds of the total subsidy payments. The proposal to limit the payment of HLCAs to a certain number of livestock units (or, indeed, to link it to the labour requirement of the farm as proposed by the Commission) would merely reduce hill land values.

5 Discussion

For heather moorland to survive, the businesses that use it must be able to exist without selling land for afforestation. We cannot, however, expect to use current economic pressures to return land use to that which was developed under past economic and technical conditions. In the context of hill farming, this means that we cannot expect to return to a fairly labour-intensive system of grazing management under a policy structure that is dominated by the EC sheepmeat regime and under which the reward for extra labour is not sufficient to justify a higher level of employment. HLCAs are something of a red herring; whilst they certainly do not discourage higher stocking rates, they cannot be effectively used to control stock numbers. Crude policy measures would be ineffective, given the narrow range of technically feasible stocking rates. If the total receipts from the sheepmeat regime and the HLCA system could be controlled, then there would be a chance of using this broad policy measure to control stock numbers, but this would require a radical revision of the sheepmeat regime, which is unlikely as sheepmeat is not currently in surplus. In 1985, the UK was 76% self-sufficient in sheepmeat, and the long-run production trend is upwards, but the underlying demand for lamb is static and, if production continues to rise at the same rate as in recent years, 100% self-sufficiency will be reached by the mid-1990s (O M Johns, pers. comm.). Some reform of the sheepmeat regime will become inevitable, but this is not a burning issue in the Commission at present. The most useful option from the NCC viewpoint would be a complete reform of the sheepmeat regime with ewe premiums. Expenditure and production could be limited by the use of a sliding scale of payments, depending on the number of ewes. This method would avoid the problem we have at present, ie HLCAs only comprising a part of the total support available, and may offer hope for reducing overall stocking rates, but would not address the issue of moorland management.

A further problem is the need to maintain confidence in the upland farming sector, which is suffering from a steep fall in land values. To propose any measure which might further shake the confidence of the industry is to invite a widening of the differential between the price of forestry planting land and hill grazing land, and so encourage coniferous afforestation. Unless there is strict control on new afforestation, which is not at all the case at present, it is irresponsible to propose any measures which might reduce hill land values.

6 References

Carroll, M. 1983. *Analysis of agricultural reforms.* Banbury: Nature Conservancy Council.

Countryside Commission. 1984. *A better future for the uplands.* Cheltenham: CC.

Crabtree, J.R., Evans, S., Revell, B.J. & Leat, P.M.K. 1986. *Agricultural structures policy and nature conservation in upland Grampian - a pilot study.* Peterborough: Nature Conservancy Council.

European Communities Commission. 1986. *Com. (86) 199.*

Farmers Weekly. 15 August 1986.

Leat, P. 1986. The changing level of support for hill and upland farming. In: *The future of agriculture in the hills and uplands.* Edinburgh: Edinburgh School of Agriculture.

MacEwen, M. & Sinclair, G. 1983. *New life for the hills.* London: Council for the National Parks.

Mowforth, M. 1986. *Moorland management, a literature review.* (Draft.) Peterborough: Nature Conservancy Council.

Nature Conservancy Council. 1984. *Nature conservation in Great Britain.* Banbury: NCC.

Parry, M.L., Bruce, A. & Harkness, C.E. 1982. *Surveys of moorland and roughland change.* Series of reports. Department of Geography, University of Birmingham.

Royal Society for the Protection of Birds. 1984. *Hill farming and birds; a survival plan.* Sandy: RSPB.

Smith, M. 1985. *Agriculture and nature conservation in conflict - the less favoured areas of France and the UK.* Langholm: The Arkleton Trust.

Yalden, D. 1981. *Sheep densities on moorland - a literature review.* (Peak District Erosion study. Phase 1 report.) Bakewell: Peak Planning Board.

Recent changes in sheep production systems in upland Britain: research note

K ATKINS and I BRADBURY
Department of Geography, University of Liverpool, PO Box 147, Liverpool, England

As the major agricultural activity in upland Britain, sheep production occupies a central position in the economy and ecology of upland areas. Changes in the nature or extent of sheep production could, therefore, have far-reaching consequences for upland environments, affecting their appearance, their ecological character and indigenous communities. In the last 10 years, policy instruments and technical innovations have combined to produce a stimulus for change in the British sheep industry, particularly its upland sector. A study is in progress to characterize recent changes in sheep production systems in 2 geographical areas, the northern Yorkshire Dales and the county of Clwyd in north Wales. The study includes an in-depth examination of over 80 farms in each locale.

The main trends identified so far in the study in Yorkshire are as follows.

1. Sheep numbers are increasing. Larger flocks, in part, reflect increases in farm size through amalgamation, but are also due to the expansion of sheep production at the expense of other enterprises on many farms, and a general intensification of sheep systems throughout the range of hill, upland and lowland farms studied.

2. Increased demand from lowland farmers for breeding ewes, traditionally supplied by hill and upland producers in Britain's highly integrated 'stratified' sheep industry, has increased market prices for breeding stock. This rise in price has enabled hill and upland farmers to increase expenditure on winter feeding and preventative medicine, with consequent improvements in flock performance.

3. A variety of farm and land improvements, and increased use of fertilizers on grassland have enabled many hill and upland farmers to alter their systems of sheep production so as to increase the proportion of their wether lamb crop sold finished, rather than as stores.

4. However, the optimism of the past 5 years now appears to be giving way to uncertainty over the future for sheep production in upland Britain.

Agroforestry research in the hills and uplands

A R SIBBALD[1], T J MAXWELL[1], J H GRIFFITHS[1], N J HUTCHINGS[1], C M A TAYLOR[2], P M TABBUSH[2] and I M S WHITE[2]
[1]*Hill Farming Research Organisation, Bush Estate, Penicuik, Midlothian, Scotland*
[2]*Forestry Commission, Northern Research Station, Bush Estate, Penicuik, Midlothian, Scotland*

1 *Introduction*

Agroforestry systems, in which grazing animals make use of pastures growing between widely spaced trees of commercial species, are now practised in many parts of the world; they have been successfully tested with sheep and conifers in Australia and New Zealand. Such new approaches offer the possibility of increasing the economic diversity in the hills and uplands of the UK.

A joint study team from the Hill Farming Research Organisation and the Forestry Commission's Northern Research Station was set up to explore, using a modelling approach, the effects of planting densities and stand management of spaced trees on upland pasture production, and to identify the most promising options in economic terms.

2 *The model*

It was assumed that trees would be planted on permanent upland pastures or on open hill pastures which can be improved, have freely drained soils and are not more than moderately exposed by forestry standards. The species of tree considered was Douglas fir (*Pseudotsuga menziesii*), because it has a fast potential growth rate, producing good-quality timber. It was assumed for the purpose of the study that the only impact of spaced trees upon pasture production would be through their shading effect, and that stocking rates of sheep would be reduced year by year as shading increased.

A tree growth model which calculates, year by year, bole and canopy dimensions was incorporated with a shading model (Satterlund 1983) to determine the amount and density of shade throughout the growing season. The effect of shading on net photosynthesis as a consequence of the spaced trees was thus calculated, and a simple assumption, that the output from a sheep flock grazing under those trees would be similarly reduced, led to an economic output which could be calculated, year by year, as the trees grew. Output of timber was calculated also, and allowance made for a premium gained for timber of high quality if a pruning regime was used. Pruning also allows more light to be transmitted to ground level, and thus increases pasture production.

The cash flows from the various options are different in time and in amount, and therefore a discounting procedure, taking account of both agricultural and timber production and leading to a comparable value in present-day terms – the net present value (NPV) – was applied. Thus, the economic performance over the whole production cycle for the various tree planting and management regimes could be ranked.

Table 1. Total net present value (£ ha^{-1}) for a range of discount rates

Stocking density	Project length (years)	Discount rate (%) 3	5	7
All forestry	45	3338	1129	126
All upland agriculture 10 ewes ha^{-1}	45	5840	4234	3241
All hill agriculture 2.5 ewes ha^{-1}	45	766	555	425

2.1 Results

Forestry is disfavoured by the use of high discount rates because of the delayed returns, and at 7% it cannot compete either with upland sheep on sown grassland, or with hill sheep on good-quality indigenous bent/fescue (*Agrostis/Festuca*) grassland (Table 1). However, at discount rates of 3% and 5%, forestry lies mid-way between these 2 agricultural options.

When wood and upland sheep production are combined on the same land, the combined revenues at a 5% discount rate equal or exceed those for either forestry or agriculture alone. The agricultural revenues are reduced, and the pattern of reduction is shown in Figure 1 as a consequence of shading. Shading is reduced significantly if trees are pruned. Figure 2 shows the patterns of reduction in agricultural production when the lowest 4 whorls of branches are removed in years 11, 15 and 19.

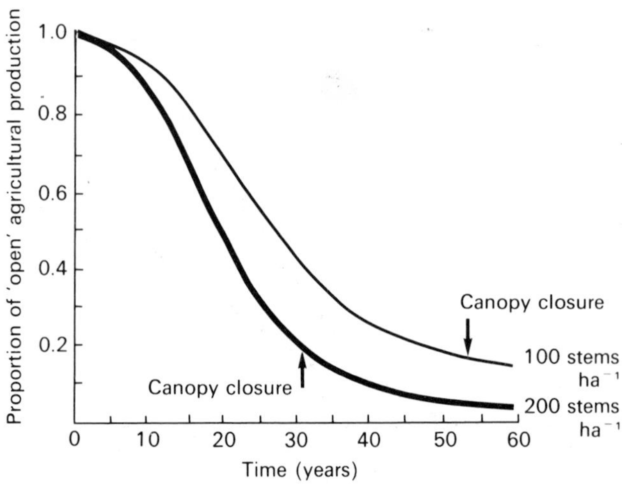

Figure 1. Patterns of reduction with time in agricultural production at 100 and 200 stems ha^{-1}

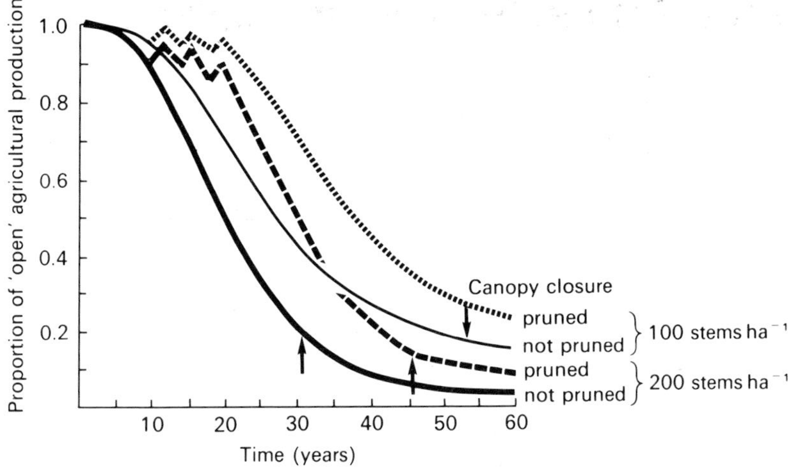

Figure 2. Patterns of reduction with time in agricultural production at 100 and 200 stems ha^{-1} with and without pruning

Canopy closure is delayed by 15 years at 200 stems ha^{-1} and is prevented, within a 60-year cycle, at 100 stems ha^{-1}. In addition to benefitting agricultural production, pruning improves timber quality by reducing the knotty core to a 10 cm diameter for a 6 m length; volume production of timber is not significantly affected, as shown in Figure 3. Table 2 shows values of NPV for pruning and non-pruning regimes and includes the assumption that high-quality, pruned timber will attract a 25% premium.

By protecting trees individually during the first years of their establishment in existing pastures, it would be possible to stock sheep on the area from the first year, rather than delaying grazing for 4 or 5 years when the leaders of the trees would be above grazing or browsing height. Such a procedure would obviously minimize disruption of an existing sheep production system. Table 2 shows the NPVs for protected and unprotected options; it is assumed that there is no agricultural return for the first 4 years in the unprotected options.

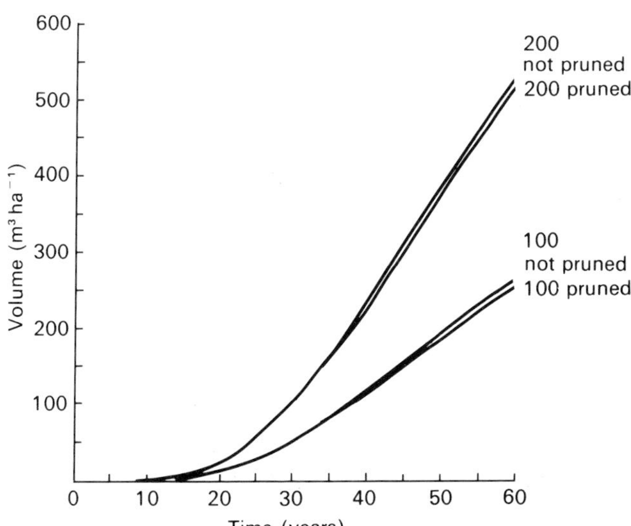

Figure 3. Pattern of increase in timber volume with time at 100 and 200 stems ha^{-1} with and without pruning

Table 2. Net present value (£ ha^{-1}) for upland sheep grazing beneath wide-spaced conifers (5% discount rate, 45-year project length)

Trees ha^{-1}		No pruning		Pruning (+25%)	
		Protection	No protection	Protection	No protection
400	Forestry	910	1310	930	1330
	Agriculture	2916	2236	3304	2625
	Total	3826	3583	4234	3955
100	Forestry	376	478	357	457
	Agriculture	3856	3174	4005	3324
	Total	4232	3652	4362	3781

The 400 stems ha^{-1} options are less favourable than the 100 stems ha^{-1} options and, by extrapolation, greater tree stocking densities would be unattractive (Table 2).

Removing trees to prolong the period before canopy closure at higher tree densities (Table 3) increases agricultural revenues, but decreases forestry revenues, and the net result is a slight decrease in total revenue. Thus, under agroforestry, the farmer would have the flexibility of felling trees to take advantage of high timber prices or to provide capital, without greatly reducing the return from the land.

2.2 Conclusions

This preliminary desk study suggests that agroforestry is worth exploring as a potential land use in the uplands of the UK. The study was based on data derived from a variety of sources, many of them from research not directly related to agroforestry. Much better data which apply directly to the British uplands are now required.

Table 3. Net present value (£ ha^{-1}) at 5% for thin and non-thin regimes on a 45-year project length with upland sheep. The initial spacing is 400 trees ha^{-1}, the trees are individually protected, pruned and a 25% premium is applied

	Non-thin	Thin[1]
Forestry	930	739
Agriculture	3304	3387
Total	4234	4126

[1] 50% of the trees are removed at canopy closure (year 32)

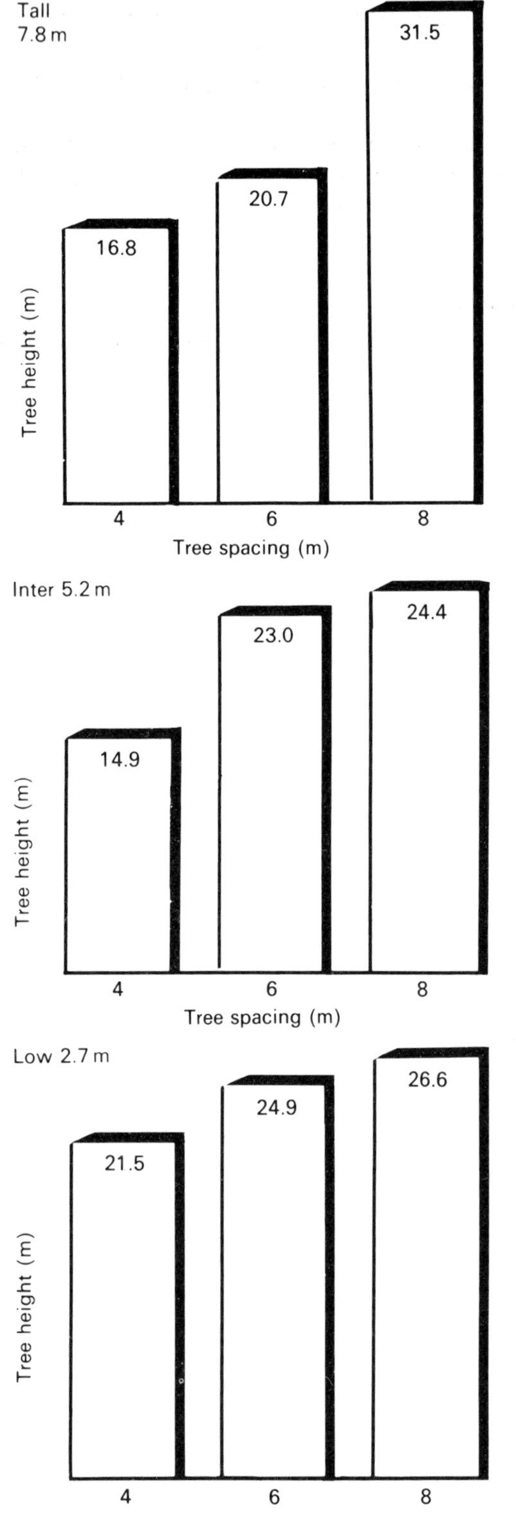

Figure 4. Herbage growth rates (6 August–27 August)

3 *Field experiment*

The biology which underlies systems of agroforestry is complex and dynamic. There are interactions between trees and grass both below and above ground level, and some of the biological components, especially those below ground, will only be fully understood with the aid of measurements made as seedling trees are established and grow in grazed pastures. However, it is possible, by respacing existing, commercial stands of trees, to represent established and well-grown agroforest tree canopies under which above-ground effects on herbage production can be measured directly, without the need to wait many years for the canopies to develop.

A field experiment, partially funded by the Commission of the European Communities, in collaboration with the Forestry Commission's Northern Research Station and Department of Forestry and Natural Resources of the University of Edinburgh, to measure the growth of pasture and to monitor the changes in the microclimate under various canopy structures of trees, is now being established and detailed measurements have been started.

3.1 Design

The experiment has been set up in an area of the Forestry Commission's forest at Glentress. Areas of Sitka spruce (*Picea sitchensis*) at 3 heights (2.7 m, 5.2 m and 7.8 m) have been respaced to 3 densities (156, 278 and 625 stems ha^{-1} – spacings of 8 m, 6 m and 4 m respectively), and an open site with no trees is also included. Growth of pasture is measured directly from sward boxes, sown with rye-grass (*Lolium perenne*) and sunk to ground level in a stratified layout, designed to measure canopy effects amongst trees as well as the effects of different canopy structure.

In addition to direct measurements of pasture growth, various microclimate parameters are also being measured at a number of locations. These measurements should enable an understanding of the effect of canopy structure on microclimate and the consequences for pasture growth to be gained.

3.2 Provisional results

Only provisional results are available at present, based on data from a limited number of sward harvests, and the microclimatic information has not yet been processed. It is possible, however, to speculate that, over certain periods, light may be the main limiting factor; a set of data which might indicate this hypothesis is shown in Figure 4. In this Figure, pasture growth increases as spacing increases at all 3 tree heights.

It is possible to identify other periods (Figure 5) in which temperature may be the factor which is limiting growth.

Figure 5. Proportion of open growth during the period 12 May–3 June

In this example, when the weather was cold and wet, most growth has been achieved at the closest spacing (4 m), where the sheltering effect may have maintained temperature above some threshold level.The other 2 spacings (6 m and 8 m) may not have buffered the temperature to the same extent and, at temperatures lower than the threshold level, light may have been a limiting factor.

3.3 Conclusion

The data presented here are provisional, and their full interpretation depends upon an analysis of the associated micrometeorological data and upon proper statistical analysis. However, it is encouraging at this stage to be able to show trends in herbage growth related to canopy structure which, if they stand up to the rigours of statistical analysis, will provide a better understanding of pasture growth in relation to canopy structure of trees in agroforestry systems.

4 Reference

Satterlund, D.R. 1983. Forest shadows: how much shelter in a shelterwood. *For. Ecol. Manage.*, **5,** 27-37.

Approaches to reinstatement of damaged footpaths in the Three Peaks area of the Yorkshire Dales National Park

N G BAYFIELD
Institute of Terrestrial Ecology, Banchory Research Station, Hill of Brathens, Banchory, Kincardineshire, Scotland

1 *Introduction*

The Yorkshire Dales National Park includes some of the most varied and interesting countryside in upland Britain, which attracts an increasing number of visitors, and is particularly popular with walkers. In recent years, footpaths linking the Three Peaks (Ingleborough, Pen-y-ghent and Whernside) have become seriously eroded because of heavy use. More than 120 000 visitors reach the summit of Ingleborough each year (Smith 1987). The area is used both by individual groups of walkers and for organized walks and races. By 1985, the extent of wear was causing serious concern, and the Yorkshire Dales National Park Committee initiated a programme to survey the damage, test reinstatement techniques, and undertake remedial work (Plate 2).

This paper outlines (i) the results of a survey of the footpaths to pinpoint the type and extent of damage, and (ii) the first summer's trials of reinstatement techniques undertaken by the Institute of Terrestrial Ecology for the National Park Committee during 1986.

The principal problem was to find a means of reinstating native vegetation on heavily disturbed sites. The methods tested included seeding, transplanting, soil amendment, and site works to improve drainage and canalize use. The results of the trials are based on less than a full season's growth, so are necessarily tentative, and the main purpose of this account is to outline the adopted approaches to reinstatement.

2 *The footpath survey*

The aims of the survey were to assess the condition of each path and to identify relationships between path condition and site factors, such as wetness, soil type, vegetation and slope. The results were to provide a baseline analysis for future monitoring and to guide the selection of revegetation techniques and of sites for reinstatement trials.

These objectives required an assessment of path widths and site characteristics along each path. The survey was completed by the end of May 1986, and preliminary analysis by the middle of June, prior to laying out the first trials in early July.

2.1 Survey methods

Recording was based on the technique described by Bayfield *et al.* (1973). Path widths (the total width of obviously trampled ground) and bare widths (the width of ground with no surviving vegetation) were measured

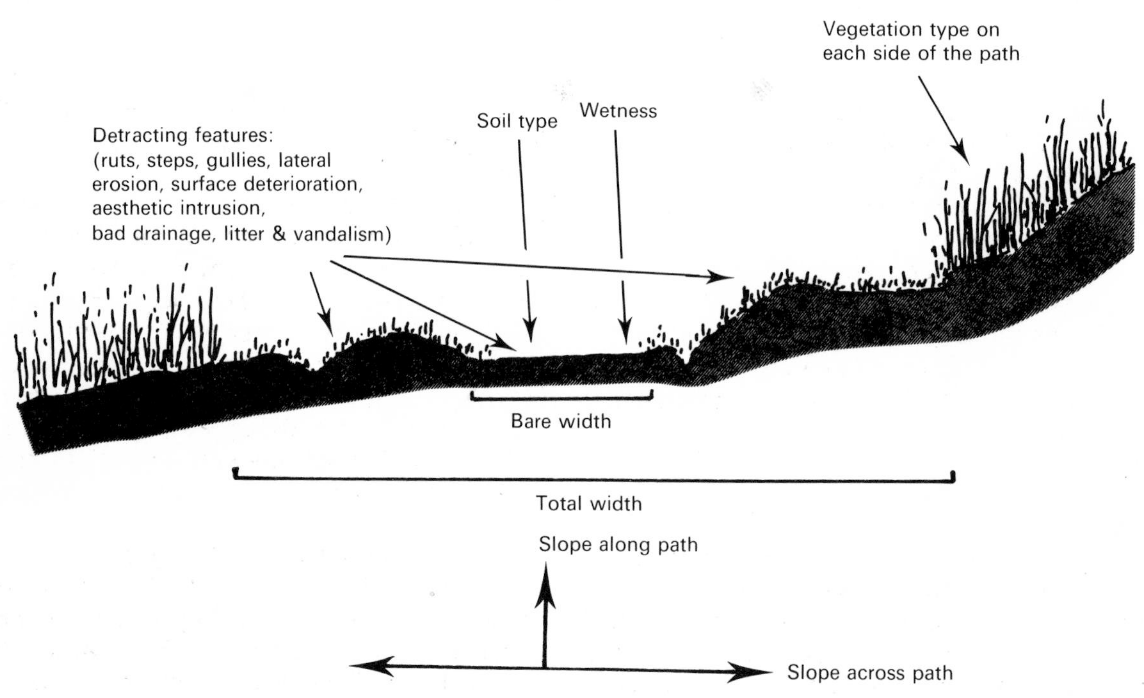

Figure 1. Path characteristics recorded at each sample point

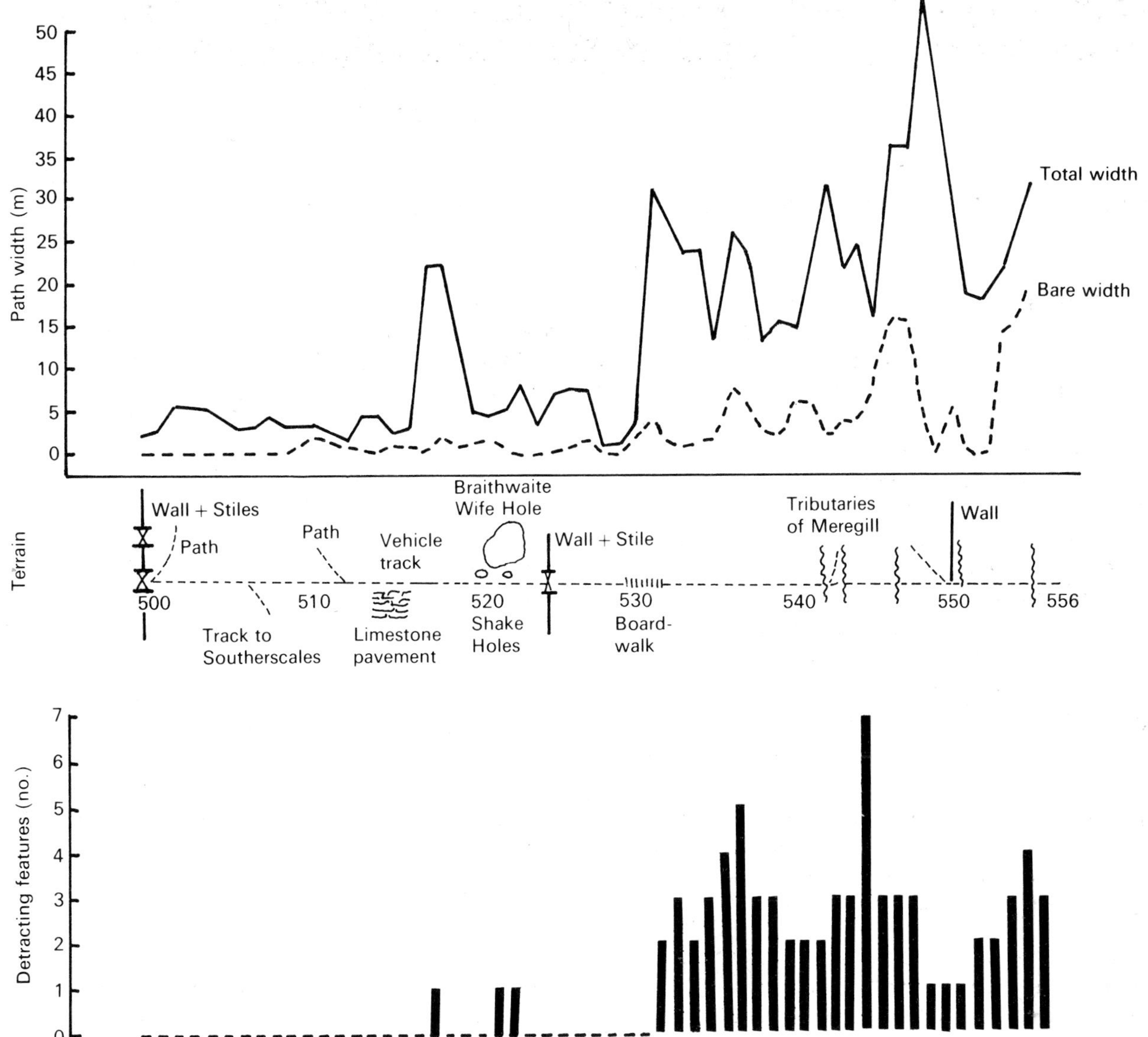

Figure 2. An example of path width data for the Southerscales–Ingleborough path. The numbered points on the terrain sketch are permanent transects

at stratified random sample points in each 50-pace (approximately 50 m) length of path. At each sample point, surface soil type, slope, wetness, adjacent vegetation, and various detracting features (features that reduced path quality) were also recorded (Figure 1). A full account of methods and definition of categories are given in Bayfield and McGowan (1986). Widths and slopes were measured using a 2 m 'A' frame, similar to a pair of large, fixed-dimension dividers with a built-in spirit level and protractor for measuring angle of slope (Bayfield 1987).

2.2 Path widths

The total length of paths surveyed was 65 km, including about 10 km where paths followed farm tracks or road, and where detailed measurements were not recorded. For each path, a listing of width and other data was drawn up to permit the rapid identification of problem sections, and corresponding soil, vegetation and other site attributes. Figure 2 is an example of such width data for the Southerscales to Ingleborough path.

The average trampled width (all paths) was 11.4 m, and bare width 2.7 m. Some sections were, of course, much more worn than others, but at over half the sample points (60%) the trampled width exceeded 5 m, and at more than a third (38%) it exceeded 10 m. Similarly, a majority (61%) of sample points had more than 2 m of bare ground, and about one in 6 (17%) had more than 5 m. These figures indicate the equivalent of about 23 km of paths that are 10 m or more wide, and 10 km with 5 m or more of bare ground.

The 11.4 m trampled width in the Three Peaks compares unfavourably with upland footpaths elsewhere. The Pennine Way, for example, although badly worn in places, averaged only 3.5 m in 1983 (Bayfield 1985). It is clear that the Three Peaks footpaths are very badly worn.

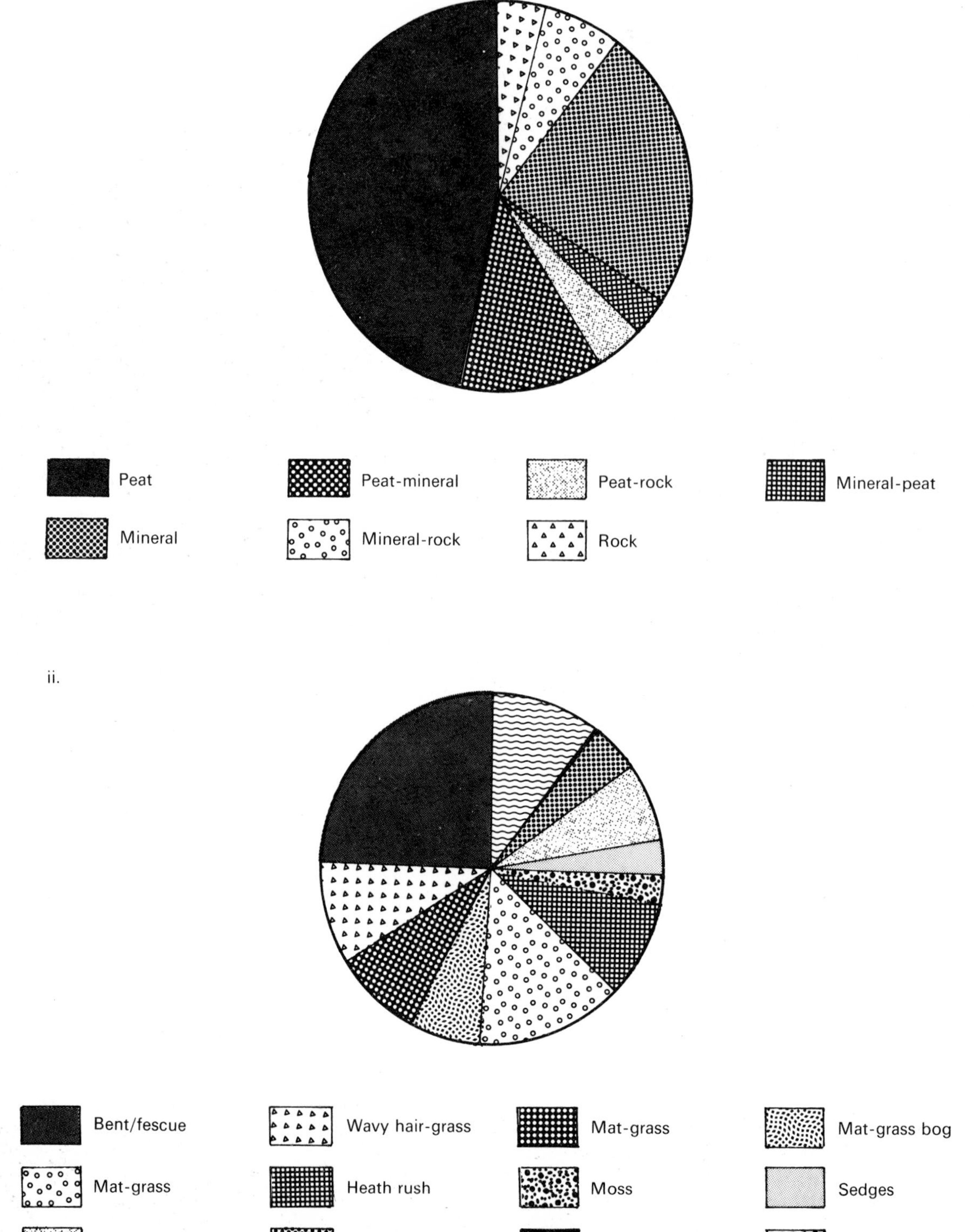

Figure 3. The percentage frequencies of (i) soil surface categories, and (ii) vegetation categories along paths in the Three Peaks area (n=1157)

2.3 Soils and vegetation

During the course of the survey, it was noticeable that badly worn sections of path were predominantly on peaty ground. The soil category with the greatest average width (>15 m) was 'peaty mineral', mainly found at sites where the peat had been worn away from part of the path to expose mineral subsoil. 'Peat' and 'peat-rock' (peat with exposed rocks) also had high average width (>10 m), whereas predominantly 'mineral' surfaces had widths less than 8 m.

Peat was also the most frequent type of surface, comprising 63% of path samples (Figure 3). The survey indicated that about 77% of badly worn sections occurred on peaty soils. The vegetation of the Three Peaks area is a mixture of heather (*Calluna vulgaris*) and

Plate 2i. Severe erosion on the path from Simon Fell to Ingleborough (Photograph N G Bayfield)

grass heaths, with the latter predominant. Twelve broad vegetation categories were recorded during the footpath survey, based on the predominant species. The single most frequent type was bent/fescue (*Agrostis/Festuca*) grassland, the characteristic vegetation of mineral soils overlying limestone (Figure 3). On peaty soils, the

Plate 2ii. Part of a trial site on Simon Fell, with a constructed gravel surface and fenced and unfenced plots of various seed mixtures (Photograph N G Bayfield)

vegetation comprised principally graminoids, notably mat-grass (*Nardus stricta*), wavy hair-grass (*Deschampsia flexuosa*), sheep's fescue (*Festuca ovina*), common bent-grass (*Agrostis capillaris*), heath rush (*Juncus squarrosus*), cotton-grass (*Eriophorum* spp.), soft rush (*Juncus effusus*), sedges (*Carex* spp.) and mosses. Heather was predominant at only 0.3% of the path sample points.

3 *The approach to reinstatement*

The principal considerations in designing the first season's reinstatement trials were:

i. to relate trial design to the main types of deterioration identified during the footpath survey;
ii. to seek, where practicable, solutions that would withstand grazing and disturbance by sheep;
iii. to use locally native species wherever possible;
iv. to conserve any surviving vegetation, and to explore means of increasing its resistance to further disturbance;
v. to explore the possibilities of transplanting established plants in order to create rapid cover, texture or pattern;
vi. to use any other readily available sources of plant material, including moss fragments, seed-rich plant litter and seeds;
vii. to treat not only symptoms but also causes, by landscaping surfaces and canalizing use to minimize further disturbance.

The initial trial sites were located at peat sites because of their apparent vulnerability. The species planted or sown were principally the graminoids and mosses predominant in the path survey. Constraints of time and resources meant that only a limited range of comparisons could be attempted in the first season, so those chosen were deliberately contrasting. The intention was that promising lines of investigation would be examined in more detail in subsequent studies. However, all trials were replicated (usually 4 replicates) to permit statistical analysis of the data. There were 3 main types of trials: seed mixtures, transplants, and the use of fertilizers to improve the resistance of vegetation to disturbance (Bayfield & Miller 1986).

The seeds and transplanting trials were laid out at 2 gently sloping peat sites on Simon Fell (about 500 m above sea level), where there was extensive exposure of bare ground (Plate 3; Figure 4). To prevent heavy disturbance of the plots, use was canalized by providing a new gravel path at one site and a boardwalk at another. To protect from the possible impact of sheep grazing, some of the trials (principally seeds trials) were fenced, but the majority of trials had no protection from sheep. No serious interference with initial plant establishment by sheep was noted, although most plots were closely grazed.

The fertilizer trials were laid out on sections of existing path with continuing use, and marked inconspicuously to avoid altering the pattern of use.

3.1 Seed mixtures trials

Replacement of vegetation by seeding bare ground is a widely used reinstatement technique, and one that has proved successful even in such harsh conditions as the Trans-Alaska pipeline system (Hubbard 1980), subalpine camp-grounds (Hingston 1982) and Scottish ski-grounds (Bayfield 1980). In most cases, however, agronomic species have been used, and there have been few attempts in Britain to sow mixtures of upland native species (Environmental Unit 1981). In the Three Peaks trials, the aim was to use mainly native species, but with some agricultural mixtures for comparative purposes and as an insurance against possible failure of the native species.

Not all the principal species identified in the path survey could be obtained commercially as seed. Some mixtures were supplemented with either chopped moss fragments or plant litter, to try and increase species diversity. There were 2 mixtures based on the agricultural grass mixtures used for reinstatement work at ski sites in Scotland (Bayfield 1980). The composition of the various mixtures is shown in Table 1.

Table 1. Seed mixtures used in the 1986 trials

		% by weight	Seeds m-2	Sowing rate (g m-2)
'I'	(Sheep's/fescue/bent/wavy hair-grass mixture			
	Wavy hair-grass (*Deschampsia flexuosa*)	27	8000	
	Sheep's fescue (*Festuca ovina*)	27	1500	
	Bent-grass (*Agrostis capillaris*)	10	9000	6
	Sweet vernal grass (*Anthoxanthum odoratum*)	34	500	
	Tormentil (*Potentilla erecta*)	1	600	
	Harebell (*Campanula rotundifolia*)	1	1200	
'N'	(Mat-grass mixture)			
	Wavy hair-grass	70	11000	
	Mat-grass (*Nardus stricta*)	14	1300	
	Bent-grass	14	11000	4.5
	Tormentil	1	400	
	Harebell	1	800	
'G'	(Agricultural mixture)			
	Red fescue (*Festuca rubra*)	48	2500	
	Meadow grass (*Poa pratensis*)	18	2400	5.3
	Bent-grass	15	12000	
	Crested dog's-tail (*Cynosurus cristatus*)	18	1900	
'GH'	(Agricultural mixture with Yorkshire fog)			
	As 'G' (80%) plus:			
	Tormentil	1	400	
	Harebell	1	800	
	Clover (*Trifolium repens*)	3	200	5.3
	Yarrow (*Achillea millefolium*)	1	500	
	Yorkshire fog (*Holcus lanatus*)	15	2000	
'IM'	('I' plus moss)			
	'I' above plus 2 g m^{-2} chopped moss fragments (bog moss (*Sphagnum* spp.), bog hair moss (*Polytrichum commune*), fork moss (*Dicranum* and *Campylopus* spp.), feather moss (*Hylocomium splendens* and *Brachythecium* spp.)			
'IF'	('I' plus litter)			
	'I' plus 0.5 l m^{-2} local plant litter			

Plate 3. A view of the 'boardwalk' site on Simon Fell Breast (Photograph N G Bayfield)

Figure 4. Interpretation key of Plate 3 - a view of the 'boardwalk' site on Simon Fell Breast.
1, fenced seed mixtures trial; 2, ditch; 3, unfenced seed mixtures trial; 4, soft rush transplants; 5, boardwalk; 6, soft rush, mat-grass and heath rush transplants

The sites were prepared by digging and raking the ground to a fine tilth, then applying 35 g m^{-2} Vitax Q4 low-nitrogen fertilizer (5.3:7.5:10 NPK) prior to seeding plots 2 m x 1 m. All the seed mixtures produced a satisfactory cover after 2½ months (mean range 58–85%), and the native species mixtures compared favourably with the agricultural mixtures. Table 2 gives an example of data for the 4 mixtures compared at the 'boardwalk' site. Of the sown grasses, bent-grass was a major contributor to cover in all 4 mixtures. The other native species, sheep's fescue and sweet vernal-grass (*Anthoxanthum odoratum*), provided much less cover, and wavy hair-grass was a very minor component. Sown herbs (broadleaved species, common tormentil (*Potentilla erecta*) and harebell (*Campanula rotundifolia*)) were only present in traces, but self-sown species (mainly soft rush) were present to some extent on all plots, and especially on the control plots (more than 20% cover).

Cores of soil from the site were found to contain a seed reservoir equivalent to about 20 000 seed m^{-2}, mainly of soft rush. Ground preparation and the addition of fertilizer appeared to have stimulated many of these seeds to germinate. The second seeds trial site had a similar seed reservoir, but produced fewer seedlings, possibly because the ground was much drier. The addition of chopped moss fragments and plant litter increased the variety and cover of mosses (Table 3), although mosses were still a minor contributor to cover. Litter was more effective than chopped moss fragments. On control plots, even higher moss cover was recorded, but this was mostly an undifferentiated filamentous mat without recognizable species.

Table 2. Percentage cover of principal species on plots sown with various seed mixtures at the boardwalk site on Simon Fell Breast. Visual estimates of cover (means of 4 replicates) after 2½ months (September 1986). Total plant cover data are back transformed from angular transformations. Details of mixtures are given in Table 1

	Mixture				
	I	IM	IL	G	C
Sown grasses					
Bent-grass (*Agrostis capillaris*)	42	55	55	29	4*
Sheep's fescue (*Festuca ovina*)	7	3	7		t*
Red fescue (*Festuca rubra*)				31	
Wavy hair-grass (*Deschampsia flexuosa*)	2	1	1		
Meadow grass (*Poa pratensis*)				1	
Sweet vernal grass (*Anthoxanthum odoratum*)	7	5	7		
Crested dog's-tail (*Cynosurus cristatus*)				t	
Sown herbs					
Self-sown species					
Soft rush (*Juncus effusus*)	7	6	5	4	24
Other species	t	t	1		1
Mosses	1	3	4	t	6
Total plant cover	65	74	78	67	34
(95% confidence limits)	(50-78)	(60-86)	(64-89)	(52-50)	(20-49)

t, trace (less than 1% cover. * not shown in these plots, seeds presumably windblown from adjacent plots

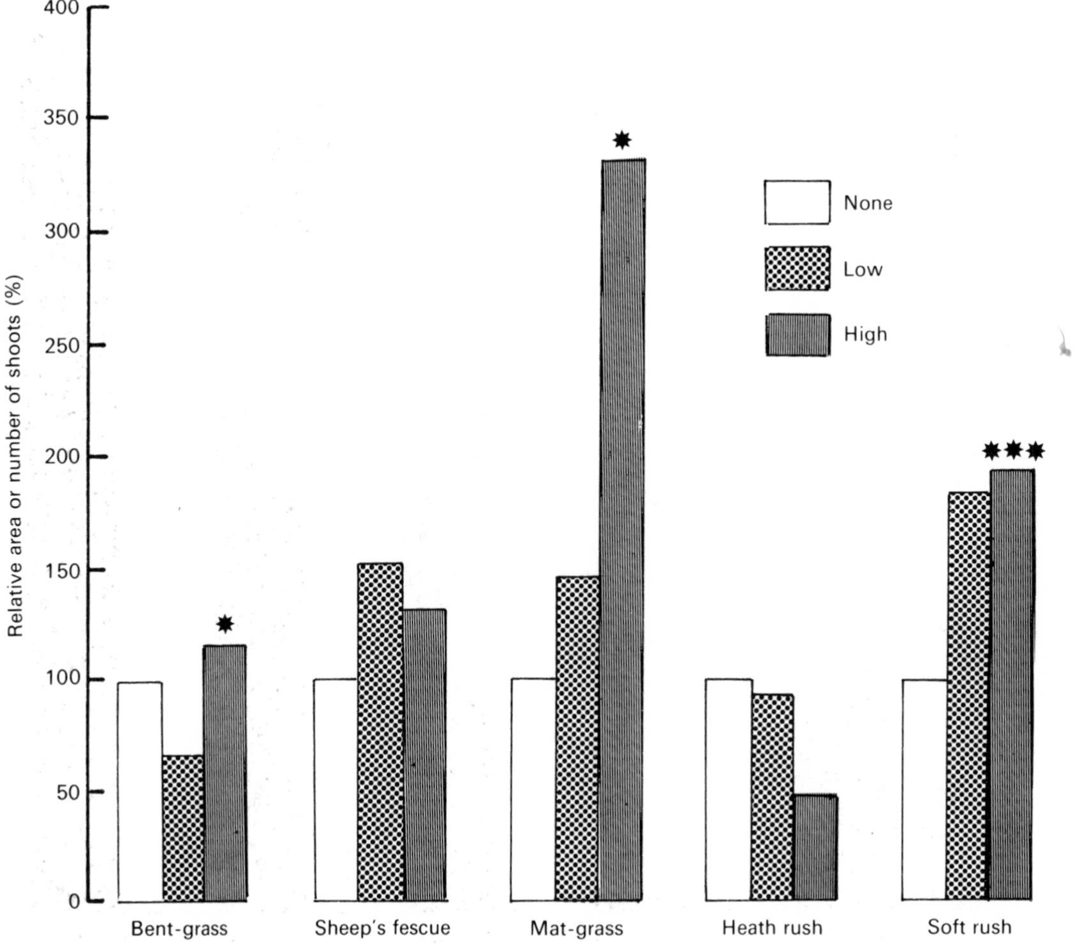

Figure 5. Effects of fertilizer (0, 70 or 140 gm m^{-2} Vitax Q4) on the areas of surviving divots. The areas on fertilized plots are expressed as a proportion of those on unfertilized plots (* $P < 0.05$; *** $P < 0.001$)

Table 3. Comparison of the numbers of quadrats in which various mosses were recorded, and the mean % cover of mosses in seeded plots at the boardwalk site on Simon Fell Breast. Eight quadrats were recorded on each seeds mixture treatment (2 quadrats on each of 4 replicates). Total moss cover untransformed. The composition of the mixtures is given in Table 1

	Mixture				
	I	IM	IL	G	C
Hair moss (*Polytrichum* spp.)	1	4	8		2
Bog moss (*Sphagnum* spp.)		1	7		
Feather moss (*Brachythecium* spp.)		2	8		
Marsh thread moss (*Aulacomnium palustre*)		1			
Fork moss (*Dicranum* or *Campylopus* spp.)		1	1		
Undifferentiated moss mat	6	8	6	5	7
Total moss cover (%)	0.9	2.6	3.6	0.6	5.7

3.2 Transplanting trials

Transplanting of alpine species has been used successfully in the United States (Brown *et al.* 1978) and spot or close turfing is widely recommended as one of the best revegetation techniques for erosion control (Schiechtl 1980). Little is known, however, of the suitability of most common British upland species for transplanting work.

These trials aimed to discover which species could be transplanted satisfactorily, the most effective size of transplant, and the effect of fertilizer on establishment. Seven species were compared (sheep's fescue, bent-grass, soft rush, heath rush, sedge (*Carex nigra*), mat-grass and cotton-grass (*Eriophorum vaginatum*). In each case, 10 cm diameter circular turves were cut and transplanted intact, 'stretched' to about double their initial area, or divided into 9 smaller rooted 'divots'. In each case, the material was planted into 0.5 m^2 plots.

Fertilizer applications were 0, 70 or 140 g m^{-2} Vitax Q4. Intact turves and stretched turves only received the lower fertilizer application and transplanted well, without any losses after 2½ months. The divots received the full range of fertilizer applications and also transplanted quite well, with 65–100% survival in most cases. An exception was heath rush, which only had a survival rate of 53% on heavily fertilized plots. The area occupied by the surviving transplants was compared after 2½ months. For bent-grass, mat-grass and heath rush, the area of divots and stretched turves slightly exceeded that of intact turves (differences not, however, significant). In the case of soft rush and sheep's fescue, the area of divots was more than double that of intact turves ($P<0.05$). The growth of cotton-grass and sedge was not analysed, as these species appear to have a flush of growth in the spring, and had made no growth since transplanting. The use of fertilizer on divots increased the area substantially in the case of soft rush and mat-grass,

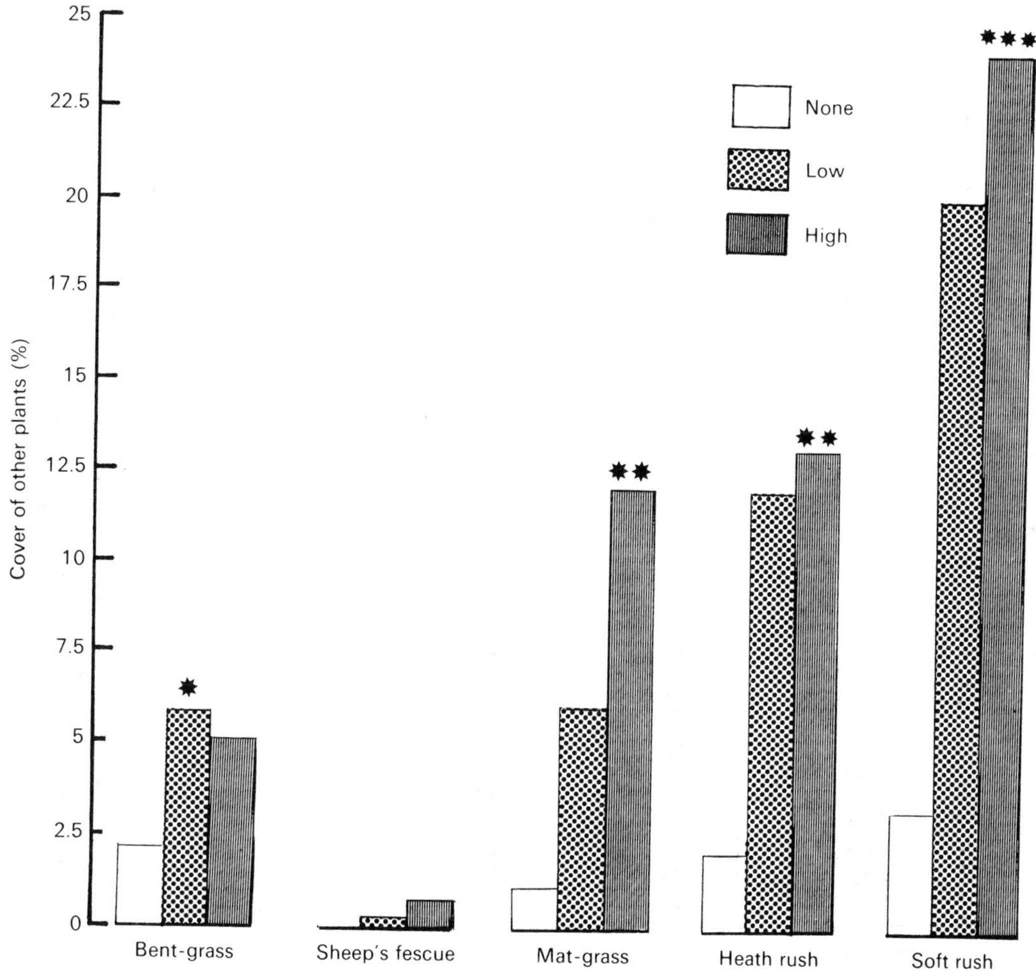

Figure 6. Effects of fertilizer on the cover (visual estimates) of other plants colonizing divot plots of bent-grass, sheep's fescue, mat-grass, heath rush and soft rush (* $P<0.05$; ** $P<0.01$; *** $P<0.001$)

affected bent-grass and sheep's fescue only slightly, and reduced the area of heath rush (Figure 5). Another important effect of fertilizer was a substantial increase in the cover of other species colonizing the transplant plots (Figure 6). The fertilizer appeared to both stimulate germination and increase growth rates of colonizing plants. The main colonizing species was soft rush, with smaller numbers of heath rush and brown bent-grass (*Agrostis canina*).

3.3 Use of fertilizers on damaged vegetation

Fertilizer is applied routinely to heavily used sports turf in order to maintain plant vigour, and has been recommended to help maintain plant cover in wilderness camp-grounds in the United States (Hendee *et al.* 1977). The aim of the present trials was to see whether the addition of fertilizer to damaged vegetation along paths could improve plant cover, and increase resistance to further disturbance. Treatments included fertilizer, lime and alginure soil improver, but some of these were not applied until late in the season, and their effects will not be analysed until 1987. At 5 sites on Simon Fell, however, the effect of fertilizer was analysed after 2½ months. Each site had 3 adjacent 2 m strips across the path dressed with 0, 35 or 105 g m^{-2} of Enmag slow-release low-nitrogen fertilizer (4.5:20:10 NPK).

The application of fertilizer increased plant cover by up to 28% (Figure 7). Detailed botanical changes were not recorded at this stage, but superficially it appeared that narrow-leaved grasses (mainly sheep's fescue) contributed the greatest improvement to cover. A similar response, although by different species, has been noted in the case of fertilized tundra vegetation (Shaver & Chapin 1986).

4 Conclusions

All 3 approaches to reinstatement (seeding, transplanting and fertilizing) showed promising results after only a few months, but it is long-term performance that will indicate which are the most satisfactory techniques. Analysis of plots after winter should be quite instructive, but performance will need to be monitored over several seasons.

As the transplanting of native species appears to be a practical possibility, it may be feasible to consider trials which combine seeding and transplanting to create reinstated vegetation with areas of contrasting texture

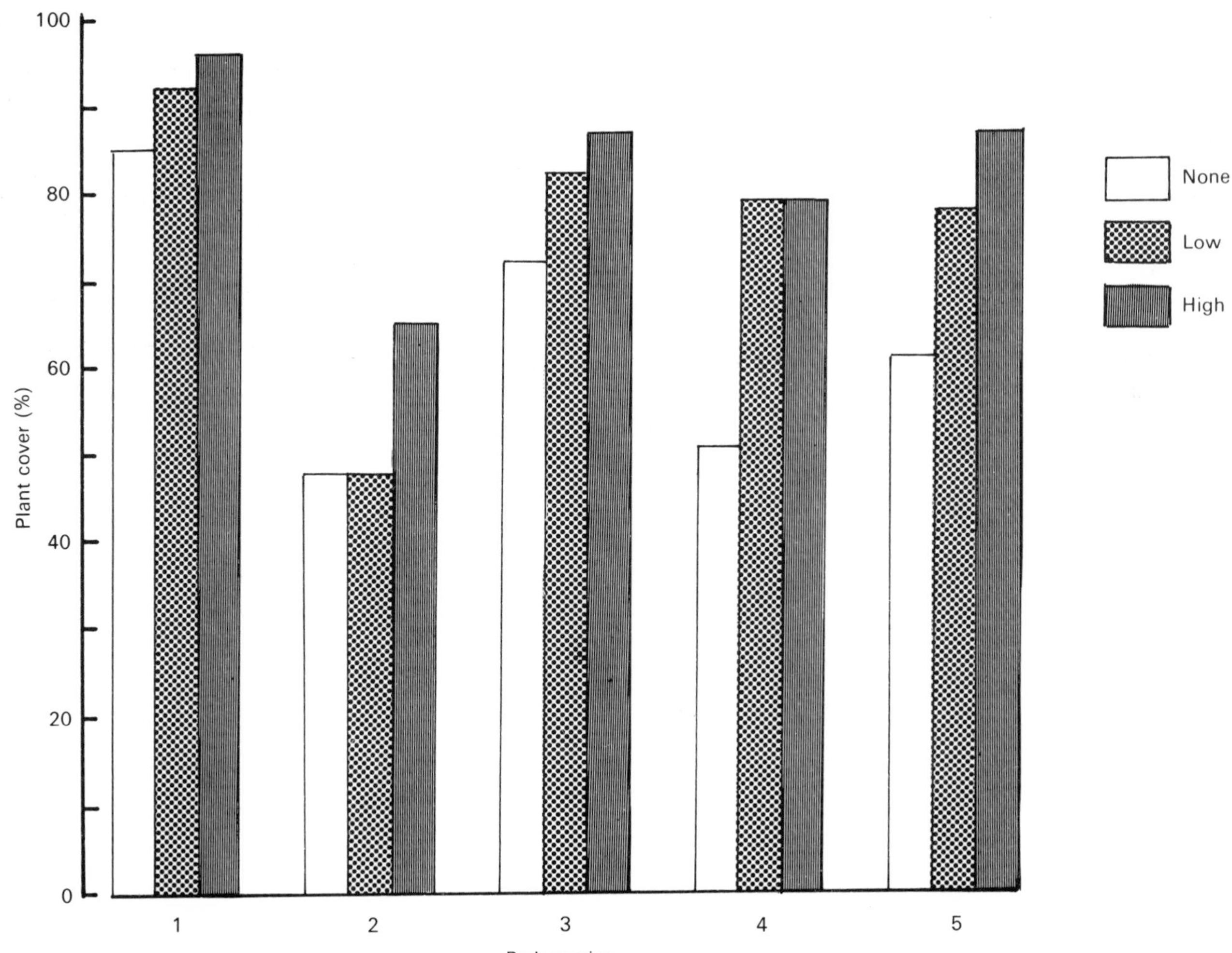

Figure 7. Effects of 2 levels of fertilizer (35 or 105 g m^{-2} Enmag) on vegetation cover at 5 damaged sections of path at Simon Fell Breast. Data are step point estimates of cover (source: Cunningham 1975)

and pattern, rather than just a uniform grassy sward. This method could be important for creating landscaped routes which blend imperceptibly with the surrounding ground. Similarly, trials with different textures, materials and colours of path surfaces need to be undertaken to establish how best to create visually acceptable path surfaces. The use of fertilizer to improve the resistance of damaged vegetation seems to be an effective and economical approach to managing paths where vegetation has been extensively damaged, but not eliminated, and could be a simple means of reducing the rate of path deterioration. Fertilizers appear to be beneficial, even where vegetation has been eliminated, in stimulating the germination of buried seed. Treatment could be easily applied to long stretches of path at comparatively low cost. Before this technique is used on a wide scale, however, it would be sensible to undertake further analysis of the trial plots to assess the persistence of the improvement, and the nature of any changes in species composition.

Some further trials on peat soils will probably be justified, but it should be possible to progress to trials on mineral and steeply sloping sites. Seed mixture trials should include, where possible, native species not tested in 1986, and transplanting should include species such as deer-grass (*Trichophorum cespitosum*), purple moor-grass (*Molinia caerulea*) and wavy hair-grass which have not so far been examined.

The contribution of buried seeds to cover at one of the trial sites indicates an important site characteristic about which we know rather little. A survey of the extent of buried seed reservoirs at different types of site could be helpful in choosing an appropriate combination of reinstatement techniques.

Finally, as reinstatment is introduced on an increasing scale, it will be important to monitor both the effectiveness and persistence of the techniques used, and the acceptability of the work to walkers and other users; we are seeking solutions which are aesthetically pleasing, and not just tidy and cost-effective.

5 *References*

Bayfield, N.G. 1980. Replacement of vegetation on disturbed ground near ski lifts in the Cairngorm Mountains, Scotland. *J. Biogeogr.*, **7,** 49-260.

Bayfield, N.G. 1985. The effects of extended use on mountain footpaths in Britain. In: *The ecological impacts of outdoor recreation on mountain areas of Europe and North America,* edited by N.G. Bayfield & G.C. Barrow, 100-111. (RERG report no. 9.) Wye: Recreation Ecology Research Group.

Bayfield, N.G. 1987. The two metre 'A' frame - a simple measuring device for rapid ecological survey. *Aberd. Lett. Ecol.* In press.

Bayfield, N.G. & McGowan, G.M. 1986. *Footpath survey 1986. The Three Peaks project.* (ITE report no. 1.) Grassington: Yorkshire Dales National Park.

Bayfield, N.G. & Miller, G.R. 1986. *Reinstatement trials 1986. The Three Peaks project.* (ITE report no. 2.) Grassington: Yorkshire Dales National Park.

Bayfield, N.G., Lloyd, R.J. & Shortridge, H.D. 1973. *Pennine Way survey.* London: Countryside Commission.

Brown, R.W., Johnston, R.S. & Johnson, D.A. 1978. Rehabilitation of alpine tundra disturbances. *J. Soil Wat. Conserv.*, **33,** 154-160.

Cunningham, G.M. 1975. Modified step pointing, a rapid method of assessing vegetation cover. *J. Soil Conserv.*, **13,** 256-265.

Environmental Unit. 1981. Previous work on restoration of moorland. In: *Moorland erosion study phase 1 report,* 208-217. Bakewell: Peak District National Park.

Hendee, J.C., Stankey, G.H. & Lucas, R.C. 1977. *Wilderness management.* (Miscellaneous publication no. 1365.) Department of Agriculture.

Hingston, S.G. 1982. *Revegetation of subalpine backcountry campaigns: principle and guidelines.* (Resource Management Report Series KR-3.) Alberta Recreation and Parks Division, Kananaskis Region.

Hubbard, G.E. 1980. Revegetation-restoration for the Trans-Alaska pipeline system. In: *Proc. High-Altitude Revegetation Workshop,* **4,** 113-125. Fort Collins, Co: Colorado Water Resources Research Institute.

Shaver, G.R. & Chapin III, F.S. 1986. Effect of fertilizer on production and biomass of tussock tundra, Alaska, USA. *Arct. Alp. Res.*, **18,** 261-268.

Schiechtl, H. 1980. *Bioengineering for land reclamation.* Edmonton, Al: University of Alberta Press.

Smith, R. 1987. The Three Peaks project. *Great Outdoors,* April, 53-57.

Agriculture, forestry and integrated land use options in south-west England

O BRANDON
Dartington Institute, Central Office, Shinners Bridge, Dartington, Totnes, Devon, England

1 *Introduction and background*

As surpluses mount and the pressures for change in the agricultural industry increase, more and more attention is being focused on ways of adverting catastrophic and uncontrolled rates of internal adjustment. Enquiry is proceeding into the prospects for alternative crops suited to growth on productive land forced out of normal agricultural production (Carruthers 1986), and there are other studies whose emphasis is on the least productive land on the farm. The object of such work is to establish a more broadly based set of enterprises within agriculture, using those resources which are currently contributing least to farm income. Such an approach is essentially a conservative, minimum risk strategy which, if successful, offers the prospect of maintaining or enhancing farm income at a time when income from conventional agriculture may be declining. What are these resources, and what is it that has apparently inhibited their exploitation to date? What are their costs and benefits, and are present policies and support measures sufficient to encourage exploitation?

There is a further question to be addressed. Are those 'marginal resources' different in the various farming areas of the country, particularly in the hills and uplands compared to the lowlands? This is an important point as policies may need to be tuned to specific locations, even within Less Favoured Areas (LFAs) of the country, as these are expanding and encompassing areas, such as the Culm Measures of Devon and Cornwall, with a maximum altitude of only 240 m. It is in the Culm that a 3-year research programme (Dartington Institute 1986) is examining the potential contribution of this marginal resource to farm income. This study has necessarily entailed a detailed analysis of all the agricultural land and woodlands on the farms of the area, and may be used to identify land marginal in agriculture and the potential for forestry. But why forestry? The simple answer is that farm woodlands come very close to being universally present on almost all farms in 'marginal' lowland areas, and equally, historically, the resource has rarely been managed or perceived as an asset of the farm. The possibility, therefore, exists of encouraging the use of this resource and utilizing it as a free injection of capital into the farm to enhance the capacity of woodlands to yield a sustainable return.

2 *Agriculture on the Culm*

The Culm Measures (Figure 1), extending to about 310 000 ha, form a geologically discrete area of carboniferous rocks running from the north-west coast of Cornwall to the Somerset border and from Bideford in the north to the slopes of Dartmoor in the south. The Culm has long been recognized as a lowland area with particular farming problems, as reflected in the recent designation of some 25% as a Less Favoured Area under European Community Directive 75/268, enabling an increased level of grant aid and support to be offered to farmers.

The boundary of the Culm LFA roughly coincides with that of land of Grade 4 or worse. Such land has a particularly high incidence of the surface water gleys so characteristic of the Culm, the management of which is exacerbated by a combination of rising groundwater and high rainfall. These features tend to curtail the grazing season by limiting access for stock to periods, and at rates, which minimize the risk of poaching.

As an aid to sampling and subsequent modelling of agriculture in the area, the 3100 km^2 of the Culm were stratified into 11 land classes (Figure 2) by the Institute of Terrestrial Ecology, using the land classification system developed over the last few years (Bunce *et al.* 1984). A proportionate random sample of 100 one km squares was selected from within the land classes, and a field survey of these areas formed the primary base upon which the assessments of agriculture and forestry potential were built. Clearly, these field data can be used to estimate the extent and distribution of a number of factors relevant to agricultural performance within the study area. Figure 2 also shows the geographical relations between the extended LFA and the land classes of the Culm. It is apparent that land classes 3, 4, 5, 7 and 11 dominate the LFA, and this fact may be employed to illustrate the salient differences between these areas and land outside of the LFA.

The combination of a higher incidence of surface water gleys and high rainfall results in the greatest restrictions to the grazing seasons within the LFA. This factor, together with the much higher incidence of rough grazing, serves to limit the mean stock carrying capacity of the land. The common response to this problem followed by farmers is to increase the use of nitrogen on that fraction of the farm least affected by problems of surface wetness. This practice requires particularly careful timing of applications, if loss through surface runoff is not to reduce benefits significantly. The net financial result is apparent in Figure 3, which shows a greater fraction of LFA land offering the poorest return.

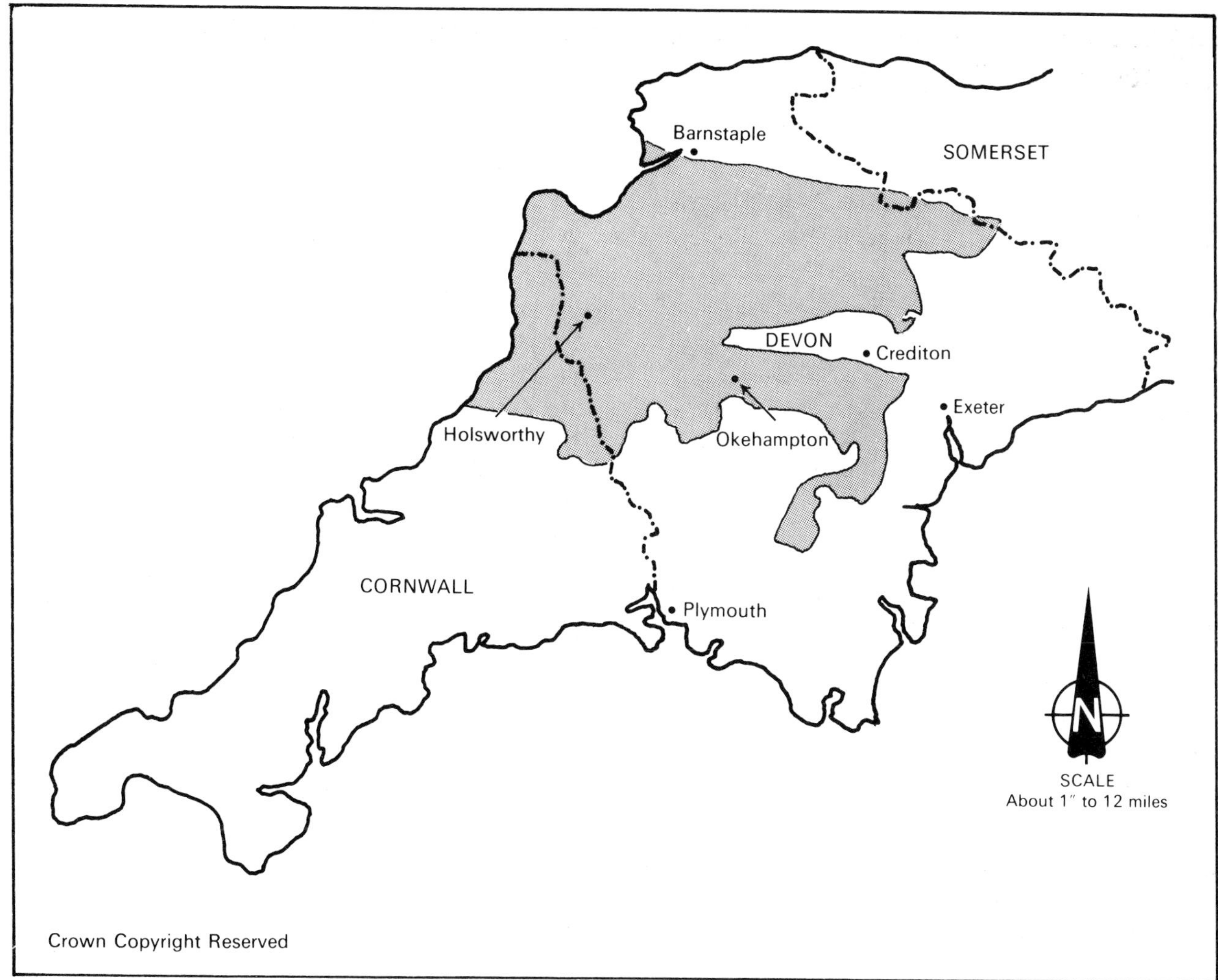

Figure 1. Map showing regional location of the Culm Measures

It would appear that these and other historical trends towards improving land management techniques have now resulted in LFA incomes being some 17% less than outside the LFA. However, this comparison may also be made in respect of potential incomes attainable if the land of the Culm were to be 'improved' through more economic use of nitrogen and judicious drainage and reseeding operations. Under these circumstances, it is apparent that the farms within the LFA have generally come close to exhausting their potential for economic improvements, given current prices and support measures. Improvement (mainly through reseeding rough grazing and a rather limited increase in nitrogen usage) might result in a 6–7% increase in farm income, whereas the farms outside the LFA exhibit a potential 20% increase (Table 1). This trend would appear to emphasize differences across the LFA boundary, with farm incomes falling to 73% of those outside.

Table 1. Mean net farm incomes (£) on the Culm Measures

	Current	After improvement	% increase
Inside LFA	6530 (±1021)	6963 (±903)	7
Outside LFA	7840 (±741)	9500 (±796)	21

Sample of 24 inside and 76 outside the LFA. Bracketed figures represent 95% confidence limits

Although the increase in income resulting from improvements was attributed only to increasing the farm stocking rates of beef and sheep (rather than dairy cattle or switching to arable), it seems fair to question the extent to which further production of these livestock products is likely to be acceptable at a time of national surplus.

The improvements shown to be economically and technically feasible would increase livestock production by about 20% overall (by about 17% in the LFA). This analysis further shows the poorer production return to investment in improvements within the LFA where the cost of increasing production by 17% results in a 6–7% increase in farm income.

It is within this agricultural context that the potential for forestry ought to be considered. Can the exploitation of existing farm woodlands and/or the afforestation of marginal agricultural land redress the balance between the LFA farms and those elsewhere? Can such measures serve to augment incomes to match those lost through a future moratorium on increased agricultural production?

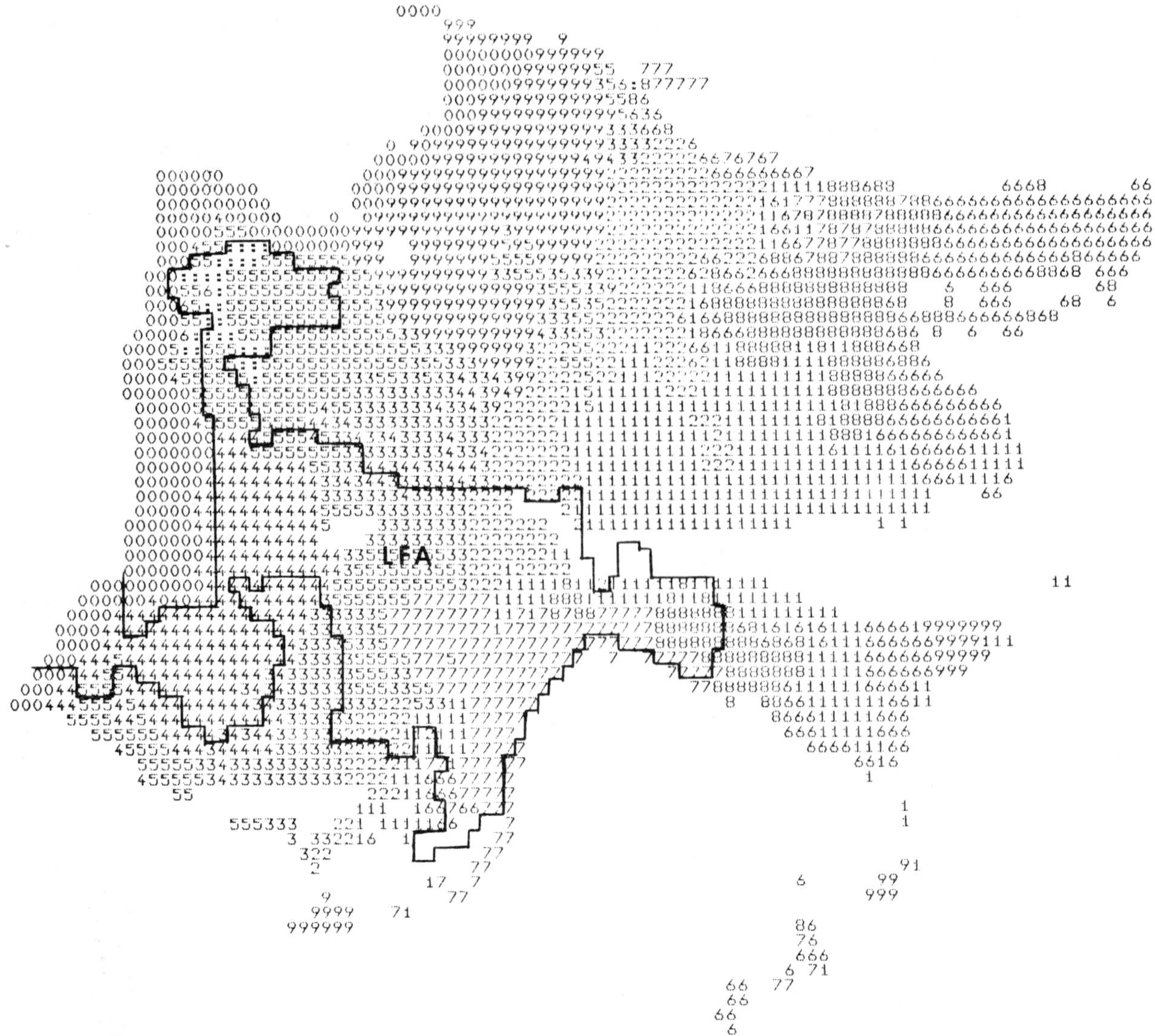

Figure 2. Map showing the location of land classes on the Culm Measures with boundary of the LFA

3 *Forestry on the Culm*

The 20 000 hectares of non-state woodlands on the Culm are characteristically scattered, small woods amounting on average to about 6% of the land area. The main woodland types are shown in Figure 4 and the distributions of the main woodland classes in Figure 5.

From analysis of the agricultural data produced by the study, it is apparent that farms within the extended LFA have, over the years, tended to exploit almost all available agricultural avenues to maintain or enhance their income. It is equally apparent that this strategy has had an impact on the woodlands of the area. In general, the farm woods within the LFA are less extensive, have a greater fraction classified as scrub, and a lower stocking rate on those areas where there is a timber crop. The implication to be drawn from these observations is that the response to agricultural pressures has tended to include the increased exploitation of farm woods as a capital resource, as a source of agricultural land by clearance, and as provision for stock shelter. This exploitation has had the effect of reducing the current value of these farm woods. The quantitative magnitude of the differences is seen in Table 2.

Clearly, management of existing farm woodlands can provide an income equivalent to that attainable through agricultural improvement within the LFA (cf Table 1), but such income is significantly less for the average farm outside the LFA. Thus, encouragement of farm forestry offers the prospect of alleviating the financial impact of a

Table 2. Estimates of the financial value of existing farm woods (£ per farm)

	Inside LFA	Outside LFA
Gross revenue (first 10 years)[1]	4 930	6 740
Net revenue (first 10 years)[2]	3 627	5 207
Net present value[3]	7 118	10 247
Annual equivalent income	356	512
% increase in current farm income	5.5	6.5

[1] Gross revenue includes grant aid as appropriate

[2] Costs exclude fiscal support

[3] NPV calculated at 5% with both grants and fiscal support included for the current crop and a complete rotation of a subsequent crop

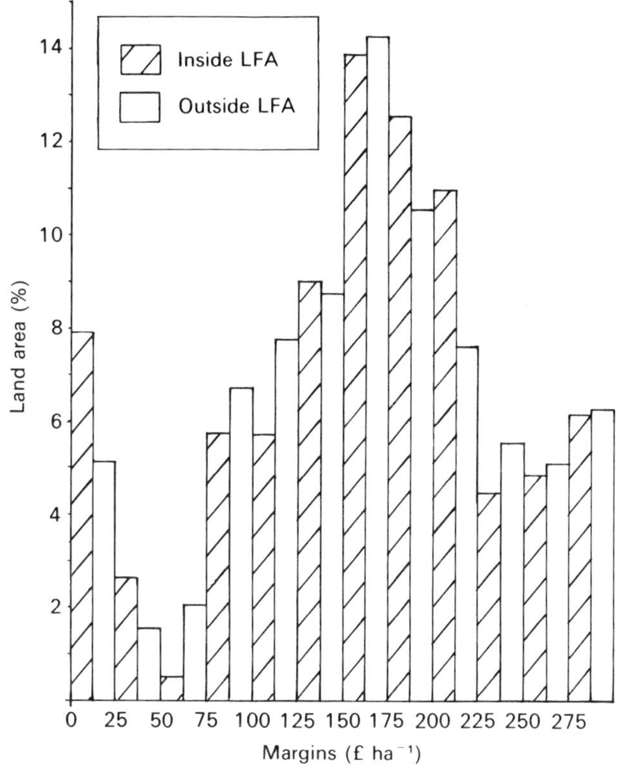

Figure 3. Net economic margins (including grants and subsidies) for agriculture on the Culm Measures

future moratorium on increasing agricultural production through land improvement.

4 *Afforestation*

A comparison of the relative financial performance of forestry with agriculture gives an indication of the total extent of economically afforestable land. This indication, too, is subject to various assumptions, particularly in respect of the provision of grants and fiscal support to forestry enterprises.

The model developed by the study identified a total of only 7150 ha (2.3%) of economically afforestable land in areas where existing designations (National Parks, Sites of Special Scientific Interest, etc) would not significantly affect a decision to plant conifers. This area is primarily determined by the limited extent of very poorly productive land on the Culm. Even the most high-yielding conifer crops do not offer an annual equivalent return of more than about £40 ha^{-1} and, consequently, their competitiveness is limited to agricultural land stocked at less than about 0.5 livestock units ha^{-1}.

It will be seen from an examination of Figure 3 that the economic potential for afforestation, given returns to agriculture, is limited to about 10.5% of the LFA and

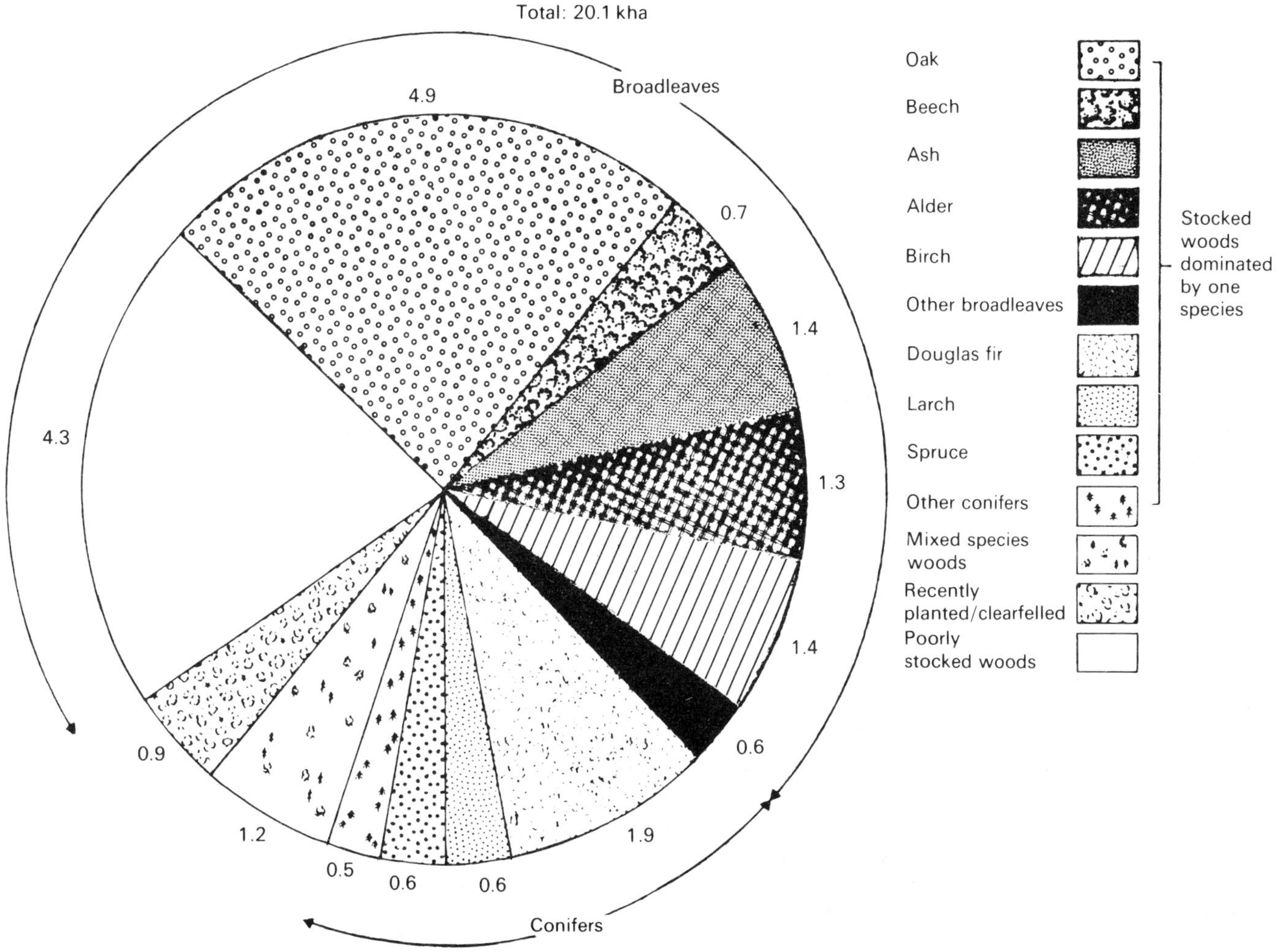

Figure 4. Area of woodland types on the Culm Measures

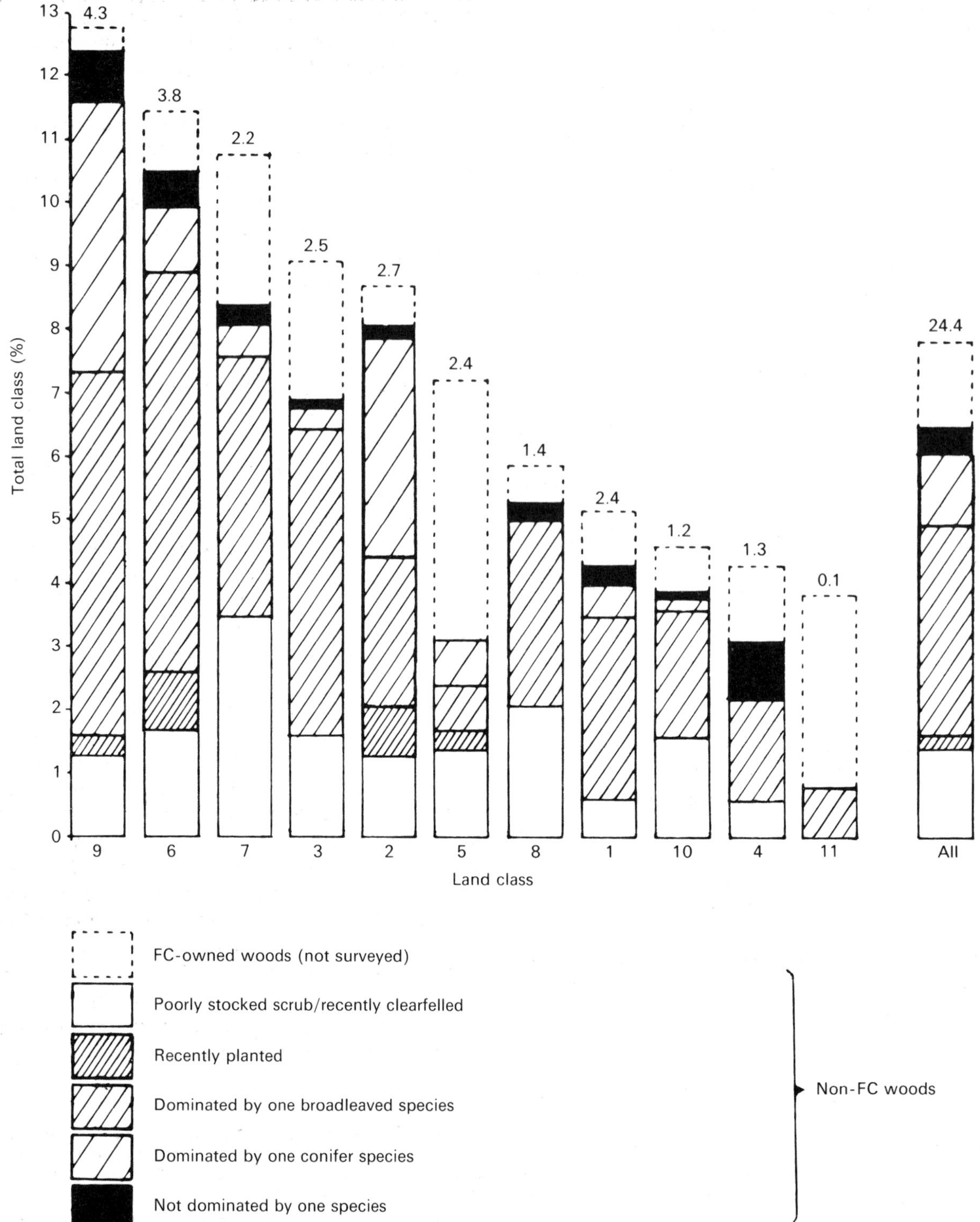

Figure 5. Distribution of main woodland classes on the Culm Measures (totals in figures, kha)

6.5% of the land outside the LFA (ie land showing a return of less than £50 ha^{-1} yr^{-1}). However, not all forestry enterprises or potential sites are capable of offering a return equivalent to the maximum that forestry may show on the Culm. Curtailed rotations due to the often high wind risk associated with plantable land severely reduce the economic potential for forestry, and this risk is particularly apparent within the LFA. The LFA is also characterized by the largest areas of 'designated' land on the Culm, and this designation, too, limits the potentially afforestable area. As a consequence, only about 2.6% of the LFA land shows an economic potential for afforestation (2.2% outside the LFA).

The exploitation of this potential by farmers would have little impact on their farm income, increasing it on average by about 0.2% net. However, equally, the loss of agricultural income would be vanishingly small, with the potential for afforestation limited to about one hectare of the poorest land on each farm. At such a scale, the capital investment required would be equally manageable (approximately £600 per farm after grants) and could

Table 3. Afforestation: area and costs

	Inside LFA	Outside LFA
Mean area per farm	1.34 ha	1.02 ha
Increase in farm income	£21 yr^{-1}	16 yr^{-1}
Net costs[1]	£675	£573

[1] Gross revenue includes grant aid as appropriate

generally be catered for by using the revenue which would result from the management of existing woods on the farm (Table 3).

5 *Labour, skills and expertise*

Past investigations seeking to establish the potential for farm forestry have invariably cited lack of time as a factor constraining the farmer from managing the woodlands on his farm. This study is no exception. However, it was equally clear that the farmers had little forestry knowledge to guide them in respect of management decisions affecting their woods. Their attitude would best be summed up as: '. . . I can and want to do it, but I don't actually know how and I haven't got the time anyway'.

6 *Conclusions*

The search for sources of alternative income capable of bolstering farm finances at a time of agricultural retrenchment has recently focused on forestry. In the context of a generally agriculturally productive area such as the Culm, it is the exploitation of the existing woodlands which is most promising, particularly where historic improvements have exhausted the farm's potential to increase income further.

However, there are many 'structural' aspects to be considered if encouragement is to be given to farm forestry in such areas.

7 *Scale and quality*

The limited extent, generally poor access and timber quality of farm woods combine to reduce the marketability of produce. The existing structure of the timber market is geared to exploiting economics of scale, and consequently it is very difficult to insert small farm woods into this framework. The solution would seem to be the development of sub-regional marketing agencies, linked to the provision of advice and, if necessary, contracting teams. In this way, it ought to be possible to market geographically associated lots in combination, having first advised and helped the owner with the devising and implementation of a management plan.

Adding value by harvesting and extracting timber can also serve to encourage interest from the existing timber market by limiting the contractor's costs to collection and haulage prior to processing. Many farmers do, in fact, have sufficient forestry equipment for such operations; most have a chainsaw and many have tractor-mounted winches that could be used for extraction.

8 *Financial incentives*

Although the calculated improvement in farm income through farm forestry included both grants and fiscal support, it is by no means clear that these support measures are overwhelmingly instrumental in affecting management decisions. The fiscal support particularly is pretty opaque to the farmer, who is generally unaware of the role that forestry could play in his tax affairs. The provision of an enhanced level of planting grant, equivalent to the current tax support on establishment and maintenance costs, would probably do much to increase interest and uptake of farm forestry.

There should also be recognition of the fact that many farm woods are of such low value that there is a net cost entailed in their initial management. Such costs may not be linked to replanting or the encouragement of natural regeneration. They might more generally be associated with a non-economic thinning coupled with scrub clearance to free a few reasonable trees. Under such circumstances, the current structures for forestry are of little benefit and could profitably be augmented with management grants for those woodlands where costs exceed revenue. Article 20 of EC Council Regulation 797/85 provides for such support, and its implementation by the UK could do much to encourage the management of lowland farm woods.

9 *References*

Bunce, R.G.H., Barr, C.J. & Whittaker H. 1984. A stratification system for ecological sampling. In: *Ecological mapping from ground, air and space*, edited R M Fuller, 39-46. (ITE symposium no. 10.) Cambridge: Institute of Terrestrial Ecology.

Carruthers, S.P., ed. 1986. *Alternative enterprises for agriculture in the UK*. Reading: Centre for Agricultural Strategy, University of Reading.

Dartington Institute. 1986. *The potential for forestry on the Culm Measures farms of south west England*. Totnes: Dartington Institute.

Prospects for people in the hills

M C WHITBY
Department of Agricultural Economics, University of Newcastle, Newcastle-upon-Tyne, England

1 Summary
The paper briefly lists the public agencies with an interest in stemming rural depopulation, and notes the main objective under which this goal is pursued through agricultural policy. It then examines the data on the structure of employment in the Less Favoured Areas (LFAs), and tentatively considers the cost-effectiveness of policies in stemming depopulation. Finally, it returns to consider the nature of the objective of such policies.

2 Agencies and policies
We have a large number of agencies and policies more or less committed to objectives of retaining people in rural Britain. A short list would include the Development Commission and Council for Small Industries in Rural Areas (in England), the Scottish and Welsh Development Agencies, the National Parks authorities, the Highlands and Islands Development Board, Mid-Wales Development, many local authorities, resource-based agencies such as the Forestry Commission, to say nothing of those with broader remits which range from the Countryside Commissions through the National Trusts to the Church of England.

In addition to that gallaxy of bodies, there is the European Community's (EC) Less Favoured Areas Directive (75/268), implementation of which is justified in the UK under Article 3(4) as:

'Less Favoured Areas in danger of depopulation: farming areas regional in character having permanent natural handicaps, essentially those of poor land where the potential for production cannot be increased except at excessive cost. To qualify, these areas must also show low productivity as reflected in crop yields or stocking of livestock and have a low population (or a dwindling one) whose economy is extensively dependent on agricultural activity.'

From this definition, I infer that the (at least implicit) objective of LFA policies is to retain populations in these sensitive areas. Our national enthusiasm for this objective alone leads us to direct some £143.1 million of agricultural public expenditure to policies in the LFAs, of £23.1M is recoverable from the EC (Ministry of Agriculture, which Fisheries & Food 1986). In addition to those direct injections, the LFAs also receive normal agricultural support worth £100M or so, and the markets for their store livestock are further enhanced by the price support systems applying to beef and sheepmeat.

Agriculture is not the sole direct beneficiary of such supports. Many other rural industries are supported in varying degrees. Forestry is one of the better-known land use alternatives within the LFAs. Recreation and tourism are encouraged in a variety of ways, through tourist boards, local authorities and the Countryside Commission. Manufacturing employment is also promoted, traditionally through the subsidized provision of premises, but also through training advice, favourable loans and other assistance. Perhaps service industries have received less public support, but many of these are in the public sector where subsidies (eg to rural health and education) are not separately identified. In the private sector, subsidies to services, such as shops, garages and pubs, are rare or non-existent. They survive depending on the economic situation of their customers.

3 Employment in the LFAs
Given the objective under which we are running LFA policies, it is notable that very few data are available to begin to indicate the success of these policies. Indeed, the Select Committee on Agriculture (1982) has produced a 2-volume report which tells us something about land use and agricultural public expenditure in the LFAs, but gives very few clues as to the economic structure of these areas. The Countryside Commission Uplands Debate (Countryside Commission 1983, 1984) produced little more of substance on these economies, because it concentrated on local land use issues rather than on people.

Department of Employment data, on employment and unemployment, are available at the level of employment exchange areas, and these provide an approximate basis for examining the structure of LFAs. Naturally, the LFA boundary does not follow those of employment exchange areas, so we either have an awkward estimation problem to convert the data to the same areal basis or we may exclude data from those areas which cross the LFA boundary. Following the latter expedient excludes rather more of the LFA in England than in Scotland and Wales, and may thus introduce a slightly distorted picture. It will also underestimate total employment in the LFAs. The resulting pattern of employment is compared with that for Great Britain in Table 1.

The data here relate to *hired* workers and exclude the self-employed. The industries which have a large self-employed component in their work force (particularly agriculture, but also construction and distribution, for example) will thus be comparatively under-represented

Table 1. Percentage distribution of employment in all employment exchange (EE) areas wholly within the LFAs, compared with Great Britain (source: Department of Employment)

Industrial sectors	EE areas wholly within the LFA boundary 1971	1981	Great Britain Total 1971	1981
Agriculture, forestry, fishing	5.7	4.8	1.9	1.6
Mining	7.1	6.2	1.8	1.6
Food, drink and tobacco	2.4	2.0	3.4	3.0
Coal, petrol and chemical products	3.4	2.3	2.2	2.0
Metal manufacture	4.6	2.0	2.6	1.5
Engineering	9.5	8.9	16.5	13.2
Textiles	6.4	4.6	4.9	3.0
Other manufacturing	2.6	3.8	6.9	5.6
Construction	6.6	6.0	5.7	5.3
Gas, electricity and water	1.7	1.8	1.7	1.6
Transport and communications	6.4	5.7	7.1	6.7
Distributive trades	9.0	10.0	11.8	12.7
Financial, professional and misc. services	25.6	33.7	26.7	35.4
Public administration and defence	7.0	8.0	6.8	6.6
Unclassified	0.0	0.2	0.0	0.2
Total	100.0	100.0	100.0	100.0

here. If we assume that there are 2 farmers per hired worker in LFA agriculture (Laxton & Whitby 1986), then the percentage of the work force accounted for by agriculture would be roughly trebled. However, this figure would still only represent 15% of the work force, which raises questions as to the dependence of these economies on agriculture. Such questions may be countered with semantic arguments about the meaning of the definitions applied. Nevertheless, it cannot be denied that these regional economies, although they are comparatively more dependent on agriculture than the rest of the country, still derive most of their employment from other sectors. Half of the 15 sectors listed in Table 1 account for more hired workers than agriculture.

Such data also offer some shreds of evidence on the possible growth sectors in the LFAs. These sectors can best be gleaned from the more detailed industrial breakdown displayed in Table 2. Here, we see that agriculture, forestry and fishing are all substantially more important in the LFAs than in Great Britain, though their share of employment is declining at about the same rate. The pattern is more mixed for the sectors connected with leisure and services where some growth has occurred. Thus, employment in cinemas and sport is low in the LFAs. Employment in hotels is very much more than in Great Britain; in restaurants, the percentage is the same as for Great Britain, whereas for pubs it is much lower. Retailing seems somewhat under-represented in the LFAs, but this situation might be corrected or even reversed by inclusion of the self-employed in retailing, who would undoubtedly be more important, because of the smaller average size of establishment in the LFAs. Perhaps the most significant finding from this rather partial examination of the data is the considerable and growing importance of employment in hotels: another sector in which self-employment will be particularly important. Indeed, sport, restaurants, pubs and other retailing have evidently increased their share of activity in the LFAs over this period.

Table 2. Percentage of total employment in selected industries, in all employment exchange (EE) areas within the LFAs compared with Great Britain (source: Department of Employment)

Industries	EE areas wholly within the LFA boundary 1971	1981	Great Britain Total 1971	1981
Agriculture	5.07	4.14	1.82	1.53
Forestry	0.56	0.50	0.06	0.06
Fishing	0.04	0.12	0.05	0.03
Cinemas	0.25	0.14	0.46	0.46
Sport	0.25	0.53	0.35	0.66
Hotels	2.93	3.79	1.01	1.24
Restaurants	0.74	0.90	0.70	0.88
Public houses	0.38	0.62	0.80	1.10
Retail food	3.19	2.91	2.75	2.72
Other retailing	4.26	4.56	5.50	5.85
Total	17.67	18.21	13.50	14.53

Despite the data in Tables 1 and 2, we still do not know the absolute numbers of workers in key industries in the LFAs: other sources must be examined. According to the Select Committee (1982), there were some 50 000 beneficiaries of Hill Livestock Compensatory Allowances in the late 1970s. Taking this figure to be equivalent to the number of farmers, we should increase it by 50% to include the hired workers in LFA agriculture, giving a total estimate of 75 000. Spread over the 6.3 Mha of the LFA used for agriculture, this would imply an average rate of employment of one person 87 ha^{-1}. The same source estimates forestry employment within the LFA as 12 500, which accounts for some two-thirds of the national (UK) employment in forestry. On the 1.25 Mha of forest in the LFA (Select Committee 1982), this is an average rate of employment of one man 100 ha^{-1}. With these estimates in mind, we may turn to examine the cost-effectiveness of LFA policies to retain people in the hills.

4 *Policy effectiveness*

Agriculture is not the sole beneficiary of public support, neither is it able to retain all of the value of the financial injections it receives, as income. Part of it goes to the suppliers of inputs and factors; part of it becomes capitalized into asset values (including flocks and herds, as well as land), and some of it returns to the exchequer in the form of tax. So, the exchequer cost is a rather crude indication of our collective wish to persuade hill farmers (and their workers) to stay in the LFAs.

Taking LFA objectives at face value, the success of the payments in stemming rural depopulation may be divided into their total cost to yield a financial cost-effectiveness criterion for the policy. The key question then is 'how many people are retained in the hills by the level of LFA payments?' The concept implied here is called 'additionality', and it is used quite generally in assessing the impact of job generation schemes. Where, for example, a factory is set up, then its direct additionality is the number employed in it minus those who would have been employed elsewhere, had the factory not existed, and any jobs lost due to competition with the new factory. In the case of agriculture, it would obviously be unrealistic to claim that all the people employed (and self-employed) in hill farming are only kept there by these subsidies. If the LFA subsidies were removed, how many people would remain in hill farming? The number of farmers plus regular workers engaged in hill farming in the north of England was recently estimated (Laxton & Whitby 1986) to be declining, at about 1–1.5% per annum over the last 20 years, which compares with steeper rates outside the LFA. If the LFA payments were not made, then it might reasonably be argued that the rate of decline would be substantially steeper.

Total agricultural employment in the LFAs was estimated above to be 75 000. Suppose we assume that 25–50% of this number are retained in the hills by the LFA payments. As long as the discussion is restricted to LFA payments alone, this seems a reasonable range: if it was considered to remove the other agricultural payments from which these farmers also benefit, then a greater fraction might be appropriate. The range in average annual per capita exchequer cost to the UK would then be £3,000 to £6,000 per annum. Such estimates may seem high in relation to average per capita incomes, but a more relevant comparison is with the cost of retaining upland populations by other methods.

To carry out precisely comparable arithmetic for forestry is much more complex, mainly because of the long production cycle in that industry. Neither do we know what proportion of the 12 500 people (Select Committee 1982) directly employed are attributable to the public subsidies to forestry. Planting grants paid this year will generate employment over a long period, but it will be concentrated at the felling stage. Furthermore, conversion of land from agriculture to forestry involves removal of agricultural labour as well as the creation of forest employment. As for managing the existing plantation, it would be appropriate to relate the current employment it provides to the accumulated subsidies of past years which have produced this work. The data requirements of such an exercise would be substantial and are beyond the scope of this paper. Suffice it to note that, where forestry has eliminated agricultural employment, its performance as a job creator is diminished to that extent. On the other hand, employment in forestry could increase over the next decade or 2 as the existing plantation matures. Whether the employment actually appears or not will depend on a number of issues, such as the rate of mechanization of felling, the extent to which contract labour is used, and so on. The potential of some further employment generation exists, but the extent of its realization is a matter of choice.

More difficult to ascertain is the extent to which forestry employment contributes to the retention of population in rural areas. Because forestry and agriculture are practised as mutually exclusive land uses, then more employment in one must mean less in the other. On balance, the impact on employment of switching land from agriculture to forestry varies widely. Thus, Laxton and Whitby found that, over a whole rotation, there would be a gain in employment from planting in Northumberland but losses in Cumbria and the north-central Pennines. It may be the case that there is more net employment to be gained from planting as we move north through Scotland. If forestry brings net gains in employment, then the annual loss it makes could be divided by the number to produce a 'financial cost per job'. However, if forest planting produced a net loss of jobs, but a financial gain, we could still measure the analogue of 'cost per job' as 'gain per job lost'. Where both jobs are lost and financial gains are negative, the situation becomes problematic: costs are incurred per job lost. The range of possibilities is displayed diagrammatically in Figure 1.

Plate 4. Biomass harvester developed by the Bord na Móna, Eire (Photograph Bord na Móna)

Plate 5. Delivery of wood gathered and processed by a purpose-designed biomass harvester (Photograph Bord na Móna)

Plate 6. Scottish border landscape steadings at about 220 m with large fields of improved grassland immediately adjacent to semi-natural hill grasses. Land class 20 in the sampling system discussed by Bell *et al.* (Photograph S Warnock)

Plate 7. Exmoor: technically improvable moorland but where heather cover is desirable. ITE has advised on vegetation management techniques and farmers have entered into contracts to produce a specific landscape (Photograph S Warnock)

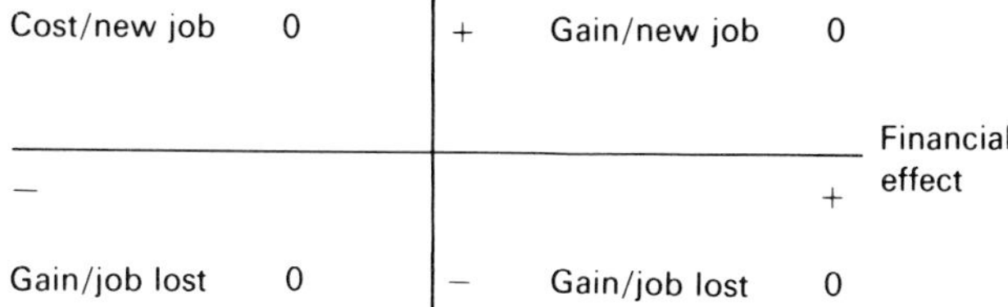

Figure 1. Range of possibilities for forestry employment and cost.

To reach conclusions about the average financial impact per net job change from conversion to forestry thus requires knowledge or assumptions about the effect of past decisions, over several decades, and levels of financial deficit, which are simply not available. In the past, such calculations have been made (HM Treasury 1972) on the basis of individual plantations, but not for the national forest estate as a whole. The calculations carried out at that time were compared with other forms of employment generation in a later report (HM Treasury 1975). In the studies reported, costs per job in forestry were much greater than the others in agriculture which, in turn, were larger than those in the manufacturing and service sectors.

Evidence on the cost per job in manufacturing over the years has been collected together (Whitby 1985) and indicates a range for rural areas of £4,500 to £6,000 per job over a 10-year period at 1985 prices. To convert to the same basis as the agricultural estimate, the costs could be annuitized (at 5%) to give 466–661 per job per year.

These more or less crude calculations suggest that support for agriculture is not the cheapest method of retaining rural populations, though past estimates confirm the cruder estimates here in indicating that it is more cost-effective in that regard than forestry.

5 *Objectives again*

What is the real justification for this concern? Why do we want to see the hills populated? A number of arguments could be adduced here. Historically, one can see a 'territorial imperative' (Ardrey 1967) at work in humans, just as in animals. Migrations have been associated with various kinds of violence and, as such, are to be distrusted, if not discouraged. A closely related attitude is the notion that people have an innate right to live where they were born. Note, however, that men *are* allowed to marry women from elsewhere; couples may settle near the home of one or other without ruffling too many feathers. Perhaps the mating imperative has to accommodate the territorial imperative! The psychic importance of place as part of the individual's personal identity kit is a theme which has been treated by many writers.

Yet the universal relevance of that value is challenged by the fact that many people, probably the majority in this country, do not live at their birth place for their whole lives. Indeed, the migration question of the 1981 population census (Davis 1983) indicated that more than 5 million people (9.6% of the UK population) changed address during the single year prior to census night. Further analysis (Brant 1984) shows that, whilst 81% of these migrations were within a region, 70% were within counties and 57% within districts. The majority of moves, particularly within urban areas, are over short distances (less than 10 km). Excluding these from the argument would still leave more than 2% of the total population moving longer distances within each year. Thus, the individual would move to a new address more than 10 km away on *average* every 50 years: that is at least once within a normal life expectancy.

Perhaps the objective is not one of territoriality but rather one of populating the countryside, irrespective of ethnic origins. If that is so, it is mere numbers of people that are needed and policy instruments should focus on the cheapest way of promoting a net return migration to rural areas. That would be a very different policy from the ethnic/territorial approach. It would be much cheaper and would certainly produce a different social ambience.

These alternative views of the LFA policy goals have been distinguished because each would imply different implementation. If the policies are responding to the innate wishes of people to live where they are born, then the very high rates of mobility detected by the population census might lead us to ask whether most people are so inflexible about where they choose to live. Also, does the electorate really have an obligation to satisfy such costly minority aspirations? On the other hand, if we wish to have people in the countryside for whatever reasons, then it is a somewhat simpler matter to adjust the incentives to produce the desired result. Such discussion may seem dangerously near to social engineering, but that is what the planning system is at least partly about. Perhaps we should recognize what we are doing, in the hope of achieving the desired result more effectively.

6 *Conclusion*

Despite the fact that we have designated our Less Favoured Areas under the definition which refers to the danger of rural depopulation, we do not, in fact, know either the present size of their population or the rate or manner in which it is changing. In such a context, the evidence on the impact of public policies in such areas is somewhat tenuous. The calculations above are, therefore, offered with some diffidence. It should also be borne in mind that they only tell part of the relevant story in that they refer to exchequer costs and not to the broader, more relevant, concepts of economic costs and benefits. The latter are much more difficult to measure and there are no recent estimates available for primary industries.

Nevertheless, this examination of the cost-effectiveness of job generation does raise important questions for the objectives of LFA policies. Although the objective relates directly to numbers of people alone, there are strong implications of territorial habits being reinforced by these policies. If that were not the case, the alternative of retaining rural populations by the cheapest means of providing employment (probably in factories) would be attractive.

7 *Acknowledgements*

The author is grateful to Dr Caroline Saunders for assistance in preparing the data reported and careful comments on the text. Errors remain his own.

8 *References*

Ardrey, R. 1967. *The territorial imperative.* London: Collins.

Brant, J. 1984. Patterns of migration from the 1981 census. *Popul. Trends,* no. 35.

Countryside Commission. 1983. *What future for the uplands?* (CCP 149.) Cheltenham: CC.

Countryside Commission. 1984. *A better future for the uplands.* (CCP 162.) Cheltenham: CC.

Davis, T. 1983. People changing address: 1971 and 1981. *Popul. Trends,* no. 32.

HM Treasury. 1972. *Forestry in Great Britain: an inter-departmental cost benefit study.* London: HMSO.

HM Treasury. 1975. *Rural depopulation appendices.* London: HMSO.

Laxton, H. & Whitby, M.C. 1986. *Employment in forestry in the northern region.* Newcastle-upon-Tyne: Agricultural Environment Research Group, The University.

Ministry of Agriculture, Fisheries & Food. 1986. *Annual Review of Agriculture.* (Cmnd 9708.) London: HMSO.

Select Committee on Agriculture. 1982. *Financial policy of the EEC, of member states and, as appropriate, of other countries, in relation to agriculture, with particular reference to poultry, horticulture, eggs and less favoured areas.* (First Report, 1981-82, Volumes I and II.) London: HMSO.

Whitby, M.C. 1985. Job creation costs and benefits: a rural to urban spectrum. *J. agric. Econ.,* **36,** 93-95.

Hill weed compensatory allowances: very alternative crops for the uplands

G J LAWSON
Institute of Terrestrial Ecology, Merlewood Research Station, Grange-over-Sands, Cumbria, England

Aur dan y rhedyn
Arian dan yr eithyn
Newyn dan y grug

A saying of Welsh hill farmers meaning 'Gold under bracken, silver under gorse, famine under heather' (Condry 1966)

1 *Summary*
UK agriculture receives £2.2 billion in subsidies, and various forms of price support permit more than one Mha in the UK to produce food which is surplus to current requirements. Rather than paying grants to drain bogs or control bracken (*Pteridium aquilinum*), it seems possible to introduce a hill weed compensatory allowance (HWCA) to permit farming to continue in the uplands, in a manner that contributes to conservation, and assists fuel rather than food production.

The potential production of biofuels in the UK is examined, and it is suggested that a number of productive weeds like bracken, gorse (*Ulex europaeus*), broom (*Cytisus scoparius*), laurel (*Prunus* spp.) and rhododendron (*Rhododendron ponticum*) could be exploited as energy crops. Some weed species increase soil fertility, or are particularly well adapted to growth in the shade. It is suggested that they could be planted as a coppiced energy crop beneath pruned and widely spaced plantations of light-demanding trees like larch (*Larix* spp.), pine (*Pinus* spp.), or ash (*Fraxinus excelsior*). Co-production of food, fuel and timber would be termed 'agrenforestry'.

2 *Introduction*
Grants of up to 60% of improvement costs are available from the Ministry of Agriculture, Fisheries and Food in the Agricultural Improvement Scheme under 67 headings ranging from 'aprons' to 'yards'. Hill livestock compensatory allowances (HLCA) of up to £62.48 ha^{-1} are payable in Less Favoured Areas, and can be payable on land planted with trees for 15 (soon to be 20) years after the last animal was removed. Grants totalling around £6 million are imminent as a payment for desisting from 'improvement' in Environmentally Sensitive Areas (Beard 1987). The Countryside Commission pays £1.75 M for amenity tree planting (Taylor 1987), and financial and fiscal subsidies for forestry may total around £30 M (Stirling-Aird 1987).

Also, there are the payments for price support and market regulation. Net farming income (NFI) first fell below the level of obvious subsidies in 1983 (Figure 1), and in 1985 the apparent agricultural deficit had widened to £1,060 M (Table 1). Farm incomes were atypically low in 1985, but no account has been taken in these figures of hidden payments to farmers, like tax concessions and free Agriculture Development Advisory Service (ADAS) advice. Furthermore, the use of NFI, rather than management and investment income, makes no allowance for the labour provided by the farmer and his family.

The 1985 figures in Table 1 represent an average subsidy of £58.45 ha^{-1} yr^{-1} on agricultural land (excluding woodlands), and an annual payment of £7,612 to each full-time or part-time farmer.

Given such munificence, what possible objection could there be to paying farmers to grow weeds? Such a payment could fit into Articles 15, 19 or 20 of the European Community (EC) Structures Regulation

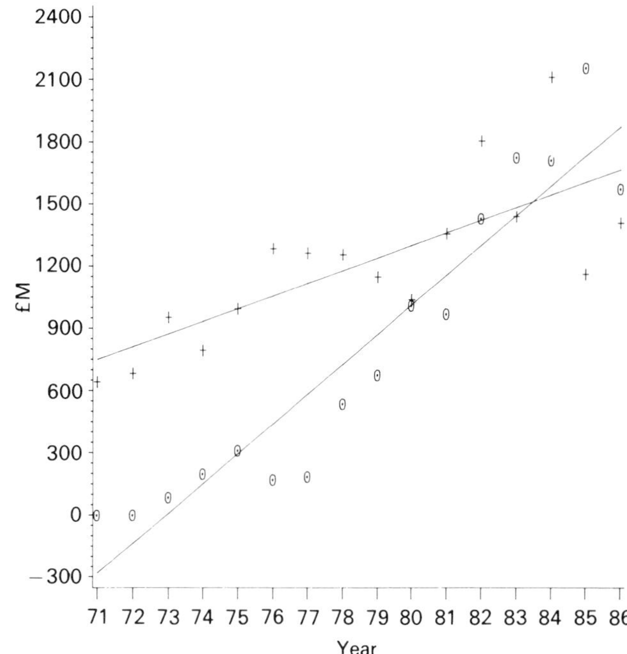

Figure 1. Changes in the relationship between net farming income (+) and Government support to agriculture (0) (source: MAFF, DAFS & DANI 1986)

Table 1. Support to UK agriculture (£M) (source: MAFF, DAFS & DANI 1986)

	1983	1985
CAP market regulation	1,374	1,893
Support for special areas	123	141
Capital and other improvement grants	221	145
Price guarantees	10	8
Total	1,729	2,215
Net farming income	1,508	1,154

(797/85), but Article 20 (Pilot schemes) would probably be the most appropriate. Necessary payments could be given the title 'hill weed compensatory allowance'.

The agricultural surpluses of the EC should be contrasted with the fact that 60% of the timber volume and 45% of the fuel used in the Community must be imported. Clearly, the current use of rural land is not based on sound economics. Yet it is unlikely that the free trade lobby (Howarth 1985) will achieve a significant reduction in the grant support given to rural communities. The farm impoverishment thesis, which propounds price controls as the main check on levels of production, seems even to have lost backing within the present Government. Agricultural subsidies will, therefore, continue as a means of social support, but this paper suggests that they should be partially diverted towards non-food crops. A hill weed compensatory allowance could make these alternative land uses viable on a proportion of the land (up to 2.6 Mha in some estimates (Brown 1987)), which may be 'set aside' from UK agriculture.

3 *Fundamental uses of land*

There are 4 fundamental uses of rural land:

- food (animal or vegetable)
- fibre (animal or vegetable)
- fuel
- pharmaceuticals

and a fifth use, fun, which incorporates a number of minor uses like fell-walking and field-sports.

Whilst this publication deals principally with the first 'f', farming for food, this paper will concentrate on the potential of a HWCA to stimulate the production of indigenous biofuel. Brief mention will also be made of the potential use of weeds as a source of chemical raw material.

4 *Growing a chemical feedstock*

Until displaced by coal and oil, all organic chemicals were made from biomass. The change took place because of the high and unstable price of biomass, and its dispersed and unreliable availability. Today, many of these factors have changed. In the developed world, plant products (like sugar, soya oil or fuelwood) are cheaper, relative to other raw materials, than they have been at any time this century. Industrial-grade ethanol can be fermented from sugar or grain crops at a price which is comparable with alcohol produced from petroleum. Direct polymerization of lactic acid, and acetic acid fermentation products offer theoretical advantages over the routes using ethanol. The dehydration of lactic acid, for example, could lead the way to cheaper production of acrylics (Sheppard & Lipinsky 1983). Many chemicals could, therefore, be produced more cheaply using the organic acid building blocks contained in biomass, rather than synthesizing them from simple hydrocarbons contained in petroleum. The technology used to produce industrial chemicals is only now improving on techniques which were available before the oil boom (Overend *et al.* 1985). In the long term, therefore, biochemical production may come to be viewed as a more valuable use for biomass than biofuel production.

5 *Biofuel production*

5.1 Theoretical potential

The total primary productivity of UK terrestrial vegetation is estimated to be 252 million tonnes of dry matter (Mt)[1]. This figure is an average of 10.5 t ha^{-1} yr^{-1}, of which above-ground production represents 6.9 t ha^{-1} yr^{-1}. Within these totals, intensive agriculture contributes 60%, productive woodland 8%, natural vegetation 26% and urban vegetation 5%. However, only 25% of total plant production is cropped by man and animals, and most of this is subsequently discarded as wastes and residues (Lawson & Callaghan 1983).

Dry biomass contains an average of 18 Gigajoules (GJ)[2] per tonne, compared with approximately 26 GJ and 42 GJ in a tonne of coal and oil respectively. If the annual growth of all vegetation in the UK were to be harvested for energy purposes, the yield would be 2.97 Exajoules (EJ)[3] of energy equivalent, compared to the 1985 UK energy demand of 8.8 EJ. It is hardly practical to use every blade of grass in Britain for energy, so another scenario is presented (Table 2), based on the complete utilization of natural vegetation, wastes, residues and catch crops. This option is purely theoretical, but it suggests that a maximum of 2.11 EJ could be harvested annually, whilst sustaining current levels of agricultural and timber production.

Coming closer to a realistic assessment of the future impact of biofuels is a recent collaborative study, based on the Institute of Terrestrial Ecology's Merlewood land classification (Mitchell *et al.* 1984), in which 6 institutes co-operated to predict the comparative profitability of a number of land uses on statistically selected areas of land throughout the country. The uses considered were: agriculture, conventional forestry, energy forestry, and a modified form of forestry which maximizes the utilization of residues. A wide range of agricultural and forestry costs and returns was modelled, together with several scenarios for movements in energy prices and discount

[1] Unless otherwise mentioned, yield figures refer to above-ground dry weights
[2] One Gigajoule = 109 joules
[3] One Exajoule = 1018 joules

Table 2. Maximum biomass resources available whilst maintaining current levels of food and timber production (source: Lawson & Callaghan 1983)

Type of biomass	Energy content (PJ)
Natural vegetation	700
Catch fuel crops	382
Crop residues and wastes	234
Industrial and commercial refuse	221
Domestic refuse	170
Urban vegetation	152
Dual-purpose crops	80
Sewage sludge	29
Forest residues and thinnings	34
Seaweed and freshwater weeds	8
Total	2121

PJ, Petajoule = 10^{15} Joules; 1 Mt coal equivalent = 26.9 PJ; 1 Mt oil equivalent = 49.9 PJ

rates. Constraints on a change of land use were imposed in sensitive areas like National Parks. The results from a central set of assumptions (Table 3) show that up to 4.6 Mha would, at 1977 prices, be more profitably used in energy forestry or in the dual production of timber and fuelwood from residues.

5.2 Energy from trees

Typically, around one-third of the weight of a tree is contained in its stem. The remainder is contained in unharvested portions of lop, top and stump. During the past 10–15 years, rapid technical progress has taken place to increase the recovery of these felling residues. North American whole-tree chipping uses mainly feller-bunchers, skidders and heavy landing chippers; the European approach employs manual felling, forwarder transport and truck-mounted landing chippers. Slash may be chipped with special chippers or crushers; or tree sections may be hauled to the mill and then processed to recover a mixture of bark and branch biomass for fuel. Continuous swath harvestors are being designed to recover slash and small-diameter coppice (Plates 4 & 5). Stump extraction is also an increasingly common part of intensive harvesting.

Using the central economic assumptions in the land availability study (Anon 1984), 8 Mm^3 is the maximum 'economic' annual yield of residues which can be achieved from modified forestry in Britain (Table 3). This figure compares to estimates of annually recoverable wood residues in the United States of 170 Mm^3 (Erickson 1975), and in Finland of 15.3 Mm^3 (Hakkila 1984). In Sweden, around 13 Mm^3 of thinnings, lop and top are currently available, but this figure would increase to 28 Mm^3 if felling techniques were modified to maximize the recovery of residues (Hakkila 1985).

Energy coppice has been investigated in temperate regions principally using clones of fast-growing species like willow (*Salix* spp.), poplar (*Populus* spp.), alder (*Alnus* spp.), eucalyptus (*Eucalyptus* spp.) and sycamore (*Acer pseudoplatanus*). Its potential in the UK will be principally in the lowlands, but it was estimated in the land availibility study that 300 000 ha of high-grade pasture could profitably be replaced by fast-growing coppice. A reduction in agricultural subsidies would increase the area of land which could be used for energy coppicing, but this increase has not been quantified.

The best UK study of energy coppice comes from Northern Ireland (McElroy & Dawson 1986), where annual yields of 12–15 t ha^{-1} have been achieved over a 9-year rotation of *Salix* x *'Aquatica-gigantea'* (a clonal willow). These experiments were performed on surface mineral-gley soils, which are marginal for agriculture. Nutrients were conserved by harvesting after leaf-fall, but nitrogen fertilizer did produce a 17% increase in yield. However, the value of this increase in production did not offset the cost of fertilizer application. It is interesting to note that the energy output from these experiments is 136 GJ ha^{-1} yr^{-1}, compared with a net energy output (utilizable metabolic energy) from grass on comparable land used for beef production of 40 GJ ha^{-1} yr^{-1}.

The UK Department of Energy have estimated that fuelwood consumption could increase from 10.4 PJ[4] at present (0.12% of gross energy consumption), to 17.5 PJ by the year 2000. This prediction assumes a continuation of current trends of agricultural and wood production; radical policy changes in favour of forestry or bioenergy production were not considered (Price & Mitchell 1985).

More than 500 000 wood-burning appliances are installed in Britain (Stevens 1984), but many of these are now fueled by coal or anthracite because of difficulties in obtaining and storing a reliable supply of fuelwood. Yet these supply problems are not universal. ADAS in Lancashire, for example, has established a scheme which induced local stove-owners to form a 'co-operative' market for fuel from an area of derelict farm woodland. The householders were guaranteed a regular supply of

[4]One Petajoule = 10^{15} joules

Table 3. Potential areas of land to be used for energy forestry, and its production before (and after) considerations of non-agricultural land uses (source: Mitchell *et al.* 1983)

Forest system	Area (Mha)	Weight (Mt)	Volume (Mm^3)
Modified conventional forestry	2.90 (1.1)	16.0 (7)	28 (11)
Single stem	1.15 (0.4)	14.0 (4)	No timber
Coppice	0.65 (0.3)	8.0 (5)	No timber
Total	4.60 (1.8)	38.0 (16)	28 (11)

seasoned wood, which they could collect as required, and the farmer gained a reliable market (Scott *et al.* 1986).

Mention should be made of the possible exploitation for fuelwood and timber of hardwood species, like birch (*Betula* spp.) and aspen (*Populus tremula*), which are currently regarded as little more than weeds. Birch woods covered 170 000 ha, or 42% of our hardwood forests in 1965 (Phillip 1978), but by the 1979–82 census their contribution had decreased to only 17.5%. Breeding and selection are proceeding to improve the form of birch (Brown 1983), and it is hoped that greater use can be made in the future of the latent advantages of this species, including rapid juvenile growth, self-thinning, and a good tolerance of infertile conditions. In catchments which are suffering the effects of acid rain, birch woods will be much preferable to conifers, because they develop a mull humus, with increased pH, more exchangeable cations and higher earthworm (Lumbricidae) populations (Miles 1986). Natural or artificial mixtures of conifers with birch or aspen are serious sylvicultural practices in central Europe and Scandinavia (Hagglund & Peterson 1985). These broadleaved mixtures are more difficult to manage in Britain than monocultures of Sitka spruce (*Picea sitchensis*), but there are likely to be areas in the uplands where improved strains of birch and hybrid aspen could be used successfully in mixture with conifers. Such mixtures would be very likely to benefit wildlife.

5.3 Energy from non-woody plants

Biofuel production strategies for herbaceous vegetation in the UK were studied in a number of reports commissioned by the Department of Energy (see Lawson & Callaghan 1983). Most options considered, such as energy catch crops or sugar beet production, do not relate to the uplands, but one feasible use of the most productive upland vegetation is as an 'opportunity energy crop', which could be exploited without planting effort.

Bracken provides an example of a productive native species, which, although an unpleasant agricultural weed, has the potential to become a viable energy crop (Lawson *et al.* 1986). It is thought to cover in excess of 300 000 ha in Britain, although one estimate puts the extent as high as 591 000 ha (Taylor 1985). Above-ground yields of 11 t ha^{-1} yr^{-1} have been recorded, and a sustained harvesting trial recorded an average 7 t ha^{-1} yr^{-1} during 4 successive years of cutting.

The pedogenic effect of this much criticized weed is important, although understudied. The high potassium content in bracken fronds has long been recognized, and they were the feedstock for potash-extracting kilns which supplied the soap and glass industries. Nutrient uptake rates in a bracken sward can be higher than in many woodlands, particularly for potassium (Table 4). It has also been shown in experimental leaching studies that bracken has a considerable ability to mobilize organic and inorganic phosphates (Mitchell 1973). It is, therefore, suggested that, rather than being a curse which occupies the best land on many upland hills, bracken is, in fact, the cause of much of this fertility. A lack of available phosphorus can limit tree growth in many upland areas, and there may be an advantage in allowing the bracken cover to remain beneath widely spaced light-demanding trees like pine, larch or ash.

Bracken could be harvested as an energy crop in summer, when its high moisture content would indicate anaerobic digestion as the most favourable energy conversion route. Later in the year, it could be harvested as a crop with a moisture content of 40% or less, requiring less drying before compression into briquettes and pellets, or thermochemical conversion to a variety of flammable gases and liquids such as methanol. These processes are described elsewhere (Lawson *et al.* 1984), and some preliminary calculations of the potential profitability of bracken are given in Table 5. With the given assumptions, a farmer collecting and briquetting his own bracken could produce a convenience fuel for the local market for around £55 t^{-1} (1983 prices). On a

Table 4. Annual nutrient uptake (g m^{-2}) and percentage returned in the annual litterfall in various ecosystems (source: Sponder 1979)

		Nitrogen	Potassium	Phosphorus	Calcium
Heather	Uptake	2.32	0.10	0.61	0.75
	Litter	110	130	33	57
Bracken	Uptake	13.4	1.0	21.3	1.35
	Litter	82	60	11	96
Scots pine	Uptake	13.9	1.1	5.8	5.6
	Litter	90	91	98	87
Beech	Uptake	7.2	0.5	4.6	3.3
	Litter	74	88	48	45
Mixed oak (*Quercus* spp.)	Uptake	9.2	0.7	6.9	20.1
	Litter	67	68	77	63
Oak/birch	Uptake	8.4	0.7	2.6	2.9
	Litter	83	75	75	72

Table 5. Costings per tonne of bracken (20 GJ or 3.4 barrels equivalent), assuming yields of 6 t ha^{-1} yr^{-1} for direct burning and gasification, or 8 t ha^{-1} yr^{-1} for anaerobic digestion (1983 prices) (source: Lawson *et al.* 1986)

	Direct burning	Gasification to methanol	Anaerobic digestion to methane
Cutting and collection	£13.00	£13.00	£12.80
Crop drying	£9.00	£9.00	NA
Densification	£26.20	£8.00	NA
Storage (1 year)	£2.00	£6.00	£32.00
Transport (20 km)	£3.00	£3.00	£12.00
Conversion costs	NA	£54.00	£30.00
Total cost	£53.20	£93.20	£76.80
Conversion efficiency	70%	50%	45%
Total cost per GJ	£3.80	£9.32	£8.53
Cost per GJ of conventional fuels	£1.58[1] £3.43[2]	£4.56[3] £10.02[4]	£2.94–5.50[5] £8.90–9.85[6]

Conventional fuel costs assume: coal to industrial[1] and domestic[2] users, pre-tax[3] and post-tax[4] motor spirit, natural gas[5] at 80–800 therms yr^{-1} (5), and propane[6] from 15–47 kg cylinders

weight basis, bracken briquettes contain only 60% of the energy in coal, but they will become more competitive as the price of coal and oil rises. A consumer preference may be expressed for biomass because of its low ash and sulphur content. It is difficult to predict the likely market for these solid-fuel briquettes, and no attempt has therefore been made to establish the enterprise gross margin.

The production of methane gas (Table 5) is unattractive because of technical difficulties in using a high-solids feedstock, and because of the high cost of storing fresh materials. Methanol production is much more feasible, both economically and energetically, particularly if some part of the petrol tax can be waived. However, non-woody crops currently have to be densified before they can be converted to the gaseous precursors of methanol. This disadvantage is not applicable to fluidized bed convertors, but these have a large intake requirement of around 60 t day^{-1}, and may not be appropriate for small-scale rural applications (Beenackers & van Swaaij 1984).

Ethanol production is not viable from bracken fronds (although it would be viable from the rhizomes), because the fermentation requires sugar or starch crops. Sugar beet, cereal grains, potatoes and Jerusalem artichoke are the most likely candidates in Britain. However, the price of fuel alcohol produced from grain in the EC, per unit of energy, is around 3 times that of petroleum. This figure is considerably in excess of the restitution payments for cereals (Sourie & Killen 1986), and it is not an economic option to allow farmers to produce surpluses for conversion into alcohol. That is not to say that the option will not be pursued by the EC, as it is in the USA and Sweden (Penrose 1985). Conversion technology is continually improving, and new physical and enzymatic techniques are being developed to convert refractory celluloses to sugars prior to fermentation (Overend *et al.* 1985). Success with these technologies would dramatically change the economics, and would certainly favour the use of productive herbaceous weeds.

5.4 Energy from shrubs and scrub

Shrub and scrub vegetation can have several advantages, in addition to the rapid production of biomass. Gorse, broom and tree lupin (*Lupinus arboreus*) are all nitrogen fixers, and have been used to reclaim mining wastes. They could become useful energy crops on derelict land. Tree lupin is rather short-lived but has recorded nitrogen fixation rates of up to 185 kg ha^{-1} yr^{-1} on china clay wastes (Palaniappan *et al.* 1979). Broom lives for around 12 years, and has been suggested as an energy crop in France, where it would be harvested on a 7-year rotation. With potassium and phosphorus fertilization, a dry matter yield of 15 t ha^{-1} yr^{-1} has been claimed (Tabard 1985). The soil underlying gorse accumulates nitrogen more rapidly than that beneath broom, and 70 kg ha^{-1} yr^{-1} has been recorded in Cornwall (Dancer *et al.* 1977). Gorse would be risky as an energy crop because of the ease with which it catches fire, but 6/8-year-old stands in Britain and New Zealand have accumulated biomass at rates approaching 10 t ha^{-1} yr^{-1}. Interestingly, the annual litterfall from gorse is almost as high as the biomass increment, indicating a considerable potential for soil improvement. Sea buckthorn (*Hippophae rhamnoides*) and Sitka alder (*Alnus sinuata*) are examples of nitrogen-fixing species which could be used in very different habitats as energy understories beneath widely spaced, and light-canopied, timber trees.

Laurel species (*Prunus lucitanica* and *P. laurocerasus*), rhododendron, and even holly (*Ilex aquifolium*) are understories which could be used as evergreen energy crops in conjunction with widely spaced timber trees. Holly has an annual recorded productivity of 12.5 t ha^{-1} yr^{-1} in an unshaded portion of the New Forest (Peterken & Newbould 1966), and rhododendron was found to grow at around 10 t ha^{-1} yr^{-1} on nutrient-poor china clay waste (Dancer *et al.* 1977). There have, however, been very few studies in Britain of the productivity in different habitats of these shrubs, and no information exists on the effects of different harvesting or fertilizing regimes.

Another problem with rhododendron is the distaste with which it is viewed by most of our foresters, farmers and conservationists. There are several reasons for this (Shaw 1984).

i. Rhododendron is an introduced alien, and the conservationists worry if such species are too successful. It was, however, native before the last glaciation.

ii. It contains an andromedo toxin which is highly poisonous if ingested. It is thus largely avoided by animals.

iii. Flowering is prolific and 3–7 thousand seeds can be produced from each flower. They are so light that dispersal of several km may be possible in turbulent conditions.

iv. Cutting has little effect on established bushes, other than encouraging coppice growth and the production of layered shoots.

v. Fire tends to favour rhododendron by creating ideal conditions for seed germination, and eliminating competing vegetation.

vi. The establishment of conventional forestry is difficult and expensive.

Rhododendron has the ideal strategy for an invasive weed, and possesses further advantages of an evergreen habit, longevity, freedom from pests and diseases, and a rather wide tolerance of environmental conditions. Once established, it can produce satisfactory growth under 5–10% of full daylight, and its physiological compensation point is less than 2% of full daylight (Nilsen 1986). These characteristics suggest it is an ideal energy crop companion to widely spaced timber trees. Indeed, only a few fully stocked conifer canopies (western hemlock (*Tsuga heterophylla*), Douglas fir (*Pseudotsuga menziesii*), Sitka spruce) are able to generate sufficient shade to eliminate rhododendron. It would also reduce the risk of grazing damage to accompanying trees, and would eliminate the need for fencing.

It is, therefore, suggested that widely spaced trees could be established in existing stands of rhododendron, after an initial harvest using a brush-cutter, and subsequent repeated application of contact herbicides around the transplants. Periodic coppicing would take place at the same time as lower branch pruning on the timber trees. The combined effect of shade and cutting would considerably reduce the problem of flowering and seed dispersal.

A general thesis is illustrated by rhododendron: the most productive and resilient energy crops are also the worst weeds. Bracken, cordgrass (*Spartina anglica*) and Japanese knotweed (*Reynoutria japonica*) are other examples in this country, and the value of weeds as producers of bioenergy is starting to be recognized abroad (Gilreath 1986).

6 *Agrenforestry*

This unfamiliar term places energy cropping in its true position: that of a land use which is intimately integrated with agriculture and forestry.

Short-rotation osier beds in Somerset are defined as agriculture by the Town and Country Planning Act, so it is semantically correct to view the coppice-with-standard system which is advocated here as a genuine mixture of agriculture, energy cropping and timber production (agrenforestry, for short). Furthermore, there is considerable potential to use the coppice, pollards, or the prunings from standard trees as fodder for animals. Several tree species have leaf protein concentrations approaching 20% of dry weight, and poplars and willows have proved to have particularly high production of the essential amino-acids for non-ruminant feed (Carlsson 1976). Indeed, it has been the practice for many years in Russia to market dried leaf meal under the name of 'mukka' (Keays & Barton 1975); 300 000 t are fed annually to cattle, poultry and pigs as a direct replacement for 5% of the standard feed. Another innovation from Russia is the use of nettles (*Urtica* spp.) as a fodder crop under Siberian larches (*Larix sibirica*) (Bogachkov 1977).

There are several possible environmental consequences of agrenforestry, and these are examined elsewhere (Callaghan *et al.* 1986). However, it is worthwhile in this paper to select one example of the advantage to wildlife of creating a diverse structure in a woodland. This

Table 6. The effect of rhododendron clearance in 1982 on bird populations in the Dinnet Oakwood, Cairngorms. An adjacent area of mixed oak/aspen/birch/bird-cherry serves as a control between years (source: French *et al.* 1986)

	Rhododendron			Other broadleaves		
2-year period	1980–81	1982–83	1984–85	1980–81	1982–83	1984–85
No. of birds	20.5	5	8	20.5	23	20
No. of species	12	6	11	11	12	15
'Bird species diversity'	2.43	1.71	2.18	2.54	2.23	2.39

Table 7. Environmental and economic comparisons of agrenforestry with intensive agriculture and forestry

	Environmental	Economic
Advantages of agrenforestry	Increased species and structural diversity Protection from wind and water erosion Leaching and denitrification reduced Floods and temperature extremes reduced Risk of fire reduced Smaller scale favours organic farming Less risk of disease and enhanced biotic control Better access for recreation and sport	Soil mixture conserved at ground level Frost and drought protection Efficient light capture in time and space Better animal performance through shelter from wind and sun Possible use of N-fixing mixtures Yield of some trees is favoured by soil cultivation Utilization of farm labour more evenly through the year Shared infrastructure costs with other land uses Use of by-products easier (eg foliage for feed and slurry for fertilizer) Preservation of rural employment Greater crop diversity and flexibility than forestry More even income flow than forestry Felling can be delayed till market prices rise
Disadvantages of agrenforestry	Uniform rows of trees may be unattractive Possible increase in total water consumption More complete harvesting may reduce soil fertility	Greater management effort and use of unknown methods Dispersed production means higher transport costs Yield of main component (eg grain) reduced Less flexible than conventional farming High fertilizer input can damage timber quality Soil compaction and bark-stripping by grazing animals Inefficient weed and pest control Less regular economic return than pure farming

example shows the dramatic decline in bird species and numbers following the clearance of rhododendron in a Scottish oak wood (Table 6). Even the partial recovery of the population in 1984–85 has been attributed to an influx of 'canopy' species, whose territories were centred on adjacent areas.

A number of advantages and disadvantages for agroforestry can be conjectured (Table 7). Considerable interdisciplinary investigation is required to verify these assumptions, but it is encouraging that an agroforestry research co-ordination group has been established which spans an increasing number of Government institutions and universities.

Perhaps it may be some time before a grant is introduced with the title suggested in this paper, but there is little doubt that the increasing pressure for 'set-aside' of agricultural land will favour the use of both energy crops and agrenforestry.

7 References

Anon. 1983. *Wood fuel: heat from the forest.* Stockholm.

Beard, N.T. 1987. MAFF grants and fiscal incentives. In: *Farming and forestry. Proc. Conf., Loughborough, 1986.* London: RASE/TGUK/FWAG. In press.

Beenackers, A.A.C.M. & van Swaaij, W.P.M. 1984. Gasification of biomass, a state of the art review. In: *Processing of biomass,* edited by A.V. Bridgewater. London: Butterworth.

Bogachkov, V.I. 1977. *Stinging nettle - an important fodder plant.* Sibirskii, Institute Sel'sko Khozyaistrava, Omsk, USSR, **3**, 58.

Brown, D.A.H. 1987. Land use changes up to the year 2000. In: *Farming and forestry. Proc. Conf., Loughborough, 1986.* London: RASE/TGUK/FWAG. In press.

Brown, I.R. 1983. *Management of birch woodland in Scotland.* Redgorton: Countryside Commission for Scotland.

Callaghan, T.V., Lawson, G.J., Millar, A. & Scott, R. 1986. Environmental aspects of agroforestry. In: *Agroforestry: a discussion of research and development requirements,* 50-76. London: MAFF.

Carlsson, R. 1976. Increased utilization of whole trees: production of protein-vitamin concentrates from leaves. In: *Premises and potential of short-rotation forestry in Sweden,* edited by G. Siren *et al.* Stockholm: Royal College of Forestry.

Condry, W.M. 1966. *The Snowdonia National Park.* London: Collins.

Dancer, W.S., Handley, J.F. & Bradshaw, A.D. 1977. Nitrogen accumulation in kaolin mining wastes in Cornwall. *Pl. Soil,* **48**, 153-167.

Erickson, J.R. 1975. Harvesting of forest residues. *AIChE Symp. Ser.,* **71**, 27-29.

French, D.D., Jenkins, D. & Conroy, J.W.H. 1986. Guidelines for managing woods in Aberdeenshire for song birds. In: *Trees and wildlife in the Scottish uplands,* edited by D. Jenkins, 129-143. (ITE symposium no. 17.) Abbots Ripton: Institute of Terrestrial Ecology.

Gilreath, J. 1986. Development of a production system for weeds as biomass crops. *Biomass,* **9**, 135-144.

Hagglund, B. & Peterson, G. 1985. *Broadleaves in boreal silviculture - an obstacle or an asset?* (Report no. 14.) Umea: Swedish University of Agricultural Sciences, Silviculture Department.

Hakkila, P. 1984. Forest chips as an energy source in Finland. *Folia for.,* no. 886.

Hakkila, P. 1985. Forest biomass as an energy resource. In: *Bioenergy '84.* Vol.I., edited by H. Egneus & A. Ellegard, 79-90. London: Applied Science.

Howarth, R.W. 1985. *Farming for farmers?* London: Institute for Economic Affairs.

Katzen, R. 1985. Large-scale ethanol production facilities. In: *Bioenergy '84. Vol.I,* edited by H. Egneus & A. Ellegard, 305-323. London: Applied Science.

Keays, J.L. & Barton, G.M. 1975. *Recent advances in foliage utilization.* (Inf. Rept. VP-x-137). Vancouver, BC: Western Forest Products Laboratory, Canadian Forest Service.

Lawson, G.J. & Callaghan, T.V. 1983. Primary productivity and prospects for biofuels in the UK. *Int. J. Biometeorol.,* **27**, 197-218.

Lawson, G.J., Callaghan, T.V. & Scott, R. 1984. Renewable energy from plants: bypassing fossilization. *Adv. Ecol. Res.,* **14**, 57-114.

Lawson, G.J., Callaghan, T.V. & Scott, R. 1986. Bracken as an energy resource. In: *Bracken: ecology, land use and control technology,* edited by R.T. Smith & J.A. Taylor, 239-248. Carnforth: Parthenon Press.

MAFF, DAFS & DANI. 1986. *Annual review of agriculture.* London: HMSO.

McElroy, G.H. & Dawson, W.M. 1986. Biomass from short-rotation coppice willow on marginal land. *Biomass,* **10**, 225-240.

Miles, J. 1986. What are the effects of trees on soils. In: *Trees and wildlife in the Scottish uplands,* edited by D.Jenkins, 55-62. (ITE symposium no. 17.) Abbots Ripton: Institute of Terrestrial Ecology.

Mitchell, J. 1973. Mobilization of phosphorus by *Pteridium aquilinum. Pl. Soil,* **38**, 489-491.

Mitchell, C.P., Brandon, O.H., Bunce, R.G.H., Barr, C.J., Whittaker, H.A., Tranter, R.B., Downing, P. & Pearce, M.L. 1983. Land availability for wood energy production in Great Britain. In: *Energy from biomass*, edited by A. Strub, P. Chartier & G.Schlesser, 159-163. London: Applied Science.

Mitchell, C.P., Trantner, R.B., Downing, P., Brandon, O., Pearce, M.L., Bunce, R.G.H. & Barr, C.J. 1987. *Growing wood for energy in Great Britain: the land availability study.* (Control report B1102.) Harwell: Energy Technology Support Unit.

Nilsen, E.T. 1986. Quantitative phenology and leaf survivorship of *Rhododendron maximum* in contrasting irradiance environments of the Southern Appalachian Mountains. *Am. J. Bot.*, **73**, 822-831.

Overend, R.P., Milne, J.A. & Mudge, L.K. 1985. *Fundamentals of biomass conversion.* London: Applied Science.

Palaniappan, V.M., Marrs, R.H. & Bradshaw, A.D. 1979. The effect of *Lupinus arboreus* on the nitrogen status of china clay wastes. *J. appl. Ecol.*, **17**, 469-477.

Penrose, J. 1985. Soak up the surplus. *Fmrs Wkly*, **103** (14), 77.

Peterken, G.F. & Newbould, P.J. 1966. Dry matter production by *Ilex aquifolium* in the New Forest. *J. Ecol.*, **54**, 143-150.

Phillip, M.S. 1978. A report of the work of the Silvicultural Group 1976-77. *Scott. For.*, **32**, 26-36.

Price, R. & Mitchell, C.P. 1985. *Potential for wood as a fuel in the United Kingdom.* (R32.) Harwell: Energy Technology Support Unit.

Scott, R., Wait, C.P., Buckland, M.P., Lawson, G.J. & Callaghan, T.V. 1986. Biofuels: the domestic market in the UK. In: *Energy for rural and island communities IV*, edited by J. Twidell, I. Hounam & C. Lewis, 115-123. London: Pergamon Press.

Shaw, M.W. 1984. Weed control and vegetation management in forests and amenity areas. *Asp. appl. Biol.*, **5**, 231-242.

Sheppard, W.J. & Lipinsky, E.S. 1983. Chemicals from biomass. In: *Energy from biomass*, edited by A. Strub, P. Chartier & G. Schlesser, 63-71. London: Applied Science.

Sourie, J.C. & Killen, L. 1986. *Biomass: recent economic studies.* London: Applied Science.

Sponder, P.M. 1979. *Nutrient cycling in heather and bracken ecosystems.* PhD thesis, University of Hull.

Stevens, R. 1984. Domestic sector of the woodburning market. In: *Growing wood for fuel.* London: RASE/ADAS

Stirling-Aird, R.J. 1987. Farm woodland. In: *New opportunities for farmland use.* London: RASE/ADAS. In press.

Tabard, P. 1985. Une plante energetique a cycle court. Le genet: *Cytisus scoparius.* In: *Energy from biomass*, edited by W. Palz, J. Coombs & D.O. Hall, 283-291. London: Applied Science.

Taylor, J.A. 1985. Bracken encroachment rates in Britain. *Soil Use Manage.*, **1**, 53-56.

Taylor, M. 1987. Grants and fiscal incentives - the role of the Countryside Commission and local government. In: *Farming and forestry. Proc. Conf., Loughborough, 1986.* London: RASE/TGUK/FWAG. In press.

Heather moorland management - a model

A R SIBBALD, S A GRANT, J A MILNE and T J MAXWELL
Hill Farming Research Organisation, Bush Estate, Penicuik, Midlothian, Scotland

1 *Introduction*

Maxwell *et al.* (1986) illustrated the potential for farming sheep, efficiently and productively, on heather (*Calluna vulgaris*) moorland, while maintaining heather dominance for conservation, sport and recreational purposes. A computer model, based on many of the requirements and constraints discussed in that paper, has been constructed with a view to defining quantitatively the potential year-round stock carrying capacity of a heather moorland for which the land resources can be described.

2 *Resource description*

The moorland is divided into 2 main classes of vegetation, grass dominant and heather dominant; each of these is subdivided into classes of different production potential.

2.1 Grass-dominant areas

There are 3 grassland classes, inbye (existing permanent pasture), good native grassland (typically bent/fescue (*Agrostis/Festuca*)), and poor native grassland (typically mat-grass (*Nardus*) or moor-grass (*Molinia*) dominant). The level of annual production and desirable levels of utilization of these classes are shown in Table 1.

Table 1. Annual production and percentage utilization of 3 classes of grassland

Grassland class	Annual production (kg dry matter ha^{-1})	Percentage utilization
Inbye	5000	80
Good grass	3500	60
Poor grass	2000	30

2.2 Heather-dominant areas

There are 4 classes of heather. Heather on blanket bog is treated separately from heather growing on drier ground; it is assumed that it will not be burned. Heather on drier land is subdivided into 3 age classes, young (less than 15 cm in height), intermediate (between 15 and 30 cm in height) and old heather (taller than 30 cm).

The model allows that, under certain conditions described below, land may be improved. It is assumed that this land will come from the heather area. The percentage of the area of young, intermediate or old heather to be used for land improvement has to be stated in the resource description.

The annual production and desirable levels of utilization assumed for these 4 heather classes are shown in Table 2.

Table 2. Annual production and percentage utilization of heather classes

Heather class	Annual production (kg dry matter ha^{-1})	Percentage utilization
Young	1750	40
Intermediate	1750	10
Old	1250	5
Blanket bog	1400	15

3 *Sheep*

Sheep are divided into 3 classes based on size. Small sheep would typically be Welsh Mountain, medium sheep would be, for example, Blackface or Swaledale, and large sheep would normally be crossbred, eg Greyface or Mules. It is assumed that these animals would be provided with supplementary feed in winter, particularly during the 6 weeks before lambing. The assumed intake of herbage from pasture for the 3 sizes of sheep are shown in Table 3.

4 *Utilization of pasture*

In order to maintain the productivity and ecological stability of heather moorland, the level of utilization of each pasture category should not exceed the relevant percentage shown in Tables 1 or 2. Research has shown that, to meet the nutritional needs of grazing ewes, at least half of the levels of annual intake shown in Table 3 should be achieved from grass swards.

The model is designed to calculate the total number of breeding ewes that fit within these constraints.

5 *Future management*

Two limiting conditions may occur. The first is that the potential stock number is constrained by the limits set for the utilization of heather. If this condition is due to an imbalance of age class, it may be resolved by a heather burning programme to create a larger proportion of young, and therefore more nutritious, heather.

Table 3. The required provision from pasture for sheep classes

Sheep class	Annual intake from pasture (kg dry matter ewe^{-1})
Small	350
Medium	450
Large	550

The second limiting condition is that there is insufficient grassland to fully utilize the heather component and, at the same time, maintain adequate levels of sheep nutrition. In this case, a limited amount of improved pasture can be created.

5.1 Heather burning

Heather may be burned in order to produce a patchwork of age classes; detailed guidelines for burning management are given in the pamphlet *A guide to good muirburn practice* (Muirburn Working Party 1977). The model offers a range of burning programmes from 8 to 15 years. The longer the burning programme, the smaller the areas to be burned in each year.

The model calculates, for each year of the burning programme, the new distribution of heather age class, and calculates a new stock number based upon it and upon the levels of utilization shown in Table 2; in doing so, it assumes that the burned areas are well distributed. This assumption ensures that the grazing animals utilize the whole resource.

5.2 Land improvement

When the proportion of grassland limits the utilization of the heather component of the area, the model offers the opportunity to improve a piece of land. The total area that may be improved has been defined above, and the model calculates some proportion of this area which is adequate to increase the proportion of the annual intake that comes from grass to half the total intake.

The balance of intake from grass and heather is altered throughout a burning programme and, under some conditions, may lead to the need to improve land. This possibility is allowed for in the model.

6 *The model*

The model is written in BBC BASIC and runs on a BBC Model B microcomputer. The inputs are limited to a description of the resource as described above, and an indication of the size of sheep involved.

Output to the computer screen shows the initial distribution of vegetation classes and the total stock number that may be carried. The model then offers a burning or land improvement programme (according to the current limitations imposed upon good management).

Table 4. Example of printed output from HFRO heather management programme

Total area = 988 acres Vegetation areas (acre)	Start	Year 14 Burned	No burn
Improved	0.00	7.31	0.00
Good grass	73.87	73.87	73.87
Poor grass	173.70	173.70	173.70
Young heather	73.87	449.57	0.00
Inter heather	298.48	59.60	0.00
Old heather	224.61	80.48	601.96
Bog heather	148.74	148.74	148.74
Ewes total	367	519	295
Ewes acre^{-1}	0.37	0.52	0.30
Acre ewe^{-1}	2.72	1.92	3.38
Burn each year on 10-year rotation			
Intermediate heather	29.85		
Old heather	22.46		

An update of distribution of vegetation class and of stock number is shown for each year in the development programme. At the conclusion of the development programme, the final stock number is shown and, for comparison, the number of stock that may be carried if no development programme is followed and, as a consequence, all the heather degenerates into the old age class.

Finally, the model produces a hard copy of the results. An example of a printed result is shown in Table 4.

7 *Conclusion*

A simple model has been developed which will calculate the appropriate stock number to carry on an area of heather moorland, while ensuring that heather remains dominant and in a highly productive state for conservation, sporting or recreation purposes, and that the area is farmed efficiently and productively.

A copy of the model on a floppy disc or a listing of the computer program is available from the authors.

8 *References*

Maxwell, T.J., Grant, S.A., Milne, J.A. & Sibbald, A.R. 1986. Systems of sheep production on heather moorland. In: *Hill Land Symposium, Galway, 1984,* edited by M. O'Toole, 188-211. Dublin: An Foras Taluntais.

Muirburn Working Party. 1977. *A guide to good muirburn practice.* Edinburgh: HMSO.

Estimating acceptable stocking levels for heather moorland

A N LANCE
Royal Society for the Protection of Birds, The Lodge, Sandy, Bedfordshire, England

1 Summary
A multiple regression model by D Welch, Institute of Terrestrial Ecology (ITE), has been adapted for predicting trends in heather (*Calluna vulgaris*) cover at different stocking densitities of sheep, cattle, and deer – alone or in combination – using input data commonly available to the land manager. Site factors are included, allowing the model to be generalized to moorland at different elevations, soils, and climatic zones. Locally high densities of small grazers (hares (*Lepus timidus*), rabbits (*Oryctolagus cuniculus*), and grouse (Tetraonidae)) can also be incorporated. Welch (1984) should be read in conjunction with the methods described here.

2 Introduction
Heather serves as self-renewing 'free capital' for British hill sheep and cattle farmers. As shelter and forage for red deer (*Cervus elaphus*) and red grouse (*Lagopus l. scoticus*), it has the same value to the owners of upland sporting estates. British heather moorland also has a distinctive flora and fauna, and is prized accordingly by nature conservationists. Its maintenance should, therefore, be valued by all these interest groups, but, instead, they often disagree over it.

Present European Community (EC) legislation adds to the dispute. The Common Agricultural Policy's system of hill livestock compensatory allowances encourages farmers in Less Favoured Areas to maximize incomes by increasing stocking densities. However, heavy grazing is well known to be detrimental to heather, causing it to decline in cover and abundance; Gimingham (1972) summarized the effects. Yet EC Directive 79/409 on the conservation of wild birds requires Member States to protect the habitats of listed birds against loss or damage by other land uses, including grazing. In the UK, the means of achieving this protection are the Wildlife and Countryside Acts 1981–85. These Acts empower the Nature Conservancy Council (NCC) to designate Sites of Special Scientific Interest (SSSI) and, within them, to compensate farmers for 'profit foregone' if their stocking levels are kept to less than the land might otherwise support.

On heather moorland SSSIs, disputes over stocking can arise in 3 ways:

i. from proposals to introduce farm stock on to previously ungrazed land;
ii. from proposals to change an acceptable existing grazing regime; and
iii. from the need to change an already unacceptable regime.

Before compensation can be agreed, figures are required for the stocking level which the land can support, and for the level at which the conservation interest will be retained. This paper is concerned with the latter, and gives a method for predicting trends in heather cover at various stocking regimes.

Despite much interest in the problem over many years, no generally acceptable basis has emerged. Figures for rates and extents of change have been produced by various studies, but most of them have been for purposes other than quantifying vegetation change *per se*, and have tended to differ widely in methods and circumstances Generalization has, therefore, been difficult, except in the broadest of terms, and practical advice has had to be based mostly on exerience with similar circumstances elsewhere.

Virtually the only study to address itself specifically to relationships between animal numbers and moorland vegetation over a typical range of variation in both has been the work by Welch at ITE's Banchory Research Station during the 1970s. However, little of this work was accessible to practical use, until Welch published a series of papers in 1984. Welch measured site occupance by hill sheep, cattle, red deer, hares, rabbits and red grouse at 32 moorland localities in north-east Scotland. He then compared these measurements with vegetation trend at each site over a 4-year period. Abiotic site factors were also measured, and the outcome has been the most comprehensive analysis of its type so far, even if still rather limited in timespan and geographic coverage, and applying only to moorland not managed by burning.

Of special practical interest has been Welch's use of regression methods with a capacity for prediction, and trends in heather cover as a yardstick of response. Trends in heather are of fundamental interest to moorland conservation, serving as a broad index of floral and faunal status.

Welch's technique compared some 7 types of independent factor against various measures of heather trend in simple and multiple regressions, narrowing down the factors and regressions step-wise to find a combination (regression model) which left the smallest residual variation ($1-R^2$) in heather trend. The most successful models were 2 which expressed heather trend in terms of logits[1] percentage cover, and herbivore

[1] Logit = ½ $\log_e (p/q)$, where p is heather cover expressed as a proportion, and q = 1 – p

site use in terms of dung deposited per unit area and time.

Dung deposition alone was a successful predictor of heather trend, but even more so when subdivided by animal of origin (ie different herbivores separately), and into different classes which distinguished light from heavy site use (Welch 1984, pp201-205, explains the rationale). R^2 increased still further when soil pH, site altitude, and an index of heather growth were added to the models as intrinsic site factors (see Welch 1984, p203, Table 4).

However, Welch's models are of little practical use in their published form. As measures of site use, dung deposition data are not likely to be available, except from field work specially designed to obtain them; the same is true for the growth index for heather production. Nonetheless, both of these drawbacks can be surmounted, although the assumptions entailed in doing so are several and less than robust.

3 *Modifications to Welch's model variables*

3.1 Stocking density instead of dung deposition

From data on mean rates of dung output per unit time per cow, sheep, deer, hare/rabbit, and grouse, respectively (Welch 1984, p192), amounts of dung expected at various hypothetical stocking densities of each herbivore can be compared with mean amounts deposited by each at the same densities. Conversion factors can then be derived to inter-relate the 2; details of the arithmetic are shown in Appendix 1. The factors are 350.0, 52.56, 96.36, and 13.14 for cattle, sheep, deer, and lagomorphs (rabbits and hares), respectively. The densities (animals ha^{-1}) multiplied by their appropriate factors then express stocking rates in terms of amounts of dung deposited, the variables to which Welch's regression coefficients apply. The principal assumptions in using these factors for practical purposes are that (i) stocking rate and dung deposition per unit area and time show the same relationship in all circumstances (site location, etc), and (ii) actual stocking levels for the heather in question are the same as the substitute figures input to the regression equation. The latter assumption is doubly relevant, because, on local areas of a moor, actual stocking levels can often depart substantially from the crude mean level for the moor as a whole (as discussed further below).

3.2 A substitute for GrI, the index of heather production

The index GrI is intended to reflect intrinsic heather production per unit area, and is the product of heather density and growth increment per unit time. Such measurements are straightforward, but, again, seldom available or easily obtainable when stocking levels are to be discussed. Site factors which affect heather growth are quicker to assess, however, and Welch considered soil pH, soil wetness, and site altitude. As a separate factor input to the regressions, soil wetness added nothing to the amount of variation explained in heather trend (Welch 1984, p201, Table 2), but pH and altitude significantly increased R^2, and so were retained in the final model. The apparent role of altitude was complex: its regression coefficient was positive, whereas heather growth is poor at high altitudes. Welch interpreted this result as reflecting weaker competition from other plants at higher altitudes, and thus a greater ability of heather to persist under grazing, despite its own slow growth. Altitude and the growth index GrI thus appear in the final model as separate and ostensibly unrelated factors. In reality, altitude and heather growth are, of course, related, and, as such, altitude can also serve as a way of estimating GrI when no growth measurements are available. Again, by regression (see Appendix 2), a substitute for GrI can be obtained for different altitudes, as (Altitude x 0.395) – 381.66. Although crude, this substitution is likely to be more realistic than simply ignoring growth or giving it some fixed mean value merely to complete the list of inputs required by the model.

4 *Classifying stocking levels*

Light grazing has long been known to benefit heather by slowing its rate of physiological ageing, and by encouraging tillering (shoot proliferation) which increases heather cover. If grazing is such that consumption by herbivores equals heather production, then heather growth will, in theory, be zero and cover will not change. In reality, as experiments confirm (Grant *et al.* 1978), consumption must be less than production, so as to offset natural winter dieback and allow further production (most of which emanates from whatever is left of the previous season's growth). Seldom is a balanced consumption/production ratio obtained in actual moor management, however, and then more often by accident than by design. A successful design must allow for the difference between heavy and light grazing, and also (if possible) demarcate the threshold between the 2. With several different herbivores to consider, Welch arrived at a demarcation empirically, by setting arbitrary threshold levels of dung deposition and then calculating separate regression coefficients for the dung totals derived from them, and repeating the process with successively higher thresholds until R^2 for change in heather cover no longer increased.

A threshold level of 24 ml dung m^{-2} yr^{-1} was found to apply for both sheep and deer, which by the above conversion (Section 3.1) is equivalent to a stocking level of 0.45 ha^{-1} for sheep and 0.25 ha^{-1} for deer. Smaller herbivores (hares, rabbits and grouse) had a higher threshold (35 ml m^{-2} yr^{-1}, converting to 2.7 ha^{-1}).

Cattle affect heather differently, however, showing no consistent beneficial effect at any stocking density. (Cattle can, in fact, suppress heather competitors, such as bracken (*Pteridium aquilinum*), by trampling, but cattle also damage heather by trampling more than sheep or deer.) A single negative coefficient, therefore, applies to cattle, and their stocking level is input separately to the model, without being classified as heavy or light.

5 The input of stocking levels, apart from cattle

If sheep and deer are both present, their stocking levels are added together (after converting to dung m^{-2} yr^{-1}). The total for sheep and/or deer is input as 'light' grazing if it is 24 ml m^{-2} yr^{-1} or less, or as 'heavy' if it equals or exceeds an upper threshold of 48. A total which lies between these values is input partly to the 'light' category and partly to the 'heavy' category, as follows:

i. 2 (Total - 24 ml m^{-2} yr^{-1}) = H, the input to 'heavy';

ii. Total - H = L, the input to 'light'.

The procedure is the same for lagomorphs and grouse (if present and if estimates of density can be obtained for them), using 35 ml m^{-2} yr^{-1} as the threshold (with no upper one) and adding the resulting sums to the 'heavy' and 'light' categories as appropriate. The inputs for animals other than cattle are thus distributed between the 'heavy' and 'light' categories according to how they straddle the difference between the 2. This method reduces the exaggerated change in predicted heather trend from rapid increase to sudden decline, which would result if 2 similar stocking levels on either side of the threshold were assigned wholly to classes representing opposing effects (+,-) on heather.

6 Inputs for site factors

Soil pH varied little between Welch's sites, and also added little to R^2. Its regression coefficients were comparatively large, however, and even small differences in pH, therefore, affect predicted heather trend too much to be ignored. Where a measured value for the site in question cannot be obtained, the use of values in the order, <4.2, 4.2-4.8, and > 4.8, for deep peat soils, peaty podzols, and mineral soils, respectively, will allow at least these major soil groupings to be differentiated.

Inputs for site altitude must allow for differences in latitude: for instance, 325 m altitude in Aberdeenshire is roughly equivalent (ecologically) to sea level in Shetland. At latitudes north of Welch's Aberdeenshire sites, therefore, altitudes must be adjusted upward, and downward for latitudes to the south. Figure 1 shows simple linear adjustment factors for different parts of Britain, based on differences between temperature zones. The factors are derived in Appendix 3. For southerly places, such as Wales and Dartmoor, these adjustments give 'altitudes' which lie below sea level for all true altitudes below 300 m. There are no standardly derived field data to compare, but, soil factors being similar, heather would be expected to grow better at sea level in south-west England than at sea level in north-east Scotland.

7 The mathematical expression to be computed

Of Welch's 2 regression models yielding similar values of R^2 for heather trend, model 3 in his Table 4 is the more straightforward, and is the one developed here for practical use. (It was also the one which Welch himself chose for discussion in his paper.) With the coefficients

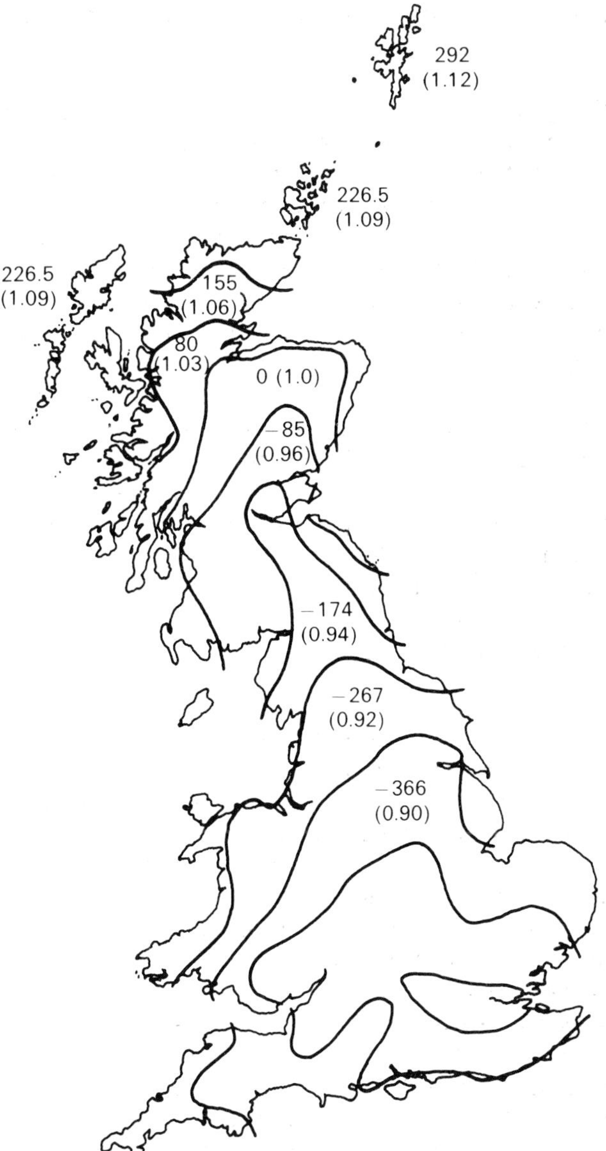

Figure 1. Adjustment factors for altitude at different latitudes. No brackets, Z-value; brackets, pdlr value (see Appendix 3 for method of use)

for this model as in Welch (1984, Table 6), the full expression to be computed is:

$$\hat{y} = 0.3298 + 0.00153\,\text{Grl} - 0.178\,\text{pH} + (0.00063 - @)\,\text{Altitude} - 0.00199\,\text{Cattle} + 0.00597\,L - 0.00114\,H \quad (1)$$

where 0.3298 is the intercept constant, @ is as defined in Appendix 3, and the inputs for grazing (L and H) are as in Section 5.

Where a measured value for Grl is unobtainable, the equation component is:

$$(0.00153\,(\text{Altitude} \times 0.395)) - 381.66 \quad (2)$$

as in Section 3.

The output value ($\hat{y}$) is the predicted mean change in heather cover over a 4-year period, and is expressed in units of logit percentage. Use of the logit transformation allows for the diminished percentage capacity of heather to increase in cover at values near to 100%, and *vice versa* for values near to zero. The equivalent percentage ŷ-value can be read from standard tables, or back-transformed from the logit value as:

$$\% = [[[1 + ((e^{2 \times logit} - 1)/(e^{2 \times logit} + 1))]/2] - 0.5] \times 100 \quad (3)$$

where e is the base to natural logarithms.

8 *Comments on the model*

8.1 Accuracy

With the various adjustment factors as well as 6 different variables, the model is a little unwieldy, yet it also contains some simplifying assumptions. Except for the altitude factor @, the model is a first-order equation throughout, even though some non-linear components could have been expected. The division of 'other herbivore' grazing into 'heavy' and 'light' is a case in point. At light to moderate densities of herbivores other than cattle, the model predicts an increase in heather cover. Above the 'threshold' density of 0.45 sheep ha^{-1} (which is still light stocking by normal hill farm standards), this beneficial effect tapers off and becomes negative as the higher stocking rates contribute increasingly to the 'heavy' category (with a negative coefficient). This result is consistent with theory, except insofar as the model, being linear, yields abrupt changes in ŷ at the threshold between heavy and light, and also at the point where the contribution from 'light' is exceeded by the contribution from 'heavy'. Figure 2 illustrates these effects. In reality, the expected changes would be gradual, giving a curving response as the maximum beneficial stocking density is approached and then passed. The model is, therefore, likely to overestimate the beneficial effect of stocking levels around the threshold, and to underestimate it at levels further below and further above (though not necessarily to the same degree, as the coefficients for heavy and light grazing differ in magnitude as well as sign).

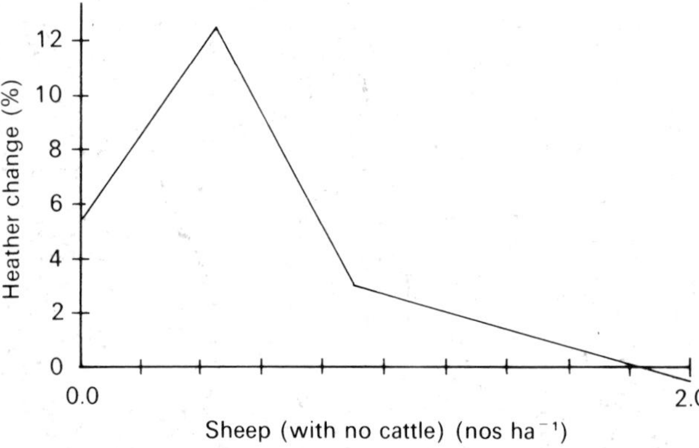

Figure 2. Predicted mean % change in heather cover at sheep stocking densities above and below the threshold (0.45 sheep ha^{-1}) between 'light' and 'heavy' grazing (values for other variables as in Welch's Table 6)

This difficulty might seem to diminish the model's practical usefulness, but there are some compensating factors. First, with sheep (or deer) considered on their own (ie no cattle present), the threshold stocking densities at which this problem arises are well below those that determine whether heather cover will increase or decline. For instance, at the point in Figure 2 where zero change in heather cover is predicted, the sheep stocking rate (1.82 ha^{-1}) is some 4 times greater than the threshold between 'heavy' and 'light' (0.45 ha^{-1}). Second, as with any regression model, prediction becomes less reliable as values depart from their means, and so, at low (and high) levels of grazing, the rates of change expected in heather will be less accurate. Hence, the model is weakest in places where its predictive strength is least essential.

8.2 Precision

In its published form, the model includes no statistical confidence limits, other than those in Welch (1984, Tables 5 & 6), for mean input values at which cover remains stable. In particular, no confidence limits are provided for the dependent variable (logit % cover change) at mean or any other values of the independent variables; and the published results of the study do not provide the statistics needed for calculating such limits. Nevertheless, the prediction of heather trend from the model is probabilistic rather than absolute, merely giving 'best estimates' within a range of other (though less likely) values. Another shortcoming of the model, therefore, is its inability to estimate the precision of any one prediction. Compared with the problem of accuracy, however, this drawback is likely to be rather slight.

8.3 The use of stocking levels instead of dung deposited

The use of dung as an index of grazing pressure presumes direct relationships between the amount of dung deposited at a site and the stocking density. Such relationships do not always hold; dung rates can vary with time and type of activity: while at one place animals may feed intensively but defecate little, while at another (eg a resting site) they may do the opposite. The use of stocking densities raises further problems. Any stocking density is, by definition, an average whose precision depends on (i) the size of area concerned, and (ii) the distribution of the animals within it. Except in controlled experiments with animals in enclosures, stocking densities are typically hard to measure, except in terms of total numbers divided by total area; indeed, in most circumstances, these are the only 2 kinds of information available. The figure thus calculated is properly termed the 'crude stocking density', to distinguish it from one based also upon information about the animals' dispersion in place and time. A stocking of 100 sheep on 100 ha thus does not imply a stocking density of one sheep ha^{-1} on all 100 ha; it must simply be treated as the best available estimate. The caution required in using it is still greater when known, but unmeasured, differences in distribution do exist, such as when the native pasture lies next to a resown one to which the stock are given

Plate 8. Long Mynd: scrub recolonization on steep land. Both ITE and the Economic and Social Research Council support work on the implications of likely reductions in farm support under the Common Agricultural Policy (Photograph R E Bryant)

Plate 9. Recolonization of land in Grampian, *c* 300 m. Grouse moor where grazing has been removed following sheep tick outbreaks. Papers in this volume consider the interplay of farm and sporting use (Photograph G R Miller)

Plate 10. Uplands of mid-Wales, *c* 400 m. Extensive improvement of land has been assisted by public financial support in order to stem rural depopulation. Dixon's paper and others in this volume discuss the potential consequences of reduced support in the future (Photograph R E Bryant)

Plate 11. Bent-grass/fescue sward in the Elan plots, mid-Wales, as recorded by Dixon (Photograph J B Dixon)

periodic access, or where exposure differs with aspect or topography. Sites at which supplemental feeding is provided within a larger area are a particular example, and will be grazed far more heavily than the crude stocking rate would indicate. No specific equation can be given, but, clearly, some adjustment of the crude stocking rate will be better than none, even when the correction is only approximate. Adjustment is most feasible when seasonal differences in rate are known: Welch's model is for year-round grazing, and shorter periods should be accommodated *pro rata*. Some allowance might also be possible for autumn and late winter grazing, which affects heather more than grazing at the same intensities at other times (Grant *et al.* 1978).

8.4 Geographic limitations

These are the most obvious limitations on reliability. Any attempt to apply Welch's coefficients to general circumstances is, in fact, to extrapolate beyond the geographic and biological limits within which they were derived. The further the extrapolation, the greater will be the risk of unrealistic results. The response of heather vegetation to similar levels of grazing in the far north and south of Britain will not necessarily be the same as in the north-east of Scotland, even when allowance has been made for latitude and other abiotic differences.

9 Finding a stocking density at which heather will remain stable

Supposing that these methods will most often be used first to predict the effect of an existing or proposed stocking level, the process can then also be used for predicting the stocking level at which cover change will be zero, other site factors being the same. The simplest way (though time-consuming) is to set the stocking rate at various arbitrarily chosen levels, to plot the corresponding predicted values for cover change, and extrapolate to zero on the y-axis (see Figure 2). Alternatively, the model can be iterated with successively increasing or decreasing stocking levels, until a value of zero cover change is obtained (see Section 11).

10 Maximum sheep or maximum cattle stocking?

For mixed stocking, as Figure 3 shows, a range of combinations exists at which heather cover should remain stable. However, not all such combinations may be equally attractive to the farmer, and an evaluation of the various options may be required. For instance, cows are worth much more than sheep, and so, other considerations being equal, a maximized stocking of cattle may pay more than a maximized stocking of sheep, even though sheep could be stocked in much greater numbers. However, a maximized stocking of cattle may not always be sought by the farmer; for instance, farm size, configuration, lack of labour, or other constraints might limit the number of cattle that could be managed, even if not necessarily their stocking density.

As in Figure 3, only 4 points are needed for showing the range of combined stockings over which heather cover

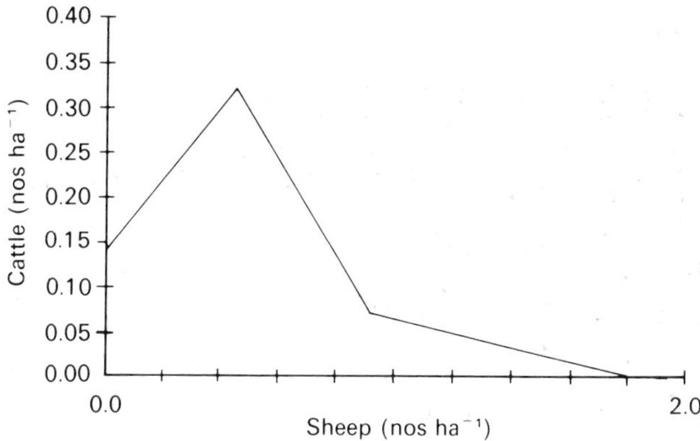

Figure 3. Combined sheep and cattle stockings at which predicted mean % heather cover change = zero (other variables as in Welch's Table 6). The slopes are, of course, particular to the site in question. They can be obtained by extrapolation or by linear programming

change is zero. The slopes of the lines in Figure 3 also give the ratios of values, cattle/sheep, at which any one combined stocking on the same line will have the same total 'value' as any other (in whatever terms the relative values of sheep and cattle might have been determined).[1] At any ratio of values greater than the slope, total value will increase as sheep density increases, and *vice versa* for a ratio less than the slope. The bigger the difference between ratio of values and ratio of stocking densities, the faster will be the change in total value per unit change in stocking ratio, and thence the greater will be the incentive to bias the stocking towards whichever animal is more financially advantageous.

11 Speeding up the calculations for practical use

None of the foregoing procedures need more than simple arithmetic, but the full sequence entails repeated step-wise calculations which are cumbersome and time-consuming, unless treated as a cyclical algorithm. This applies especially to the iterative procedure in Section 9, which otherwise depends on graph-plotting or efficient guesstimation of the appropriate input points if the number of repeat calculations is not to be excessive. A program in BBC BASIC is available on request.

12 Concluding remarks

These procedures are meant to be a supplement to judgement and local knowledge, not a substitute for them. Although they yield specific predictions from particular inputs, the predictions are at best indicative approximations. Furthermore, they relate only to moorland not being managed by burning. They constitute no evidence of change in any particular instance, even when input values have changed during a period of time. In the absence of measured values for stocking level and heather trend on moorland at a wider range of locations

[1] 'Value' here is a notional term for the profit per animal, and total value the notional profit for the flock, herd, or combination of the 2. The relevant matter in this context is the ratio between cattle and sheep returns, and how this can be compared with stocking ratios to differentiate amongst an otherwise equally feasible choice of stocking regime. How the profits might be calculated is a separate issue.

than is available so far, the assumptions in Section 8 remain untested, and therefore also the method itself.

Until such time as something more robust becomes available, however, the procedures described here may still prove useful for estimating trends in heather, and for aiding the choice of stocking levels in management agreements. They may also be a useful adjunct to models for planning land management at the individual farm level, as described by Sibbald *et al.* (1987). Lastly, predictions from the model can be used to estimate the sampling intensities required when heather cover is being monitored. For instance, the expression:

$$n \geq (2(t_{\alpha} + t_{2(1-\beta)})^2 s^2)/d^2$$

estimates the sample size (n) needed for detecting a difference of size d between 2 means at a chosen level of statistical assurance. In the case of heather cover change, d represents the amount of change predicted via the model (see any standard statistical text for other details). Data from monitoring can, in turn, give the necessary feedback for judging the method's general reliability.

13 References

Gimingham, C.H. 1972. *Ecology of heathlands.* London: Chapman & Hall.

Grant, S.A., Barthram, G.T., Lamb, W.I.C. & Milne, J.A. 1978. Effect of season and level of grazing on the utilisation of heather by sheep. 1. Responses of the sward. *J. Br. Grassld Soc.*, **33,** 289-300.

Miller, G.R. & Watson, A. 1978. Heather productivity and its relevance to the regulation of red grouse populations. In: *Production ecology of British moors and montane grasslands,* edited by O.W. Heal & D.F. Perkins, 277-285. Berlin: Springer.

Sibbald, A.R., Grant, S.A., Milne, J.A. & Maxwell, T.J. 1987. Heather moorland management - a model. In: *Agriculture and conservation in the hills and uplands,* edited by M. Bell & R.G.H. Bunce, ?-?. (ITE symposium no. 23.) Grange-over-Sands: Institute of Terrestrial Ecology.

Spence, D.H.N. 1960. Studies on the vegetation of Shetland. *J. Ecol.,* **48,** 73-95

Welch, D. 1984. Studies in the grazing of heather moorland in north-east Scotland. I-III. *J. appl. Ecol.,* **21,** 178-225.

Appendix 1. Factors for converting stocking rate into its equivalent in dung deposition[1]

I	Mean dung output per animal h^{-1} (from Welch 1984, p192)	cow	444 ml	$= 3.893 \times 10^6$ ml
		sheep	60	= 0.5256
		deer	110	= 0.9636
		hare/rabbit	15	= 0.1314
II	Mean deposition yr^{-1} at one animal ha^{-1} ($I \times 10^{-4}$)	cow	389 ml m^{-2} yr^{-1}	
		sheep	52	
		deer	96	
		hare/rabbit	13	

[1] For cattle, 444 ≅ 800/1.8, where 800 is the mean output quoted by Welch (1984, p192), and the division by 1.8 adjusts for the greater moisture content (and hence volume) of cattle dung compared with the pelleted dung of the other animals. However, Welch (1984, Table 6) gives the mean deposition by cattle as 91 ml m^{-2} yr^{-1} at mean stocking rate (0.26 ha^{-1}), which gives a conversion factor (II) of 350.00 (ie 10% lower). This lower factor is used in Section 7 so as to maintain parity with the value in Welch's Table 6 (which contains the mean values of the independent variables from which regression model 3 was derived).

Appendix 2. A substitute for Welch's Grl

Miller and Watson (1978) collated estimates of heather production (in kg ha^{-1}) from 8 field studies, standardized the estimates to a uniform cover abundance of 100% and found a significant relationship between these standardized estimates and the attitude to which they pertained. The equation was:

$$\text{Production} = 3565 - \text{Altitude} \times 3.69$$

For the mean altitude of 294.3 m by Welch (1984, Table 6), this equation gives a standardized heather production of 2479.03 kg ha^{-1}, as compared with 265.4 for Welch's mean value of Grl at the same altitude. The ratio between Miller and Watson's equation coefficients for kg ha^{-1} and the coefficient for Grl's is 0.10706, viz:

$$(0.10706 \times 3565) - (0.10706 \times 3.69 \times \text{Altitude}) = 381.66 - 0.395 \times \text{Altitude} \quad (4)$$

All but one of the production estimates quoted by Miller and Watson were from sites in north-east Scotland, and so the relationship with altitude would not have been much confounded by latitude. The equation above must, therefore, be further adjusted for latitude when used at places outside north-east Scotland, as explained in Section 6 and Appendix 3.

Appendix 3. Allowing for differences in latitude

As shown, for instance, in the depression of the hypothetical tree-line with increasing latitude, plant growth rates differ with altitude according to (i) latitudinal differences in mean temperature at sea level, and (ii) differences in lapse rate (rate of temperature decline with altitude). Allowance for both at different localities can be made as follows.

1. Lapse rates differ from north to south, apparently in a regular manner, becoming steadily faster as mean July temperatures decline northward (Figure 4).

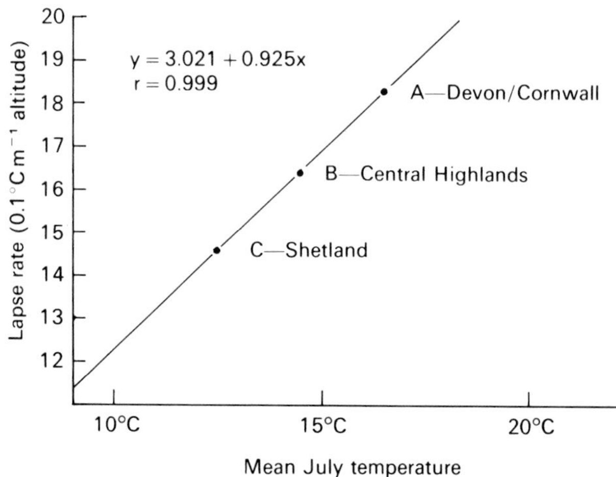

Figure 4. Change in lapse rate with latitudinal differences in mean July temperature (source: A, calculated from Meteorological Office data; B,C, Spence 1960)

Accordingly, temperature differences between latitudes become wider as altitude rises. The differences are negligible for localities near to one another, but more substantial for places further apart. From the line in Figure 4, lapse rates can be interpolated for each of the 9 zones in Figure 1, and the difference from the rate in north-east Scotland can be expressed as a proportion (pdlr. shown as a bracketed value for each zone in Figure 1). Thus, at 9/10th of the lapse rate in north-east Scotland, 300 m in south-west England (eg Exmoor) corresponds to 270 m altitude in north-east Scotland.

2. Published Meteorological Office isotherms for daily mean temperature in July (the warmest month of the growing season) divide the whole of Britain into zones at 0.5°C intervals, standardized to sea level temperatures. North-east Scotland differs from Shetland by about 2.0°C, and from Devon (Exmoor) by the same amount. Multiply by the local lapse rate then converts these differences into their equivalents in local altitude:

   $$Z = dt \times llr \qquad (5)$$

   Where Z is the equivalent difference in altitude (m), dt is the latitudinal difference in temperature (°C), and llr is the local lapse rate (m $1.0°C^{-1}$) for the temperature zone in question. Values of Z for each of the zones are shown on Figure 1.

3. For a given altitude within a particular zone, the equivalent altitude in north-east Scotland is thus:

   $$Alt' = (Alt + Z) \times pdlr \qquad (6)$$

Where no measured value for Grl is available, Alt' should be used in place of true altitude when substituting for Grl in equations 1–4. As Welch's model includes altitude as a factor in its own right, values for it should, in theory, be adjusted twice – once in the substitute for Grl and again directly. However, the effect of this adjustment is to offset most of the adjustment to Grl, enough in the case of Orkney and Shetland to produce ŷ-values bigger than those for the same true altitudes on the mainland. (Indeed, for northerly latitudes generally, increasing heather cover would be predicted for altitudes at which heather has ceased to occur.) Whether adjusted for latitude or not, a linear coefficient for altitude is probably much too simple a model of the 'competition' factor (Section 3.2) to suffice for representing it on moorland generally. Whatever its influence at low or medium altitudes, any competitive advantage of heather can be expected to decline to zero as the plant itself nears its limits of occurrence. In the absence of data showing what the form and rate of decline might be, the coefficient for altitude is, therefore, progressively reduced in equations 1 and 2 by a factor of @ at site altitudes above 300 m (the mean altitude in Welch's Table 6). With Grl as in equation 2, no grazing, and other site inputs at Welch's means, the setting of @ at

$$@ = 18.25 \times 10^{-8} (Altitude - 300)^{-1} \qquad (7)$$

forces ŷ-values to decline evenly to zero at an adjusted altitude of 1000 m (approximately the upper limit of heather in Britain).

The use of goats in hill pasture management

M LIPPERT, A J F RUSSEL and S A GRANT
Hill Farming Research Organisation, Bush Estate, Penicuik, Midlothian, Scotland

1 Summary
The productivity of hill sheep flocks can be markedly increased by the integrated use of reseeded and indigenous pastures, as in the Hill Farming Research Organisation (HFRO) '2-pasture' system of management described in the Organisation's 1979 report. The maintenance of areas of reseeded grass and clover (*Trifolium* spp.) in a productive and weed-free state can, in some situations, prove difficult when grazed only by sheep. Recent research has shown that, where weed encroachment is a problem, strategic grazing by goats may aid pasture management to the potential benefit of sheep production. Goats may also graze certain plant species less readily eaten by sheep, and thus both increase dry matter utilization and, if the grazing is controlled, help maintain a more desirable species balance.

2 Control of rushes in enclosed reseeds
One of the most common problems of hill reseeds is infestation with rushes (*Juncus* spp). In an experiment carried out over 3 consecutive grazing seasons on a wholly enclosed red fescue/white clover (*Festuca rubra /Trifolium repens*) reseed infested with rushes, stock numbers were adjusted to maintain sward surface heights of 3-4 cm on plots grazed by either sheep or goats, and of 5-6 cm on plots grazed only by goats. Initially, rush stem height averaged more than 70 cm on all plots with a green stem density of about 4000 m^{-2}. Rush cover was approximately 12%. On both treatments involving goats, the green rush stems were virtually all grazed within 2 weeks of the plots being stocked, and on the 3-4 cm plots few green stems remained visible above ground.

The effect of the first year's grazing treatments, which were imposed for only some 8 weeks, was evident at the beginning of the following grazing season; the density and height of the green stems on the 5-6 cm goat treatment (1190 m^{-2} and 25 cm respectively) were considerably reduced in comparison to the 3-4 cm sheep treatment (4400 m^{-2} and 36 cm), and on the 3-4 goat treatment the rush stems were so scarce that measurements could not be made (see Table 1). By the end of the second season, it was only with extreme difficulty that the locations formerly occupied by rushes could be identified.Comparisons in the final year were again between the 3-4 cm grass height sheep plots and the 5-6 cm goat plots. Overall, the results presented in Table 1 show that, while some grazing of rushes by sheep was observed, particularly in the latter part of each season, it was insufficient to have any real effect on their vigour or density. The grazing by goats on the 5-6 cm grass height treatment progressively weakened the vigour and density of rushes over the 3-year period, while the heavier goat grazing (3-4 cm grass height) effectively eliminated the rushes early in the second grazing season.

In practice, it may be desirable to control rushes by the combined grazing of sheep and goats, and an experiment designed to study the complementary grazing by sheep and goats of 2 areas of common bent-grass (*Agrostis capillaris*) which had been invaded by rushes has recently been completed. Goats were stocked on plots at rates equivalent to 10, 20 and 30 ha^{-1}, and sufficient numbers of sheep were added to each plot to maintain sward heights at 4-5 cm. In the first year, the proportion of green rush stems grazed and the closeness of grazing increased as goat stocking rate increased from 10 to 20 ha^{-1}; rush control was effective at 20 goats ha^{-1} and differed little at the end of the season from the 30 ha^{-1}

Table 1. The effects of separate grazing by sheep and goats on the vigour and density of rushes in enclosed reseeded hill pasture

Sward height (cm)	Sheep 3-4	Goats 3-4	Goats 5-6
Year 1			
Grazing days (ha^{-1}) sheep	2593		
goats		4030	2215
Pre-grazing: rush stem height (cm)	72	71	71
Mid-season: proportion green stems grazed	0.34	0.99	0.97
height grazed green stems (cm)	57	12	38
End season: proportion green stems grazed	0.82	0.94	0.95
height grazed green stems (cm)	50	7	18
Year 2			
Grazing days (ha^{-1}) sheep	1865	325	225
goats		2095	1905
Pre-grazing: green stem density (m^{-2})	4400	0	1190
green stem height (cm)	36	0	25
End season: proportion green stems grazed	0.58	-	1.00
height grazed green stems (cm)	55	-	12
Year 3			
Grazing days (ha^{-1}) sheep	1955		
goats barren		1505	100
with single kids		1365	1680
Pre-grazing: green stem density (m^{-2})	3766	0	969
green stem height (cm)	51	0	20
End season: proportion green stems grazed	0.79	-	0.98
height grazed green stems (cm)	53	-	7

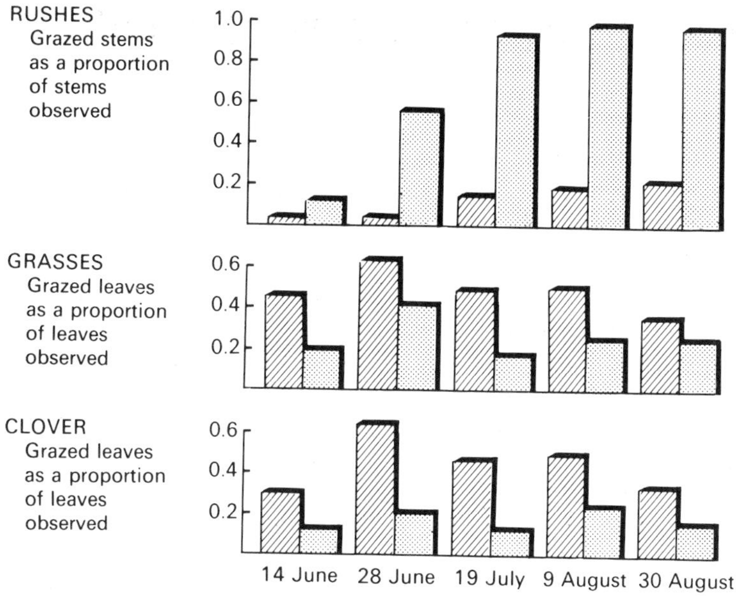

Figure 1. Reseeded pasture. The proportions of grazed leaves of rushes, grasses and clover on plots grazed by sheep or goats

treatment. At the end of the second season, the proportions of green stems grazed on the 3 treatments were 0.87, 0.92 and 0.92, and grazed stem heights were 49, 30 and 13 cm respectively. The ratios of goat to sheep grazing days to achieve these levels of rush control were 0.5, 2.4 and 5.4. These results and those of the experiment described above indicate that high goat grazing pressures can effectively control rushes in sown pasture. Further investigations are required to determine the type of subsequent grazing management needed to prevent reinfestation of clean pasture by seedling rushes.

3 Grazing choice in mosaic improvements

The maintenance of areas of reseeded pasture which, because of difficulties of drainage and topography, are sown as patches or mosaics within a larger enclosed area of indigenous vegetation can pose particular

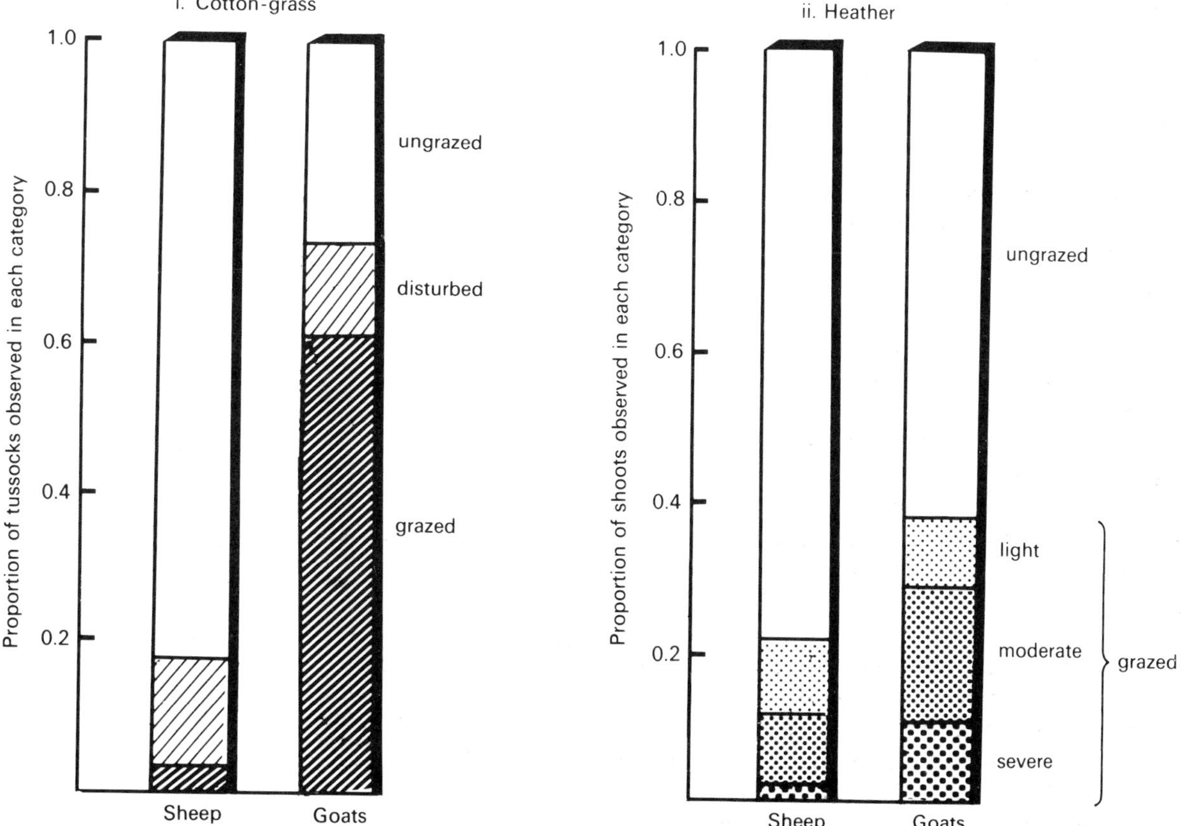

Figure 2. Proportions of (i) cotton-grass tussocks, and (ii) heather shoots in the designated categories in July

problems. The improved areas of sown grass and clover tend to be grazed by sheep in preference to the unimproved areas, and are often invaded by rushes, thistles (*Cirsium* spp.) and indigenous species. In an experiment reported by Grant *et al.* (1984) and conducted on such reseeds on blanket bog vegetation, sheep and feral goats were separately grazed on plots comprising half reseeded pasture and half indigenous vegetation. On the reseeded areas, the goats grazed grass and particularly clover to a lesser extent, and rushes to a markedly greater extent, than did sheep (Figure 1). On the unimproved areas, the goats grazed the 2 dominant species – cotton-grass (*Eriophorum vaginatum*) and heather (*Calluna vulgaris*) – heavily early in the season when grass on the reseeded area was plentiful and in contrast to the pattern shown by sheep (Figure 2).

More detailed studies of the grazing of grass/heather mosaics by goats on freely drained heather moor have also been conducted. These studies have shown marked differences in the grazing habits of goats on grass/heather mosaics to those noted previously with sheep; whereas sheep preferentially graze grass, so that at a given stocking rate they graze most heather where there is least grass, goats exhibit a preference for heather, and utilize it to the greatest extent where it forms only a small proportion of the available grazing (Figure 3). The appreciation of this major difference in grazing preference between sheep and goats has led to experiments in which one of the variables has been the number of goat grazing days required to achieve utilization of 40% of the current season's growth.

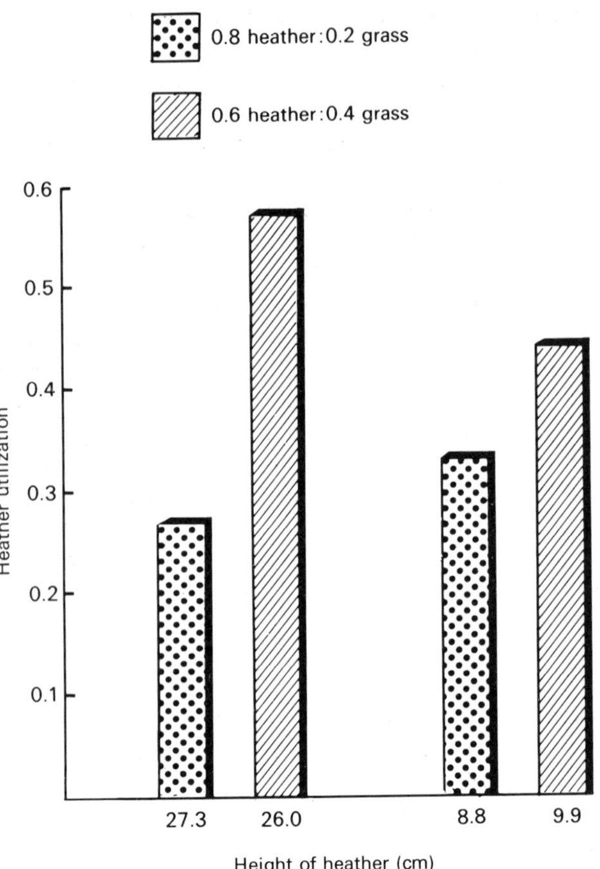

Figure 3. On heather/grass mosaic reseeds, the utilization of heather by goats varies inversely as the proportion of heather in the mosaic. Plots (0.2 ha) each stocked with 4 feral goats (28 kg live weight) on 2 July; utilization records for 15 August

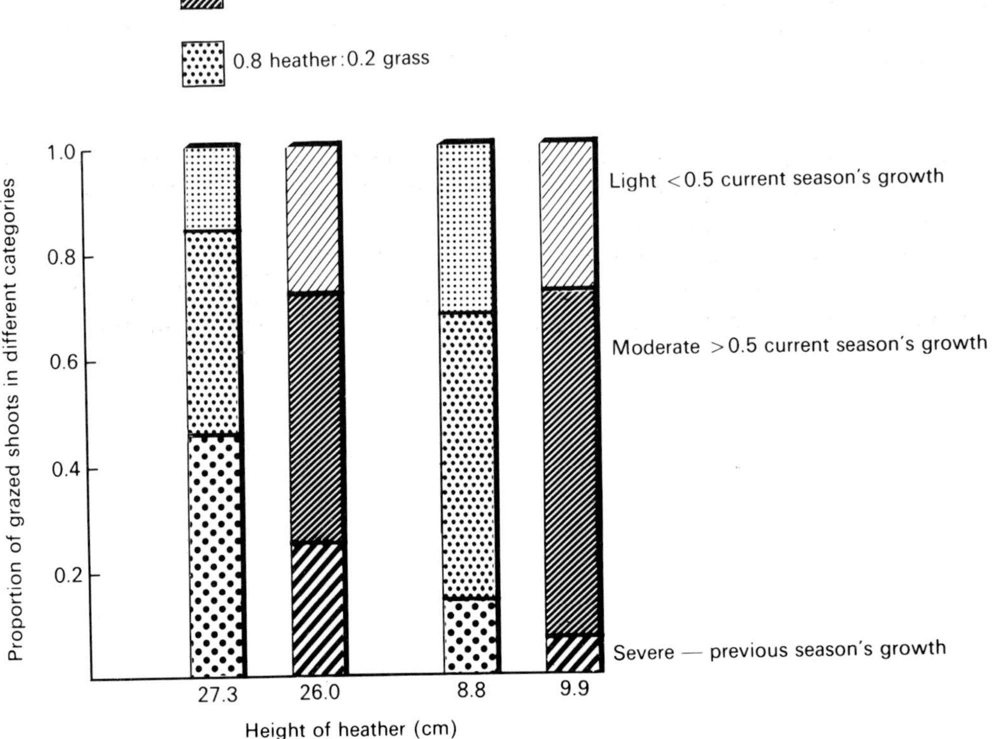

Figure 4. Goats graze a greater proportion of previous season's growth on tall than on short stands

These requirements have been of the order of 1000–1600 grazing days ha^{-1}, varying according to the proportion of heather in the mosaic. Patterns of utilization on short and tall heather stands have shown that, although restricted to consuming not more than 40% of the current season's growth, goats will eat into the woody tissue of the previous season's growth to a significant extent on long heather, but to only a negligible degree on short stands (Figure 4). These results indicate a very considerable potential complementarity between sheep and goats in the grazing management of grass/heather mosaics. Although the risk of over-grazing heather, and thus adversely affecting subsequent production, must be greater with goats than with sheep, this need not constitute a problem once the preference of goats for heather is recognized. Indeed, providing grazing can be controlled, there would appear to be opportunities for using goats to advantage in the management of heather resources.

4 *Manipulation of hill communities*

The use of goats to control white bent or moor mat-grass (*Nardus stricta*) has also been examined in an experiment over the last 3 years. The numbers of goats grazing areas of mat-grass were adjusted twice weekly as necessary to maintain between-tussock grass heights of 4.5, 5.5 and 6.5 cm, and for comparison sheep were also grazed on other areas to maintain a grass height of 4.5 cm. The results, illustrated in Figure 5, show clearly that, as goat grazing pressure was increased to reduce between-tussock grass height, both the proportion of mat-grass leaves grazed and the severity with which these leaves were grazed increased. It is also evident that, under equivalent management, goats graze more mat-grass and do so more closely than do sheep. These results indicate that mat-grass can be controlled more effectively by grazing with goats than with sheep, and other work (Grant *et al.* 1984) has demonstrated that goats can be almost as effective as cattle in this respect.

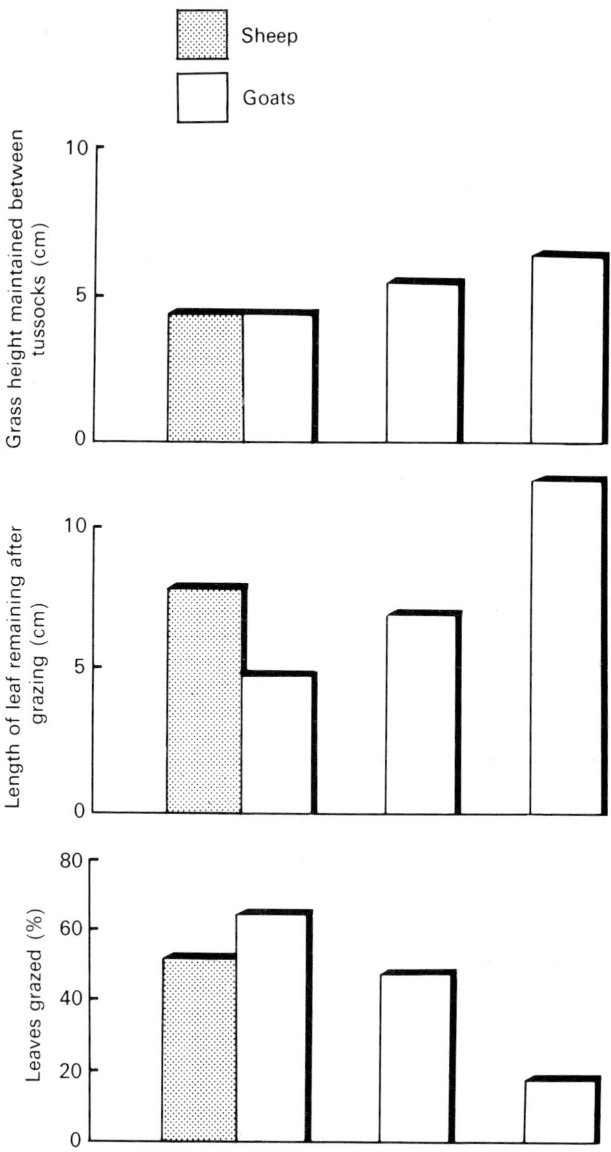

Figure 5. The effect of between-tussock sward height on the grazing of mat-grass by goats in comparison to sheep

5 *Conclusion*

In conclusion, it is clear that goats can be used to bring about changes in the vegetational composition of hill pastures such that undesirable plant species can be controlled and in some cases eliminated. It is evident that there is a considerable potential complementarity between the grazing of sheep and goats and that this could be used to benefit sheep production, as well as to sustain production from goats on hill sheep enterprises.

6 *Reference*

Grant, S.A., Bolton, G.R. & Russel, A.J.F. 1984. The utilization of sown and indigenous plant species by sheep and goats grazing hill pastures. *Grass Forage Sci.*, **39,** 361-370.

Nature conservation and rural development

A MOWLE
Nature Conservancy Council, 12 Hope Terrace, Edinburgh, Scotland

1 Introduction

A considerable amount of time at conferences is spent making statements of the problem under study, but real progress depends on entering a more prescriptive phase. The remarks which follow will float some ideas for consideration and comment (Mowle 1986).

This conference has focused its attention on the 'hills and uplands'. Working in Scotland, with most of Britain's uplands, it makes more sense to talk of the Less Favoured Areas (LFAs). These Areas are the main target of the European farm structures policy within the Common Agricultural Policy (CAP), and are designated under the European Community (EC) Directive 75/269. Most of Scotland is designated as LFA, and so 'the uplands issue', in the sense it has been used at this meeting, begins at sea level. The primary focus of this conference on agricultural land use can also be questioned because for a number of years in Scotland (and now in northern England) extensive afforestation has been an important source of concern. Forestry and agriculture cannot be placed in watertight compartments in the LFAs, and so there will be passing reference to forestry in this paper.

2 Conservation and the rural community

If we look at the LFAs, a considerable number of celebrated conservation cases attracting media attention in recent years can be identified. In Wales, there are the Berwyn Mountains, in northern England the north Pennines, in Scotland Lurcher's Gully, Creag Meagaidh, Duich Moss, Orkney, Shetland, the Caithness and Sutherland 'Flow country'. In all these cases, the status of the local rural community faced with conservation constraints has been a major issue. Local opinion has been quoted questioning the right of interfering outsiders to influence the direction, scale or pace of development.

At one level, this is fair comment.The substantial political support for the conservation lobby is undoubtedly urban-based, not least because that is where 80% or more of the population lives. In a Scottish context, the support for conservation is skewed towards the south-east of England and towards the articulate middle classes (Lowe & Goyder 1983).

The danger is that this situation sets up a completely false dichotomy. Rural and urban are not independent, or even all that different. If you go into a crofthouse in Shetland, you are just as likely to find a video, colour TV, automatic washing machine and deep freeze. The rural community has similar material aspirations to its urban counterparts, watches the same television soap operas, reads the same newspapers, votes for representatives to the same Parliament. Rural land uses are industrial operations carried on in the countryside, governed by the same economic rationale as urban industries. Farmers, and especially foresters, are increasingly dependent on urban capital, supplies of fuel, and other inputs and demand from urban markets for their economic survival. The rural policies set in Whitehall, Edinburgh and other urban centres are funded from the same exchequer, to which urban and rural taxpayers alike make contributions. The countryside is simply that element of our urban/industrial civilization where there happens to be more space, land, natural resources and fewer people. It is a focus of attention for urban conservationists simply because such thinly populated areas are, by definition, much closer to 'wild nature', therefore containing wildlife and landscapes whose future is the subject of concern.

This uncomfortable interdependence holds lessons for all of us. Those identified in the press as the rural community – farmers, foresters, landowners and those living in rural areas – must accept their interdependence and not try to portray themselves as an independent yeomanry threatened by alien bureaucratic intervention and red tape. The increasing political significance of the green vote is a factor with which these interests must come to terms. If the rural community were to look for allies in the urban community, where can it turn? Those urban dwellers who have some concern and are motivated to address the problems of the countryside are the core of the green vote. Surely, the conservation lobby and the rural community are natural allies?

To bring about such a reconciliation, certain home truths must be accepted by the conservation lobby. Setting aside areas of ground as nature reserves, special sites, various species of park where conservation needs are to be the primary consideration of management is one thing. When this inventory is expanded to include a substantial proportion of the land area in a locality, one can legitimately ask how other factors can be brought into balance. There must be a limit on the inventory of designations, and yet present policies and legislation provide for little else. There is a limit beyond which conservation designations cannot protect environmental interests, and this limit is being reached in parts of Britain's Less Favoured Areas.

Second, the conservation lobby is largely urban-based and tends to have an urban outlook. Generally speaking, town dwellers overlook the connection between the barley in the field and the steak on the table or the whisky on the bar. Most people have a low awareness of their physical dependence on the countryside, and when this lack of awareness is coupled with television and Sunday colour supplement images of rural charm (McLaughlin 1986), those who actually make a living in rural areas have legitimate cause for concern. While it is possible to envisage a rural arcadia founded upon the principles derived from the World Conservation Strategy, if it denies opportunity to the rural community relative to the urban majority, it can be no more than a subtle form of tyranny. To take one obvious example, the calls one often hears to preserve 'traditional' forms of agriculture in some of our more picturesque areas are a completely inadequate economic and cultural solution to an ecological problem.

Therefore, any prescriptions for the rural sector derived from environmentalist thinking must be evaluated in terms of social justice, as well as ecological rectitude. Any wide-ranging ecological policy must take account of the fact that the primary concern with the health of the natural environment *via* wildlife and amenity issues necessarily raises issues of distributional justice, of personal and public rights, and of social and cultural values in the human communities concerned.

While I have spoken of the conservation lobby and the rural community as 2 distinct and coherent entities, life is not really that simple. The rural community is often cited as a voice which must be heard, but there is little agreement on which body or bodies can legitimately represent its views. In practice, the rural lobby can be subdivided in many ways into various types of landed interest, large- and small-scale agriculture, commercial forestry, the various game pursuits, landed estates, and so on. Rural dwellers can equally be subdivided into owners, tenants, farm and forestry workers, shopkeepers, other service workers in transport, telephones, post office and so on, rural-dwelling urban commuters and their 2 LFA subspecies, the second-home owners and the retired 'white settlers'. These diverse groups certainly do not agree amongst themselves. There could be a similar litany for the green lobby, from Government-funded conservation agencies to animal liberation fundamentalists, but the point is made.

3 The desire for integration

When attention is focused on reconciliation of these diverse interests, the word integration springs readily to the lips. The problem with integration is that no recognized definition of the term has ever been widely accepted. As a result, we have calls for 'integrated rural development' (Ulbricht 1986) and the like, without any clear idea whether the word is simply a fashionable slogan or whether it has any real meaning. As a way of shedding light over this confusing picture, it is helpful to consider integration of conservation and development at 3 levels – policy, programme and practical. The policy level is the most fundamental because it sets the overall framework of legislation.

Integration requires at least an extension and elaboration of existing liaison between the sectoral agencies, and some see a need for some overall 'Ministry of Rural Affairs'. There must be doubts about such a monolithic approach yielding many benefits, but there is certainly a gap in the present arrangements, with no official body charged to develop an overview, in a sense to arbitrate the conflicts which arise and to promote a framework of integration.

Attempts to secure integration at the programme level are hindered by this policy failure. The only attempt at a large-scale 'integrated' programme in Britain has been the Western Isles Integrated Development Programme (IDP), which was supported from the European farm structures policy under EC Regulation 1939/81. The Nature Conservancy Council (NCC) was commissioned by the EC Environment Directorate (DGXI) to report on the environmental effects of the Programme, and their final report was submitted to Brussels in 1986. In practice, the IDP simply labelled existing patterns of expenditure as integrated, with little real attempt to co-ordinate the expenditure of different agencies on the ground. In particular, there was no attempt to manage the diverse funding mechanisms under a single budget line, which would make 'integration' possible. Indeed, it is difficult to see how this could be achieved short of a wholesale restructuring of the existing sectoral agencies. Under present circumstances, the local authorities' role in rural land use is extremely limited. There must surely be a potentially far greater role for them in implementing integrated programmes, but they would have to be provided with some form of guidelines steering the balance of local and national interests.

On the ground, in practical terms, individual initiative, motivation and commitment are the key factors for the success of any integration strategy. Over-regulation will work against these factors, while an inadequate or inappropriate package of incentives will tend to stifle such energies or direct them in ways which fail to secure objectives. If we take the example of farming, it is quite clear that the underlying direction of policy of recent decades towards increasing output must be changed. No similar single dominant purpose for future policy can be identified, and the range of other interests mentioned earlier are all pressing for their say. The result must be multiple-objective policies. The farmer will need public support to maintain an economic enterprise, while meeting a range of other explicit objectives in relation to wildlife, landscape, local employment, tourism, and so on. He will receive public support in so far as he works to a management plan which reconciles these various aims. This prospect may be set alongside other present trends in farming. Farmers have increased their productive capability enormously over the last 20 years by adopting new machinery and technologies such as spraying, and by introducing plant varieties and animal breeds capable of exploiting these management regimes. In future, attention will be focused on improving management skills within the established technologies. Problems will be solved through better management rather than by the adoption of new gadgetry.

Such multiple objectives are demanding for the farmer, who must take in a wider range of needs in day-to-day management. In these circumstances, the practical manager has the right to expect clear signals in terms of policies, legislation and public expenditure programmes to support his acceptance of the challenge. At present, we are some way from providing practitioners with such clear guidance. Take the example of the farmer considering diversification into woodland management, faced with a bewildering array of overlapping and conflicting sources of advice and grant aid. Such circumstances are a strong disincentive to multiple land use, yet this seems to be the logical end point of the desire to meet wider objectives and secure this elusive thing called 'integration'.

4 *Indicative strategies*

Politicians, quite understandably, express doubts that such a reconciliation of interests can really be achieved. The sorts of changes that are required are not going to be achieved overnight, or as the result of some centrally imposed master-plan or blueprint. The key lies in local or regional responses to local or regional problems, and these, taken together, can create a climate of opinion in which the overall changes required will be generally seen as both desirable and necessary. There is no sense in waiting for the grand solution, because none can emerge when the necessary frameworks of policy are inappropriate. The idea of local indicative strategies springs from this perception of the situation.

What is an indicative strategy? Like integration, this strategy has also lacked any real definition of terms. In Scotland, one or 2 local authorities have taken cautious steps towards establishing a local framework of liaison between the various interests involved, adopting the role of broker. Through its local plan, one has declared its intention 'to investigate opportunities for agreeing an integrated framework ..., to resolve conflict and competing objectives in rural land use' (Argyll & Bute District Council 1985). So, indicative strategies are a means of achieving integration and multiple objectives in land use. They are local, referring to some generally accepted geographical boundary. This focus on a geographical area and the range of interests it contains needs a systems view to establish a common basis for analysis. Such an analysis, in turn, requires a continuing dialogue involving the local community, various land use and conservation interests, and others, which will help to overcome misunderstandings and thereby more precisely identify real conflicts of interest. These discussions will identify issues requiring further research and elucidation, leading to better understanding of the system and its dynamic relationships.

An indicative strategy is, therefore, a process, not a statement. At different stages, reports and written statements of the current understanding of the strategic relationships will aid the process, but cannot replace it. This has been a primary failing of calls for land use strategies to date, which have tended to think in terms of a preliminary horse-trading of interests, for which each is then expected to sign up, and thereby become irrevocably committed. This expectation is certainly unrealistic, and ignores the constantly changing circumstances of the real world.

5 *Accommodating the conservation interest*

Speaking from a conservationist viewpoint, what does such a process offer the conservation interest, faced with the limits and hostility I reviewed at the outset? At present, a national system of site safeguard is administered by the Nature Conservancy Council (1984) as one of the range of sectoral agencies. The NCC does not have any real access to national Governmental policy-making, but must play within the present sectoral rules. This approach has clear limitations in localities where site designations are constraining economic activity on a significant proportion of the land area.

NCC's designation of Sites of Special Scientific Interest rests entirely on a statement of the ecological importance of the defined areas, set against the nationally determined criteria for designation. In future, and particularly where these limitations of the site safeguard approach are encountered, making the case for conservation will have to go much further. Most important, the ecological evidence will have to be placed in the context of its interactions with other associated interests, land uses, local industries and communities. In addition, the relative strengths and importance of these different interests must be the subject of critical review. These 3 stages provide a basis for presentation of the conservation case in the indicative strategy process.

With such a multi-stage approach to the presentation of the conservation case, it is possible to speculate on the form of the indicative strategy process of which it will be a part. The logic of the approach is towards some sort of zonal management for the locality under consideration. That cannot be successful if it can only corral the different interests behind artificial boundaries delimiting exclusive use zones. The complexity of inter-relationships requires a more sophisticated approach, within constraints of practicality and subject to monitoring and periodic review to account for changing circumstances. The kind of zoning required will be founded upon a degrees of constraint principle rather than exclusive use.

From a nature conservation viewpoint, the result will be a number of zones ranging from the statutory sites, where nature conservation is regarded as the primary focus of land management, through one or more zones of specified environmental sensitivity, where economic activity will be supported with certain constraints, to a zone where codes of practice and design standards defined to protect the natural environment are to be followed. Thus, there should be no land entirely free of constraints on activities which might adversely affect the natural environment, but the degree of constraint will reflect the degree of environmental sensitivity. It may be that the proposed Environmentally Sensitive Areas (ESAs) set up under the European Structures Regulation (797/85) and the Agriculture Act 1986 will provide experience of establishing an intermediate level of protection. Some conservation bodies (including NCC) have taken the view that ESAs are a test bed for new agricultural support measures sensitive to the needs of the environment, which may be more widely adopted in due course.

From the agricultural point of view, a similar staged approach to presentation of its case is required. The primary assessment of the agricultural interest will be founded upon knowledge of present use in relation to a statement of land capability. This assessment will have to be set in the context of the other interests on that land, and then alongside these other interests in the same way. The same system of zones will define a range from the prime agricultural resource, essential to sustain the local structure of agriculture, through intermediate supporting zones, to those in which agriculture is clearly secondary to another primary interest. In the same way, there are no zones from which agriculture is automatically excluded, although there may be extremes of constraint which make agriculture impracticable at particular times and in certain places.

Similar arrangements are required for forestry, local industry, tourism, services and other interests falling within the concerns of the indicative strategy. The whole concept is thus one of dialogue and continuing engagement, rather than the sterile confrontation which is all too common within the present arrangements.

6 *Conclusion*

So, back to reality. The reality is that we have sectoral policies and programmes which impede integration in practice. The existing agencies and vested interests have not generally been prepared in the past to indulge in the self-appraisal necessary to make indicative strategies a reality. As Theodore Roszak put it with appropriate imagery, is this not rather like butterflies making demands of dinosaurs?

To end on a positive note, there are a few encouraging signs to be seen. In agriculture, there is a fundamental reappraisal of policy objectives. There are questions being asked about the basis of forestry policy, of the status of rural communities, of the place for conservation in the 90% of the countryside which is not already designated. Looking back, the present structures date largely from the post-war reconstruction of the late 1940s. People are now asking how long this structure can continue to be useful, and what circumstances will be required to bring about the modern equivalent of the learned committees of the 1940s from which flowed our town and country planning system, together with the basic frameworks of agriculture, forestry and conservation policy. At risk of over-extending the analogy, the task facing us all is to retrain the dinosaurs of present policy to face a new reality.

7 *References*

Argyll & Bute District Council. 1985. *Islay, Jura and Colonsay local plan.* Kilmory, Lochgilphead: The Council.

Lowe, P. & Goyder, J. 1983. *Environmental groups in politics.* London: George Allen & Unwin.

McLaughlin, B. 1986. Rural policy in the 1980s: the revival of the rural idyll. *J. Rural Stud.*, **2**,81-90.

Mowle, A. 1986. *Nature conservation and rural development - the need for new thinking about rural sector policies.* (Focus on Nature Conservation no. 18.) Peterborough: Nature Conservancy Council.

Nature Conservancy Council. 1984. *Nature conservation in Great Britain.* Peterborough: NCC.

Ulbricht, T., ed. 1986. *Integrated rural development. Proc. European Symposium, September 1985, Wageningen.* National Raad voor Landbouwkundig Onderzoek.

An assessment of amenity tree planting in England and Wales: research note

J M SYKES and D R BRIGGS
Institute of Terrestrial Ecology, Merlewood Research Station, Grange-over-Sands, Cumbria, England

Since 1974–75, the Countryside Commission for England and Wales has paid grant aid amounting to over £9 million on about 30 000 amenity tree planting (ATP) schemes. In the summer of 1985, the Institute of Terrestrial Ecology carried out a survey to appraise the success of 288 schemes drawn from 3 counties in each of the Commission's 8 Regions. An assessment of the schemes included estimates of survival percentages and condition of trees; effects of post-planting maintenance on survival; effect on survival of planting by experienced or inexperienced individuals; and the potential contribution to the landscape of each scheme. Analysis of the data sought for differences between Regions and between planting years, and the sample was divided equally between the 3 planting years 1976–77, 1979–80, 1982–83.

Frequency distributions of percentage survival of trees were calculated for England and Wales for the 8 Regions and for the 3 planting years. The distributions were markedly skewed towards the highest survival class (90–100%) and, in order to best represent the central tendency, survivals were ranked and the median value was calculated. Non-parametric statistical tests (Kruskal-Wallis and Kendall coefficient of concordance) did not reveal any significant differences between years or Regions. When all years and Regions were considered together, the median survival was 77% with an interquartile range of 49–96%. Whilst 57% of schemes had 70% survival or better and complete survival had been achieved in 17% of schemes, 10% had less than 30% survival.

Several factors are thought to have affected the longevity of planted trees. Thirty per cent of schemes showed evidence of recent maintenance (weeding, repair work, etc) and had a median survival of 88%. This result was significantly different ($P<0.01$) from those schemes which did not show such evidence of maintenance (73%). Post-planting maintenance grants, offered as an incentive for grantees to continue caring for their trees, have become less commonly available since 1978, and in only one of the local authority areas sampled were such grants paid. The small sample available did not have a significantly higher survival than other schemes and, if this result were confirmed in a larger sample, it would suggest that, whilst post-planting maintenance leads to higher survival, the availability of maintenance grants *per se* does not necessarily do so. Perhaps surprisingly, no significant differences were shown to exist when the survival of trees planted by individuals or groups of varying expertise was examined. Although survival is the most important single criterion to be used in judging the success of an ATP scheme, the condition of surviving trees will also determine a scheme's eventual contribution to the landscape. The condition of individual trees was assessed in order to determine the proportion of healthy to unhealthy trees and to establish the principal causes and extent of damage. Using the Forestry Commission's criteria, trees were assigned to one of 3 health categories, and it was found that 75% of surviving trees were healthy, 12% moderately healthy and 13% unhealthy. Apart from environmentally determined tree damage (eg exposure, frost), which was apparent in 23% of schemes, domestic, farm and wild animals affected a further 14% and human or unknown causes were recorded in 7% of schemes. Of all the schemes affected by damage, 28% suffered at least some serious damage and half of those were unlikely to make any contribution to the landscape without replanting.

Seventeen per cent of schemes required some restocking, but the most common maintenance need, affecting 20% of schemes, was adjustment of tree ties and stakes. Fifteen per cent of schemes required weeding or mulching, etc, and an additional 14% needed some other form of attention. Only 34% of schemes did not require attention at the time of survey.

Schemes were most commonly planted along field boundaries (35%), an encouraging trend toward regeneration of hedgerow features, with planting around existing features such as buildings and silage pits also being common in most Regions (23%). Planting beside thoroughfares, including public and farm roads, private drives, footpaths and bridleways, was at about the same level (18%) as in field corners.

More detailed facts and figures are available from the authors or from the Countryside Commission, which funded this work.

Grazing in broadleaved upland woods

F J G MITCHELL
Hill Farming Research Organisation, Bush Estate, Penicuik, Midlothian, Scotland

The shelter and grazing provided by upland broadleaved woods can play an important role in upland agriculture. However, these woods are also prime sites for nature conservation, and overgrazing by large herbivores is normally blamed for the lack of natural tree regeneration. The current conservation response is the total exclusion of large herbivores by fencing. It is proposed that a reduction in grazing, rather than its cessation, may be a better course of action environmentally and would allow some continued use of the woods by stock.

The aim of this project is to assess the impact of controlled variations in intensity and seasonality of grazing on tree regeneration and on the ground flora in upland broadleaved woodland on a site in Naddle Low Forest, Cumbria. The site covers 36 ha of a north-west/north-east facing slope (250–400 m OD). Sessile oak/common ash (*Quercus petraea/Fraxinus excelsior*) woodland grades into open downy birch (*Betula pubescens*) wood with rising altitude. Swaledale x Herdwick yearling wethers are grazed at 3 different intensities (1, 2 or 3 sheep ha^{-1}), designed to remove nominally 20%, 40% and 60% of annual herbage accumulation in fenced plots. Each plot runs upslope to cover the full altitudinal range, and thus contains the major variations in vegetation. Plots at each utilization level are grazed April–October or October–April in order to assess the effect of seasonality of grazing.

All plots are monitored at the beginning and end of each grazing season. Naturally occurring established seedlings are recorded on permanent transects which run diagonally upslope. The height and evidence of past grazing of each seedling are recorded. The ground vegetation is monitored in quadrats spaced along the transects. No comparative data are yet available, as the experimental treatments were only initiated in May 1986; prior to this date, the wood was uniformly grazed by free-ranging sheep. Of the seedlings recorded, 60% were rowan (*Sorbus aucuparia*), 22% were birch, 14% were ash, and 0.6% were oak. Proportions of corresponding mature trees were calculated from 36 400 m^2 quadrats spread throughout the wood; 8% of these were rowan, 48% were birch, 5% were ash and 15% were oak. The project will investigate how the various grazing treatments affect these seedling proportions, the good rowan and poor oak seedling establishment being of particular interest. The tree canopy is sufficiently open throughout most of the wood that light is not a limiting factor in seedling survival.

To make up for the lack of saplings in the wood, 420 whips of oak, holly (*Ilex aquifolium*), ash and birch were

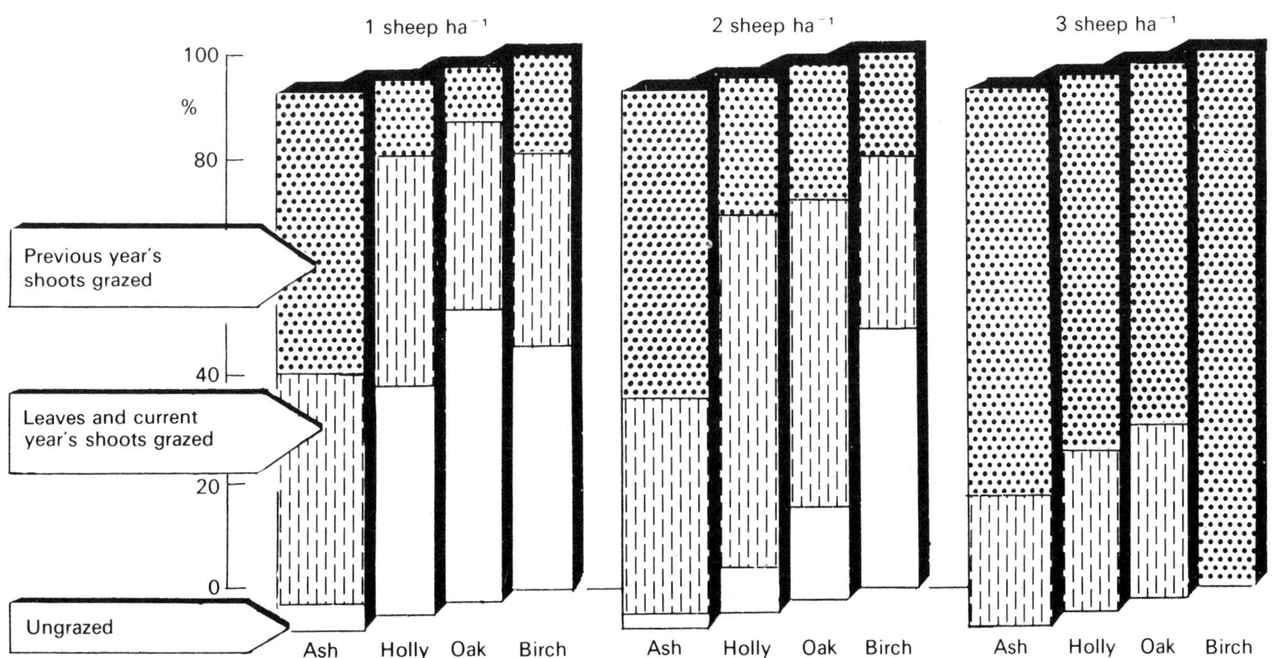

Figure 1. The incidence of browsing of planted saplings during the summer grazing period under 3 different sheep grazing intensities

planted in the summer grazing plots. Weekly monitoring indicated a trend of increased browsing with an increase in grazing intensity, ash being the species most favoured by sheep (Figure 1). Ash also exhibited the greatest capacity to recover from browsing and produce new leaves, while holly was the least capable. Oak was intermediate both in browsing incidence and recovery capacity. Similar quantities of saplings will be planted in the winter grazed plots and will be monitored accordingly.

The object of this poster presentation was primarily to illustrate the aims and methods of the project, and to present preliminary results on sapling browsing. The project, which is funded by the Nature Conservancy Council, will run initially for 2 years. To put the experimental data in a wider context, it is intended to survey other woods in Cumbria, north Wales and Argyll to investigate their regenerative status under varying grazing conditions.

Section 43 maps of moor or heath: a tool for conservation

C SWANWICK
Land Use Consultants, Levric, North Road, South Kilworth, Leicestershire, England

1 Introduction
In 1985, Land Use Consultants were asked by the Countryside Commission (CC) to carry out a review of the way in which the 10 National Park authorities had implemented Section 43 of the Wildlife and Countryside Act 1981, which required maps to be prepared identifying areas of moorland or heathland considered to be 'particularly important to conserve'. This review was instigated as a result of the Countryside Commission's own evidence to the House of Commons Environment Committee (Countryside Commission 1984b), and as a contribution to its examination of the operation of the Wildlife and Countryside Act. The work we undertook involved discussions with officers in the National Parks, and brief site visits in each Park to a selection of areas which had been included in the maps, and others which had not. Some of the conclusions of this work, relating particularly to the policy implications of Section 43, are summarized in this paper.

2 The origins of Section 43
Section 43 of the Wildlife and Countryside Act required National Park authorities to prepare maps showing 'areas of moor or heath the natural beauty of which it is, in the opinion of the authority, particularly important to conserve'. The origins of the Section in the long run up to the passing of the Act appear to be somewhat obsure. It must be remembered that Section 42, allowing Moorland Conservation Orders to be made, had been in the Bill from the beginning, although Ministers had indicated that it would not be used unless the situation in a National Park was as serious as, or worse than, Exmoor. Introduction of the new Section 43 followed the somewhat belated recognition of the work of Dr Martin Parry of Birmingham University in compiling historical evidence about moorland change. It also related to continuing attempts to secure provision for the compulsory notification of agricultural improvement in all National Parks, as for Sites of Special Scientific Interest (SSSIs). Such a move was resolutely opposed by the Government, and Section 43 seems to have emerged somewhere in the process.

It has been suggested (G Coggins, pers. comm., who was involved throughout the passage of the Act) that Section 43 was intended to do 3 things:

i. to complement Section 42 so that there would be a ready-made area in which Moorland Conservation Orders could be applied, if Ministers ever decided to operate the provisions;

ii. to provide a data base to show the state of moor or heath, and to allow for monitoring of change;

iii. to focus attention on moor or heath, and on the losses taking place, and to provide a greater measure of protection for it.

At the same time, it seems probable that Section 43 owes something to Lord Porchester's proposals, relating to Exmoor (Porchester 1977), for defining a category of moorland where 'change from the traditional appearance should be firmly resisted'. This suggestion eventually became enshrined in the Porchester maps 1 and 2 compiled by the Exmoor National Park Authority. The fact that Section 43 specifically refers to moor or heath whose natural beauty it is *'particularly important to conserve'* must, even though it is not explicit, imply some intention to conserve the traditional appearance, as in Porchester, by the definition of special areas.

Most of the National Park authorities did put such an interpretation on Section 43, either implicitly or explicitly. For example, the published statement accompanying the map for the Brecon Beacons (Brecon Beacons National Park Committee 1985) states that the purpose of the map is:

> 'to show areas which the National Park Authority will as a matter of policy seek to conserve as moor or heath when it is consulted (or receives planning applications) about proposed changes affecting their character or natural beauty'.

Policy statements for other Parks express a similar intention.

The major problem with Section 43 is the fact that no-one has been entirely sure what it was intended to achieve. Its objectives are certainly not made clear in the Act, and no further guidance has been forthcoming. In particular, there was no indication as to what sorts of areas of moor or heath the legislation was aimed at or how important an area had to be in order to qualify for inclusion. It was left to the discretion of the National Park authorities in exercising their 'opinion' of importance.

3 Implementation of Section 43: preparing the maps
All of the Parks have been influenced to some degree by the way that the Porchester exercise was carried out for Exmoor, and the majority have adopted some form of 2-stage approach, involving initial definition of all moor

or heath, followed by the selection of areas particularly important to conserve. This approach has the advantage of providing a full record of everything considered to be moor or heath, which is useful for monitoring purposes, as well as a description of special areas to which conservation and management policies can be applied. Only half of the Parks have shown the full extent of moor or heath on their published map. The others show only areas which are most important to conserve.

Definitions of what is moor or heath relied heavily on the statements made by Porchester that:

i. the approach should not be too theoretical;

ii. the principal factor should be vegetation;

iii. those responsible should look at the area as informed laymen and should identify broad tracts of land which would commonly be regarded as moorland or heath.

In practice, each National Park authority adopted a definition to suit its own circumstances. Some used very general definitions; for example, Dartmoor included:

> 'any areas which would normally be considered as moor and heath, including unimproved grassland with and without rushes, heather, bracken, whortleberry and gorse'.

Others used detailed ecological definitions. The Exmoor National Park Committee (1979) examined the subject in detail and came up with a useful comprehensive definition of the terms, as follows.

> *Moor*
> 'An area of acid soil with a peaty surface horizon of variable depth, bearing plant communities typical of bog or moss formations, or acid grassland in which ericaceous species are not abundant but bracken may be present as an invasive species.'
>
> *Heath*
> 'Area where trees or tall shrubs are sparse or absent, and in which the dominant life form is that of the evergreen dwarf shrub, particularly represented by the Ericaceae.'

Definitions used by other Parks who adopted an ecological definition are summarized in Table 1, which relates them to this Exmoor definition. Interesting points to note are:

i. inclusion of limestone and maritime grassland;

ii. Northumberland's use of enclosure size to determine whether bent/fescue (*Agrostis/Festuca*) grassland should be included;

both of which lead to a very liberal interpretation; and, by contrast,

iii. Snowdonia's adoption of a very selective definition which excluded acid grassland.

Assessment of whether an area, once defined as moor or heath, is considered particularly important to conserve required the National Park authorities to develop criteria for judging value. Approaches to identification of particularly important areas fall broadly into 2 groups:

i. those concentrating exclusively or largely on landscape criteria, eg Dartmoor, Exmoor, and the Lake District;

ii. those giving equal weight to a range of factors, including landscape value, nature conservation

Table 1. Ecological definitions of moor or heath

Type of community (from Exmoor definition)	Brecon Beacons	Northumberland	North York Moors	Pembrokeshire	Snowdonia
Moor i. Bogs, mosses, etc	Blanket mire and wetland species	Peat bogs and other mire vegetation	Blanket bogs, valley bogs	Moor	Cotton-grass/ heather
ii. Acid grassland	Coarse grassland with mat-grass, purple moor-grass, wavy hair-grass, bent/fescue grassland	Acid grassland Bent/fescue grassland in enclosures of more than 10 ha	Mat-grass moor Purple moor-grass	Grasslands Grass moor	(Only to consolidate areas of shrubby heath)
Heath	Dwarf shrub heath	Dwarf shrub heath	*Calluna* heath *Vaccinium* heath	Dry heath Wet heath Grass heath	Heather/bilberry and purple moor-grass Heather/bilberry and wavy hair-grass Dry *Calluna* heath
Other	Limestone grassland areas with up to 70% tree or shrub cover	Areas dominated by bracken, gorse and rushes	Scrub woodland with up to 25% tree cover Areas dominated by bracken	Maritime and other grasslands	

Table 2 Criteria used in identifying 'areas particularly important to conserve'

Group of criteria	Brecon Beacons	Dartmoor	Exmoor	Lake District	North York Moors	Pembrokeshire Coast	Snowdonia
LANDSCAPE QUALITIES							
Physical and topographical factors		Relationship to topography	Pattern in relationship to topography				
Extent and continuity	Continuity	Protect extent and continuity	Real and apparent extent				
Enclosure	Unenclosed or large	Size of enclosure	Openness and enclosures				
Colour and texture	Be attractive to walk through, taking account of colour, diversity and naturalness		Colour and texture	Seasonal changes in colour Contrasting texture of vegetation			
Boundaries			Nature of edges				
CONTRIBUTION TO WIDER LANDSCAPE							
Importance as part of wider landscape	Scenic value as distantly viewed object		Views to moorland from other areas	Contribution to landscape	Areas of visual importance, viz i. high moorland on plateaux ii. on shoulders of valleys and skylines iii. visible from roads and rights of way	High value as distantly viewed object	
Views	Be attractive to walk through, taking account of viewpoints		Panoramas, framed and sequential views of moorland				
PERCEPTUAL QUALITIES							
General moorland experience		Need to maintain moorland experience for drivers					
Qualities of openness, remoteness and wilderness	Feeling of openness is essential. Be attractive to walk through, taking account of qualities of remoteness	Wilderness experience	Remoteness	Feelings of wildness and openness		Qualities of openness, remoteness, wilderness	Imbibe a psycho-logical feeling of solitude
ECOLOGICAL FACTORS							
General wildlife appeal	Be attractive to walk through, taking account of wildlife appeal		Special features of wildlife interest			Enable wild-life to be experienced at first hand	
Nature conservation	Important for wildlife conservation or have features of scientific interest	(Only a subsidiary factor)		Ecological features (SSSIs and NNRs)	Areas of natural history importance, ie all unploughed moorland and all designated or known sites	Be important for nature conservation, including all SSSIs, NNRs, etc	All SSSIs, NNRs, LNRs
ARCHAEOLOGICAL FACTORS	Be attractive to walk through, taking account of features of historical interest	(Only a subsidiary factor)	Special features of historical interest	Archaeological features (Scheduled Ancient Monuments)	Areas of archaeol-importance, including Scheduled Monuments	Archaeological heritage of the area	All Ancient Monuments and recognized areas of archaeological importance
RECREATION AND ACCESS							
General access	Access routes to adjoining areas		Public access Rights of way Road access	Opportunities for walking with freedom in challenging environment	Importance for recreation and amenity		
Special areas					Areas of particular significance for forms of recreation		

value, archaeological value, importance for recreation, etc, eg the North York Moors and Pembrokeshire.

Whatever the criteria adopted, they have mainly been used in defining the edges and in assessing marginal areas of moor or heath.

Table 2 summarizes the criteria adopted by those National Park authorities who were explicit about the basis for their judgements of value. In addition to these general criteria, some Parks also included special considerations. Dartmoor and Snowdonia both automatically included all commons. Snowdonia also included moor or heath which was Crown land or National Trust land, was covered by Section 42 Moorland Conservation Orders, or which had not been improved for 20 years.

Application of these criteria led to inclusion of different proportions of each National Park in the maps, as shown by Table 3. In this Table, figures for the estimated total area of rough pasture are given in those cases where no map 1 was prepared. This figure is therefore a substitute for the total extent of moor or heath measured from map 1 in the other Parks. Both Northumberland and the Yorkshire Dales stand out, with over 50% of the total Park area included on the maps, and Dartmoor is not far behind. By comparison, only 15% of the area of Snowdonia is included on the maps.

In general, land identified as particularly important to conserve represents between 70% and 90% of land mapped as moor or heath, or of the estimated extent of rough pasture. Snowdonia, however, is an exception. Although areas important to conserve represent 83% of land identified as moor or heath on map 1, the very restrictive definition adopted, which excluded acid grassland from this map, means that, in fact, only 23% of the total area of rough pasture in the Park is included.

4 Section 43 as a basis for policies

Lines on a map in themselves mean little, of course, but the fact that particularly important areas have been defined means that the maps can be used to provide the basis for policies to conserve them. There is, however, no stated requirement for the map to be accompanied by policies, and the Parks vary widely in their approach. All are using the maps to assess Farm Grant Notifications, whether or not they have any stated policies towards

Table 3. Areas covered by Section 43 maps (in ha)

National Park	1 Total area of Park	2 Total area of rough pasture	3 Rough pasture which is shrubby heath	4 Total extent of moor and heath in S43 (map 1)	5 Area particularly important to conserve (map 2)
Brecon Beacons	134 000	68 000 (51%)	28 140 (21%)	Not applicable	53 000 (77% of rough pasture) (39% of Park)
Dartmoor	95 000	Not applicable	26 600 (28%)	52 761	48 277 (91.5% of map 1) (49.6% of Park)
Exmoor	68 635	Not applicable	14 490 (21%)	19 555	16 036 (82% of map 1) (23% of Park)
Lake District	224 000	120 960 (54%)	49 280 (22%)	Not applicable	106 753 (88% of rough pasture) (8% of Park)
Northumberland	103 000	Not applicable	27 750 (25%)	66 686	52 720 (79% of map 1) (53% of Park)
North York Moors	143 000	Not applicable	57 200 (40%)	50 340	47 785 (95% of map 1) (33% of Park)
Peak District	140 000	64 400 (46%)	25 200 (18%)	Not applicable	49 140 (76% of rough pasture) (35% of Park)
Pembrokeshire	58 350	Not applicable	6 380 (11%)	7 586	7 412 (98% of map 1) (13% of Park)
Snowdonia	217 000	136 710 (63%)	49 910 (23%)	37 350	31 000 (83% of map 1) (23% of rough pasture) (15% of Park)
Yorkshire Dales	176 000	Not applicable	26 400 (15%)	126 238	88 500 (70% of map 1) (50% of Park)

All figures in columns 2 and 3 from Sinclair quoted in Brotherton (1985) (% figures are of whole Park). Figures in columns 4 and 5 from discussions with the National Park authority or published Section 43 statements, except Peak District, from Roberts (1985)

agricultural activities in the Section 43 areas. Otherwise, to varying degrees, the maps are accompanied by:

i. policies dealing with attitudes to conservation of moor or heath and to forms of agricultural improvement;

ii. policies towards land which is shown as moor or heath (map 1) but is not identified as being particularly important to conserve;

iii. policies relating to afforestation and, particularly, the relationship between Section 43 map areas and existing forestry policy maps;

iv. positive policies concerning the management of moor or heath on the map.

Review of these policies reveals a number of issues of particular interest.

4.1 Forestry policy

The majority of the Parks have some form of forestry policy or forestry agreement map which was drawn up, usually over a considerable period of time, by consensus between the interested parties. These maps take various forms, but usually include a zone with a strong presumption against new afforestation, a zone with a presumption against but where some planting may be acceptable, and either a neutral zone, with no presumption either way, or a zone with a presumption in favour of forestry.

The preparation of Section 43 maps inevitably demonstrates a change of thinking since these maps were originally agreed, and indicates that, in some cases, the areas where forestry is acceptable may be too generous. There is inevitably a contradiction in terms where the Section 43 maps overlap with zones which do not bear a presumption against forestry planting. If Section 43 areas are identified as moor or heath whose natural beauty it is particularly important to conserve, then, one would imagine, there should be no part of them which does not bear a strong presumption against afforestation. With the existing forestry agreement maps this is far from the truth, and in the Brecon Beacons, Dartmoor, Exmoor, the Lake District, Northumberland and Snowdonia there are varying degrees of overlap between the Section 43 maps and land which does not carry a presumption against afforestation.

The National Park authorities have tackled this problem in different ways. At one extreme, Snowdonia proposes that, in future, there should be a presumption against tree planting throughout the Section 43 map area, thus effectively reducing the area which formerly bore a presumption in favour of planting by 12 300 hectares or 13%. However, as the forestry agreement maps are prepared by a consensus approach, it is difficult to see how such an approach will find support. In Northumberland, 20% of the Section 43 map 2 moor and heath coincides with the neutral zone where there is no presumption either way in terms of forestry planting, and, in these areas, the decision is left open 'with particular attention being given to matters of siting and scale to minimize the loss of moorland and any damage to the wider landscape setting'.

In the Lake District, the overlaps with the zone which has a less stringent policy towards new planting are limited to some of the outer fringes of the fells. Officers are aware of the problem and are treating cases on their merits. In Dartmoor, there are also a few areas where this problem exists and, again, proposals are to be treated on their merits, but a statement is likely to be added to the text accompanying the map to clarify the position. There are significant problems in the Brecon Beacons, and the National Park authority are giving further thought to this issue as part of their current work to develop a landscape strategy for the Park.

Exmoor represents the opposite approach to Snowdonia, in that, where land in the Section 43 map coincides with areas on the afforestation policy map which bear a strong presumption that forestry will be acceptable, then forestry planting will take precedence, although in every other respect there will be the strongest possible presumption in favour of moorland conservation. In the absence of planning controls over forestry, and bearing in mind the considerable amount of time and effort required to reach even the present agreement on forestry policy maps, it seems unlikely that these contradictions will be resolved easily. Suffice it to say that, at present, the Section 43 maps mean different things for forestry in a number of the Parks.

4.2 Agricultural improvements

There also appear to be difficulties concerning the approach to agriculture within the Section 43 map areas. The issue here is the extent to which agricultural improvements can be accepted within areas where the specific aim should now be clearly stated as the conservation of moor or heath character. Should this land be a virtual 'no-go' area in terms of any form of agricultural management beyond the traditional forms of grazing and burning? Some would doubtless argue that it should, but it seems that the picture is by no means as clear as that because of the generally liberal definition of moor or heath which has been adopted. Two types of vegetation appear to pose particular problems, namely grassland and bracken (*Pteridium aquilinum*).

Much of the grassland within the map areas is poor-quality acid grassland, of relatively low grazing value, which is not subject to significant management. However, in the limestone belt of the Yorkshire Dales, to a limited extent in the limestone area of the Peak District, and in the Cheviots and the Whin Sill areas of Northumberland, substantial areas of better-quality grassland have been included, which are already subject, to varying degrees, to forms of management such as liming and fertilizer application, and sometimes, especially in Northumberland, direct seeding and fencing. If these operations are already taking place on land which has been included as being 'particularly important to conserve', then it might seem unreasonable and inconsistent to prevent them from continuing in the future.

No clear solution to this question emerges. One of these grassland areas in the Peak District has been contested by the owner as not suitable for inclusion on the map of moor and heath in the first place. Northumberland has deliberately drawn a liberal line on its Section 43 map, in the knowledge that it would be linked to a series of liberal policies allowing existing forms of grassland management to continue and perhaps to be extended, while protecting heather (*Calluna vulgaris*) moorland.

Bracken occurs in association with grassland and heathland in a variety of situations in the Section 43 map areas. It is a particular landscape feature of the Lake District fells, of the Pembrokeshire coastal belt, of the valley-sides of the North York Moors, and of some parts of Exmoor and the Brecon Beacons. It is particularly associated with the soils of the lower slopes, and therefore often occurs in the marginal areas where pressure for change is most likely. Because of its seasonal colour changes, it is a visually important component of many moor and heath landscapes and yet, because of its invasive qualities, it is an anathema to farmers. For this reason, all the Parks seem to allow for bracken clearance operations within their Section 43 areas.

Bracken areas seem to pose the greatest problems in the North York Moors, but for reasons related to afforestation rather than agricultural change. Here, afforestation proposals have been permitted on a small scale on bracken-covered slopes, on the grounds that it will actually improve their wildlife and landscape value. As a result, serious thought has been given to pulling back the Section 43 boundaries to exclude these bracken-covered slopes, leaving them as map 1 land where proposals will be treated on their merits.

The other issue which appears to be the subject of some uncertainty is moorland gripping within Section 43 land. Gripping to improve drainage is already a feature of some areas included within Section 43 maps, but there is concern at its detrimental effects on moorland ecology and on landscape, as well as doubts about its effectiveness. Northumberland has specifically mentioned this concern in its policies, deeming it to be an acceptable feature of moorland management, while Snowdonia has stated a presumption against it on Section 43 land in its guidelines for assessing Farm Grant Notifications. Elsewhere, individual judgements will presumably be made depending on whether it is considered to change the moorland character. In the Yorkshire Dales, it may be resisted because of its ecological effects, but not because of its impact on the landscape.

Overall, the question arises as to the extent to which the Section 43 maps should have been drawn purely on merit in terms of the importance of the moor or heath, and how much they should have been influenced by thinking about the policies which might apply. Practice within the Parks again seems to have varied. Some authorities seem to have drawn their maps reasonably independently of any thoughts about policy, whereas Northumberland always saw the 2 aspects as inseparable and intentionally linked liberal policies with a liberal definition. By contrast, Snowdonia chose a very selective definition of its area, influenced at least in part by the belief that tight policies over a wider area would be untenable. Having drawn a very tight boundary, it was then able to put forward very tight policies towards afforestation and other change, including seeking to persuade the Secretary of State to make a blanket Moorland Conservation Order over the entire Section 43 area.

These issues demonstrate above all that there is no simple black and white answer to the question of policies for Section 43 land, simply because so many different situations have to be covered. In future, it may well be that a much more subtle response will be needed, perhaps necessitating different sets of policies for different types of vegetation. This differentiation is already beginning to emerge in some cases, with an implicit understanding that heather moorland is subject to the strictest policies.

5 Attitudes of National Park authorities to Section 43

The officers of the National Parks hold very different views about this part of the 1981 legislation. Some consider it to be an irritating and irrelevant requirement, which has little to do with the real problems facing their National Park, and which has diverted resources from other pressing work. Some positively disapprove of it, believing that, by picking out important areas, others not so described will be devalued. This is a particular concern for areas shown only as map 1 moor or heath, and is one of the reasons why a number of the Parks have not shown these areas. Others do believe that Section 43 has been a positive step forward. It is seen as making a real contribution to thinking about landscape conservation, providing a very useful tool for assessing Farm Grant Notifications and other proposals, and giving added impetus to the development of a comprehensive data base in some areas. One officer even expressed the view that the exercise represented the most important step forward in National Park planning for 35 years.

However, there is also almost unanimous concern that the maps, in themselves, do not mean anything and do not have any additional powers to go with them. Considering the time and effort that has gone into preparing them, this shortcoming is widely regretted and most officers would like to see the maps backed up by a suitable policy framework and by some form of 'last resort' power to protect moor or heath by use of binding Moorland Conservation Orders.

These different views are demonstrated by the following 2 extracts from letters from National Park authorities, written during the review exercise.

The Lake District Special Planning Board wrote:

'Preparation of the map generally has been considered as an unfortunate and sometimes irritating requirement because the wording of the Act is ambiguous and its purpose unclear, and because conversion of moorland through agricultural improvement was not a major issue locally. The requirement risked fuelling unnecessary controversy, yet offered no obvious benefits or reserve powers to protect areas so defined. The doubt that the map would devalue areas outside it has only been overcome by drawing it very broadly. In consequence, it is not possible to be dogmatic about what is and is not acceptable in a particular locality, and individual proposals continue to be considered on their merits against the background of statutory objectives and policies related to forestry, landscape, access, nature conservation and the like. This approach would have been pursued had the requirement to produce a map not reached the statute books.'

The North York Moors National Park wrote:

'The task of producing the map was greeted in various ways by National Park authorities, depending upon the extent to which the future of moor and heath was seen as a problem in the particular Park. In the North York Moors, we were already involved in a very similar exercise as part of the National Park Plan Review, and therefore the requirement of Section 43 was clearly relevant. Indeed, it helped us in our dealings with the farmers and landowners in demonstrating the need for preparing the map.'

The Pembrokeshire Coast National Park wrote (referring to our report (Land Use Consultants 1985), and a meeting held with officers from all the National Parks to discuss it):

'On a concluding note the report and meeting confirmed that Section 43 has been inadequately thought out and framed by the legislators; implemented within a policy vacuum and should have been accompanied by guidance at a national level... I would propose that the Commission:

i. emphasizes to Government the need for Section 43 maps to be prepared within/ backed up by a suitable policy framework and by some form of "last resort" power to protect these areas;

ii. accepts the Consultants' finding that some basic ground rules would have been helpful in co-ordinating the preparation of the Section 43 maps of moor and heath by the individual National Parks and takes steps to issue such guidance as and when the Amendment Bill is finally passed;

iii. draws up such ground rules in full consultation with the National Parks and issues these in the form of guidance, not instructions, to the Parks to enable them to make an individual response whilst broadly conforming to a more comparable "model".

The new Section 43 maps should then enable the Commission to construct a much stronger case for using them to argue for more resources and greater commitment by MAFF towards conservation at the national level.'

6 Views of the Countryside Commission on Section 43

Our review of the implementation of Section 43 was instigated as a result of the Countryside Commission's own evidence to the House of Commons Environment Committee on the operation of the Wildlife and Countryside Act. In this evidence, the Commission (1984b) expressed the view that the Section 43 maps will be 'used increasingly to influence decisions on such matters as afforestation proposals, Farm Grant Notifications and Capital Transfer Tax applications', and also that 'the national credibility of such policy tools will be difficult to support when the variations in approach are realised'. The evidence went on to say: 'The Commission believes that Section 43 maps must not be allowed to fall into disrepute because of administrative problems. The maps are vital for the conservation of those wild open areas which form the heartland of our National Parks; the process of defining such areas and associated policies must stand up to public scrutiny and command respect at a national level'.

At the end of our review exercise, the Chairman of the Commission wrote to the Minister, noting that the National Park authorities clearly needed and, indeed, would have welcomed, a clear indication on the reasoning behind the exercise which they were statutorily required to conduct. The letter further noted that: 'Clarification would also be welcomed on the relationship of Section 43 with Section 42 of the Act which is concerned with Moorland Conservation Orders. The same terms "moor and heath" are used in both of these juxtaposed sections in the Act but the inter-relationship of the 2 tends to be confused. If the maps are to be effective as a special designation rather than as a mere inventory, there is a need for back-up powers to support them. Section 42 would seem to offer that possibility although this has never been tested'.

Apart from its views on the way that Section 43 has been implemented in the National Parks, the Commission clearly believes that the approach is useful, and in its report (Countryside Commission 1984a) recommended that legislation be introduced requiring that Section 43 maps be prepared by County Councils for all the Less Favoured Areas. The Commission went much further than that, indicating that Section 43 was seen as having a clear 'policy' role, by recommending that the Ministry of Agriculture, Fisheries and Food grants for drainage and land improvement should be withdrawn in these areas and that they should be used to help in assessing stocking levels for the hill livestock compensatory allowance payments. This recommendation, coming as it did when most National Park authorities were in the midst of preparing their own maps, caused a great deal of consternation in the National Parks. There has been no progress in these proposals to extend the application of Section 43.

7 Changes since the 1985 review

The Commission's 1985 review of the implementation of Section 43 was largely overtaken by events with the passage of the Wildlife and Countryside (Amendment) Bill through Parliament. As a result, Section 3 of the Wildlife and Countryside Act 1985 amends Section 43 of the 1981 Act. The new Section requires that the National Park authorities prepare maps showing 'any areas to which this Section applies whose natural beauty it is, in the opinion of the authority, particularly important to conserve'. The Section is defined as applying to 'mountain, moor, heath, woodland, down, cliff or foreshore', ie 'open country' as defined in the 1949 National Parks and 1968 Countryside Acts. The other significant changes are that the Countryside Commission is required to issue guidelines after consulting interested parties, the Authorities preparing the maps are required to consult interested parties, and the review period for the new maps is changed to 5 years rather than one year.

The new Section answers a number of the criticisms which have been made of the former Section 43, in that the provisions are no longer limited to moor or heath. In particular, they now extend to woodland, and to coasts which are such important features of the Parks. Perhaps the greatest remaining omission is that they do not embrace special features such as wetlands or meadows which do not fall within the open country definition.

The Countryside Commission issued its guidelines in October 1986. It suggests that 2 objectives might apply to land identified on the new maps:

i. adoption of positive steps to ensure the conservation of natural beauty;

ii. a presumption against changes detrimental to natural beauty, from new development or land management.

By way of example, for mountain and moorland, the guidelines suggest that specific policies might (not should) be developed along these lines:

i. promotion/adoption of management aimed at keeping characteristic vegetation in good health;

ii. a presumption against afforestation which would be detrimental to natural beauty;

iii. a presumption against agricultural operations aimed at converting the land to improved grassland or arable use and which would be detrimental to natural beauty.

So, clearly, although these are only guidelines, there is now a much clearer view of the purpose of the maps. The National Park authorities must produce the maps 2 years from the issue of these guidelines.

Although this amendment in Section 3 is an improvement over the original Section 43, it nevertheless leaves a number of questions unanswered. First of all, why should the provision apply only to National Parks, and not to other areas of open country in Areas of Outstanding National Beauty, and for that matter in the remainder of the countryside? Second, what about the important landscape features which are not covered by the definition of open country, such as meadows and wetlands? Finally, is this approach of considering individual components of the landscape really the most appropriate one, or should we be looking at landscapes in a more integrated way? New initiatives such as Environmentally Sensitive Areas appear to encourage this broader approach.

In all, then, Section 43 (and now Section 3) is certainly a tool for the conservation of important landscape features, but it is a partial tool, and a flawed one.

8 References

Brecon Beacons National Park Committee. 1985. Statement accompanying Section 43 maps of moor or heath.

Brotherton, I. 1985. Changing landscapes in National Parks. In: *Moor and heathland: its conservation and management.* (Conference report.) Snowdonia National Park Authority.

Countryside Commission. 1984a. *A better future for the uplands.* (CCP 162.) Cheltenham: CC.

Countryside Commission. 1984b. *Evidence to the House of Commons Environment Committee on the operation of the Wildlife and Countryside Act.* Cheltenham: CC.

Exmoor National Park Committee. 1979. *Porchester map one, explanatory notes.* Exmoor.

Land Use Consultants. 1985. *Maps of moor or heath: a report on the implementation of Section 43 of the Wildlife and Countryside Act 1981.* Report to the Countryside Commission. (Unpublished.)

Porchester, Lord. 1977. *A study of Exmoor.* London: HMSO.

Roberts, G. 1985. Section 43 maps of moor and heath. In: *Moor and heathland: its conservation and management.* (Conference report.) Snowdonia National Park Authority.

Environmental education in hills and uplands

E CLARK
Environmental Education Unit, Old Brathay, Ambleside, Cumbria, England

1 *Introduction*

People who live and work in the uplands cannot help but be aware of the large numbers of young people visiting these areas. It is perhaps more usual for negative effects of this invasion to be stressed, rather than the positive. The results which stem from visits are not immediately obvious, neither are all the purposes of visits apparent to the farmers and foresters who see groups about in the countryside. This paper looks at some of the ways in which young people are educated in, about, and for the upland environment and considers implications of recent developments.

2 *Why such use of uplands?*

The uplands are chosen for a range of activities because:

- they are the only areas left which resemble true wilderness;
- they are a part of each individual's heritage, even though many of us will not choose to avail ourselves of their attractions;
- many uplands are beautiful and aesthetically stimulating areas;
- they present physical challenges such as difficult terrain, cliffs, fast-moving waters, etc;
- people can experience solitude within them in a way which is not now possible for the majority of the population;
- there is greater freedom to move within them than in more intensively used areas;
- they contain many features studied in school subjects such as geography, history, biology and environmental science.

3 *Uplands as an educational resource*

Depending on specialism and interest, teachers could have one or more of the following perceptions of the upland environment.

A teacher of primary school children might see it as an exciting place for journeys of exploration into unfamiliar surroundings, with lots to see and do. Pupils would lay by a store of experiences which would enrich their learning for years to come.

Very many groups of young people are brought to the uplands because of the opportunities they present for mastery of new skills like climbing and canoeing. Furthermore, in residential courses such as those provided by the Brathay Hall Trust and the Outward Bound movement, leaders use these experiences in development training. Young people acquire confidence in their own ability to cope with testing situations in other places and at other times in their lives.

In a similar way, the upland environment can be seen as a place where groups of young people can be taken away from the support systems - shops, entertainment, transport, comforts - of modern urban existence. During development training courses, they work in groups to, for instance, navigate themselves across unfamiliar and difficult terrain. The impact of such experiences and the effect they have on learning about self and group relationships is well known and respected, so much so that the Government, as recently as in its declared intention to develop City Technology Colleges, expects students to take part in residential courses with both physical and intellectual challenge.

Teachers of biology, geology, geography and history look upon the upland environment as a major learning resource where vivid first-hand learning takes place.The field study movement is well established and, over the years, many hundreds of thousands of young people have journeyed to the uplands to carry out studies of farming, ecology, geomorphology, etc.

4 *New approaches*

Changes now taking place in schools and wherever young people are being educated or trained have been described as revolutionary.

Students in schools are embarking on new courses leading to the General Certificate of Secondary Education. These courses make it essential for learning to be based on practical first-hand experience. Schools are developing close links with their local communities and there is a great deal of to-ing and fro-ing of people and ideas. The Manpower Services Commission-sponsored Technical and Vocational Education Initiative schemes lead to students spending periods of time in work experience and at out-stations like the Cumbria College of Agriculture and Forestry. Residential courses for personal and social development are an essential feature of many TVEI and Youth Training Schemes, and field courses continue to play an important part in subjects such as geography and biology.

Examination syllabuses are changing and man/environment issues are being given a much more important role in education than used to be the case. This development is all part of a wider environmental education movement.

Many people are concerned that there is insufficient knowledge and understanding of environmental matters among all sectors of the population. Informed and wise concern develops as a consequence of first-hand sensory experiences, growing knowledge and understanding of the nature of man's relationships with his environment, and appreciation of the fact that conflicting interests often necessitate compromise and sacrifice. Syllabuses and methods of teaching now increasingly reflect these interests.

Another trend is a lessening of single-minded purpose in outdoor educational activities. For example, scientific studies of moorland vegetation would introduce consideration of upland land use and management, and those who visit the uplands to learn rock-climbing would be encouraged to understand more about the environment and to consider their own impact on it. These trends are seen in the new emphasis on environmental adventure in the Duke of Edinburgh Award schemes and also in the embryonic outdoor education degree course now being prepared for teachers in training at Charlotte Mason College of Education at Ambleside.

5 Some implications

Very probably, young people will come to the uplands in increasing numbers for part of their education or training. Will they be welcomed or regarded as nuisances?

Society must surely benefit from there being a more informed and caring generation coming from schools and training institutions. Wisdom and balance will remain difficult to achieve, without deliberate effort to encourage interest and involvement.

There must be long-term good effects for farming, in general, if young people have, as would be the case during courses at Brathay, walked the ground the shepherds walk, learned from people who live and work in the hills, and been given time and and opportunity to reflect on their own relationships with the hills.

Some farmers have already developed enterprises to cater for the educational market. The hills and uplands are a resource which is used not only for farming and forestry but also for learning. Farmers and foresters should seize opportunities to become involved in upland environmental education.

Soil fertility and commercial forest felling: research note

J K ADAMSON
Institute of Terrestrial Ecology, Merlewood Research Station,Grange-over-Sands, Cumbria, England

In upland Britain, large areas of nutrient-poor, former sheep grazing land has been planted with Sitka spruce (*Picea sitchensis*). Many of these plantations will be clearfelled before the end of the century.

Clearfelling results in:

i. changes in soil decomposer activity, because of changes in temperature and moisture regimes;

ii. increases in material for decomposition (branches, etc);

iii. cessation of nutrient uptake by roots.

Research around the world indicates that these processes may cause a significant loss of plant nutrients in drainage water, resulting in reduced soil fertility. There are, however, no published data for British forests.

To determine if the clearfelling of spruce plantations will have a signficant impact on soil fertility, research is being conducted at Kershope Forest in Cumbria. Water is collected for analysis from 6 ditch systems, each of which drains a separate plot of approximately 2 ha. All plots are on a peaty gley soil which has never been fertilized and which was planted with Sitka spruce in 1948. Three plots have now been felled. Sampling began 2 years before felling was completed and continues at weekly intervals, on standing and felled plots.

Concentrations of all major nutrients increased following felling (relative to standing forest). These increases were compounded by increased drainage water discharge, resulting from reduced evaporation caused by tree removal. Thus, the annual export of nutrients increased markedly, as a result of felling, although more data will be required to determine the impact on soil fertility.

Annual export of nutrients (kg ha^{-1} yr^{-1})

	1982		1983		1984		1985	
	C	E	C	E	C	E	C	E
Potassium	2.9	2.0	1.8	2.9	3.6	18.3	5.7	21.8
Phosphate-P	0	0	0.09	0.04	0.02	0.23	0.08	0.42
Nitrate-N	9.4	10.5	6.0	7.8	8.5	38.7	15.2	41.1
Ammonium-N	1.0	0.6	0.5	0.3	0.9	7.6	1.6	3.0

C, control plot; E, experimental plot where felling took place in 1983

Increased acidity of drainage water from commercial forests has been attributed to the trapping of atmospheric pollutants by the tree canopy. However, so far at Kershope, no reduction in acidity has been found as a result of tree felling. At no time did the concentration of nutrients in the drainage water exceed pollution standards.

To determine the sources of nutrient fluxes and likely effects on the next forest rotation, water is also sampled at all stages in its passage through the standing and felled forest systems (including 4 soil horizons).

This work forms part of a programme of field and laboratory work to determine the effects of felling on soil processes. A parallel site is at Beddgelert Forest in Gwynedd. Staff involved are from the Institute of Terrestrial Ecology's Merlewood and Bangor Research Stations and from the Forestry Commission research stations.

Soil fertility and nature conservation: research note

R H MARRS
Institute of Terrestrial Ecology, Monks Wood Experimental Station, Abbots Ripton, Huntingdon, England

The loss of species diversity in many infertile semi-natural communities, such as grasslands, heaths and moors, is often ascribed to the effects of increased fertility, sometimes described as soil eutrophication. If these infertile habitats are to be conserved, the solutions are obvious: (i) prevent fertilizer additions, and (ii) manage the site to remove more nutrients in the crop than are added by natural inputs. However, on sites which have already suffered from fertilizer additions during agricultural improvement, there is an increasing desire by conservation bodies to restore semi-natural plant communities. This demand should increase if future economic policies dictate land use changes from intensive agricultural production to less productive uses, and will be especially marked in areas of marginal land, where production is limited by climatic or soil factors.

There is an enormous range of potential methods which could be used to reduce soil fertility, including grazing, burning, cropping, topsoil stripping, topsoil burial and introducing species which degrade the surface soil. Only limited quantitative information is available for a few of these methods, and few attempts have been made to use any of these techniques on a large scale for the specific objective of reducing soil fertility. This note reports some results of one such attempt at Roper's Heath in Suffolk. An agricultural field separated 2 heathland nature reserves, and the aim of the Nature Conservancy Council was to restore heathland vegetation. Two methods for reducing soil fertility were investigated:

i. cereal cropping. Here, cereal rye was grown without fertilizer additions. The effectiveness of the treatment was assessed by measuring the nutrients taken off in the crop and by measuring soil fertility in cropped and uncropped areas using a combination of chemical analyses and bioassays. The cereal crop removed more P and K, but not N in grain, compared to the inputs, but, if the straw was also removed, there was also a net loss of N. The bioassay results suggested that the fertility of the soil was reduced by treatment.

ii. topsoil stripping. Results of similar studies on the fertility of the different depths of soil on the site suggested that, if the surface 20 cm of soil was removed, then there would be a significant and immediate reduction in fertility.

The studies at Roper's Heath have, unfortunately, come to an end, but are reported in detail by Marrs (1986). The work has highlighted many areas of ignorance; in particular, we do not know how infertile soils need to be in order to support specific plant communities. Further research on this topic is planned on a wider range of sites.

Reference

Marrs, R.H. 1986. Techniques for reducing soil fertility for nature conservation purposes: a review in relation to research at Roper's Heath, Suffolk. *Biol. Conserv.*, **34,** 307-332.

Long-term studies of vegetation change at Moor House NNR: research note

R H MARRS
Institute of Terrestrial Ecology, Monks Wood Experimental Station, Abbots Ripton, Huntingdon, England

Moor House National Nature Reserve was bought by the Nature Conservancy in 1952 specifically as a centre for scientific research on the ecology of upland communities. The quality of research done at Moor House by the Nature Conservancy staff in the 1950s and early 1960s was recognized by the designation of Moor House as one of the main British sites in the International Biological Programme (IBP - Tundra Biome study). A major part of the research emphasis during this early period was the setting up of long-term experiments on a range of upland vegetation types; these experiments were designed to detect:

i. long-term changes in species composition, structure and function;

ii. long-term effects of management by man, especially the effects of burning and sheep grazing.

These experiments, and some new ones set up more recently for the same purpose, were monitored at varying levels of intensity until 1982, when the Moor House Research Station was closed. At this point, the Institute of Terrestrial Ecology took over the responsibility for monitoring these long-term experiments, and for subsequent data analysis.

There are, however, 3 major problems with long-term experiments of this kind. First, their duration (at present 15–32 years) means that changes in observers are bound to occur. Second, with the demise of the station facilities at Moor House, it was thought unlikely that detailed intensive studies could be carried out in the longer term, because of financial constraints, and, third, the data were available only on field data sheets and were difficult and costly to analyse. Since 1982, we have tried to overcome these problems by:

i. setting the range of 10 available experiments into a 10-year rotational sampling programme, and monitoring one experiment per year. This approach allows information to be collected at minimum expense.

ii. producing a detailed methods handbook (Marrs *et al.* 1986), which involved the collaboration of both the 'old' and 'new' observers. Moreover, the first draft of the methods handbook was produced from the available information within the experimental notes, and then 'debugged' in the field, to make sure that a new observer in the future would be unlikely to make mistakes.

iii. transferring all the accumulated data to computer storage on the Natural Environment Research Council's VAX computer at Keyworth. It is hoped to start analysing some of the recent trends shortly.

Reference

Marrs, R.H., Rawes, M., Robinson, J.S. & Poppit, S.D. 1986. *Long-term studies of vegetation change at Moor House NNR: guide to recording methods and database.* (Merlewood research and development paper no. 109.) Grange-over-Sands: Institute of Terrestrial Ecology.

The flow country: is there room for everyone?

N BLACK
Highland Regional Council, Glenurquhart Road, Inverness, Scotland.

1 Introduction

Highland Regional Council (HRC) is the planning authority for the largest Local Authority area in western Europe. The Region covers 2.5 Mha (9805 square miles), is larger than Wales, and supports a population of under 200 000 people.

The Council regards existing and future land use as a key structure plan issue because of the implications of change on the diverse landscape, wildlife and cultural heritage of such a vast Region. As a result of this interest, the Council has recently examined claims that there is increasing conflict between forestry, agriculture, crofting, peat extraction and nature conservation in Caithness and Sutherland. A location map is given in Figure 1.

This paper summarizes the key findings of an objective assessment of existing and potential land uses undertaken by the Council, using a computer-based land classification system and data base developed in conjunction with the Institute of Terrestrial Ecology (ITE) at its Merlewood Research Station (HRC 1985a).

2 Summary of findings

Land use changes in Caithness and Sutherland will largely result from increased afforestation (the most dynamic land use at present). The extent to which the potential for new commercial afforestation in Caithness and Sutherland is affected by safeguards on agriculture, crofting and nature conservation designations is shown in Figures 2–6. If recent local planting rates were to continue, the 25% of potential in Caithness and 21% in Sutherland represent 37 years of planting reserve in Caithness and 35 years in Sutherland.

The overall conclusion from this assessment is that there is room for a wide range of land uses (both existing and potential) and safeguarding for conservation to co-exist without conflict in Caithness and Sutherland. The stages involved in this assessment are described below, and included:

i. assessing forestry potential;

ii. identifying agricultural land quality and applying different levels of safeguarding;

iii. identifying and safeguarding crofting land;

iv. identifying existing and proposed Sites of Special Scientific Interest (SSSIs) and assessing the implications of safeguarding them.

3 Forestry

The first stage in the overall assessment is to identify the potential for forestry, as this is the most dynamic land use in both Districts. This assessment is undertaken using a computer model developed by HRC, which is designed to predict the location of land that is theoretically suitable for forestry.

The model initially assesses the forestry potential within each of the 27 915 one km grid squares in the Highland Region, using data recorded and stored in the course of setting up the HRC/ITE land classification system. The data base includes information on altitude, exposure, and land covered by water, buildings and existing woodland which can be used to constrain forestry within each grid square.

As a result of applying these constraints, the theoretical potential for planting is shown in Table 1.

4 Agriculture

After the removal of land technically unsuitable for planting, the next stage is to identify and assess the implications of safeguarding different classes of agricultural land.

The Council's computer data base contains information extracted from the land capability for agriculture maps produced by the Macaulay Institute for Soil Research. The effect on forestry potential of safeguarding for agriculture land of Classes 3–5 (there is no Class 1 or 2 land) and Classes 3 and 4, which correspond with the land release policy recently revised by the Department of Agriculture and Fisheries for Scotland, is shown in Table 2 and illustrated in Figure 7.

An alternative approach has been developed utilizing the land classification system to assess the implications of land changing from an agricultural use to a forestry use. This method involves allocating financial values to different types of agricultural and forestry enterprises, within each land class, and, by applying different discount rates, identifying the amount of land being taken over for forestry. The results are shown in Figure 8.

Table 1. Percentage of District suitable for forestry

District	Theoretically suitable
Caithness	76.2
Sutherland	43.1

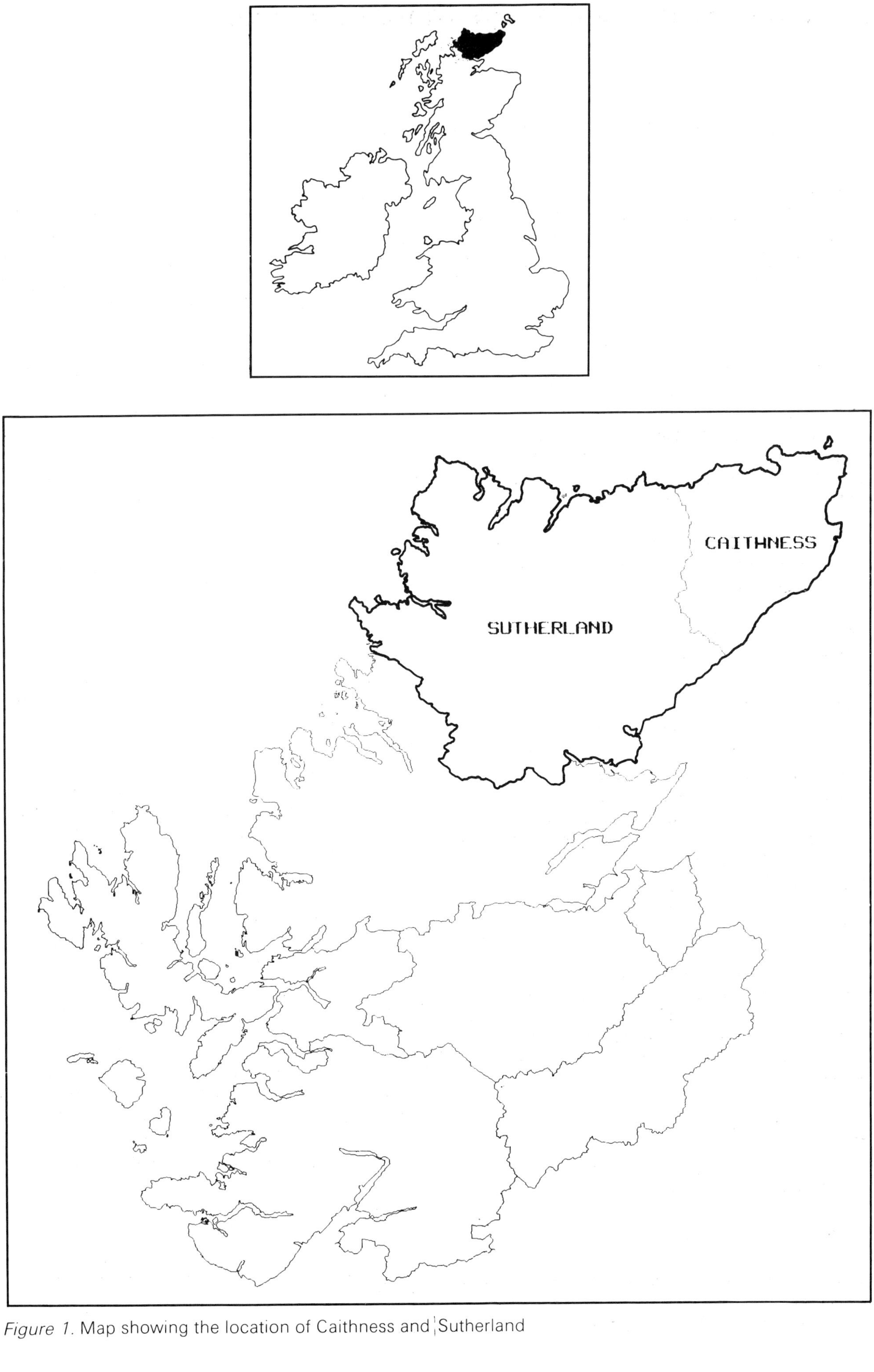

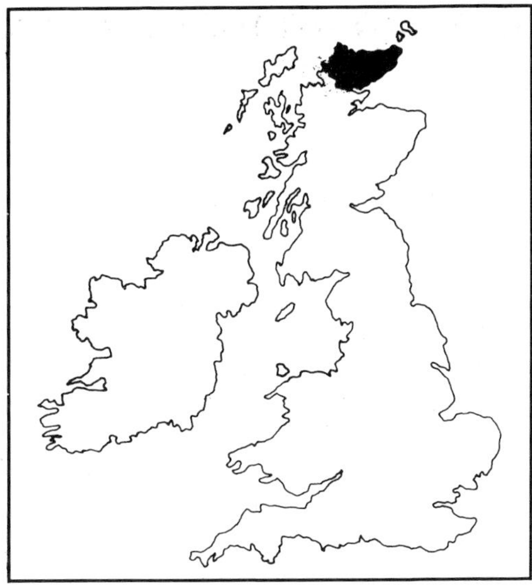

Figure 1. Map showing the location of Caithness and Sutherland

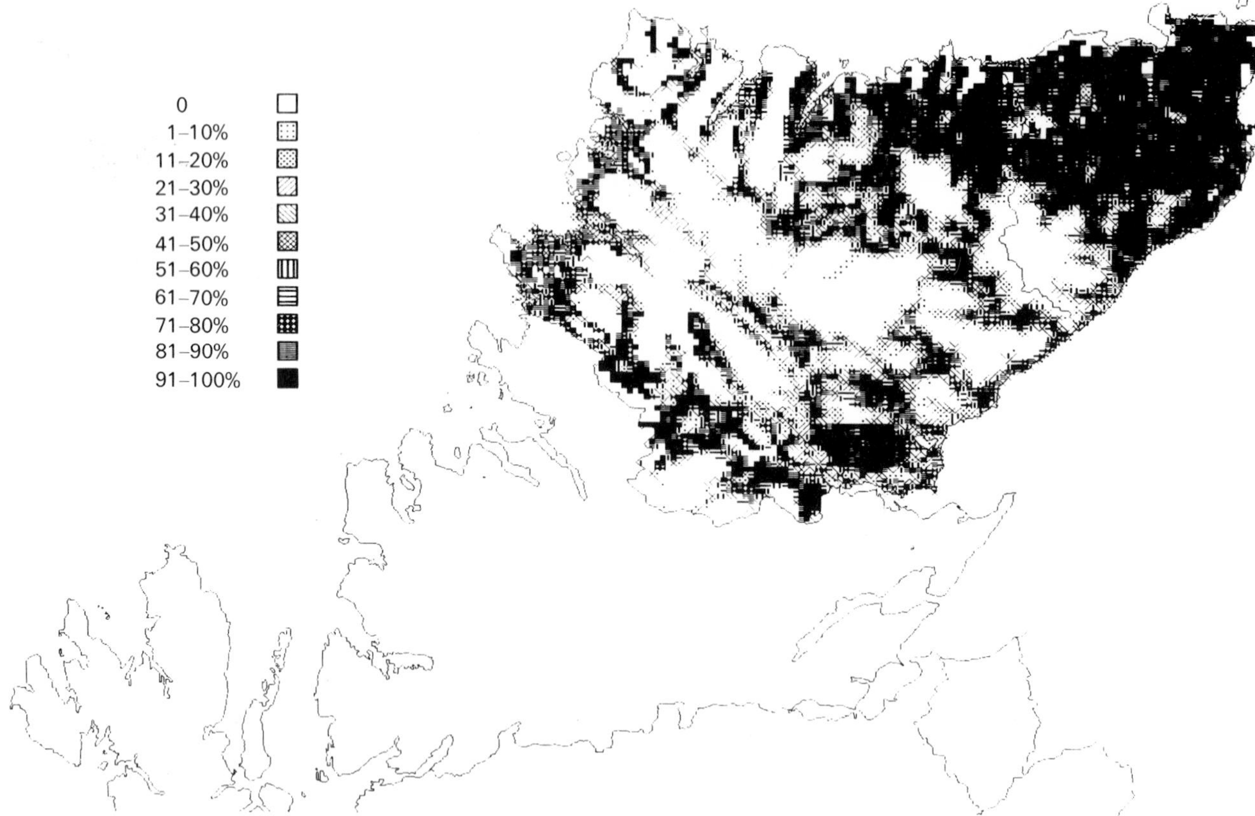

Figure 2. Map showing land theoretically suitable for forestry in Caithness and Sutherland

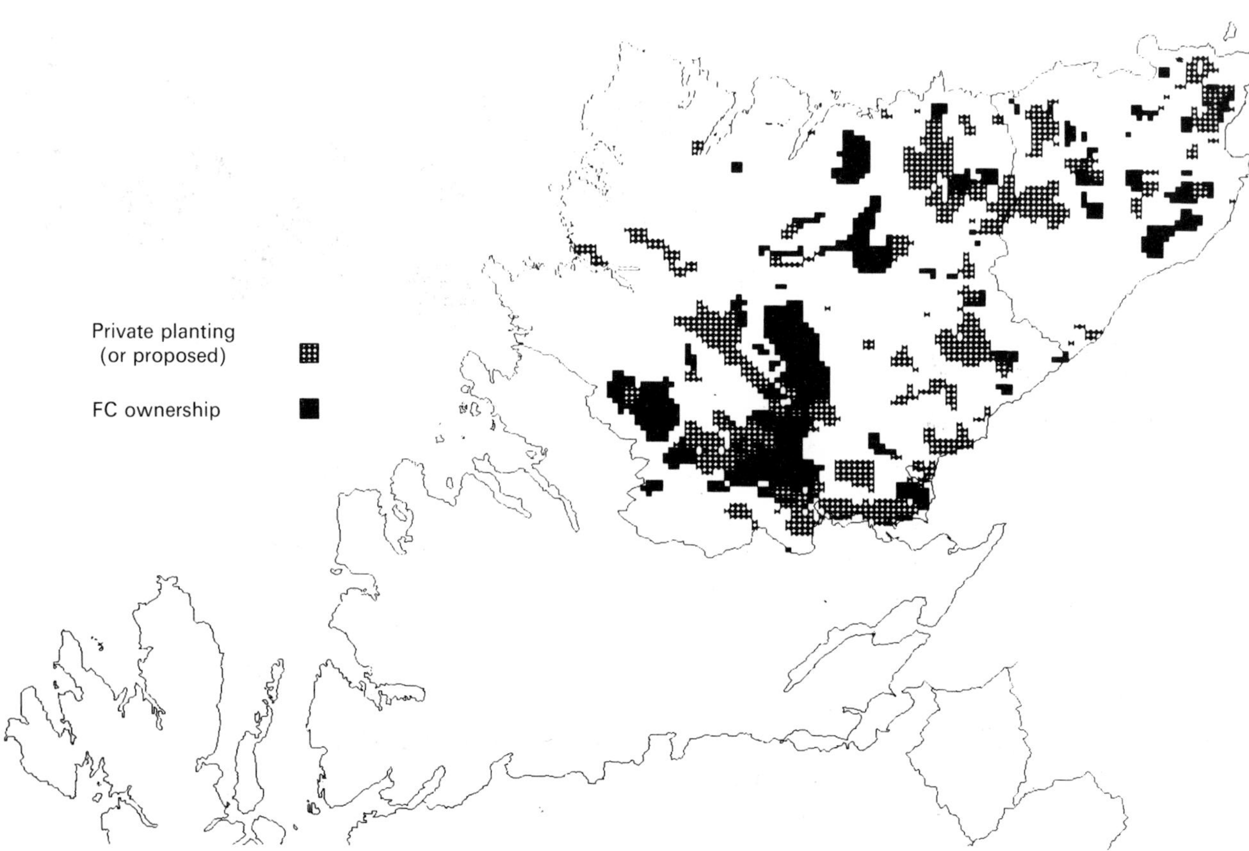

Figure 3. One km grid squares containing forestry in Caithness and Sutherland

Figure 4. Peat core areas in Caithness and Sutherland

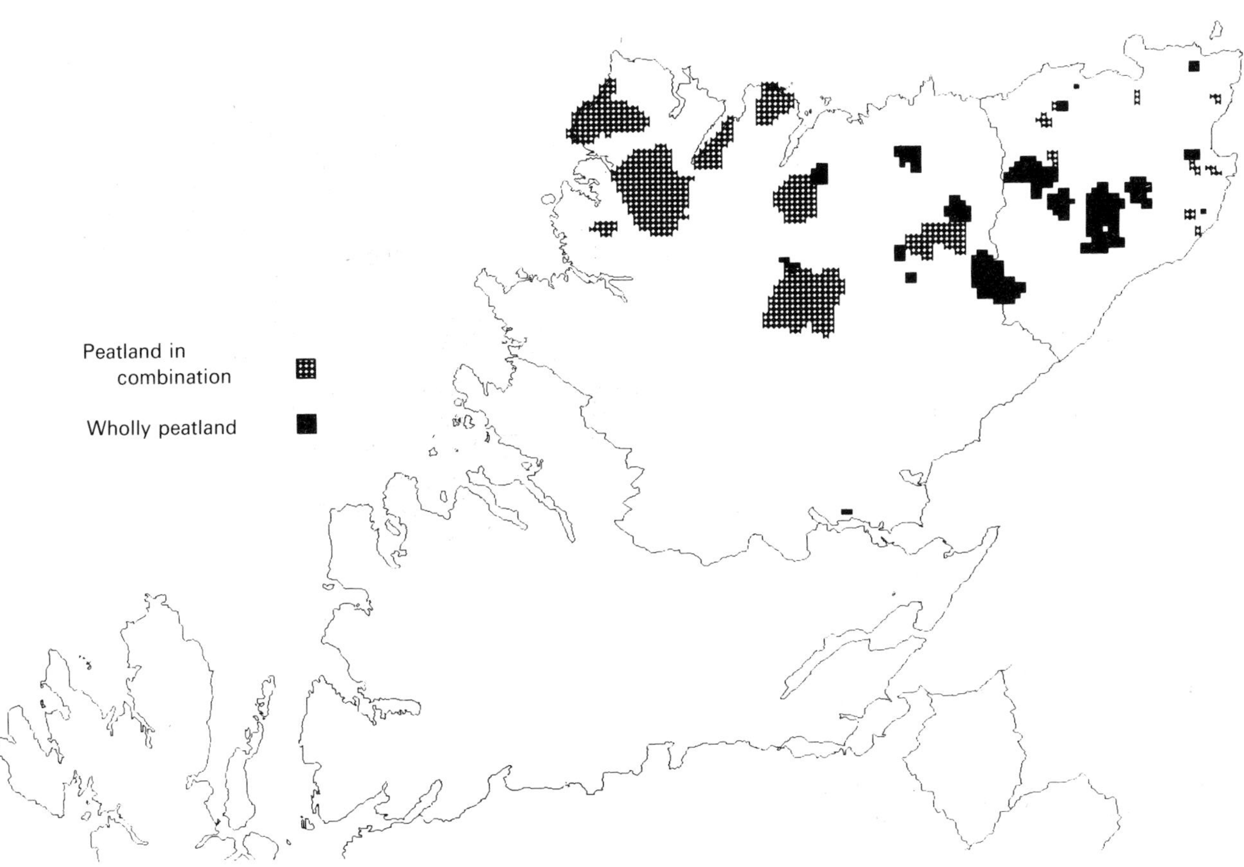

Figure 5. Map showing peatlands with habitat interest in Caithness and Sutherland

Figure 6. One km grid squares containing notified SSSIs in Caithness and Sutherland

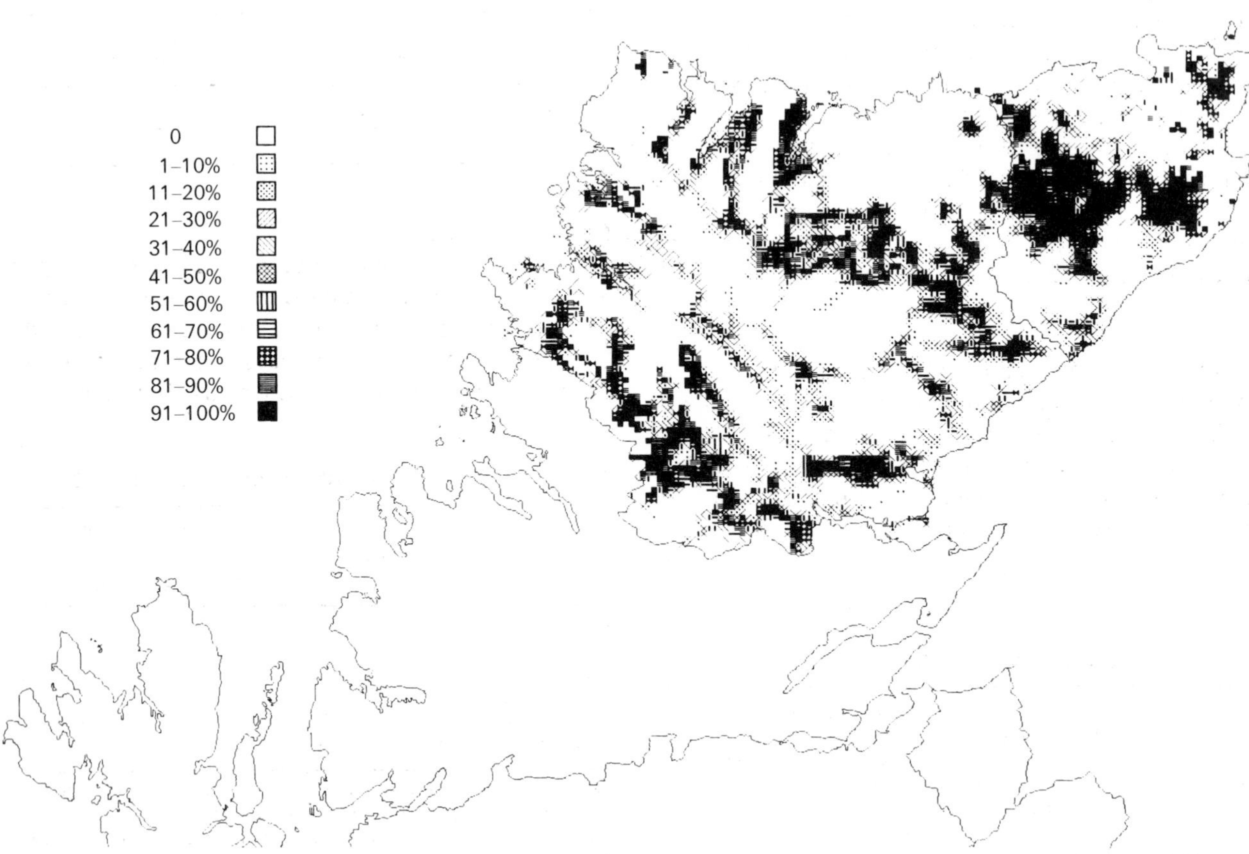

Figure 7. Areas of land with potential for forestry after removal of Macaulay land classes 2–4 and crofting in Caithness and Sutherland

Figure 8. Land available for forestry after competition with agriculture in Caithness and Sutherland (discount rate 3% constant)

5 *Crofting*

Crofting is an important social and economic activity, particularly in Sutherland District. At present, there are legal restrictions on crofters planting trees and, therefore, croft land is currently regarded as a constraint on commercial forestry. The recently formed Scottish Crofters' Union has produced a discussion paper identifying action that is required to enable crofters to play a more active part in forestry. In the meantime, any assessment of forestry potential should exclude croft land.

Information on the distribution of land under crofting tenure (both inbye and common grazings) is difficult to obtain. The Council has added a 'broad-brush' assessment of the distribution of croft land to its computer data base. Table 3 shows the effect of the exclusion of croft land on forestry potential, and Figure 7 illustrates the geography.

Table 2. Percentage of District suitable for forestry

	Theoretically suitable	After exclusion of Macaulay classes 3–4	3–5
Caithness	76.2	49.7	33.7
Sutherland	43.1	40.1	21.0

Class 3 = land capable of producing a moderate range of crops
Class 4 = land capable of producing a narrow range of crops
Class 5 = land capable of use as improved grassland

Table 3. Percentage of District suitable for forestry

	Theoretically suitable	After exclusion of croft land
Caithness	76.2	48.7
Sutherland	43.1	26.0

6 *Peat deposits*

In Caithness and Sutherland, there are extensive peat deposits, some of which have been surveyed as having potential for commercial extraction. Since 1981, the Council has been safeguarding the most important deposits which it has called 'core areas'. The distribution

Table 4. Peat and SSSIs in Caithness (CA) and Sutherland (SU)

Categories	District total (ha) CA	SU	Current SSSIs (%) CA	SU	Proposed SSSIs (%) CA	SU
All peat[1]	82 520	109 480	12.9	9.7	0	25.5
Reconnoitred bogs[2]	5 506	31 727	42.0	10.0	0	15.0
Surveyed bogs[3]						
i. Non-core areas	11 016	9 021	34.0	4.0	0	58.0
ii. core areas[4]	10 230	0	4.0	0	0	0

[1]Includes peat with a minimum depth of 0.5 m, as recorded on the Macaulay maps – it includes reconnoitred and surveyed bogs
[2]Includes peat deposits identified by the Scottish Peat Survey but not surveyed in detail
[3]Includes peat deposits surveyed in detail by the Scottish Peat Survey
[4]Includes those areas identified in local plans for safeguarding for possible commercial peat extraction

Table 5. SSSIs at November 1986

District	No. of SSSIs	SSSI area	District area (ha)	% of District area under existing SSSI designation	% of District under existing or proposed SSSI designation
Caithness	49	18 976	177 576	10.69	10.69
Sutherland	53	78 682	586 518	13.42	18.16
Region	279	365 682	2539 122	14.40	

of the various categories of peat deposit in each District is shown in Table 4. At present, only information on the core areas has been added to the computer data base. The safeguarding of the core areas (only found in Caithness) has an insignificant effect on forestry potential. However, even so, 17% of the core areas have been lost to forestry already.

The relationship between peat deposits and existing and proposed SSSIs is shown in Table 4.

The proposed increase in SSSI designation in Sutherland from 4% of the non-core areas to 62%, and from 10% of the reconnoitred bogs to 25% is unlikely to prejudice possible large-scale commercial peat extraction, because these deposits are considered to be of low potential, as a result of their location, depth and accessibility. The Regional Council has already decided not to safeguard the non-core and reconnoitred areas in its local plans.

7 *Nature conservation*

The next stage in the assessment is to examine the implications of nature conservation sites, both existing and proposed, on forestry potential. Caithness and Sutherland are internationally important, having been singled out in the World Conservation Strategy (Allen 1980), the Nature Conservation Review (Ratcliffe 1977) and, more recently, by the International Mire Conservation Group.

It is estimated that Great Britain contains one-seventh of the world's blanket bog, with Caithness and Sutherland possessing more than one-quarter of the Scottish total. Ratcliffe (1977) describes this area of flow country as 'the largest area of undamaged *Sphagnum*-rich blanket mire in Britain and the conservation of representative examples of the range of variation is of highest importance'.

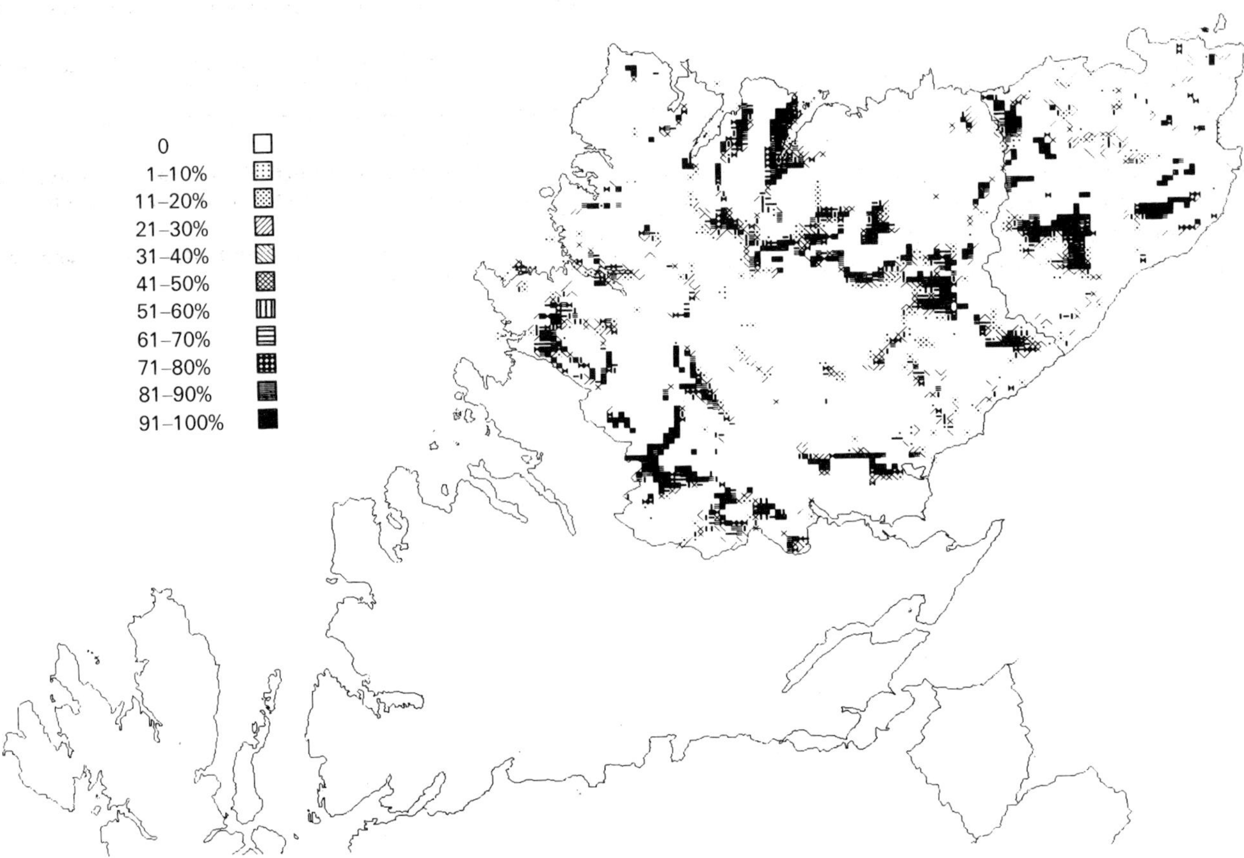

Figure 9. Potential areas of forestry outwith all constraints in Caithness and Sutherland

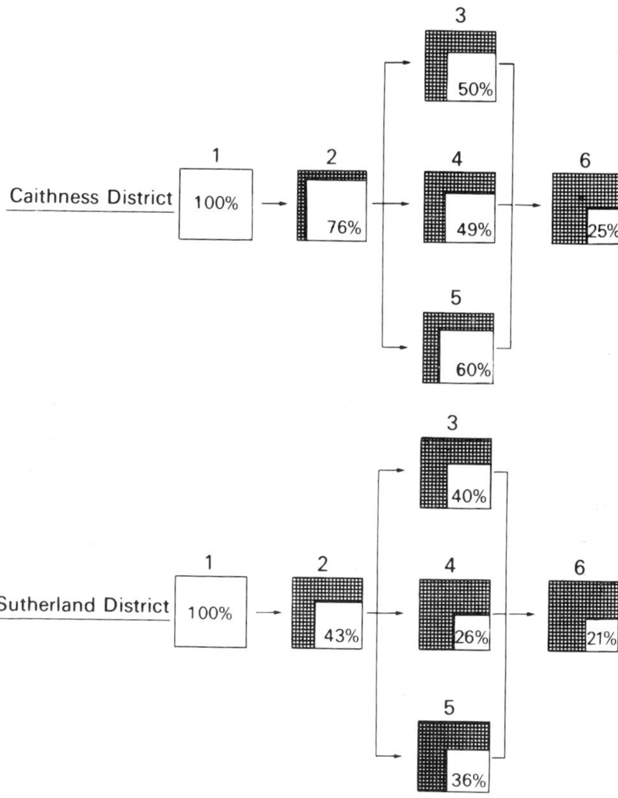

1 Theoretical maximum potential (100%)
2 Remove technicaly unsuitable land (TUL)
3 Remove TUL and Macaulay classes 3 and 4
4 Remove TUL and land in crofting tenure
5 Remove TUL and land under SSSI designation
6 Remove TUL, Macaulay Classes 3 and 4, crofting land and SSSIs

Figure 10. Reductions in forestry potential due to various contraints

The distribution of existing and, where known, proposed SSSIs in Caithness and Sutherland is shown in Table 5.

The implications of existing and proposed SSSIs on forestry potential are shown in Figures 9 and 10, which bring together all the constraint information. The computer data base excludes information on proposed

Table 6. Percentage of District suitable for forestry

	Theoretically suitable	After excluding existing SSSIs[1]	After excluding existing and proposed SSSIs[1]
Caithness	76.2	60.0	60.0
Sutherland	43.1	36.1	34.1

[1] This represents an underestimate because of the way SSSIs are recorded for one km grid square in data base

SSSIs (to respect the NCC's wishes for confidentiality at this stage) but a manual assessment has been undertaken.

In summary, it is necessary to emphasize that the whole interlinkage and interdependence of rural land uses, including conservation, will continue to be studied comprehensively and analysed through the Council's structure plan review (HRC 1985b). In this policy document relating to strategic issues in the Region, it is envisaged that a strategy based upon land use and conservation will be formalized and adopted. This land use and conservation strategy will be formulated within a positive framework, whereby the Council considers that conservation should be seen in the overall context of good land management – agriculture, forestry, recreation and sporting interest – which will support a healthy rural economy sustaining community services, infrastructure and facilities, meet the needs of visitors, and ensure effective conservation and management of the Region's resources.

8 *References*

Allen, R. 1980. *How to save the world: strategy for world conservation.* London: Kogan Page.

Highland Regional Council. 1985a. *HRC/ITE land classification system.* (Information Paper no. 5.) Inverness: HRC.

Highland Regional Council. 1985b. *Structure plan review - issues paper.* Inverness: HRC.

Macaulay Institute for Soil Research. Various dates. *Soil maps, land capability for agriculture maps and handbooks.* Aberdeen: Macaulay Institute.

Ratcliffe, D.A. 1977. *A nature conservation review.* Cambridge: Cambridge University Press.

Changes in the hills and uplands: research note

C J BARR[1] and G DEANE[2]
[1]*Institute of Terrestrial Ecology, Merlewood Research Station, Grange-over-Sands, Cumbria, England*
[2]*Hunting Technical Services, Boreham Wood, Hertfordshire, England*

The original concept of this research note had been to compare and contrast results from 2 independent estimates of landscape change. However, for reasons that will become apparent, it has proved extremely difficult, if not impossible, to carry out any useful form of comparison of published results, due in large measure to differences in survey dates and methodology. Further work will allow results to be co-ordinated but, for the time being, this note will focus on the factual differences of approach adopted by the 2 research teams, not so much as a critical examination but more by way of clarification. Some examples of results are given. The research under review has been carried out quite independently by the Institute of Terrestrial Ecology (ITE) and Hunting Technical Services (HTS), the former as part of a continuing policy of monitoring the rural environment, and the latter under contract to the Department of the Environment and the Countryside Commission for England and Wales.

Because of ITE's existing brief to cover Great Britain, and the requirements of Huntings' customers being restricted to England and Wales, the geographical extent of the landscape change detection exercises was different. This difference is especially significant when considering changes in the uplands. Both organizations accepted the inevitability of adopting a sampling strategy for land use work at the national scale, but ITE sampled at the GB scale, using its own 'land classification' as a form of stratification, while HTS sampled at the county level, employing a soil-based stratification developed by the Forestry Commission.

The sampling unit used by ITE was a one km square, while HTS used variable-sized blocks usually totalling 5 km^2. One of the major differences between the approaches was in the methods of landscape change detection which, in turn, reflects the sampling intensity of the 2 systems. ITE used field survey (as part of a wider ITE project comparing survey methods), while HTS employed aerial photography supported by field survey. As a consequence, HTS were able to obtain information from 707 sites in England and Wales (giving a sampling rate of 2.4% by land area), while ITE visited only 256 sites in GB (less than 0.1% cover by area).

The trade-off for the ITE system was in its ability to detect a far greater level of detail within each site, surveyors recognizing more than 340 features (including dominant vegetation species), while the aerial photograph interpretation undertaken by HTS revealed 41 broader categories of land cover and linear feature.

Perhaps the major reason why comparison of results is difficult is the relative timespans for which landscape change was estimated. ITE compared results from a field survey undertaken by its own staff in the summer months of 1984 with similar data from surveys during the 1977 and 1978 field seasons. Because of the availability of aerial photographic coverage, HTS chose the target dates of 1947, 1970 and 1980 for comparison. Although average annual rates of change can be estimated from both studies, they are not strictly comparable as they take no account of variation within the broad timespans.

By way of example, the following Table shows figures for some predominantly upland landscape changes from these 2 projects.

	Areas (km^2)		
	HTS 1947-69	HTS 1969-80	ITE 1978-84
Loss of 'upland heath, grass and bog' in England and Wales	1900	1100	-
Loss of 'rough grazing'			
GB	-	-	1480
Scotland	-	-	480
Wales	-	-	150
Northern England	-	-	125
Increase in 'coniferous woodland' in GB	-	-	1800
Wales	400	400	43
Northern England	692	76	150
Scotland	-	-	1360
Loss of 'broadleaved woodland'			
Wales	30	100	-
Northern England	46	35	-
Loss of 'broadleaved woodland and scrub'			
GB	-	-	248
Scotland	-	-	12
Wales	-	-	13
Northern England	-	-	4

Looking to the future, ITE (which is a part-Government-funded organization within the Natural Environment Research Council) will continue to monitor changes in the countryside, both to update its data bases for research purposes and to provide change statistics. As a result of a recent contract awarded by the Department of Environment, it will be required to incorporate the results of the HTS work into its own land classification system - a positive step in data integration.

The relative costs and statistical accuracy of the approaches described here have yet to be assessed. However, whatever the outcome, it is apparent that there are 'horses for courses'. Some assessments will require greater statistical accuracy at the expense of a detailed level of information, while the converse may be true in other circumstances, especially where detailed ecological descriptions are fundamental to the study in hand.

Socio-economic survey in upland areas: field work based upon the Merlewood land classification system: research note

M BELL, J LANCASTER and J S WARNOCK
Institute of Terrestrial Ecology, Merlewood Research Station, Grange-over-Sands, Cumbria, England

1 The Merlewood land classification system

A team of research workers based at the Institute of Terrestrial Ecology's Merlewood Research Station has developed a sampling system for Britain. The system is based upon the careful analysis of the environmental characteristics of one in 45 of the one km squares from the National Grid. Each of these squares is allocated to one of 32 'land classes'. The land classes were derived by computer analysis, which split the whole set into dichotomous groups: first the 2 groups most unlike each other, then 4, then 8, and so forth. Thirty-two was felt to be a reasonable number to handle. The system provides arguably the best sampling framework for land use or ecological purposes available, and is described in detail in a number of publications (Bunce *et al.* 1981; Heal & Bunce 1984; Bunce 1987).

2 The land use surveys

In 1978 and 1984, field work was undertaken which involved detailed recording of the land use and ecological characteristics of 8 squares from each land class (ie 256 squares). In the 1984 survey, 4 more squares from each class were resurveyed to permit partial replacement, if required. Comparison with other, independently derived, figures from censuses or surveys using larger samples has shown the system to be remarkably robust. The 1978–84 survey figures also permit statistics of land use change to be derived (Barr *et al.* 1986).

3 Adding in socio-economic data

From 1985–87, the Economic and Social/Natural Environment Research Councils (ESRC/NERC) established their first joint fellowship, based at Merlewood. A connecting theme of the work was to explore the past, present and future influences of the Common Agricultural Policy on the countryside. Aspects of this work are discussed in various publications by Bell (1985a, b, c, 1986, 1987a; Bell & Elliott 1985; Bell & Payne 1987). Within this context, exploration of the potential for incorporating socio-economic data within the ITE sampling frame was a major part of the brief. The success in this regard, particularly as part of a joint study with the Centre for Agricultural Strategy, is discussed elsewhere (Bell 1987b; Centre for Agricultural Strategy 1986).

A further related aspect of work within the fellowship has involved a first examination of the nature of the human sample involved in the squares. A related block of land classes was selected (nos 17–21), covering a range of hill and upland sites. An attempt has been made to identify and contact the owners and occupiers of the land within those 40 squares (ie 4000 ha). Normally this has involved a field visit and a questionnaire survey covering such aspects as:

- tenure
- farm or estate enterprises and capitalization
- agricultural and forestry management
- fertilizer and pesticide use
- attitudes and practice regarding landscape or habitat features
- explanation of land use change
- likely response to proposed European Community policies such as pre-pensions, extensification, or limitations on hill livestock compensatory allowances.

Each farm has subsequently been allocated to its appropriate farm management survey categories. This process gains the benefit of relating land in the sample squares to their appropriate farm management data for their size and type, collected annually by agricultural colleges and universities. This wide range of economic information is used for the compilation of, and in large part is published in, the annual farm income 'Blue Books' (Ministry of Agriculture, Fisheries & Food, annual). More detailed and regionally discriminated data are published by relevant universities or colleges. These sources are working tools of agricultural economics, but we have not previously had the ability to utilize them in conjunction with a carefully stratified land use survey. The data could have been fitted as a desk exercise, with expert assessment of the likely farm or estate system, but this exercise could not necessarily be expected to pick up the many socio-economic factors which influence land use practice; for example,

- tenancy conditions precluding land use change;
- other special tenures or ownerships by conservation-oriented landlords;
- areas of small, pressured or part-time farms;
- large, especially sporting, estates purchased with no intention of ever showing a profit;
- the importance of production quotas;
- aims and objectives of the farmers.

The analysis of the survey data is being undertaken in

conjunction with the ESRC-supported Rural Areas Database (RAD) at Essex University, and it is intended that it will be accessible via RAD in due course. In parallel, Dr Clive Potter and colleagues at Wye College have carried out a similar exercise for 2 land classes distributed in the lowlands. This project is part of the ESRC-supported work on setaside as an environmental and policy instrument, and represents a significant link between 2 of the leading institutions in countryside research. A good deal of follow-up work may be generated, and this will be one aspect to be covered in a final report to both Research Councils.

4 References

Barr, C.J., Benefield, C., Bunce, B., Ridsdale, H. & Whittaker, M. 1986. *Landscape change in Britain.* Grange-over-Sands: Institute of Terrestrial Ecology.

Bell, M. 1985a. *Farm diversification in the EEC.* (Report of the Rural Life Conference). London: National Council for Voluntary Organisations.

Bell, M. 1985b. *Agriculture environment and rural life.* (Submission to the Environment, Public Health and Consumer Protection Committee of the European Parliament. Public Expert Hearings, September 1985). Grange-over-Sands: Institute of Terrestrial Ecology.

Bell, M. 1985c. New CAP angles from the EEC. *Chart. Surv. Wkly,* **12,** 373-374.

Bell, M. 1986. Making it all come right together. *Ecos: Rev. Conserv.,* **7**(2), 2-5.

Bell, M. 1987a. Agriculture and the environment: the EEC dimension. In: *Environmental problems and policies in rural societies,* edited by T. Marsden & D. Evans. (Paper given to Rural Economy and Society Study Group, Loughborough.) In press.

Bell, M. 1987b. *Forestry: always on the land left to Cain?* (Paper given to a conference on Farming and Forestry, Loughborough.) Royal Agricultural Society of England.

Bell, M. & Elliott, A.H. 1985. Changing agricultural policy and the countryside: for better or worse? In: *Environmental issues, Seminar D, 13th, 1-9.* (Publication P261.) London: Planning and Transportation Research Computation Ltd (PTRC).

Bell, M. & Payne, M.J. 1987. *Agriculture and the environment: an objective summary report on the position in the UK.* (Report prepared for a seminar on Agriculture and the Environment, Fredeburg, West Germany.) Brussels: Centre Europeean pour la Promotion et la Formation en Milieu Agricole et Rural.

Bunce, R.G.H., ed. 1987. *Rural information for forward planning.* (ITE symposium no. 21.) Grange-over-Sands: Institute of Terrestrial Ecology.

Bunce, R.G.H., Barr, C.J. & Whittaker, H.A. 1981. *Land classes in Great Britain: preliminary descriptions for users of the Merlewood method of land classification.* Grange-over-Sands: Institute of Terrestrial Ecology.

Centre for Agricultural Strategy. 1986. *Countryside implications for England and Wales of possible changes in the Common Agricultural Policy.* Reading: CAS.

Heal, O.W. & Bunce, R.G.H. 1984. Landscape evaluation and the impact of changing land use on the rural environment: the problem and an approach. In: *Planning and ecology,* edited by T.M. Roberts & R.D. Roberts, 164-188. London: Chapman & Hall.

Ministry of Agriculture, Fisheries & Food. Annual. *Farm incomes in the United Kingdom.* London: HMSO.

Do they do things better in France?

M E SMITH
Nature Conservancy Council, Plas Penrhos, Bangor, Gwynedd, north Wales

To the title given for this paper, the obvious answer is *'Yes,* of course they do'!

For over a decade, the UK Agriculture Departments have had the capacity, within the framework of the European Community (EC) Agricultural Directives in which policies are formulated, to support a healthy agricultural economy in the uplands, without causing such widespread destruction of many landscape and nature conservation features. However, they have pursued ways of implementing these agricultural guidelines which have:

i. substantially reduced the number of small farms;

ii. given most financial incentives to the wealthiest farmers, who least need them because they farm the more productive land in the least rugged parts of the uplands;

iii. significantly reduced wildlife-rich moorlands, wetlands and traditionally managed hay meadows;

iv. threatened the long-term survival of most of the upland broadleaved woodland that still exists in the UK.

In 1986, a draft EC Regulation on agricultural structures came hard on the heels of the previous year's Regulation 'on improving the efficiency of agricultural structures'. The UK's Agriculture Departments thus had a golden opportunity to redirect their policies.

Almost 10 Mha of UK upland are designated as Less Favoured Area (LFA) under the original 1975 EC Directive on hill farming. In Wales, it includes over 20 000 farms, occupying 1.4 Mha (Figure 1). Most of the Auvergne region in south-central France, a predominantly upland area comparable in many ways with Wales, is also designated as LFA under the same Directive (Figure 2). The Auvergne has 1.6 Mha of agricultural land, supporting nearly 57 000 farms, nearly 3 times as many as in Wales. The majority are small – many are part-time units – but, apart from some reorganization and amalgamation of very small land parcels to produce more manageable farms, the number is likely to stay fairly constant in the foreseeable future.

The agriculture/nature conservation conflict so obvious in the UK's uplands in the last 20 years simply does not exist in the French uplands (Figure 3), even though both countries, as EC Member States, operate their agricultural policies and financial incentives under the very same Directives. Much of this difference can be attributed to the ways in which hill livestock compensatory allowances (HLCAs) – headage payments for sheep and cattle – are paid in the 2 countries.

The UK's boundaries for the LFA are based in good part on a rather arbitrary 'hill cow line' drawn up in the 1940s and hardly modified since. The level of HLCA payment depends on whether a farm is in what the UK Agriculture Departments call the 'severely disadvantaged' or the 'disadvantaged' part of the LFA. There is a stocking density limit on sheep (6 ha^{-1} of land), above which no further HLCAs are paid to a farm. However, because much rough upland would struggle to support even 2 sheep ha^{-1}, and because most farms in the LFA have an abundance of rough grazing and little good pasture, this limit is reached by very few farmers.

What I contend to be the most inequitable policy, and the one which has in large part encouraged farm amalgamations, rural depopulation and agricultural developments damaging for wildlife conservation, is the failure of the UK Agriculture Departments to put a limit on the number of livestock per farm on which HLCAs are paid. There is, as a result, every incentive for a farmer to stock his land heavily, to buy more land and increase the size of his holding, and to develop what he has agriculturally, by ploughing rough grassland and moor or by draining wetlands, all to produce, at high cost, grass monocultures which support more livestock but no wildlife. In a study in 1983 for the Council for National Parks, McEwen and Sinclair found that the largest farms received the lion's share of the HLCAs. In 1981–82, the 759 largest farms in the England and Wales LFA received an average of £13,192 each. At the other extreme, the 11 213 smallest farms received an average of just £590 each. Until December 1984, when the Government publicly acknowledged that it was no longer politically acceptable to pay enormous capital grants to the agriculture industry when most other industries were being left to their own devices, these costs were met substantially by the taxpayer. The high levels of grant, in themselves, were a strong incentive for agricultural intensification; coupled with the HLCA payments, they were irresistable to most farmers.

As a result, the Powys county of Wales (almost all of it in the LFA) lost over 60 000 ha of rough grazings, most of it to agricultural intensification, between 1955 and 1982. In Snowdonia, 80% of the broadleaved woodland is grazed so heavily by sheep that it fails to regenerate,

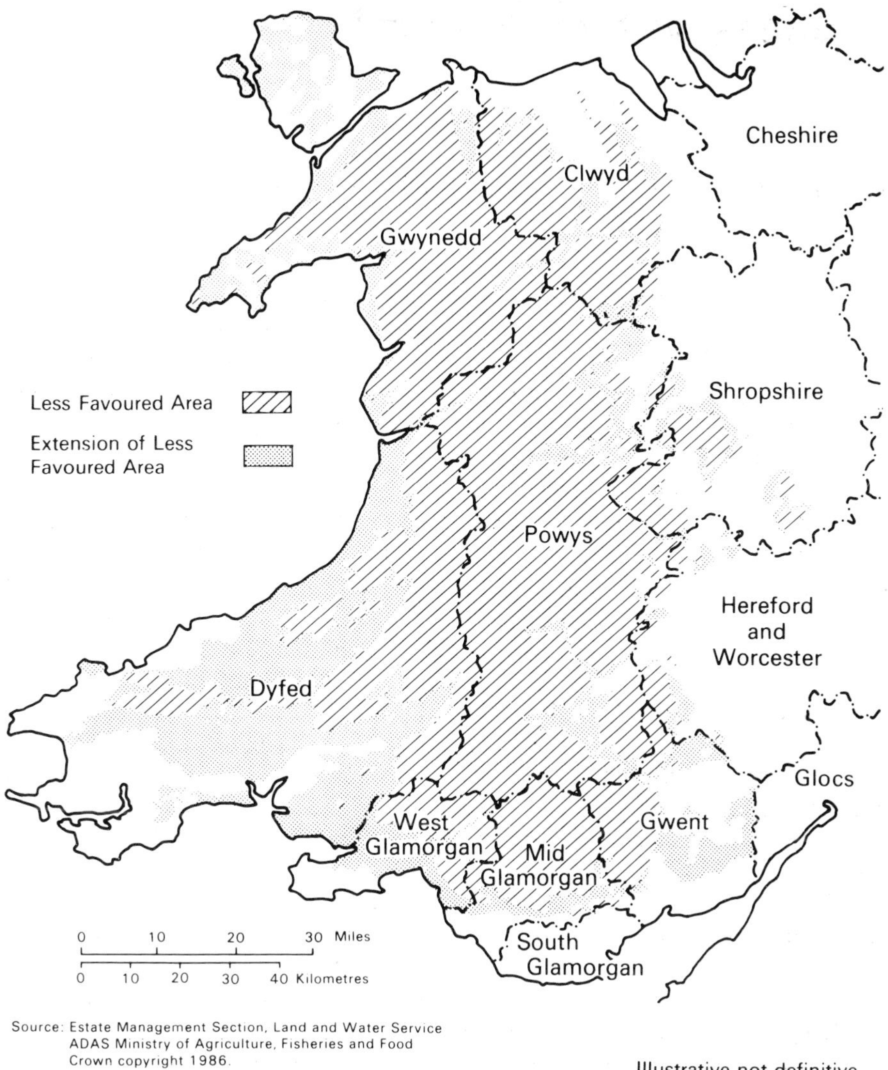

Figure 1. Map showing Less Favoured Areas in Wales designated under EC Directive 85/268

threatening its future survival. The plight of these woods is mirrored throughout the UK uplands.

The French do it differently. Their zonation of the LFA, upon which HLCA levels are based, is more thorough than in the UK. In the Auvergne, for instance, 3 zones are distinguished. Unlike in Britain, the French put an upper limit in each zone on the number of livestock for which HLCAs are paid per farm: 40 livestock units (40 cows or 267 sheep) in the Haute Montagne and Montagne zones; 30 cows or 200 sheep in the Piedmont and Hors Montagne zones.

The upper limit per farm in France means that a farm in the high mountain zone can attract a maximum of 24,000 FF per annum (around £2,400); a mountain zone farm 14,000 FF; and a foothills zone farm no more than 4,500 FF. These limits provide no incentive for a farmer to increase the intensity of his operation or to buy more land to keep more livestock. Coupled with lower levels of capital grants (usually around the 30% mark) but with the emphasis on low interest loans, plus the inevitable French bureaucracy, official agricultural policies and financial incentives have not stimulated agricultural developments and intensification. As a result, there is no nature conservation/agriculture conflict in the French uplands. Areas of rough grassland and moor have hardly declined; wetlands survive. Most pastures are traditionally managed without inorganic fertilizers; rich in flowering plants, they also support good insect, small mammal and bird populations.

What is needed in the UK is for the Agriculture Departments, for the first time, to link HLCA payments properly with the degree of agricultural handicap in the LFA and to apply a limit per farm.The means to do it exist at present under the EC legislation, as witnessed by the French system. All that the current proposed Regulation on improving agricultural structures does is to adjust the minimum and maximum HLCAs per head of livestock permissible throughout the Community. The proposed minimum is approximately £19 per cow (£2.85 per sheep) and the maximum £74 per cow (£11 per sheep).

There should be a proper zonation of the LFA based on the Ministry of Agriculture, Fisheries and Food's existing hills and uplands land classification. The upland LFA could be divided into 3 zones: a mountain zone based on

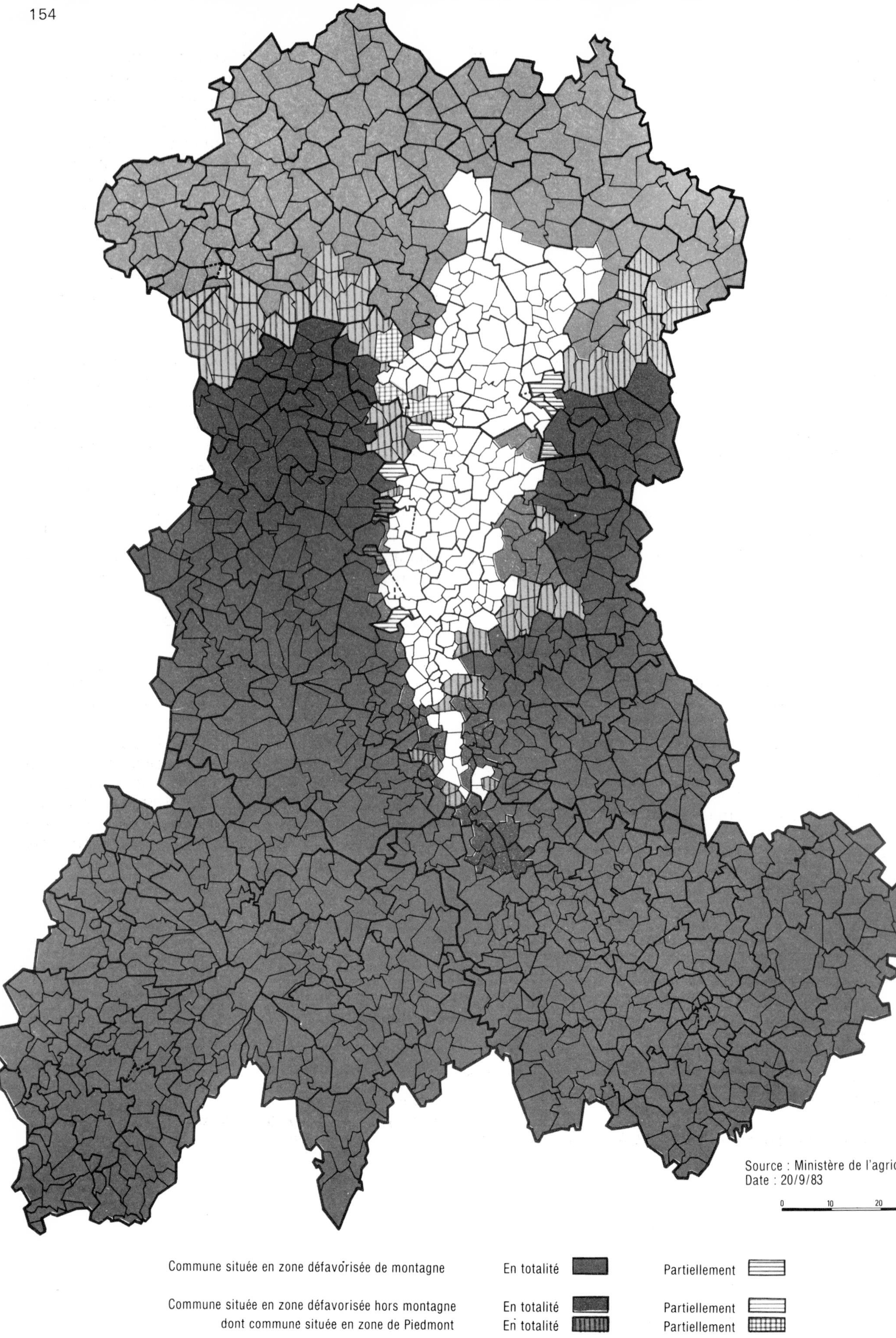

Figure 2. Map showing Less Favoured Areas in Auvergne designated under EC Directive 85/268

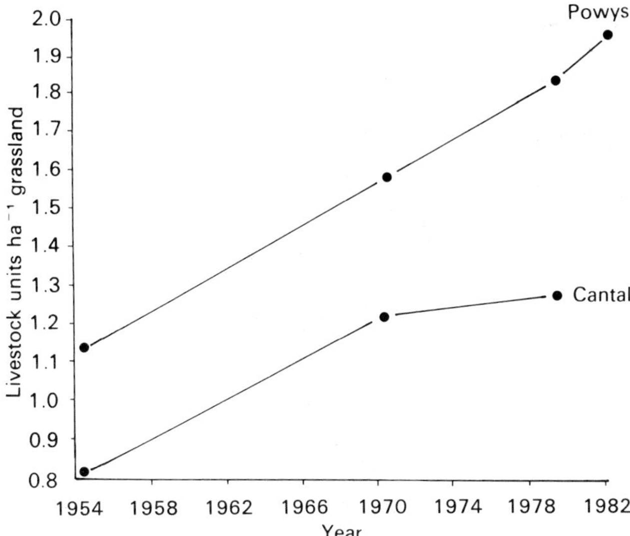

Figure 3. Graph showing numbers of livestock units ha^{-1} of permanent grassland in Powys and Cantal, 1954-82

land grades H3 and H4 (poorer rough grazing); an intermediate zone using land grades H1 and H2 (better rough grazing); and a marginal zone using land grades U3 and U4 (poorer inbye land). Levels of HLCAs paid would be linked to the zonation.

If there is a requirement to lower grazing levels on particular parts of a farm, perhaps a flower-rich pasture or moorland, the loss of HLCAs can be accommodated at present in a management agreement with the agency promoting the reduction, be it the Nature Conservancy Council or the National Park authority. The draft Regulation does, however, contain a clause proposing a 50% increase in the HLCA payment for agreed levels of grazing reduction, a mechanism which potentially gives scope for adjusting livestock numbers without compensatory management agreements.

Of the Community countries, only Belgium and Luxembourg, apart from the UK, fail to equate handicap with compensation by zoning their LFAs, and, because these 2 countries account for little over 1% of the EC's HLCA expenditure, the UK's position is anomalous. The Department of Agriculture and Fisheries for Scotland has conducted individual farm assessments for its LFA for many years, with appeal committees on which farmers are represented. A more complex system is operated in Austria.

The limit per farm on which HLCAs are paid should, I suggest, be pegged at 50 livestock units (50 cows or 333 sheep, or combinations thereof). A farm in the mountain zone could then not receive more than £3,700 per annum; an intermediate zone farm no more than £2,300; and a marginal zone farm no more than £950. Accountancy fiddles, such as notionally splitting units into several 'on-paper' farms to claim on 50 livestock units several times over, would need vigilance by the Agriculture Departments. The proposal to limit HLCAs per farm to 50 livestock units would not take support from the farms that most need it; 54% of all LFA farms in England and Wales have less than this number of animals.

The cut-off per farm would act as a disincentive to enlarge the holding by buying up more land. It might mean the larger farms on the better LFA land shedding some of the relatively small amount of labour they employ, but this short-term effect would be more than offset by a gradual increase in the number of small family farms in the UK uplands, which would be better supported than they are presently. There would be little incentive for an upland farmer to improve much of his land agriculturally because, once the livestock ceiling was reached, no more HLCAs would be paid, a trend which would be in line with present surplus-conscious agricultural thinking of extensifying output.

Lower grazing levels and less agricultural improvement would take the pressure off wildlife-rich moorlands, upland grasslands and wetlands, especially when combined with the reduced levels of capital grants which have been operational since the end of 1984. With more capital incentives for managing broadleaved woods on hill farms, a general reduction in grazing levels could also help to guarantee their survival. Conservation of the countryside, the maintenance of a viable rural population and hill agriculture could be in balance for the first time in at least 40 years.

Acknowledgement

The research for this paper was supported by the Arkleton Trust. The editors are grateful to the Trust, and to the Ministry of Agriculture, Fisheries and Food, for permission to reproduce figures. A fuller report of Dr Smith's findings can be obtained from the Trust at Enstone, Oxfordshire.

Reference

McEwen M. & Sinclair, G. 1983. *New life for the hills.* London: Council for National Parks.

Upland land use: the quest for the elusive balance

C PRICE
Department of Forestry and Wood Science, University College of North Wales, Bangor, Gwynedd, north Wales

1 *Introduction*

Everyone is in favour of balanced land use. No-one stands up in conference and says 'I am here this morning to present the case for unbalanced land use'. Furthermore, we all know what we mean by balanced land use: it is that mix of uses which gives due regard to the legitimate interests of all relevant parties. As to the exact proportions of the mix, they vary with circumstances: terrain, climate, location, tenure, human dimensions, and so forth. However, in principle, given the goodwill of all concerned and a readiness to give and take a little, a reasonable and satisfactory compromise can always be reached.

How often have we not been subjected to such platitudes at conferences, through the media, in the pages of journals? It all sounds self-evident: yet *apparent* balance is a function of the *status quo*, of perceived political trends and of what is, in fact, a very singular and distorted viewpoint.

Let me give an example. If, 50 years ago – at the height of the controversy over afforestation in the Lake District – I had proposed an expansion of productive forest cover in Britain to 2 Mha, the foresters would have hailed me as a prophet and the amenity lobby would have reviled me as an unbalanced fanatic. When in the mid-1980s I propose that the productive forest cover of Britain should be *restricted* to 2 Mha, the foresters revile me as an unbalanced fanatic and the amenity interests applaud enthusiastically. 'Balance' is all a matter of securing advantageous change from the present position, either nationally or upon some particular piece of ground.

'Balance' also justifies multiple use on *someone else's* particular piece of ground. Sensing favourable winds of political change, naturalists are vigorously promoting the merits of creating features of conservation value in agricultural holdings: it is a more balanced use. One hears few naturalists advocating a more balanced use through partial afforestation of National Nature Reserves. This is an expected political propensity, but let us not pretend that real balance has anything to do with it.

Even for commentators with no particular axe to grind, 'balance' is not always a helpful concept. I have a very clear idea of what I regard as a balanced forestry strategy for Britain: the difficulty is that neither the Forestry Commission nor the Ramblers' Association share that idea. In order to achieve a shared idea of balance, we require shared premises of merit – at the simplest, a common perception of the national needs for each of the products of the uplands, but our search founders on even the most objective data. The present forest area of Britain could supply nearly 50% of our timber consumption requirements, but amenity and forestry lobbies diverge in their views of how these requirements will change in future, and, indeed, on how fatal to national well-being a reduction in consumption would be. What chance, then, for agreement on whether cosmetic tampering with the boundaries of Sitka spruce (*Picea sitchensis*) plantations meets the nation's needs for aesthetic fulfilment?

It was for this reason and no other that I became an economist. The market mechanism is a tool of balance, requiring individuals to make considered sacrifices of what they value, in order that they may afford to consume what they value *more*. Cost-benefit analysis is a tool of balance, enabling its practitioners to quantify environmental values in terms comparable with market values, and to combine in one measure the legitimate and quantified interests of all relevant parties. Economics requires no agreed premise, except that people are the best judges of their own well-being, no trade-off except what is implicit in those people's choices. If economics could not reconcile my love for the landscapes of the uplands with their value for timber production, it could at least apportion to each interest that elusive due regard. So, in my naivety, I believed.

However, to simplify the quest for balanced land use, economics and its devotees make certain assumptions. This fact is of no great consequence, as everyone subscribes to them, but I shall list a few.

i. The food surpluses of Europe have no relevance to the famines of Africa and elsewhere.

ii. The distant future does not matter in the slightest.

iii. Given enough data and degrees of freedom, one can readily infer cash values for environmental services.

These being so, it would be instructive to devote the remainder of this paper to presenting the details of what data are to be collected, and how the computer will set about mapping the one optimal and balanced land use pattern for the whole of the uplands.

However, there are always sceptics in any audience. Let me enlarge on these premises.

2 Environmental values

Human willingness to pay for experiences is a function of the value of those experiences. Thus, the decisions of ornithologists to visit bird locations can be modelled as follows:

$$\frac{V_{ij}}{P_i} = F(C_{ij}, Q_{1j}, Q_{2j}, \ldots, Q_{sj})$$

where V_{ij} is the number of visits to location j from a geographical zone, i, with population P_i; C_{ij} is the cost of travel from i to j; Q_{sj} is the number of birds of species s ($s=1 \rightarrow S$) at j.

On the basis of about 300 bird species, 50 visitors from each zone and the normal breakdown of visitors on social and economic dimensions, a mere 500 000 observations on ornithological trips should, in theory, provide sufficient data to determine, by regression analysis, the willingness to pay for, shall we say, the greenshank (*Tringa nebularia*). The addition of flowers, beetles, landscape, etc, makes it more difficult, of course, and we do need to assume linearity and additive separability of our functional forms.

Whether or not this esoteric stuff is intelligible, the point I am trying to make is, I hope, clear. Anyone with experience of travel cost analysis knows that the best that can be expected of a multivariable model is to discover that the sign of a parameter is significant. In other words, we might hope to find evidence that, all else being equal, ornithologists prefer sites with greenshank to sites without greenshank – but, again, experience with landscape evaluation techniques would not lead me to offer any guarantees of that conclusion.

Furthermore, there are systematic reasons, to do with the existence of alternative destinations for visits, from which we could expect travel cost analysis to underestimate the absolute value of a visit to any site. In addition, the armchair conservationist – an oft but unjustly derided stereotype – experiences great and real pleasure from knowing the greenshank remains as a breeding British species. Travel cost analysis cannot even attempt to capture this value. It is very likely that what is left out of cost-benefit analysis of wildlife (and equally of landscape) will exceed what is put in (Price 1978).

This news will come as a great relief to those who would prefer to evaluate wildlife by informed intuition and blind prejudice. You see, a reliable technique of *quantifying* balance scientifically would not, in practice, be welcome.

Nonetheless, someday someone is going to try to value greenshank in this way, and my guess is that their resultant cash value will be too low to outweigh the cash benefits of afforestation, say in the flow country of north Scotland: the balance of advantage, on the basis of this very incomplete figure, lies with afforestation. At this stage, the conservation movement will protest 'But the greenshank has a **right** to live'. For a sceptical old economist, this assertion needs decoding. Do we speak of greenshank as rarity, greenshank as ingredient of ecosystem, or greenshank as individual? As a rarity, the greenshank has economic value to humanity, partly reflected, as noted above, in the willingness of humanity to travel to see it. As an ingredient of the ecosystem, I am not sure that the greenshank is pivotal: its very rarity suggests that we can get by without it. In both roles, the greenshank is perceived as *instrumental*; this perception has no bearing on its **own** right to live. Ah, but the greenshank as an individual, whose life and the lives of whose progeny would be snuffed out by afforestation, that is a matter on which we need to argue a point, if our view of land use is not to be blighted by anthropocentric imbalance.

On the other hand, afforestation brings a fresh habitat for other birds, like the cheery chaffinch (*Fringilla coelebs*). Loss and gain balance. False! false! comes the retort: the chaffinch and the greenshank cannot be equated, for one is increasingly common, the other increasingly rare. Granted, and this is a relevant argument, *in so far as we are considering the chaffinch's value to humanity*. However, the notion that being a greenshank is more valuable than being a chaffinch, just because chaffinches are common, is not an argument likely to appeal to a chaffinch, which equally has the right, as an individual, to live. There are philosophical parallels with judging the 'worth' of human individuals. Are they to be assessed according to the market wage they can command, which depends on their marginal contribution to gross national product, which in its turn depends on the scarcity of their skills? Or do we look to the legal or religious ideals of treating everyone equally? Of course, we laugh at this style of thought, because the alternative of taking it seriously is intolerably problematic, and, in the meantime, we shamelessly exploit the imputed right to life of this or that species, merely as a means to weight our own side of the balance.

3 The future

To reinforce the greenshank stratagem, conservationists nowadays defend threatened country by arguing that, in discounted cash flow terms, afforestation is not a profitable investment (Grove 1983). More than ever before, economists and conservationists appear to be speaking the same language in the quest for the elusive balance. The discount rate is 5%. It's official: the Forestry Commission use it to determine all their silvicultural operations, and the Institute of Terrestrial Ecology use it in generating their optimal land use patterns.

Discounting is a device to balance the interests of different time periods – of different generations. No balanced land use strategy can be without it, and the implication of discounting at 5% is quite straightforward and uncontroversial. The value ascribed to greenshank, timber, landscapes, soil fertility, fossil fuels and people in 100 years' time is for all practical purposes nil. Yes, fellow ecologists, that's the balanced judgement at which so many conservationists have arrived in their bid to wipe conifer afforestation off the map.

Of course, discounted cash flow does make life easier. We can go for car-borne nature-loving jaunts and promote the benefits of recreation in the remote uplands, without considering the long-term cost in depleted oil reserves. We can replace semi-natural ecosystems by grass monocultures and drain our wetlands wholesale, with never a thought for permanent loss to the gene pool. We can balance the timber production of high-yielding species against the nutrient drain they impose, without looking further than the effects on soils and watercourses over the first forest rotation. Saving exquisite landscapes and unique ecosystems for all future generations is good political rhetoric, but to balance them against present cost puts a terrible strain on scientific prediction and economic evaluation.

So, we hunt a rationale for discounting, and find it in technological advance and the increasing affluence of future generations, which will enable them to sacrifice material consumption with less pain than we would experience. This is the ideal argument for conservationists, for it allows them to discount timber and food values, while values of wildlife and landscape – which are in constant or diminishing supply – can be assumed equally or even more valuable to future generations. The case for conservation cannot lose under such a dispensation. Surely no-one could begrudge us the assumption that natural resource limitations will become less and less significant to material production as time goes on, or deny our right to squander the timber and soil and oil resources within our own life-time? Well, maybe future generations will.

Alternatively, we dispense with discounting, and perhaps three-quarters of the uplands become apparently economic to afforest. Would we see this as a balanced land use mix?

4 The world of food and wood

A few days ago I was at a conference called to celebrate the triumph of the environmental movement over irrational subsidy to agricultural surpluses in Europe. At least, that was the way it felt. However, during the evening session, one timid soul – the one ghost at the banquet – arose and said 'I wonder, am I being naive, but isn't it strange to talk about agricultural surpluses when so many people are starving?' Well, of course, he was being naive, and, goodness, aren't we glad that we are so much more sophisticated: because if there *were* some relationship between food grown *here* and food eaten *there*, then some of us might suffer a bad conscience over a decision to protect an interesting wetland ecosystem from the indignity of overproduction.

In the same way, the uninformed layman might find it strange that, within the covers of one book (Dudley 1985), the deforestation of the tropics and the afforestation of the British uplands are attacked with equal passion. I wonder, am I being naive, he might say, but won't growing our own timber reduce the need to destroy the forests of the tropics?

We, who are wise, however, know that the solution to famines and the rape of the tropical high forest lies not in what we do, but elsewhere, in systems of land tenure and ecologically sound crop management. We know that the meagre product of upland soils is too small to affect the total world food and wood production; that, in any case, there are far more efficient ways of increasing world production; that there is plenty of food in the world already, what it needs is better distribution; and, above all, that if we give a man a fish we feed him for a day, but that if we *teach* a man to fish we feed him for life.

Oddly enough, a few days previously I had been called upon to sign a petition against the dumping of European surpluses in Africa, on the grounds that this would lead to a fall in food prices, undermining the domestic agricultural economy. The suggestion was that European surpluses are not so much irrelevant as positively harmful to the developing world. (Of course, by the same token, we should not be producing timber either, because that will damage the price received by firewood producers in the Third World.)

If I were a Sahelian, starved of everything but information, I think I should be a little puzzled about the petition, and I should reason thus. I am untroubled by the prospect of food prices falling, because I do not produce enough food to sell: that is one of the reasons that I and my family are starving. I have no personal objection to European surpluses being dumped in my region, though I do understand that it will erode the profits of the prosperous farmers in the east of the country. Higher prices, on the other hand, could do little to improve the agricultural economy round here: if we tried to increase food production, then what is left of the soil would fall apart. I suppose it is all more complicated than that.

Similarly, I should be forced to assume that the wise ones who had declared that the food surpluses of their own country did not provide the best solution to my problems were using their utmost powers and all available finance to pursue *better* solutions – to improve land tenure in my country, to increase world food production in efficient ways, to distribute existing world food production more equitably; and **that** was why they were declining to subsidize food production in their uplands. I should assume that they were not giving me a fish, because they had plans afoot to teach me to fish, and to create for me a lake or river as an adjunct to this technology. (Of course, the chances were that they would mis-read the ecology of the lake, and soon there would be no fish, but at least it would feed me for more than a day.) When these actions failed to materialize, I should begin to wonder if their wise assertions had been made simply because they wished to excuse themselves from considering my nutritional needs, when they made decisions about land use in the uplands of Europe.

Of course, we are not the monsters that the cynical Sahelian imagines. We take no action, because the effects of well-meant action are so miniscule, and so prone to be swamped by the dominant, uncaring actors in the world economic and political scene. Actually, it is not that European surpluses are not the right solution, but simply that they do not change anything. This is one argument, of course, but it is strange to me that ecologists, who spend so much time explaining that the biosphere is an interacting system in which everything relates to everything else, do not automatically assume that the politico-economic system will be the same. No doubt, the simple economic model of supply, demand and price has to be worked out through much political and bureaucratic inertia and a complex web of negative feedbacks. Yet even my most distorted and labyrinthine model (Price 1987) of the world economy suggests, with inexorable logic, that, if more food is produced in a small project, then more food is eaten by a few consumers.

5 *The trade-off*

The balancing of the issues I have been talking about may be represented as follows.

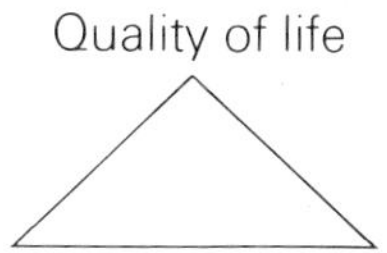

The upland debate, however, seems to be largely confined to making a balance on an axis perpendicular to the plane of the triangle – a debate on the constitution of the quality of life: how much food for us, how much wood for us, how much conservation, of what things, for us. The other dimensions of balance are invoked only to support *our* interest: greenshank and sustainability for the conservationist, feeding the world for the farmer. Likewise, the subject matter of this conference focuses (and it is a very proper concern) on this corner and on *transformations* – the technical data and managerial skills required to exchange one product for another.

The other aspect of balance is *substitution* – the process of weighing preference for one position within the triangle against another. It is a barely discussed topic, largely, I conjecture, because these are choices which we have neither the criteria nor the stomach to make. It is not so much that there is no such thing as a perfect countryside, but that we should not be able to recognize it if it arose. Most of the time we do not even seem conscious that there is a choice.

For example, the food production potential of the world is, they say, enough to support many times the present population. The uplands could assist that expansion, at some cost to diversity of ecosystem and (perhaps consequently) to the sustainability of food production. Yet our interest seems mostly to be directed at forgone diversity. We know a little about long-term sustainability, but emasculate the knowledge with the conventions of discounted cash flow. What of the benefits of increased quantity of life? It seems axiomatic to me that 10 billion people being happy means twice as much happiness as 5 billion people being happy, and, if the latter is good, then the former is twice as good (Price 1977). I am continually surprised to find that others (ecologists and economists equally) disagree, not just with my evaluation, but with the whole concept of even asking the question.

6 *Conclusion*

Don't mistake me: I don't know the answer. I offer no solutions, no strong defence of my position. The connection of single-minded conservation with starvation is so tenuous that we can almost forget it: the triumph of technology in giving future generations the food, and materials and energy they need is so plausible (Price 1984), that we can almost accept discounting – almost, but not quite.

Thus, the only thing I am sure of, after 20 years of economic research, is still the pattern of upland landscape which would be directly congenial to me, and which, together with a diverse flora and fauna, forms an important part of why life is worth living. I could have given a paper which competently rationalized that pattern, with a pick-and-mix bag of arguments such as is available at the Woolworth's sweet-counter of the Great Uplands Debate. I could have hoped, for my conscience's sake, that the irrelevance of food supplies and of future generations would be taken as read, but the mere fact of my hoping suggests that the presumption of irrelevance is a matter of convenience rather than of truth.

In other areas of human enquiry, the absence of knowledge is taken as good reason to initiate research. Here, it is different: where doubt exists, we can continue to argue for what is comfortable and convenient; we can evade ideas – ideas about the community of things living and yet to live – which have the effrontery to lie outside the resolution of the scientific method, the market mechanism or the democratic process.

That, of course, is why we have responded so eagerly to the brave new opportunities offered by change in the uplands: change diverts our thoughts from the profounder realities into which they are in danger of lapsing when things stay the same for long enough.

7 *References*

Dudley, N. 1985. *The death of trees.* London: Pluto Press.

Grove, R. 1983. *The future for forestry.* Oxford: British Association of Nature Conservationists.

Price, C. 1977. Total net benefit and the quantity of life: a query. *Environ. Plann., A,* **9,** 813-816.

Price, C. 1978. *Landscape economics.* London: Macmillan.

Price, C. 1984. Project appraisal and planning for overdeveloped countries. I: The costing of nonrenewable resources. *Environ. Manage.,* **8,** 221-232.

Price, C. 1987. *Does shadow pricing go on for ever?* Bangor: Department of Forestry and Wood Science, University College of North Wales.

Management of change in the hills and uplands: concluding comment

O W HEAL
Institute of Terrestrial Ecology, Bush Estate, Penicuik, Midlothian

This seminar has been organized by ITE, sponsored by the Countryside Commission for England and Wales, supported by 6 national organizations, involved 150 participants from national, regional and local organizations and universities, and was based on a joint NERC/ ESRC initiative. Why? There were 3 main reasons which were recurrent themes in the papers and discussions:

i. acceptance that the rate of change in land use is increasing and will continue to do so, with social, economic and environmental consequences;

ii. recognition that in order to manage change it is necessary to move from sectoral interests and advocacy towards greater interaction and collaboration;

iii. concern to improve communication and understanding between disciplines and interests, and particularly to improve the exchange of information between research and management.

The papers, poster displays and discussions ranged far and wide in subjects, but there were some important distinctions which can be made and which point to ways forward. Debate on *methods of management* was dominant, and distinguished between those for policy implementation, eg headage payments, improvement grants and designated areas; for planning, eg cost-benefit analysis and optimization models; and for practical management, eg stock control, burning and erosion control. As emphasized by various speakers, the tools already exist for many of the current challenges of management. The problem is primarily that those involved in policy, planning and management are either not aware of the range of methods and their applicability or do not have the expertise available to use them, especially when different disciplines are involved. The solution lies in training and communication.

However, the situation is not quite as simple as indicated for 2 reasons. First, the cause–effect or dose–response relationships are sometimes uncertain, as in defining the level of subsidy that will induce a particular shift in the level and distribution of a product, or in the intensity of grazing required to produce a specified change in the composition of the vegetation. Whilst the general principles may be known, their application to particular situations or sites must take into account other factors and must also recognize that there is often a long time-lag in response. Second, alternative types and combinations of land use are required, as emphasized particularly by Dr Maxwell. The time to develop and test those can take a decade or more, especially where trees are concerned. Thus, although potential new options can be readily identified, there is a danger that expectations are raised, and not fulfilled, because the methods are not tried and tested. Application of options such as agroforestry or biofuels requires not only the development of suitable management systems, but also the assessment and development of market systems and of training and advice. Again, there is a significant time-lag in response, in this case between research and application.

An important distinction between the papers presented was in the *spatial scale* under consideration: a distinction which, if not clearly related to objectives, can lead to confusion and frustration. At a national and regional scale, information is required with precision but not detail for strategic planning, eg the amount of land suitable for, and sensitive to, a particular use. This requirement contrasts with the local site-specific detail required for management practice, eg the fertilizer application or stock density to conserve a particular vegetation on a particular soil. The objectives, methods and information requirements are quite distinct at the different levels of resolution. An analogous situation is in the finer level of detail required by the research worker, as distinct from the policy-maker, planner or manager.

A main conclusion was, therefore, that communication and an understanding of the needs of different interests and disciplines were key requirements for the future management of the hills and uplands. This does not mean simply more meetings. It will involve the use of a full range of techniques from field demonstrations, through advisory leaflets, to computer models and expert systems. The danger, particularly for the man on the ground, is in receiving too much information! There was some consensus in discussion that effective communication required interpretive and advisory groups to act as an interface, particularly between the research worker and the manager, an interface that benefited from the meeting and from the subsequent contacts that were planned.

Appendix: List of participants

Mrs P Anderson, Gwynfa, Buxton Road, Chinley, Stockport, Cheshire, SK12 6DR.

Mr Armstrong, Hill Farming Research Organisation, Bush Estate, Penicuik, Midlothian, EH26 OPY.

Ms K Atkins, Department of Geography, University of Liverpool, Roxby Building, PO Box 147, Liverpool, L69 3BX.

Dr I Bainbridge, Royal Society for the Protection of Birds, 217 Regent Terrace, Edinburgh, EH7 5BN.

Sir D Barber, Countryside Commission, John Dower House, Crescent Place, Cheltenham, Gloucestershire, GL50 3RA.

Ms T Barret, Farming and Wildlife Advisory Group, Houghhall Farm, Houghall, Durham, DH1 3SG.

Dr P Beckett, Department of Agricultural Sciences, University of Oxford, Parks Road, Oxford, OX1 3PF.

Ms S Bell, Country Landowners Association, 16 Belgrave Square, London, SW1X 8PQ.

Dr M Bell, Economic & Social Research Council/Natural Environment Research Council Fellow, Merlewood Research Station, Grange-over-Sands, Cumbria, LA11 6JU.

Mr G Berry, 27 Greenside, Kendal, Cumbria.

Mr N Black, Highland Regional Council, Department of Planning, Regional Buildings, Glenurquart Road, Inverness, IV3 5NX.

Mr J Blackwood, Nature Conservancy Council, Northminster House, Northminster, Peterborough, PE1 1UA.

Miss A Bondi, East Cumbria Countryside Project, Unit 2C, The Old Mill, Warwick Bridge, Carlisle, Cumbria, CA4 8RR.

Dr I Bonner, Nature Conservancy Council, Blackwell, Bowness-on-Windermere, Cumbria, LA23 3JR.

Mr J Bowers, School of Economic Studies, University of Leeds, Leeds, West Yorkshire, LS2 9JT.

Dr I K Bradbury, Department of Geography, University of Liverpool, Roxby Building, PO Box 147, Liverpool, L69 3BX.

Mr O Brandon, Dartington Institute, Central Offices, Shinners Bridge, Totnes, Devon, TQ9 6JE.

Mr T Bryson, Winterbourne House, Wye, Ashford, Kent.

Ms A Burn, Nature Conservancy Council, Plas Penrhos, Ffordd Penrhos, Bangor, Gwynedd, LL57 2LQ.

Dr N Buxton, Nature Conservancy Council, Achantoul, Aviemore, Inverness-shire, PH22 1QD.

Mr E Carter, Farming and Wildlife Advisory Group, The Lodge, Sandy, Bedfordshire, SG19 2DL.

Mr R N Cartwright, Cumbria County Planning Department, County Offices, Kendal, Cumbria, LA9 4RQ.

Mr R A Challenor, Messrs Davis & Bowring, 6–8 Main Street, Kirkby Lonsdale, Cumbria.

Ms E Christie, Farming and Wildlife Advisory Group, Bonnygate, Cupar, Fife, Y15 4HN.

Ms A Clark, Royal Society for the Protection of Birds, Highland Office, Munlochy, Ross & Cromarty, IV8 3ND.

Mrs E Clark, Brathay Hall Trust, Brathay Hall, Ambleside, Cumbria, LA22 OHR.

Mr C G Coggins, Countryside Commission, Warwick House, Grantham Road, Newcastle-upon-Tyne, NE2 1QF.

Mr & Mrs J Corlett, Ben Fold, Field Head, Outgate, Ambleside, Cumbria.

Ms H Corrie, World Wildlife Fund, 11–13 Ockford Road, Godalming, Surrey, GU7 7QU.

Mr J R Cowan, Ministry of Agriculture, Fisheries & Food, Great Westminster House, Horseferry Road, London, SW1P 2AE.

Dr J R Crabtree, Aberdeen School of Agriculture, 581 King Street, Aberdeen, AB9 1UD.

Mr H Currie, Ministry of Agriculture, Fisheries & Food, Government Buildings, Otley Road, Lawnswood, Leeds, West Yorkshire LS16 5PY.

Mr I Dair, Nature Conservancy Council, Northminster House, Peterborough, PE1 1UA.

Mr J Dixon, Department of Applied Biology, University of Wales Institute of Science and Technology, Llysdinam Field Centre, Newbridge-on-Wye, Powys, CD1 6NB.

Mr M J Dodds, Cumbria County Planning Department, County Offices, Kendal, Cumbria, LA9 4RQ.

Mr J Dodgson, Gurnel Beck, Millside, Witherslack, Grange-over-Sands, Cumbria.

Mr P J D Donnelly, Lyme Park, Disley, Stockport, Cheshire, SK12 2NX.

Ms I Dunn, East Cumbria Countryside Project, Unit 2C, The Old Mill, Warwick Bridge, Carlisle, Cumbria, CA4 8RR.

Mr J Dunning, Lower Chapel, Orton, Penrith, Cumbria.

Mr K P Durrant, Cumbria County Planning Department, County Offices, Kendal, Cumbria, LA9 4RQ.

Mr J Eadie, Hill Farming Research Organisation, Bush Estate, Penicuik, Midlothian, EH26 OPY.

Ms S Evans, Nature Conservancy Council, Northminster House, Peterborough, PE1 1UA.

Mr M Felton, Nature Conservancy Council, Northminster House, Peterborough, PE1 1UA.

Mr A Fishwick, Lake District Special Planning Board, Busher Walk, Kendal, Cumbria, LA9 4RH.

Ms P Gatto, Department of Agricultural Economics, The University, Kings Walk, Newcastle-upon-Tyne, NE1 7RU.

Mr P G Duff-Pennington, National Farmers Union, Muncaster Castle, Ravenglass, Cumbria.

Dr S Grant, Hill Farming Research Organisation, Bush Estate, Penicuik, Midlothian, EH26 OPY.

Dr W Grayson, Cheshire County Council, 108 Greenbank Lane, Northwich, Cheshire, CW8 1JS.

Mr A Griffiths, University of Exeter, Mayflower Close, Plymstock, Plymouth, Devon, PL9 8SJ.

Mr L Grisedale, 93 Cinder Hill, Broughton-in-Furness, Cumbria.

Mrs V Harris, Lake District Special Planning Board, Busher Walk, Kendal, Cumbria, LA9 4RH.

Mr L H Harwood, National Trust, Rothay Holme, Rothay Road, Ambleside, Cumbria, LA22 OEJ.

Mr D Hickson, 218 Carlisle Road, Dalston, Carlisle, Cumbria.

Ms S Hooper, Department of Agricultural Economics, The University, Kings Walk, Newcastle-upon-Tyne, NE1 7RU.

Mr W J Hopkin, Nature Conservancy Council, Plas Penrhos, Ffordd Penrhos, Bangor, Gwynedd, LL57 2LQ.

Mr P Howarth, Department of Environmental Studies, Manchester Polytechnic, Chester Street, Manchester, M15 6BH.

Mr L Howson, Windsor Farm, Wasdale, Seascale, Cumbria, CA20 1EU.

Sir T Jackson, Routen, Ennerdale, Cleator, Cumbria.

Prof J N R Jeffers, Ellerhow, Lindale, Grange-over-Sands, Cumbria, LA11 6NA.

Mr B Jones, Farming and Wildlife Advisory Group, Agricultural Department, Penrallt, Caernarfon, Gwynedd, LL55 1EP.

Mr B Jones, Ramblers Association, Department of Physics, University of Lancaster, Lancaster, Lancashire, LA1 4YB.

Ms B Jones, Nature Conservancy Council, Achantoul, Aviemore, Inverness-shire, PH22 1QD.

Ms G Kerby, Agricultural Training Board, 1 Red Cottage, Elsfield, Oxford, OX3 9UL.

Mrs H Kerry, Cumbria College of Agriculture & Forestry, Newton Rigg, Penrith, Cumbria.

Miss J Ketchen, Cumbria Trust for Nature Conservation, Church Street, Ambleside, Cumbria, LA22 OBU.

Mr I R Kibble, Swathgill, Coulton, Hovingham, York, North Yorkshire, YO6 4NG.

Ms J Lancaster, Department of Agriculture, The University, Kings Walk, Newcastle-upon-Tyne, NE1 7RU.

Dr A Lance, Royal Society for the Protection of Birds, The Lodge, Sandy, Bedfordshire, SG19 2DL.

Ms A Lane, ESRC Data Archive, University of Essex, Wivenhoe Park, Colchester, Essex.

Ms M Lippert, Hill Farming Research Organisation, Glensaugh, Nr Laurencekirk, Kincardineshire.

Mr D J L Lee, Timber Growers UK, Holker Estates Co Ltd, Estate Office, Cark-in-Cartmel, Grange-over-Sands, Cumbria, LA11 7PH.

Dr R Lovegrove, Royal Society for the Protection of Birds, Frolic Street, Newtown, Powys.

Mr J Loxham, Beckfoot, Ennerdale, Cleator, Cumbria.

Mr P Lyth, Farming and Wildlife Advisory Group, Block 7, Government Buildings, St Georges Road, Harrogate, North Yorkshire.

Ms E McIntosh, Farming and Wildlife Advisory Group, College of Agriculture, Kirkley Hall, Ponteland, Newcastleupon-Tyne.

Ms E McKenzie, Countryside Ranger, 126 Meadow Street, Wheelton, Chorley, Lancashire.

Ms F MacLennan, Farming and Wildlife Advisory Group, 22 Hall Lane, Longton, Preston, Lancashire.

Mr K McNaught, Nature Conservancy Council, Blackwell, Bowness-on-Windermere, Cumbria, LA23 3JR.

Mr J Marsden, Nature Conservancy Council, Blackwell, Bowness-on-Windermere, Cumbria, LA23 3JR.

Dr T J Maxwell, Hill Farming Research Organisation, Bush Estate, Penicuik, Midlothian, EH26 OPY.

Mr B Mercer, Nature Conservancy Council, Thornborough Hall, Leyburn, North Yorkshire.

Ms J Meredith, Countryside Commission, John Dower House, Crescent Place, Cheltenham, Gloucestershire, GL50 3RA.

Mr J B Miles, Royal Society for the Protection of Birds, Carlisle, Cumbria.

Mr G Miller, Association of Countryside Rangers, Field Head Cottage, Grindsbrook Booth, Edale, via Sheffield, South Yorkshire, S30 22D.

Dr S A Milne, Hill Farming Research Organisation, Bush Estate, Penicuik, Midlothian, EH26 OPY.

Dr F Mitchell, Hill Farming Research Organisation, Bush Estate, Penicuik, Midlothian, EH26 OPY.

Mr G Morries, Lancashire County Council, Planning Department, East Cliff County Offices, Preston, Lancashire, PR1 3EX.

Miss S M Morris-Eyton, National Farmers Union, Agriculture House, Knightsbridge, London, SW1X 7NJ.

Mr D Morris, Nature Conservancy Council, Northminster House, Peterborough, PE1 1UA.

Dr A Mowle, Nature Conservancy Council, 12 Hope Terrace, Edinburgh, EH9 2AS.

Mr A Nicholson, East Cumbria Countryside Project, Unit 2C, The Old Mill, Warwick Bridge, Carlisle, Cumbria, CA4 8RR.

Mr M O'Hanlon, Department of Geography, University of Liverpool, Roxby Building, PO Box 147, Liverpool, L69 3BX.

Ms C Osmaston, Farming and Wildlife Advisory Group, ESCA, Greycrook, St Boswells, Roxburgh, TD6 OEU.

Mr G Paget, Department of Environmental Studies, Manchester Polytechnic, Chester Street, Manchester, M15 6BH.

Miss J A Palmer, Cumbria Trust for Nature Conservation, Church Street, Ambleside, Cumbria, LA22 OBU.

Mr P Park, National Trust, 2 Awelon, Trallong, Brecon, Powys, LD3 8HP.

Mr J Pattinson, Lake District Special Planning Board, Busher Walk, Kendal, Cumbria, LA9 4RH.

Dr C Price, Department of Forestry and Wood Science, University College of North Wales, Bangor, Gwynedd, LL57 2UW.

Miss R Queen, Department of Geography, University of Lancaster, Lancaster, Lancashire, LA1 4YW.

Miss J Randell, West of Scotland Agricultural College, St Mary's Industrial Estate, Dumfries, DG1 1DX.

Ms F Reynolds, Council for the National Parks, 45 Shelton Street, London, WC2H 9HJ.

Ms S Reynolds, Department of Geography, University of Lancaster, Lancaster, Lancashire, LA1 4YW.

Mr W H Robinson, Holmescales, Old Hutton, Nr Kendal, Cumbria.

Mr M Scrowston, National Trust, Rothay Holme, Rothay Road, Ambleside, Cumbria, LA22 OEJ.

Dr A R Sibbald, Hill Farming Research Organisation, Bush Estate, Penicuik, Midlothian, EH26 OPY.

Mr G Sinclair, Environment Information Services, Glede House, Martletwy, Narberth, Dyfed, SA67 8AS.

Dr M E Smith, Nature Conservancy Council, Highthorn, Northcliffe Avenue, Old Colwyn, Clwyd, LL29 9AF.

Dr R S Smith, Department of Agricultural & Environmental Science, The University, Kings Walk, Newcastle-upon-Tyne, NE1 7RU.

Mr I Sloane, Nature Conservancy Council, Deauville, Spa Road, Llandrindod Wells, Powys.

Mr P Spencer, Farming and Wildlife Advisory Group, Staffordshire College of Agriculture, Rodbartan, Penkridge, Stafford, Staffordshire, ST19 5PH.

Ms N Stedman, Yorkshire Dales National Park, Yorebridge House, Bainbridge, Leyburn, North Yorkshire.

Ms C Swanwick, Land Use Consultants, Levric, North Road, South Kilworth, Lutterworth, Leicestershire, LE17 6DU.

Dr J Tait, Systems Group, Technology Faculty, Open University, Walton Hall, Milton Keynes, Buckinghamshire, MK7 6AA.

Dr P Tattersfield, Gwynfa, Buxton Road, Chinley, Stockport, Cheshire, SK12 6DR.

Mr P Taylor, National Trust, Rothay Holme, Rothay Road, Ambleside, Cumbria, LA22 OEJ.

Mr P Taylor, Lake District Special Planning Board, Busher Walk, Kendal, Cumbria, LA9 4RH.

Mr D Thompson, Soil Survey of England and Wales, Shire Hall, Mold, Clwyd.

Dr D B A Thompson, Nature Conservancy Council, 12 Hope Terrace, Edinburgh, EH9 2AS.

Mr E G Thompson, Nature Conservancy Council, 43 The Parade, Cardiff, South Glamorgan, CF2 3UH.

Mr B Tobin, Yorkshire Dales National Park, Yorebridge House, Bainbridge, Leyburn, North Yorkshire.

Mr S Toomer, East Cumbria Countryside Project, Unit 2C, The Old Mill, Warwick Bridge, Carlisle, Cumbria, CA4 8RB.

Ms L Torvell, Hill Farming Research Organisation, Bush Estate, Penicuik, Midlothian, EH26 OPY.

Mr P Turkentine, The National Trust, High Peak Estate, Edale End, Hope, Sheffield, South Yorkshire.

Mr J Walne, Ministry of Agriculture, Fisheries & Food, Eden Bridge House, Lowther Street, Carlisle, Cumbria.

Ms M Walsh, 110 The Avenue, Wivenhoe, Colchester, Essex.

Dr S D Ward, Nature Conservancy Council, 12 Hope Terrace, Edinburgh, EH9 2AS.

Dr J M Way, Ministry of Agriculture, Fisheries & Food, Room 388, Great Westminster House, Horseferry Road, London, SW1P 2AE.

Dr A Weir, Northumberland National Park Authority, Eastburn, Southpark, Hexham, Northumberland.

Mr M C Whitby, Department of Agricultural Economics, The University, Kings Walk, Newcastle-upon-Tyne, NE1 7RU.

Mr D White, Nature Conservancy Council, Plas Penrhos, Ffordd Penrhos, Bangor, Gwynedd, LL57 2LQ.

Dr K Whitehead, Natural Environment Research Council, Polaris House, North Star Avenue, Swindon, Wiltshire, SN2 1EU.

Mr J Williams, Lake District Special Planning Board, Busher Walk, Kendal, Cumbria, LA9 4RH.

Mr D Wilson, National Trust, High Peak Estate, Edale End, Hope, Sheffield, South Yorkshire.

Ms V Wood, Farming and Wildlife Advisory Group, Imperial House, Imperial Arcade, Huddersfield, West Yorkshire, HD1 2BR.

Mr A Woods, Royal Society for the Protection of Birds, The Lodge, Sandy, Bedfordshire, SG19 2DL.

Mr R G Woolmore, Countryside Commission, John Dower House, Crescent Place, Cheltenham, Gloucestershire, GL52 2QR.

Mr P Wright, Yorkshire Dales National Park, Yorebridge House, Bainbridge, Leyburn, North Yorkshire.

The following staff from the Institute of Terrestrial Ecology were also present:

Merlewood Research Station, Grange-over-Sands, Cumbria, LA11 6JU

Mr J K Adamson, Mr C J Barr, Mr J Beckett, Mr C B Benefield, Mr D R Briggs, Mr A H F Brown, Dr R G H Bunce, Mr P A Coward, Dr J Dighton, Dr A F Harrison, Dr O W Heal, Mrs G Howson, Dr P Ineson, Miss S E Jewell, Mr G J Lawson, Mrs C McClure, Mr R Scott, Mr J M Sykes, Ms M Whittaker

Monks Wood Experimental Station, Abbots Ripton, Huntingdon, PE17 2LS

Dr R H Marrs

Hill of Brathens, Banchory, Kincardineshire, AB3 4BY

Dr N G Bayfield, Dr J Miles